Web-Spinning Heroics

Web-Spinning Heroics

*Critical Essays on the History
and Meaning of Spider-Man*

Edited by
ROBERT MOSES PEASLEE *and*
ROBERT G. WEINER

Foreword by Tom DeFalco
Afterword by Gary Jackson

McFarland & Company, Inc., Publishers
Jefferson, North Carolina, and London

ALSO OF INTEREST

*In the Peanut Gallery with Mystery Science Theater 3000:
Essays on Film, Fandom, Technology and the Culture of Riffing*
(2011; edited by Robert G. Weiner and Shelley E. Barba)

*Graphic Novels and Comics in Libraries and Archives: Essays on Readers,
Research, History and Cataloging* (2010; edited by Robert G. Weiner)

*Captain America and the Struggle of the Superhero:
Critical Essays* (2009; edited by Robert G. Weiner)

*Marvel Graphic Novels and Related Publications:
An Annotated Guide to Comics, Prose Novels, Children's Books, Articles,
Criticism and Reference Works, 1965–2005* (2008; Robert G. Weiner)

LIBRARY OF CONGRESS CATALOGUING-IN-PUBLICATION DATA

Web-spinning heroics : critical essays on the history and meaning of Spider-Man /
edited by Robert Moses Peaslee and Robert G. Weiner ;
foreword by Tom DeFalco ; afterword by Gary Jackson.
p.   cm.
Includes bibliographical references and index.

ISBN 978-0-7864-4627-8
softcover : acid free paper ∞

1. Spider-Man (Fictitious character)   2. Comic books, strips, etc.—Moral and ethical aspects.   I. Peaslee, Robert Moses, 1973–   II. Weiner, Robert G., 1966–
PN6728.S6W425 2012   741.5'973—dc23   2012014322

BRITISH LIBRARY CATALOGUING DATA ARE AVAILABLE

© 2012 Robert Moses Peaslee and Robert G. Weiner. All rights reserved

*No part of this book may be reproduced or transmitted in any form
or by any means, electronic or mechanical, including photocopying
or recording, or by any information storage and retrieval system,
without permission in writing from the publisher.*

Cover illustration ©2012 Digital Vision

Manufactured in the United States of America

*McFarland & Company, Inc., Publishers
Box 611, Jefferson, North Carolina 28640
www.mcfarlandpub.com*

Acknowledgments

The editors would like to thank Tom DeFalco and Gary Jackson for their support of the project and their generous contributions to it.

Robert Moses Peaslee:

This volume is dedicated to all the mentors who have guided me as a student and a scholar, and who have in the process refrained from steering me too rigidly way from the diversionary projects that have, in time, become my fields of study: Donna Berghorn, Patrick Anderson, Ann Page Stecker, Joe Kelly, Janice Peck, Polly McLean, Andrew Calabrese, Paul Gordon, Liz Skewes, Ann Hardy, Tim Oakes, Lynn Clark, Stewart Hoover, and Shu-Ling Berggreen.

I would especially honor the memory of Dr. Donald Coonley, who first introduced me to critical media studies and, in effect, opened my eyes.

Thanks to Brian Hamilton and Jacob Copple, whose generous and skilled assistance during the editing process was invaluable to bringing the project together more or less on time.

Many friends and family members have stoked my interest in the topic of superheroes and their attendant milieu: among them I would mention TJ Davis, Jon Zimnick, the late Kirk Zimnick, Curtis Coats, and, of course, Rob Weiner. Rob, you are a scholarship machine, an encyclopedia, an expert, and a true inspiration. Thank you for your overwhelming generosity in all things, but especially in bringing me into this important project.

Robert G. Weiner:

This book is dedicated to the memory of my father Dr. Leonard Weiner, who always supported my scholarship and never once made light of my various projects (even as a forty-something studying comics and film).

Thanks and love to Marilyn Weiner and Larry and Vicki.

Thanks to Elizabeth Figa, Cynthia J. Miller, The Southwestern Popular Culture Association (Ken Dvorak, Sally Sanchez, Lynnea Chapman King, Kelli Shapiro), John Cline, Flint Marko, KD, Jessica Drew, Ben Reilly, Tom Gonzales, Sara Dulin, Joe Ferrer, John Oyerbides, Ms. Conni Kitten, Dan Watkins, Dr. Sam Dragga, Marina Oliver, Shelley E. Barba, Kaley Daniel, Mr. Ryan Litsey, Lynn Whitfield, David Marshall, Fredonia Paschal and Dr. Peter Coogan. Thanks to Dean Dyal, Dr. Joan Ormrod, Dr. David Huxley, and the *Journal of Graphic Novels and Comics*. All my love to Rachel (you are my Sunday Morning Sunshine).

Thanks to the staff of the Texas Tech Libraries and in particular the staff of Document Delivery!

Thanks to my supervisor Laura Heinz for good advice always and to my colleagues in the Research, Outreach and Instruction department (Ryan Cassidy, Kimberly Vardeman, Arlene Paschall, Jon Hufford, Tom Rohrig, Minerva Alaniz, Brian Quinn, Jack Becker, Donell Callender, Sandy River, Innocent Awesome, Carrye and Jake Syma, Sheila Hoover, Ms. Cynthia Henry, Susan Hidalgo, ER, and Mr. Samuel Dyal).

Thanks to my magical critters for always putting a smile on my face! I would like to give tribute to the memory of Sunshine, Remy, and Captain, who are missed.

An honest dedication to those Spidey scribes who influenced me: Tom DeFalco, J.M. DeMatteis, Steve Ditko, John Romita, Sr., Alex Ross, Stan Lee, Roy Thomas, Gerry Conway, Brian Michael Bendis, Roger Stern, Gil Kane, Marv Wolfman, and Len Wein. And thanks to *all* the writers and artists who have ever worked on a *Spider-Man* comic.

Finally, I would like to thank my friend, colleague, teacher, and co-editor Dr. Robert Moses Peaslee. Thanks for believing in this project, your eye for detail, and for so much hard work. You are truly a "gentleman and a scholar." It is an honor to work with you.

Table of Contents

Acknowledgments v

Foreword: My Pal Pete
    Tom DeFalco 1

Elegy for Gwen Stacy
    Gary Jackson 3

Introduction
    Robert G. Weiner *and* Robert Moses Peaslee 4

I. Historical, Cultural and Pedagogical Angles

Donald Glover for Spider-Man
    Phillip Lamarr Cunningham 22

Have Great Power, Greatly Irresponsible: Intergenerational Conflict in 1960s *Amazing Spider-Man*
    Peter Lee 29

"Continually in the Making": Spider-Man's New York
    Martin Flanagan 40

Hegemonic Implications of Science in Popular Media: Science Narratives and Representations of Physics in the *Spider-Man* Film Trilogy
    Lisa Holderman 53

Teaching Peter Parker's Ghosts of Milton: Anxiety of Influence, the Trace, and Platonic Knowing in *Ultimate Spider-Man Volume 1*
    James Bucky Carter 63

II. Considering Specific Graphic Novels

Weaving Webs and True Lies: Revisiting *Kraven's Last Hunt* Through the Lens of *Brooklyn Dreams*
    David Walton 70

The Hermeneutics of Spider-Man: What Is Peter Parker Doing in Elizabethan England?
    Christina C. Angel 74

Strategies of Narration in Jeph Loeb and Tim Sale's *Spider-Man: Blue*
  DEREK PARKER ROYAL 81

III. The J. Jonah Jameson Problem

Spider-Man: MENACE!!! Stan Lee, Censorship and the 100-Issue Revolution
  AARON DRUCKER 90

J. Jonah Jameson — Hero or Villain? Spider-Man's Nemesis Hard to Pigeonhole
  ANDREW A. SMITH 101

Spider-Management: A Critical Examination of the Business World of Spider-Man
  MATTHEW MCGOWAN *and* JEREMY SHORT 113

IV. Spider-Man and Other Sequential Art Characters

Anti-Heroes: Spider-Man and the Punisher
  CORD A. SCOTT 120

The Sinister Six: Anti-Villains in an Anti-Heroic Narrative
  RICK HUDSON 128

Spider-Man and Batman, Disordered Minds: Friendship Through Difference
  PHILLIP BEVIN 134

V. Trauma Textual and Extra-Textual

The Loss of the Father: Trauma Theory and the Birth of Spider-Man
  FORREST C. HELVIE 146

Artificial Mourning: The *Spider-Man* Trilogy and September 11th
  TAMA LEAVER 154

VI. Issues of Gender in the Spider-verse

Three Stories, Three Movies and the Romances of Mary Jane and Spider-Man
  ROBERT G. WEINER 166

Women's Pleasures Watching Spider-Man's Journeys
  EMILY D. EDWARDS 177

The Incorrigible Aunt May
  ORA C. MCWILLIAMS 187

Spidey Meets Freud: Central Psychoanalytic Motifs in *Spider-Man* and *Spider-Man 2*
  ROBERT MOSES PEASLEE 195

VII. Under-Examined Spider-Texts

Reinterpreting Myths in *Spider-Man: The Animated Series*
 DAVID RAY CARTER 210

Finding the Milieu of the *Spider-Man* Music LPs
 MARK MCDERMOTT 222

Games Are Not Convergence: *Spider-Man 3*, Game Design and the Lost Promise of Digital Production and Convergence
 CASEY O'DONNELL 234

Afterword
 GARY JACKSON 249

About the Contributors 251

Index 255

Foreword: My Pal Pete

Tom DeFalco

Peter Parker, better known to the rest of the world as the amazing Spider-Man, holds a very special place in my heart. I first encountered him when I chanced upon a copy of *Amazing Fantasy #15*. The year was 1962 and I bought all my comic books off the spinner rack at my local soda shop. (No, I didn't live in Riverdale, but Pop Tate-style soda shops were where you bought your candy bars, comics, magazines, malteds, vanilla egg creams, root beer floats, lime rickeys, hamburgers and even school supplies back in the day.) I spied the cover to *AF #15* on the rack and couldn't resist a chance to read the introduction of Spider-Man. Why not? I was already a loyal Marvel fan, having begun on the day I purchased *Fantastic Four #3* and *#4* and every succeeding issue.

Needless to say, like many a comic book fan, I immediately identified with Pete. He wasn't a geek or a loser. He just liked to read, had trouble attracting girls, and wasn't the most popular kid in school. He was the first comic book character who shared a lot of the same problems I did. (Robin lived in a mansion, Archie was surrounded by Betty and Veronica, and Superboy was, well, SUPERBOY!) In many ways, I would have ended up a lot like Pete if the radioactive spider had bitten me. (I say a lot like Pete, but the truth is he was always much smarter and braver than me. I doubt I would have survived the Chameleon in *Amazing Spider-Man #1* and certainly would have gotten knocked off by the Vulture in *#2*.)

I later learned that Stan Lee always intended Spider-Man to be the first realistic teenage superhero. Stan wanted Pete to be a real teenager with real problems. No sooner did Pete gain his powers than he tried to make money off them. (How many of us would have done the same?) With fame and fortune, Pete got a little arrogant. That's why he let a burglar run past him — a mistake that later returned to haunt him and teach him a most valuable lesson about personal responsibility.

Knowing Stan the way I do, I can see how he put a lot of himself into Pete's character. (I can also see a lot of Stan in Aunt May and J. Jonah Jameson.) The origin of Spider-Man is a simple little morality play, a basic plot that Stan had used in many of his mystery/fantasy titles. The protagonist allows his ego to get the better of him and later pays for it at the end of the story.

What makes Spider-Man so special is the theme of personal responsibility that runs throughout the entire series. Before Spider-Man, most comic books focused on some gimmick — a magic word, a special talent or power. Spider-Man may have been the first that centered on an idea. Yes, Spider-Man has special abilities and gimmicks, but his stories are usually more than simple slugfests. The good ones discuss various aspects of responsibility. We often find Pete torn between his responsibilities, forced to decide between what he wants to do and what he should do. He's constantly juggling his duties to his beloved aunt, his girlfriend, his job, his studies, and his life as Spider-Man.

His choices always have consequences. It's like real life. Our responsibilities may differ, but we've all got them. That's why we still identify with Pete. He's just like us.

Tom DeFalco • May 2012

Tom DeFalco is a former editor-in-chief of Marvel Comics with over thirty books in print. He has written comic books, graphic novels, short stories, prose novels and books including *Spider-Man: The Ultimate Guide*, *Comic Creators on Fantastic Four*, and *Comic Creators on Spider-Man*. He is known for writing stories featuring Spider-Man and Spider-Girl.

Elegy for Gwen Stacy

GARY JACKSON

Spider-Man appeared ... I knew he would save her. That was what they did. They saved innocents.—Phil Sheldon from *Marvels #4*

I can't stop dying.
The first time was 1973—
fell off the Brooklyn Bridge,
killed by my lover
as he tried to catch me
with his webs.
It was an accident,
he didn't understand terminal
velocity, sudden stops, whiplash.
It wasn't the Green Goblin
who killed me, or the falling,
but my hero.

Some people never forget
the way you laugh
or the way your body burns
as you walk away.
People never forgot the way
I died. They told their friends,
re-read those issues
until the staples fell out
and fingerprints dulled the covers.
I died a lot in 1987.
Peter got married that same year.

I still get thank-you letters
from people who claim
if it wasn't for me,
they would have closed
this world off, abandoned it
like so many highway gas stations.
But it's not me.
I didn't restore their faith
in the funny books. It's my dying.
Always my dying.

Gary Jackson, "Elegy for Gwen Stacy" from *Missing You, Metropolis*. Copyright © 2010 by Gary Jackson. Reprinted with the permission of The Permissions Company, Inc. on behalf of Graywolf Press, Minneapolis, Minnesota, www.graywolfpress.org.

Introduction

ROBERT G. WEINER *and* ROBERT MOSES PEASLEE

In his 50 year career, Spider-Man has become the unquestioned flagship character of Marvel Comics and, next to Batman and Superman, the best known superhero across the globe. With movies, toys, books, video games, clothing, children's products, websites, animated television programs, a (beleaguered) Broadway musical, fan films, and of course, comic books, Spider-Man has permeated the popular culture landscape in a way that few superheroes have. One could say that Spider-Man has also finally made a mark in the world of academia: the august Modern Language Association announced its hosting of a special session, "The Material History of Spider-Man: A 50th Anniversary Observance," at its 2012 meeting. This illustrates the importance of sequential art as a legitimate object of cultural and historical study. Spider-Man is now "part of our collective consciousness ... (and) probably would be recognized anywhere in the world regardless of differences in race, language, creed or any other grouping, and whether or not the individuals had read a story, seen a movie, watched a television program or played a video game related to him" (Weiner, 2009: 458).

At the time of this writing, Online Computer Library Center's WorldCat, a world catalog of materials, books, articles, videos, music, and websites often used as a tool by librarians and academics, lists the phrase "Spider-Man" as occurring 5,018 times; with "Spider-Man" and "comic" occurring together on 2,220 occasions. "Spider-Man (Fictitious character) — Comic books, strips, etc." occurs 1,176 times and encompasses books, serials, internet, visual, sound and even one lone archival record for the Stan Lee papers. Spider-Man as a subject heading resulted in 2,173 items and even included a musical score, *Peter Parker: für Klavier sol*. There are 74 listings for Spider-Man and computer games.

In addition to graphic novels, children's books, Internet web sites, prose novels, and film books, Spider-Man is the topic of a wide variety of popular secondary literature. Several of those sources are worth mentioning here, including Steve Saffel's (2007) *Spider-Man The Icon: The Life and Times of a Pop Culture Phenomenon*, which looks at Spider-Man as the representative superhero of our times. The character has received the "how to" treatment in *The Spider-Man Handbook: The Ultimate Training Manual* (2006) by Seth Grahame-Smith. This guide gives readers what they need to know about how to function like Spider-Man. Tom DeFalco published his definitive collection of Spider-Man-related artist/writer interviews, *Comic Creators on Spider-Man* (2004), as well as *Spider-Man: The Ultimate Guide* (2007). Marvel Comics even got into the act of Spider-Man support literature by publishing *The Amazing Spider-Man: The Official Index to the Marvel Universe* (Sjoerdsma, 2010) and *The Official Handbook of the Marvel Universe: Spider-Man* (Couper-Smartt, 2006). Longtime Spider-Man scribe Gerry Conway published a collection of essays called *Webslinger: Unauthorized*

Essays on your Friendly Neighborhood Spider-Man (2006). Edward Gross (2002) published *Spider-Man Confidential*, his analysis of the Spider-Man phenomena shortly before the debut of Sam Raimi's *Spider-Man* in 2002. Longtime *Amazing Spider-Man* artist John Romita, Sr. (who took over when Steve Ditko left and is the artist other than Ditko most associated with the character) has been the subject of a number of studies, including the *Art of John Romita* (1996), which was a limited edition hardcover and included a signed Spider-Man drawing, and *The Romita Legacy* (2010) by Tom Spurgeon.

Spider-Man has been the subject of scholarly interest as well. This includes entries in diverse journal titles: *Communication Quarterly* (Meyer, 2003); *Continuum: Journal of Media and Cultural Studies* (Koh, 2009); *International Journal of Comic Art* (Weiner, 2009); *Journal of Child Abuse & Neglect* (Garbarino, 1987); *Journal of Criminal Justice and Popular Culture* (Adkinson, 2008); *Journal of Popular Culture* (Kaplan, 2011; Mondello, 1976; Palumbo, 1983; Richardson, 2004); *PsyArt: An Online Journal for the Psychological Study of the Arts* (Peaslee, 2005) and *Reconstruction: Studies in Contemporary Culture* (Blumberg, 2003). Spidey also appears as an important case study in a number of studies concerned with the superhero as a literary, cinematic and political phenomenon (DiPaolo, 2011; Lang and Trimble, 1988; Morris and Morris, 2005; Peaslee, 2006). This is by no means a complete catalogue, but the reader will, we hope, get some sense of the scope of popular and academic interest taken in a character who began his existence inauspiciously.

Amazing Fantasy 15 and the Rise of Spider-Man

Like most "happy accidents," the rise of Spider-Man almost did not happen. Initially, it was a throwaway story in a magazine that was about to be cancelled. *Amazing Fantasy 15* first appeared in 1962 with the cover blurb "Introducing Spider-Man." Martin Goodman, the publisher of Marvel comics at the time, was skeptical that a hero like Spider-Man would appeal to anyone. After all, why would a hero based on the repellent arachnid be appealing? However, since *Amazing Fantasy* was to be cancelled with its 15th issue, he clearly felt there was little risk. Then a strange thing happened—when the sales figures for the magazine came in, the accountants found that *Amazing Fantasy 15* sold better than any previous issue. Something about Spider-Man resonated with the reading public. This was a superhero character that was different from all the others in comicdom and one to whom everyone could relate. Ditko and Lee had hit upon the proverbial pot of gold in their storytelling.

Peter Parker (Spider-Man's alter ego) was a teenager who had money, relationship, and family problems with which he had to struggle in spite of his "amazing" powers. In high school, he still had to learn some hard life lessons. When Parker first obtained his powers, he used them to make money and get fame, but when he failed to stop a burglar who eventually killed his Uncle Ben, he learned that "with great power comes great responsibility." Since Stan Lee wrote that line in 1962, it has become one of the most quoted lines in the history of sequential art.

Spider-Man was both young and a solo hero; he was not the teenage sidekick to some other superhero like Batman's Robin or Captain America's Bucky. Yet Spider-Man was a teenager. There was an everyman quality about Parker/Spider-Man that the reading populace found appealing, and which went on to make Spider-Man the most well-liked superhero of all time. Readers found they could empathize with and understand Parker better than superheroes who were wealthy socialites or highly educated scientists. The sales of the Spider-Man comics show this. According to the web site The Comics Chronicles, since 1966 *The Amazing Spider-Man* has sold an estimated 145–150 million copies compared to Superman (110–115 million) and Iron Man (65–75 million) (Miller 2011). The story continued in *Amazing Spider-Man 1* (1963), and the soap-opera-like plots continued to increase the character's popularity. Parker graduated from high school, went to college, got a job as a photographer for a newspaper (whose publisher, J. Jonah Jameson, harbored a seething hatred of Spider-Man), and when not battling villains, he wrestled with problems of everyday life. He was often financially dependent on others, and he was scrawny — at least in those early Ditko/Lee issues (Easton, 2010: 204). Here was a character who was far from perfect, and that is precisely what made Spider-Man so popular among kids and adults of both sexes.

Another aspect that sets Parker/Spider-Man apart is that Parker pines for a father figure, having lost two (his father and his Uncle Ben). He has a mother figure in Aunt May, who, especially in the early issues, consistently dotes over him as though he were the sickliest teenager in the world. Parker/Spider-Man had both the "boyish elements of the sidekick ... absorbed into the dual identity of the superhero. (He) combined the feminine along with the boyish and adult masculine" (Easton, 2010: 204).

The Creation of Spider-Man: Controversy?

At least four people have claimed a hand in the creation of Spider-Man (although Lee and Ditko are usually given the full credit). Jack Kirby said he created Spider-Man during a 1982 interview published in Will Eisner's *Spirit* magazine. Kirby claimed: "Spider-Man was not a product of Marvel." He went on to say that the "idea was there when I talked to Stan" in the early sixties (Kirby quoted in Simon and Simon, 2003: 182–183). In a 1989 interview with Gary Groth, Kirby said, "I created Spider-Man. We decided to give it to Steve Ditko. I drew the first *Spider-Man* cover. I created the character. I created the costume..." (Groth, 2003: 39). It is true that Kirby did the cover artwork on the published version of *Amazing Fantasy 15*. In fact, comics historian Greg Theakston, in his article "The Birth of Spider-Man," points out there is evidence that Kirby produced a "five page story ... (featuring) the characters of Uncle Ben, Aunt May and Peter at home." He goes on to say that "Kirby's SPIDER-MAN design looked a great deal like the Night Fighter" (a previous Kirby production that could walk on walls) (Theakston, 1990: n.p.). Lee admits that, when he saw Kirby's work on a few pages, "he wasn't the guy for Spider-Man. I didn't want the character to look like your usual superhero.... When Jack drew him, Spider-Man looked like all Jack's other heroes" (DeFalco, 2004: 12).

Joe Simon, Kirby's longtime artistic partner, described how he created a version of Spider-Man in 1953 (Kirby claimed to be involved too) called the Silver Spider who had the powers of a human spider. He was eventually going to be called "Spiderman," as opposed to Marvel's hyphenated Spider-Man. The project never got off the ground, but Simon did create a logo for the Spiderman and several story outlines with art for the Silver Spider, who looked more like a combination of Archie and Captain Marvel than Peter Parker/Spider-Man. Kirby and Simon did create a hero with the powers of a fly (called, simply, the Fly). The first issue featured the Fly against a villainous Spider Spry. The center spread for the issue featured the Fly on a spider's web with the Spry taunting the superhero (Simon and Simon, 2003: 173; Theakston, 1990: n.p.).

Ditko dismisses Kirby's claims of having created Spider-Man. Ditko argues that Kirby came up with "five unused pages of an unfinished story. It existed as a part of a fragment of some undisclosed whole. The story, characters, legend, 'ideas' are incomplete, unknown. Jack's whole Spider-man 'idea' is unexplained, non-existing, uncreated" (Ditko, 2002: 58). Ditko goes on to point out that Kirby's version of Spider-Man is not the same one that he and Lee worked on. Kirby's cover for *Amazing Fantasy 15* came after Ditko had drawn one that wasn't used and after the story was already written. "Spider-man had a costume used in the story, the web-designed costume I brought into existence. So I am the creator of it and the published Spider-man costume is my creation" (Ditko, 2002: 59). Of everyone who claims to have had a hand in creating Spider-Man, Ditko is the one most offended by Kirby's comments and not, perhaps, without some justification.

Lee, for his part, has always said that his inspiration for Spider-Man was the old pulp hero the Spider. In an interview with Tom DeFalco, Lee had no problem sharing credit for Spider-Man with Ditko, calling him "the co-creator." Lee further amplifies that statement with this one: "Even though Spider-Man was my idea.... Spider-Man needed Steve to transform him from an idea into artwork on paper. Steve had to design the look of the character" (DeFalco, 2004: 14). As Spider-Man continued, Ditko took more control in terms of writing. Lee admitted as much in early 1966: "I don't plot *Spider-Man* any more. Steve Ditko the artist has been doing the stories. I guess I'll leave him alone until sales start to slip.... We were arguing so much over plot lines, I told him to make up his own stories..." (quoted in Wells, 2002: 76).

Perhaps it doesn't really matter who actually created Spider-Man. One could argue that all four of them did. Today, so many people have taken a turn at writing or drawing Spider-Man that it seems almost a moot discussion. Spider-Man endures as one of the most popular heroes in the modern world. The character is tailored to changing trends. As technologies get better, the character continues to be adapted to films, video games, toys, clothing, and animation, but his core remains the same. Theakston remains philosophical about the creation of Spider-Man: "Spider-Man was molded by many hands over many years. No one man can lay full claim to the character's creation, but they can all share the glory" (1990, n.p.).

Spider-Man: A Superhero

Spider-Man fits firmly within the definition of a superhero. Comics scholar Peter Coogan, in his groundbreaking work on the superhero (2009, 2006), argues that four unique characteristics differentiate the superhero from other heroes (pulp, western, science fiction, horror, biblical, etc.). The characteristics are (1) powers, (2) identity, (3) costume, and (4) generic distinction. Spider-Man clearly has powers from being bitten by a radioactive spider. Having such powers is "one of the most identifiable elements of the superhero genre" (Coogan, 2009: 78). Spider-Man has super strength and agility, the ability to walk up and down on walls, a "spider-sense" that tells him of danger, and the enhanced intellectual and scientific acuity that led to the creation of his webbing. In addition, Coogan identifies "mission" as an important dimension of the superhero's identity. After the death of his uncle at the hands of a burglar, Parker/Spider-Man could have stopped; instead, he learns that "with great power comes great responsibility" and launches his mission to help others and stop criminals so no one else has to experience his anguish. The task of making the world a better and safer place in the face of his guilt helps spur on the decision to use his powers for the betterment of humanity. Spider-Man's identity also "comprises the codename and the costume" (Coogan, 2009: 78). He takes the codename Spider-Man and usually swings around in a bright blue and red costume that indicates his kinship to the spider. In the costume, Spider-Man clearly has what Coogan calls the "chevron"—a unique identifier (Coogan, 2009: 79). In fact, Theakston praises Spider-Man's costume as a "wonderful example of design skills" (2002, n.p.). Ditko himself reinforces this point: "I've always felt that you should be able to identify a hero by a small part of the costume. The best characters have costumes like that: Speedball, The Thing, and Spider-Man" (Ditko, quoted in Theakston, 2002: n.p.). Generic distinctions, finally, "...mark the superhero genre off from the rest of the adventure meta-genre" (Coogan, 2009: 91). Clearly because Spider-Man fits within the parameters of the superhero character type, he is different from other heroes like Buffy the Vampire Slayer, Rooster Cockburn, Luke Skywalker, the Shadow, or the Green Hornet, all of whom do amazing things but would fall outside Coogan's taxonomy.

Spider-Man Media

Since 1962, there have been no less than 10 different sequential art titles featuring Spider-Man, six different animated series (Spider-Woman also had an animated series), a live action television program, animated movies, and three very successful blockbuster feature films grossing a total of just under $2.5 billion. Spider-Man also has the distinction of being teamed up with President Obama in *Amazing Spider-Man 583*, published in January, 2009. This issue became one of the biggest selling comics of all time, requiring more than five printings. There are also numerous fan films online and on DVD (such as Dan Poole's *Green Goblin's Last Stand*, based on the "Death of Gwen Stacy" storyline). Spider-Man has also been a popular video game character, including the 2011 release of *Spider-Man: Edge of Time* (in which Spidey must team up with his 2099 alternate-universe self), and Stan Lee with his brother Larry Lieber is still publishing the Spider-Man newspaper strip. That all of these media have enjoyed varying but consistently above-average levels of success "is a sign of the continued importance of Peter Parker's story to us" (Harrison, 2010: 256).

Meanwhile, things show no sign of slowing down. A "rebooting" of the film franchise, starring Andrew Garfield (and not Donald Glover, as Phillip Cunningham discusses in this volume), is scheduled for a 2012 release. In the fall of 2011, a new sequential art series, *Avenging Spider-Man* by Zeb Wells and Joe Madureira, debuted as a team-up book with the Red Hulk, Wolverine, and Spider-Woman. And then, of course, there's that Broadway thing ... but we'll save that for later.

Since 1962, literally hundreds of writers and artists have told thousands of Spider-Man stories. Some of the most notable storylines and graphic novels include the *Death of Gwen Stacy, The Wedding, One More Day, The Clone Saga, Birth of Venom, The Death of Spider-Man, Spider-Man: Noir* and *Kraven's Last Hunt*. The writers and artists who have worked on various Spider-Man projects represent a virtual who's who of sequential art. These include Brian Michael Bendis, Paul Benjamin, Sal Buscema, Tom DeFalco, J. M. DeMatteis, Gerry Conway, Steve Ditko, Neil Gaiman, Mark Gruenwald, Paul Jenkins, Stan Lee, Howard Mackie, Frank Miller, Joe Quesada, John Romita, Sr., John Romita, Jr., Roger Stern, Dan Slott, Roy Thomas, Marv Wolfman, and so many others that deserve a mention. Spider-Man is one of those characters sought out by talent.

Spider-Man has worked with nearly every hero in the Marvel Universe. Although he usually flies solo, Spider-Man has at times been a part of teams including the Avengers and, most recently, the Fantastic Four (renamed the Future Foundation, for which Spider-Man wears a white costume). Spider-Man even worked alongside Marvel's "distinguished competition," DC Comics' Superman, in 1976, and has also teamed up with Batman on occasion. He has seen several well-known character spin-offs — including Spider-Woman, Spider-Girl, Cosmic Spider-Man, Arena, Spider-Ham, Spider-Man Doppelganger, Scarlett Spider, and Spider-Man 2099 — and Spider-Man comics have been adapted to different cultural contexts, including the series *Spider-Man: Manga* and *Spider-Man: India*. Spider-Man appeared in a Japanese live-action television series. Some unauthorized uses include an Italian version and a Turkish film. In the Turkish version, Spider-Man is a villain who battles Santo and Captain America. This demonstrates the character's worldwide appeal (and his cultural flexibility).

Spider-Man Villains

In superhero storytelling, heroes are often only as good as their villains. In Spider-Man's case, as Rick Hudson discusses below with regard to the Sinister Six, the villains against which he battles often share many of his character flaws. Many villains in the *Spider-Man* series remain memorable, including the Green Goblin, Doctor Octopus, Carnage, Kraven, Venom, the Jackal, Hobgoblin, Sandman, Scorpion, and many others. Stan Lee admits the villains' central role: "...I always start with the villain. Who is the villain? What terrible thing does he want to do? What are his problems? Once I work that out, I try to figure how the hero can stop him" (DeFalco, 2004: 22). Villains in the Spidey-verse are usually complex characters who are not strictly evil and are sometimes capable of doing great good. In Spidey's world, most of the villains have complex motivations for what they do. One of the most telling examples of this occurs during the *Clone Saga* storyline when Doctor Octopus does everything he can to save Spider-Man from a lethal chemical virus. He saves his "greatest enemy" so they can continue their "dance." Octopus recognizes the hero in Spider-Man when he tells his girlfriend "Spider-Man has always been my perfect foil: Courageous, Decent, and Self Sacrificing! In so many way he was the man I could have been ... might have been..." (DeFalco, 2010: n.p.). Ock recognizes his own shortcomings, but in doing so realizes that he needs Spider-Man so they can continue to fight another day. He thinks to himself, "I need you Spider-Man. I need the challenge and meaning only you can provide" (*ibid.*). In some sense Spider-Man is a part of his family (Octopus once almost married Aunt May). He has been involved in Peter Parker's life for many years and needs to have the back and forth between them to find meaning in his own life.

Spider-Man: A Hero for Education

Very early in Stan Lee's tenure writing the *Spider-Man* title, he received letters from parents telling him that their child's "...reading skills have improved ever since he started reading *Spider-Man*" (DeFalco, 2004: 21). Spider-Man was one of the first major superhero characters to be adapted for education by appearing on the 1970s program *The Electric Company* in three-to-six minute episodes. Spider-Man communicated using word balloons, which encouraged young people to read and conceptualize the action. Actor Morgan Freeman sometimes provided narration and acted in numerous episodes. To further this educational component, Marvel created the comic book series *Spidey Super Stories* in conjunction with *The Electric Company*.

The series lasted 57 issues, running from 1974 until 1982. These were designed as easy-reader comics to teach and foster a love of reading in very young children (Weiss, 2010). A graphic novel, *Best of Spidey Super Stories*, was also published (Thomas, 1978). There have also been numerous easy-reader Spider-Man related books published over the years (Weiner, 2008). James Rourke, in the *Comic Book Curriculum*, includes a chapter on Spider-Man using the graphic novel *Kraven's Last Hunt* as a teaching tool. He even includes a lesson plan complete with discussion questions and vocabulary list, based upon the graphic novel (2010: pp. 27–34, 145–150). James Bucky Carter describes in this volume how he used *Ultimate Spider-Man* in the classroom.

Spider-Man: Turn Off the Dark

The seven-plus-years-in-the-making Spider-Man musical *Spider-Man: Turn Off the Dark* (*TOD*) represents a rare attempt at combining comic book mythology with the trappings of the Broadway theater musical, a project tried before with modest success in 1966. That production, *It's a Bird ... It's a Plane ... It's Superman,* has a varied history, including a television broadcast based on the musical and revival performances over the years, as recently as 2010. Unlike *TOD*, *It's a Bird...* was received positively, with three Tony Award nominations during its 1966 run. *TOD*, on the other hand, has had numerous false starts, rewrites, production problems and set accidents. Its pre-production costs ballooned to $75 million (the most expensive Broadway musical in history). Its co-writer and director, the auteur Julie Taymor, was eventually fired. Some critics vehemently decried the play during previews, with *New York Times* critic Ben Brantley critiquing the show as "not only the most expensive musical ever to hit Broadway; it may also rank among the worst" (2011). Perhaps even more damning was Brantley's summation that the production was "just a bore." National Public Radio, while agreeing that the play had its boring parts, was slightly more generous in its praise of the opening, saying that the musical does have "plenty of thrilling moments in the production." NPR goes on to qualify, however, that it is the effects — and not the story — that is the true star of the show, a "musical that is not much of a musical at all" (Blankenship, 2011).

Taymor, for her part, was critical of the producers for being too quick to listen to focus groups, blogs, and social media like Facebook and Twitter. She argued that there is "always something people don't like" and that in its revised version the "production today has become simpler." She also pointed out that "Shakespeare would have been appalled" by the way producers listen to amateurs instead of allowing artistic creativity and originality to reign (Healy, 2011). Because of the perceived problems with the script, comic book writer, Spider-Man scribe, and playwright Roberto Aguirre-Sacasa was brought in for rewrites (DeBenedetto, 2011; Marshall 2011) and to work with playwright Glen Berger (Aguirre-Sacasa also wrote a successful update to the Superman musical). In revamping the original script, writers Berger and Aguirre-Sacasa wanted to provide the fan base with more entry points. Aguirre-Sacasa told MTV.com, "We put in a few inside jokes for the Marvel fans, some references that true die-hards will get, but if you blink you miss them" (Marshall, 2011).

As Daniel Mendelsohn points out in his *New York Review of Books* article about the play, "Why She Fell," only two genres feature humans transformed into monsters: "Classical Greek and Roman myth and American comic books" (2011). He sees Taymor as a bad fit for the project given her general disdain of popular culture, suggesting that there is "very little about *Spider-Man* (that) suggests an ideal vehicle for Taymor's talents" (2011). Taymor's attempts at making Spider-Man's transformation echo the Greek transformations of man into animal seemed destined for failure. (Director Ang Lee succeeded in making the 2003 *Hulk* movie a Greek/Shakespearian tragedy, much to the displeasure of movie-going audiences.)

Musically the production employed top-notch talent with U2's Bono and the Edge writing the score, but Mendelsohn's initial reaction to a preview was that the music was "banal" (2011). The composers themselves appeared onstage at the 2011 Tony Awards to deliver the self-deprecating line, "we used to be famous for being in U2." Literally thousands of news stories (and even a few parodies) have covered *TOD*'s trials and tribulations. A Google search at the time of this writing for "Spider-Man: Turn Off the Dark" yielded 8,680,000 hits, illustrating the interest in the production. Seventeen-year-old Adam Brodhiem wrote *Spider-Man: Turn Off the Lights*, a satirical script based upon the distressed production and a winning entry in the 2011 Blank Theatre Company's Young Playwrights Festival in Hollywood—honored the same month of *TOD*'s official opening. *Mad Magazine* poked fun at the musical in its June 2011 issue.

With 183 preview performances, multiple false starts, seemingly interminable script doctoring, rewritten music, highly publicized stage disasters, and the attempt to design the most elaborate theater set in history, it is perhaps amazing that *TOD* has survived. One news commentator further reiterated this point on the eve of the official opening on June 14th, 2011 saying, "if nothing else (*TOD* is) a major spectacle, including acrobatic stunts where actors literally float above the audience" (Brown, 2011). Talking to Jeffrey Brown, *The New York Times*' Patrick Healy said the musical was an attempt to bring to the theater something novel and spectacular:

> They wanted to create something that Broadway had never seen. They wanted to blend circus, music, flying stunts, sort of create like a Cirque du Soleil meets Broadway. And they wanted to tell a story sort of that they saw as a post–9/11 story about a young boy from Queens who was finding something within himself to face a very difficult world (Brown, 2011).

Like the character for which it is named, *TOD* will no doubt endure and be popular regardless of how critics view it. The early previews made $1 million despite bad reviews, and the show continues to do big business after its official opening regardless of its seeming mediocrity. *TOD* is already, at the time of this writing, the third-highest grossing show on Broadway after *Wicked* and *The Lion King* (Associated Press, 2011). If only because of its notoriety, it seems assured a successful run. One is tempted to imagine the Broadway old guard shaking their incredulous fists in *TOD*'s direction with all the vigor and spite of J. Jonah Jameson.

The "Death" of Spider-Man

In the highly praised *Ultimate Spider-Man*, which debuted in 2000, Spider-Man was updated for a post-millennial audience. The rationale was to try and bring in new readers by creating a separate "Ultimate" Marvel Universe where the previous 50 years of continuity would not be an issue. Those who wanted to start reading comics, but were put off by having to know a tremendous amount of history, could dive in. The *Ultimate* line was a great success, with *Ultimate Spider-Man* being one of the key titles. Written by Brian Michael Bendis, the title was a hit. Bendis' writing captured the imagination of readers old and new, but what really sets him apart is the bomb he drops in *Ultimate Spider-Man #160*, where Peter Parker is killed at the hands of the Green Goblin while saving both his Aunt May and Gwen Stacy (in a unique twist on the original Gwen Stacy story). Bendis was so intimate with the character he had written for over ten years that he told *USA Today*: "Listen, I sat there typing this thing with tears in my eyes like a big baby.... I went upstairs to my wife, and I go, 'I am so embarrassed. I think I've literally been crying for 45 minutes.' I've had real things happen in my life I didn't cry about, and yet I'm crying about this" (Truitt, 2011). Bendis said he was more "professionally and personally" involved in this version of Parker than characters he himself created. A new Spider-Man will arise from the ashes of Parker's death, influenced by the "great responsibility" Peter showed at saving his loved ones (Truitt, 2011). It remains to be seen whether this version of Parker will indeed remain dead. Superhero narratives are notorious for never keeping a character dead for too long. Captain America, the original Human Torch, Green Goblin (Norman Osborne), Bucky, Jean Grey, Jason Todd (Robin), Green Arrow, and Superman have all "died" and been brought back. But for the moment, it seems that this version of Peter Parker is really, truly dead.

Exploring the Spider-verse

What follows, then, is a necessarily incomplete collection of analyses focusing upon the popular culture phenomenon we've come to know, in hundreds of manifestations, as Spider-Man; an exercise in capturing the dynamism of what Henry Jenkins (2003) has called "transmedia storytelling." We begin, appropriately enough, with a foreword by Tom DeFalco, one of the true giants on the short list of industry professionals who have substantively influenced Spidey's development and a former editor-in-chief at Marvel Comics.

Part I begins the collection with a series of articles dealing with relationships between the world of Spider-Man and the culture within which he exists. In his article entitled "Donald Glover for Spider-Man," Phillip Lamarr Cunningham explores the recent episode surrounding the supposed "candidacy" for the role of Peter Parker/Spider-Man on the part of African American actor Donald Glover. Although largely farcical, Glover's campaign to portray the Webslinger in Columbia Studios/Marvel's 2012 film "reboot," *The Amazing Spider-Man* offers, Cunningham suggests, an opportunity to consider the role of race in casting (and drawing) superheroes and (especially) their alter egos. As Cunningham states, "the strong reactions of those who argued that casting Glover as Parker was inappropriate due to his race speaks with equal volume to concerns about continuity, fidelity and racial identity that have been a hallmark of comic book superhero fandom. As such, the discourse on Donald Glover's campaign to audition for *The Amazing Spider-Man* provides a meaningful context in which to consider the competing desires for diversity and universality (an interesting paradox on its own), on the one hand, and for continuity and fidelity, on the other, when it comes to comic book superheroes." These desires, it might be said, are present in all cases where adaptation occurs, and so Cunningham's analysis offers an interesting starting point for further investigation of these questions.

Peter Lee reaches back much further in his piece analyzing the place of Spider-Man comics within 1960s counterculture, with particular emphasis on Parker's role as mouthpiece of a generation: "as an outsider, Parker—and Spider-Man—serves as a commentator of the changing social milieu during the 1960s." Addressing issues such as race, drugs, campus unrest, and other contemporary topics, Marvel provides, through the experiences of Parker/Spider-Man, a teen-aged perspective often left aside in mainstream news coverage. Moreover, the narrative choices made by Stan Lee, Steve Ditko and others served, Lee suggests, to critique a conservative power structure even as the Spider-Man texts existed unproblematically within the confines of the Comics Code. In Lee's summation, the adults of the Spider-Man world, or the "establishment," provide countless examples of how not to act; though they had great power, "they were greatly irresponsible."

Martin Flanagan shifts the analytical lens from the historical to the spatial context, exploring Spider-Man's New York, in print and on celluloid, alongside the concept of the "spectacular city" so often utilized in contemporary action cinema. Flanagan argues that "what all of these cities hold in common, across different sub-generic articulations of the adventure-fantasy spectrum, is their capacity to be spectacularly destroyed, with attendant implications both for audience pleasure, and anxiety," particularly in a Western, post–9/11 milieu. Writing about the trilogy of cinematic adaptations beginning with *Spider-Man* (2002), Flanagan points out: "Raimi understands that what counts in a superhero story is the way the protagonist navigates their way around the city; not only how they interact with people but how they incorporate an intimate knowledge of urban space to their advantage (and how the city facilitates their omnipotence)." Moreover, the article outlines some crucial differences between sequential art and cinematic approaches to the urban, particularly with regard to how each approached (or failed to approach) the events of September 11, 2001.

Moving to a different dimension of the extra-textual, Lisa Holderman asks us to consider the impact upon popular understandings of science produced by the $2.5 billion-grossing teaching tool known as the *Spider-Man* film trilogy, exploring her central proposition "that popular media, including (and perhaps especially) high-budget Hollywood science fiction films ... contribute to a denigration of science in the public sphere, and by extension, to a general anti-intellectualism that has hegemonic implications." Important to her discussion is Holderman's insistence that such a process is best understood theoretically through the Gramscian concept of "hegemony," an approach that allows for the exploration of nuance and negotiation in meaning-making rather than simply ascribing blame or responsibility for what she sees as the three most prominent ways in which viewers are alienated from science: fear-mongering, the negative depiction of practitioners, and misrepresentation of facts.

Closing Part I, James Bucky Carter shares his experiences using *Spider-Man* texts — in particular, *Ultimate Spider-Man Volume 1*— as classroom tools effective in bringing students into contact with Platonic philosophy and Derridean theory. In this series, subtitled *Power and Responsibility*, "students find an adolescent male on the cusp of adulthood living out the tensions and ties among these poets, philosophers and critical theorists." The results, Carter suggests, are not limited to a more insightful grasp of concept; also, "students attend to each additional graphic novel we read in class, regardless of genre, cognizant to textual detail and with an aim of considering how every graphic novel reveals important elements of human thought and contemporary theories of living and knowing."

Beginning Part II, in one of three pieces analyzing specific graphic novels within the larger Spidey-verse, David Walton takes on J.M. DeMatteis' *Kraven's Last Hunt* (a collaboration with penciler Mike Zeck), asking us to consider whether we might more fully understand Kraven's full dimensionality as a character and attain greater understanding of the story within which he appears by turning to DeMettais' later autobiographical effort, *Brooklyn Dreams*, chief among other works. Kraven, Walton suggests, is best seen as a channeling of DeMatteis' effort to explore, understand, establish, and perhaps theorize his own authorship against the backdrop of a narrative philosophy Walton characterizes as "true lies."

The reader next finds Christina C. Angel's analysis of Neil Gaiman's *Marvel 1602*, a text that "manages to address Elizabethan/Jacobean politics and religion using quintessentially

American and famous Marvel comic characters from the 20th century." For Angel, the book, in which we find not Spider-Man but rather Parker (Parquagh) amidst a stable of other anachronistic Marvel heroes, "stands not only as a critically-acclaimed comic series, but as a crossroads of interpretive values, not the least of which is how these two disparate chronotopes (Renaissance England and 20th century America) can be in dialogue with one another in meaningful ways." In particular, Angel prosecutes a critique of those analyses, finding an easy isomorphism between Spider-Man and the Christian savior, suggesting, from a hermeneutical perspective, that "Spider-Man is not so much Christ-like as he is *like* Christ (a fine but important distinction)" in his capacity to be interpreted — and therefore present — in narratives from which he is nominally absent (like *Marvel 1602*).

Derek Parker Royal's analysis of *Spider-Man: Blue*, finally, finds — in authors Jeph Loeb and Tim Sale's removal of the traditional omniscient narrator — "a significant shift in the narrative strategy, one that allows us an intimate and more immediate association with the hero." The story, Royal suggests, is told solely from Parker/Spidey's perspective, a strategy that is enhanced visually by first-person, point-of-view composition, and which sets *Blue* apart from previous, much-loved Spider-Man stories.

Opening Part III, which considers the colorful *Daily Bugle* editor J. Jonah Jameson, Aaron Drucker argues for a reading of Jameson in which the character's function extends beyond his well-documented status as both a foil for Parker/Spidey and a narrative embodiment of Stan Lee himself. In what Drucker calls a "manifesto as metaphor," Jameson is deployed by Lee as the embodiment of conservative, Comics Code censorship (perhaps as a synecdoche of Dr. Frederic Wertham himself), and therefore, in his frequent buffoonery, stands as Lee's critique of that censorship. According to Drucker, it is only once Lee shows *Spider-Man* can succeed without Code approval that Jameson ceases to perform this function. At this pivot, we see a change in "the dynamic of Jameson's character from a pure antagonistic foil and single-issue critic to a powerful voice in the media generally. Lee offers a model for cultural critique and opens the door for later writers to criticize, lampoon, and castigate the polemical media of their day."

Andrew A. Smith continues the exploration of Jameson's character by posing the question, "hero or villain?" After exploring the genesis of the character and cataloguing his litany of reprehensible (perhaps villainous) deeds, Smith goes on to show how Jameson has, over time, developed into a multi-dimensional character capable of altruism, nobility, and perhaps even heroism. Although Smith finally suggests that "hero" is too kind a term for the irascible editor, the essay, a detailed and comprehensive analysis of Jameson's character history, does make a case for his narrative indispensability.

Finally, Jameson is examined by Matthew McGowan, a working journalist, and Jeremy Short, a scholar of business administration, as an example of high profile, metropolitan journalism management. McGowan and Short "provide a critical perspective on the similarities and differences between the workplace environment found in *Spider-Man* texts, and the realities of the modern workplace — especially in regard to the newspaper publishing industry," and in so doing further clarify the degree to which Jameson's character ambiguity reveals more than simple narrative play. For the authors, Jameson's management style and (in)ethical decisions serve as a trenchant reminder that the old chestnut about power and responsibility also applies to those who, instead of tights, wear ties.

Part IV, which explores specific relationships between Spidey and other superheroes and villains, begins with Cord A. Scott's analysis of the Punisher — how he and Spider-Man "became symbols of a dystopic America that dealt with corruption following the Vietnam

War." Scott explores the similarities, contrasts and interactions between the two characters, suggesting that in many ways, the Webslinger and his vigilante counterpart are distorted mirror images—two answers to the same question. Scott examines in particular detail the maxi-series *Civil War*, pointing out that many of the same discourses that constituted the pair's interactions at the outset remain in place—though their roles in the narrative (as savior and saved) are reversed—and that they continue to offer different answers to the same question: what becomes of American ideals in the "War on Terror"?

Rick Hudson explores the notion of the "anti-villain" in his examination of the nefarious "hexahedral harem of hate," the Sinister Six. Hudson suggests that, "unlike the somewhat 'gothic' or perhaps even 'operatic' villains of the Batman comics, the villains Spider-Man faces show qualities similar to the hero and supporting characters." They are "in many ways 'ordinary guys' living in a fantastical world where extraordinary things happen" and who exhibit a "flawed likeability." While the attraction to Peter Parker as a super-heroic alter ego based on his realism is well-documented, Hudson calls our attention to the Spider-Man universe as an "empathic narrative" in which *both heroes and villains* "must contend—alongside the mythic struggles that form the backbone of the story—with the mundane disasters and tragedies we all face."

Philip Bevin closes the section with a return to the work of J.M. DeMatteis and a Judith Butler-influenced analysis of the 1995 crossover book *Batman and Spider-Man: Disordered Minds*. Anticipating many of the theoretical considerations explored in our later section on gender, Bevin utilizes Butler's work on "performativity"—that is, "performance of a given role that is enacted unconsciously and with absolute faith in the reality of the identity traits being performed on the part of the 'performer'"—"to demonstrate that both Batman and Spider-Man are defined by their awareness and fear of the fact that the characteristics and personality traits that constitute their own senses of self are contingent, and by their efforts to make these character traits appear to themselves as fixed and immutable in order to prevent their own identities from being lost."

Bevin's piece is also very interested in the somewhat paradoxical role of loss in the creation of identity, a more general dimension of superhero character construction, and so his piece also acts as a bridge to Part V, addressing the concept of trauma. Forrest C. Helvie begins the segment with an articulation of trauma theory and its applicability to studies of popular culture: "in bringing to light the presence in comics of [traumatic] experiences ... we might better understand how sequential art can provide a voice for those who experience it in the real world." In particular, Helvie's analysis aims to illustrate "how the traumatic events in Peter's life changed him, how the death of his Uncle Ben serves as the moment of his being fractured apart from his community, and his continual attempt to return that broken community to its original state of wholeness."

Moving from personal to national trauma, Tama Leaver considers 9/11 and the role of the Raimi film trilogy in facilitating what he terms "artificial mourning," a term, as Leaver puts it, that should be read not as "necessarily positioning mourning facilitated through popular culture as 'unreal' or necessarily 'less' than trauma in the 'real' world," but rather "as a signifier of unstable boundaries, where easy binary divisions no longer make sense." For Leaver, Spider-Man's "artificiality is evident in the seeming incompatibilities of being both a human subject and a technological object, being both a hero and an everyday person with everyday problems, and being both a means of escapism for audiences, while engaging on some level with serious political and cultural concerns." Leaver positions the Spider-Man films as significant texts for understanding the post–9/11 environment, suggesting that "the films do not seek to re-vision the historical event of September 11th, but rather address the West's Long September not just metaphorically but in an allegorical manner that, to some extent, attempts to remake the past of the Marvel comic book franchise."

In Part VI, dealing with gender in the world of Spider-Man, we begin with Robert G. Weiner's look at the various manifestations of the Peter Parker/Mary Jane Watson romance and their importance for examining Susan Wood Glucksohn's contention that the role of the female lead in superhero narratives is essentially that of obfuscation. Comparing Mary Jane's characterization in the *Amazing Spider-Man* comic oeuvre with her cinematic manifestation, Weiner suggests that in the latter case the romantic relationship is far more central to the story, reflecting a long-standing bias in American narrative cinema, not to mention an effort by Universal Studios, to attain the Holy Grail of high-concept filmmaking: a "four-quadrant" audience.

It is with audience in mind that Emily D. Edwards moves the discussion forward with her examination of the under-researched area of female superhero spectatorship, specifically that surrounding the *Spider-Man* film trilogy. Weaving together textual and reception analyses, Edwards asks whether the films provide yet another example of Laura Mulvey's "male gaze," or if, in fact, other "visual pleasures" are built into the text and therefore available to and attained by the women she interviews. She suggests that "for some viewers Peter Parker can be interpreted as a manifestation of the animus, allowing the viewer to identify with the masculine side of herself but not suffer 'masculinization' of the male gaze."

Alongside Mary Jane and J. Jonah Jameson, the character of Aunt May is among the most long-standing and narratively fecund supporting players found within the pages and frames of the *Spider-Man* textual apparatus, and Ora C. McWilliams continues the examination of gender by asking how me might read the "incorrigible" May in feminist terms. McWilliams' archaeology of May's development is expansive, reaching from canonical beginnings to more recent adaptations within the sequential art tradition, suggesting, in part, that "Aunt May represents an intersectionality between expectations of feminine gender roles and expectations of the elderly" and "a reflection of how we feel about mother figures and women in general from the 1960s through the 2000s."

Robert Moses Peaslee closes the section with his reading of the first two *Spider-Man* films, analyzing the many crucial psychoanalytic motifs present in them. He first analyzes the many Oedipal triangles present in the narratives, with special emphasis on that set up between the alter ego, the female, and the superhero. Peaslee goes on to posit that the female, while clearly a maternal character in Oedipal terms, also fulfills other Freudian roles such as the madonna/whore and an Oedipal role of her own. Peaslee concludes with a look at the overarching construct of the conscious/unconscious split as it is so plainly illustrated in many characters, both heroic and villainous. The chapter ends with some observations on the importance of a psychoanalytic interpretation, primarily given its utility in exploring the changing nature of the superhero genre.

Part VII concludes the selection of articles with attention to derivative Spider-Man texts beyond the various manifestations in sequential art and cinema, the majority of which have languished in a state of relative inattention. David Ray Carter begins by considering the politics of adaptation and "retroactive continuity" at play in the creation of *Spider-Man: The Animated Series*. *SMAS*, Carter contends, is an example of the benefits of narrative synthesis, "weaving a more perfect web" out of thirty years' worth of fragmented storytelling. Carter takes us on a detailed tour of the *SMAS* narrative arc and makes a case for its inclusion among the best realizations of the character and his story.

Mark McDermott, jumping off from the press surrounding U2's involvement with the *Turn Off the Dark* project, takes readers on a connoisseur's tour of the vast, obscure trove of Spider-Man–related music recording. Part history, part critical review, McDermott's chapter represents a missing piece added to the puzzle of sequential art scholarship, providing an important example of how relationships between the comics industry and those to which it contributes might fruitfully be examined.

Casey O'Donnell concludes with an important and timely look at Spider-Man's presence in the world of electronic gaming. Discussing ethnographic data collected during extended fieldwork among game developers working on the Vivacious Visions game studio release, *Spider-Man 3*, O'Donnell provides a case-study analysis asking us to reconsider the easy ascription of the term "convergent" to networked technologies of play: "This project is exemplary of what most cross-platform/cross-media production looks like. There is more divergence than convergence when examined from the perspective of media producer." Critiquing the work of Henry Jenkins, O'Donnell argues that convergence represents "a labor space where media producers work extensively to keep media technologies, digital encoded data in proprietary formats, and media organizations with little interest in cooperating with one another beyond economic gain, from flying apart into their 'component parts.'"

Finally, we are very fortunate to end the volume with an afterword by poet Gary Jackson, whose book *Missing You, Metropolis* explores issues of race, gender, and identity in superhero texts and was awarded the 2009 Cave Canem Prize. Jackson's approach to this material is raw and personal, and we are proud to include his summative essay as part of this collection.

What follows, in sum, is a collection defined by a deliberately expansive and inclusive approach to capturing what it means to be a scholar, interpreter, teacher and fan of all things Spidey. Our hope is that the volume provides new insight, contributes to the theory and history of Spider-Man and superheroes generally, and gives Spidey-philes of both academic and historical persuasion reason to keep turning pages.

Should Stan Lee or Steve Ditko ever read these words, I hope they will accept our gratitude for creating a character worthy of such prolonged discussion.

Works Cited

Adkinson, Cary D. "The Amazing Spider-Man and the Evolution of the Comics Code: A Case Study in Cultural Criminology." *Journal of Criminal Justice and Popular Culture* 15:3 (2008): 241–61.

Associated Press. "Spider-Man Musical Not Hurt by Poor Reviews," *Sacramento Bee Online*. 6/20/2011. Accessed 6/22/2011. http://www.sacbee.com/2011/06/20/3714571/spider-man-musical-not-hurt-by.html.

Bagge, Peter. "Spider-Man Sucks." in Ben Schwartz ed., *The Best American Comics Criticism*. Seattle: Fantagraphics, 2010: pp. 117–121.

Blankenship, Mark. "'Spider-Man': Worked Over and Reworked, Does It Work Better Now?" *NPR.org*. 6/15/2011. Accessed 6/16/2011. http://www.npr.org/blogs/monkeysee/2011/06/15/137194403/spider-man-worked-over-and-reworked-does-it-work-better-now.

Blumberg, Arnold T. "The Night Gwen Stacy Died: The End of Innocence and the Birth of the Bronze Age." *Reconstruction: Studies in Contemporary Culture*. 3:4 (Fall 2003). Accessed 6/5/2011. http://reconstruction.eserver.org/034/blumberg.htm.

Boehm, Mark. "Student Playwright Spins a 'Spider-Man' Tale," *LATimes.com*. 5/31/2011. Accessed 6/6/2011. http://articles.latimes.com/2011/may/31/entertainment/la-et-spider-man-satire-20110531.

Brantley, Ben. "Good vs. Evil, Hanging by a Thread." *NYTIMES.Com*. 2/8/2011. Accessed 6/3/2011. http://theater.nytimes.com/2011/02/08/theater/reviews/Spider-Man-review.html?src=tptw&pagewanted=all.

_____. "1 Radioactive Bite, 8 Legs and 183 Previews." *NYTimes.com*. 6/14/2011. Accessed 6/16/2011. http://theater.nytimes.com/2011/06/15/theater/reviews/spider-man-turn-off-the-dark-opens-after-changes-review.html?adxnnl=1&hpw=&adxnnlx=1308139831-8zKqptJWQgNkhP638FtjFQ.

Brown, Jeffrey. "Broadway Holds Its Breath as 'Spider-Man' Musical Officially Debuts." *PBS.org*. 6/14/2011. Accessed 6/6/2011. http://www.pbs.org/newshour/bb/entertainment/jan-june11/Spider-Man_06-14.html.

Conway, Gerry ed., *Webslinger: Unauthorized Essays on Your Friendly Neighborhood Spider-Man*. Dallas: BenBella Books, 2006.

Coogan, Peter. "The Definition of a Superhero," in Jeet Heer and Kent Worcester eds., *A Comics Studies Reader*. Jackson, Miss: University of Mississippi Press, 2009: 77–93.

_____. *Superhero: The Secret Origin of a Genre*. Austin, TX: Monkeybrain Books, 2006.

Couper-Smartt, Jonathan. *Official Handbook of the Marvel Universe: Spider-Man*. New York: Marvel, 2006.

DeBenedett, Paul. "Caught in Critics' Web, Spider-Man Musical Finds New Writer." *NBCNewYork.Com*. 2/17/2011. Accessed 6/3/2011. http://www.nbcnewyork.com/news/local/Spider-Man-Musical-Finds-New-Writer-116403594.html.

DeFalco, Tom, and Matthew K. Manning. *The Amazing Spider-Man: The Ultimate Guide*. New York: DK Publishing, 2007.

DeFalco, Tom. *Comic Creators on Spider-Man*. London: Titan, 2004.

DeFalco, Tom, J.M. DeMatteis, Tom Brevoort et al. *Spider-Man: The Complete Clone Saga Volume 2*. New York: Marvel, 2010.

DiPaolo, Marc. *War, Politics and Superheroes: Ethics and Propaganda in Comics and Film*. Jefferson, NC: McFarland, 2011.

Ditko, Steve. "An Insider's Part of Comics History: Jack Kirby's Spider-Man." in Ditko, Robin Synder eds., *Avenging World*. Bellingham, WA: Robin Snyder and S Ditko, 2002: 57–60.

Easton, Lee. "Boy Trouble: The Sidekick Problem in the Superhero Comic," in Lee Easton, Richard Harrison. *Secret Identity Reader: Essays on Sex, Death and the Superhero*. Hamilton, ON: Wolsak and Wynn Publishers Ltd, 2010: 191–208.

_____, and Richard Harrison. *Secret Identity Reader: Essays on Sex, Death and the Superhero*. Hamilton, ON: Wolsak and Wynn Publishers Ltd, 2010.

Garbarino, James. "Children's Response to a Sexual Abuse Prevention Program: A Study of the Spider-Man Comic." *Child Abuse & Neglect* 11: 1 (1987): 143–148.

Gross, Edward. *Spider-Man Confidential: From Comic Icon to Hollywood Hero the Unauthorized History*. New York: Hyperion, 2002.

Groth, Gary, ed. *The Comics Journal Library: Jack Kirby*. Seattle, WA: Fantagraphics Books, 2003.

_____. "Interview III: I've Never Done Anything Halfheartedly." in Gary Groth ed., *The Comics Journal Library: Jack Kirby*. Seattle, WA: Fantagraphics Books, 2002: 18–49. (originally published in 1989).

Harrison, Richard. "The Heroic Narrative in Crisis." In Lee Easton, Richard Harrison. *Secret Identity Reader: Essays on Sex, Death and the Superhero*. Hamilton, ON: Wolsak and Wynn Publishers Ltd, 2010: 253–262.

Healy, Patrick. "As 'Spider-Man' Opens, Its Former Director Shows Up. And a Former President," *NYTimes.com*. 6/15/2011. Accessed 6/16/2011. http://www.nytimes.com/2011/06/15/nyregion/julie-taymor-at-spider-man-opening-bill-clinton-too.html?_r=1&ref=reviews.

_____. "Taymor Tries to Reclaim a Reputation." *NYTimes.com* 6/19/2011. Accessed 6/21/2011. http://www.nytimes.com/2011/06/20/theater/julie-taymor-discusses-spider-man-and-twitter-critics.html.

Jenkins, Henry. "Transmedia Storytelling." *Technology Review*. January 15th 2003. Accessed 11/6/2011. http://www.technologyreview.com/Biotech/13052/.

Kaplan, Richard. "Spider-Man in Love: A Psychoanalytic Interpretation." *Journal of Popular Culture* 44: 2 (April 2011): 291–313.

Koh, Wilson. "Everything Old Is Good Again: Myth and Nostalgia in *Spider-Man*." *Continuum: Journal of Media & Cultural Studies* 23:5 (October 2009): 735–47.

Lang, Jeffrey S. & Trimble, Patrick. "Whatever Happened to the Man of Tomorrow? An Examination of the American Monomyth and the Comic Book Superhero." *Journal of Popular Culture* 22:3 (Winter 1988): 157–73.

Lee, Stan, Larry Lieber. "Spider-Man." *Houston Chronicle*. 6/4/2011. Accessed 6/6/2011. http://www.chron.com/apps/comics/showComick.mpl?date=20110604&name=Spider-Man.

Marshall, Rick. "*Spider-Man: Turn Off The Dark* Writers Explain How The Script Changed," *MTV.com*. 6/16/11. Accessed 6/21/2011. http://splashpage.mtv.com/2011/06/16/spider-man-turn-off-the-dark-musical-premiere-script/.

_____. "'Spider-Man' Musical Hires Comic Book Writer To Rework Story," *MTV.com*. 2/16/2011. Accessed 6/3/2011. http://splashpage.mtv.com/2011/02/16/spider-man-musical-hires-comic-book-writer-to-rework-story/.

Mendelsohn, Daniel. "Why She Fell." *The New York Review of Books*. 5/12/2011. Accessed 5/14/2011. http://www.nybooks.com/articles/archives/2011/may/12/why-she-fell/?page=1.

Meyer, Michaela D.E. "Utilizing Mythic Criticism in Contemporary Narrative Culture: Examining the 'Present-Absence' of Shadow Archetypes in *Spider-Man*." *Communication Quarterly* 51: 4 (Fall 2003): 518–529.

Miller, John Jackson. *The Comics Chronicle*. Accessed 7/11/2011. http://www.comichron.com/.
Mondello, Salvatore. "Spider-Man Superhero in the Liberal Tradition." *Journal of Popular Culture* 10:1 (Summer 1976): 232–238.
Morris, Tom, and Morris, Matt eds. *Superheroes and Philosophy: Truth, Justice and the Socratic Way*. New York: Open Court Press, 2005.
Palumbo, Donald. "The Marvel Comics Group's Spider-Man Is an Existentialist Superhero, or 'Life Has No Meaning without My Latest Marvels.'" *Journal of Popular Culture*. 17:2 (Fall 1983): 67–81.
Peaslee, Robert Moses "Superheroes, Moral Economy, and the Iron Cage: Morality, Alienation, and the Super-Individual" in Angela Ndalianis and Wendy Haslem eds. *Super/Heroes: Myth and Meaning*. Melbourne: New Academia, 2006: 37–50.
_____. "'With Great Power Comes Great Responsibility': Central Psychoanalytic Motifs in *Spider-Man* and *Spider-Man 2*" PSYART: *A Hyperlink Journal for the Psychological Study of the Arts*. (July 2005) Accessed 6/10/2011. http://www.psyartjournal.com/article/show/m_peaslee-with_great_power_comes_great_responsibil.
Richards, Niall. "The Gospel According to Spider-Man." *Journal of Popular Culture* 37:4 (May 2004): 694–703.
Romita, John, Sr. *The Art of John Romita*. New York: Marvel, 1996.
Rourke, James. *The Comic Book Curriculum*. Santa Barbara, CA: Libraries Unlimited, 2010.
Simon, Joe and Jim Simon. "The Birth of Spider-Man" in Joe Simon and Jim Simon. *The Comic Book Makers*. Lebanon, NJ: Vanguard Productions, 2003: 173–185.
Saffel, Steve. *Spider-Man: The Icon: The Life and Times of a Pop Culture Phenomenon*. London: Titan, 2007.
Smith, Seth-Grahame, Stan Lee, Carlo Barberi et al. *The Spider-Man Handbook: the Ultimate Training Manual*. Philadelphia: Quirk Books, 2006.
Sjoerdsma, Al, Stuart Vandal; Chris Buchner et al. *The Amazing Spider-Man: The Official Index to the Marvel Universe*. New York: Marvel, 2010.
Spurgeon, Tom, Brain Cunningham, Alex Ross et al. *The Romita Legacy*. Runnemede, N.J.: Dynamite Entertainment, 2010.
Theakston, Greg. "The Birth of Spider-Man: The Final World on the Creation of Marvel's Greatest Hero." *Pure Images 1*. 3:1, 1990: np.
_____. "The Road to Spider-Man" in Steve Ditko and Greg Theakston. *The Steve Ditko Reader*. Brooklyn, NY: Pure Imagination, 2002.
Thomas, Jean, Win Mortimer, Mike Esposito, et al. *The Best of Spider-Man Super Stories*. New York: Simon and Schuster, 1978.
Truitt, Brian. "*Avenging Spider-Man*' Swings into Action in November," *USAToday.com*. 6/13/2011. Accessed 6/14/2011. http://www.usatoday.com/life/comics/2011-06-13-Avenging-Spider-Man-series-swings-into-action_n.htm.
_____. "Ultimate Spider-Man Meets an Ultimate Fate," *USAToday.com* 6/21/2011. Accessed 6/21/2011. http://www.usatoday.com/life/comics/2011-06-21-Ultimate-Spider-Man-meets-his-ultimate-fate_n.htm.
Weiss, Brett. "Spider-Super Stories: Back Stage Pass!" *Back Issue* 44 (October 2010): 23-28.
Weiner, Robert G. *Marvel Graphic Novels and Related Publications: An Annotated Guide to Comics, Prose Novels, Children's Books, Articles, Criticism, and Reference Works*. Jefferson, NC: McFarland, 2008.
_____. "Sequential Art and Reality: Yes Virginia There is a Spider-Man," *International Journal of Comic Art* 11:1 (Spring 2009): 457–477.
Wells, Earl. "Essay III: Once and For All Who Was the Author of Marvel," in Gary Groth ed., *The Comics Journal Library: Jack Kirby*. Seattle, WA: Fantagraphics Books, 2002: 75–87.

I. Historical, Cultural and Pedagogical Angles

Donald Glover for Spider-Man

Phillip Lamarr Cunningham

Today, if someone were to describe to a person unfamiliar with comics a superhero who lives with his elderly aunt in Queens after the tragic deaths of his parents and uncle, who was ostracized from his peers because of his intelligence and humble beginnings, and who spends much of his life working low-wage jobs and living in crummy apartments, that someone most likely would not assume that this superhero was white. Indeed, given how well these characteristics fit in with generalizations often made about minorities, this someone very likely may conclude that the superhero is either African American or Latino.

Of course, the above description is of none other than Peter Parker, Your Friendly Neighborhood Spider-Man, who typically is depicted as a white male. Two exceptions exist: in 1992, Marvel Comics began publishing *Spider-Man 2099*, which featured a Spider-Man (Miguel O'Hara) of Irish and Mexican ancestry. Then, in 2005, Marvel published the four-issue series *Spider-Man: India*, which featured an Indian Spider-Man (Pavitr Prabhakar). The former series, which covered the adventures of the Spider-Man of an alternate timeline, was quite popular and lasted 46 issues. Furthermore, *Spider-Man 2099* has found his way into other media, including video games such as 2010's *Spider-Man: Shattered Dimensions*. The latter series, as Sukhdev Sandhu (2005) points out, caused a bit of a stir: "On chat boards and across the blogosphere, comics fans have been competing with each other to see who is the most indignant. It's claimed that Spider-Man's purity will be sullied. That he's a uniquely American superhero. That the very idea of Indian graphic fiction is a bit of a joke" (n.p.).

However, in both series, the man behind the mask is not Peter Parker, Spider-Man's traditional alter ego. Thus far, in every medium in which he has appeared, Parker has been depicted as white (presumably Irish-American). In May 2010, however, the first possibilities of a non-white Peter Parker emerged when blogger Marc Bernardin of popular science-fiction blog io9 suggested that producers of *The Amazing Spider-Man*—the 2012 reboot of the popular film franchise—should consider casting a non-white actor, primarily because of the lukewarm reception to the white actors (three of whom were British) first considered for the role. Bernardin sarcastically remarked, "So why couldn't Peter Parker be played by a black or a Hispanic actor? ... I'm not saying that the producers need to force the issue; that they need to cast a minority just for the sake of it—but in the face of such underwhelming options like Billy Elliot [actor Jamie Bell] and the kid who played young Voldemort [actor Frank Dillane], why not broaden the search?" (n.p.). A vigorous debate ensued on the discussion thread, and one poster recommended African American actor/comedian Donald Glover for the role. Subsequently, Glover himself began campaigning for an audition on Twitter, and thousands of fans created several variations of "Donald Glover for Spider-Man" pages on Facebook.

Though Glover was not granted an audition, his campaign and the significant support he received from fans speaks volumes not only about his popularity but also — and perhaps more importantly — the perceived universality of Parker and Spider-Man. Conversely, the strong reactions of those who argued that casting Glover as Parker was inappropriate due to his race speaks with equal volume to concerns about continuity, fidelity and racial identity that have been a hallmark of comic book superhero fandom. As such, the discourse on Donald Glover's campaign to audition for *The Amazing Spider-Man* provides a meaningful context within which to consider the competing desires for diversity and universality (an interesting paradox on its own), on the one hand, and for continuity and fidelity, on the other, when it comes to comic book superheroes. As will be argued here, the support for Glover's campaign signifies a dynamic shift in fans' ability and willingness to see some of themselves in an unlikely other, a shift only capable through a character such as Spider-Man.

Of Everymen and Nerds

J.M. DeMatteis — who wrote many of the most important story arcs in *Amazing Spider-Man* in the 1990s — wrote in 2010 that "Peter Parker is perhaps the most emotionally and psychologically authentic protagonist in any super-hero universe. Underneath that mask, he's as confused, as flawed, as touchingly human, as the people who read — and write — about him: the quintessential Everyman." DeMatteis' comments reflect not only conventional wisdom bred by several decades of Spider-Man adventures but also the intent of Spider-Man co-creator Stan Lee, who notes, "I tried to make him typical of all young boys — guys who are insecure about how they'll earn a living, about their love life, about what the future holds, etc." (Kenney, 2007: n.p.). As both DeMatteis and Lee's comments suggest, Spider-Man always has been intended to be a character to whom most — particularly male — readers could relate. Given his humble beginnings and modest present, Parker resonates with a great number of readers, filmgoers, and television viewers, especially given that many probably come from similar backgrounds.

In most media forms — particularly cartoons and movies — Parker is typically portrayed either as an awkward, bookish teenager or as a struggling college student who freelances as a photographer for *The Daily Bugle* (though, until recently, he also had been a science teacher at his former high school in his ongoing comic book series). In each case, Parker can consistently be read as a bit of a nerd. As Lori Kendall (1999) suggests, beginning in the 1980s, the nerd identity began to be incorporated into traditional concepts of masculinity: "The reconfiguration of hegemonic masculinity to include aspects of the once subjugated masculine stereotype of the nerd relates both to changes in economic and job prospects for middle-class white males, and to the growing pervasiveness of computers in work and leisure activities" (261). While Kendall cites films such as *Revenge of the Nerds* (1984) as important in this reconfiguration, Parker obviously serves as a precursor — especially since Parker as teen scientist and hero appears over two decades before *Revenge*'s computer science student protagonists Lewis Skolnick (Robert Carradine) and Gilbert Lowe (Anthony Edwards). Indeed, Parker arguably epitomizes the conflation of everyman and nerd better than any popular culture figure.

Nonetheless, Kendall is correct when she asserts that *Revenge of the Nerds* accomplishes "this transformation of the word nerd from a stereotypical representation of a single type of white male to an all-inclusive term for anyone who isn't on top of the power hierarchy" (268).

As evidence, she points to the inclusion of Lamar Letrell (Larry B. Scott), a gay African American who plays a pivotal role in the film. Though she concedes that Lamar is a problematic character because of the rather strong gay stereotyping, Kendall rightly suggests that he is evidence of the inclusive nature of nerd-hood. As a result, *Revenge of the Nerds* is not only an important film for establishing the nerd as everyman and hero but also an important film for opening up the nerd persona as one inclusive of others, including African American men. Indeed, the Lamar character would open the door to the appearance of other black nerds, most notably the foremost black nerd in popular culture, Steve Urkel (Jaleel White) of the hit ABC sitcom *Family Matters*. Ron Eglash (2002) contends that part of Urkel's appeal "derives from a combination of popular American fascinations: on the one hand, opposing the myth of biological determinism, on the other, continuing the myth of Horatio Alger, who in this case must pull himself up not the financial ladder but the social status rungs of youth subculture" (55). Given his similarities with *Revenge of the Nerds*' main characters, it is of little surprise that Urkel has joined the pantheon of nerds occupied by the Skolnicks and Lowes of popular culture. As black nerds such as Lamar, Urkel, Stevie Kernaban (Craig Lamar Traylor) of *Malcolm in the Middle,* and a number of others prove, nerd-dom in popular culture is no longer the sole province of white men.

Thus, Donald Glover has emerged at a time in which the black nerd is an accepted archetype within popular culture. Indeed, so far, Glover has built his career and public persona on being a black nerd, publicly declaring himself as such in his 2010 Comedy Central special. A former writer for *The Daily Show* and *30 Rock*, Glover is perhaps most noted for his role as community college student Troy Barnes in the NBC series *Community*. Barnes is a former jock who later embraces an identity as a nerd; however, what is most significant about his role as Barnes — particularly for this study — is that the character was originally supposed to be white. In his *Village Voice* profile of Glover, Bill Jensen (2011) writes, "the character of Troy was actually written for a white guy, but [Glover] made it his own" (n.p.). Of course, this fact is not particularly surprising given the relatively recent trend of black actors filling roles originally intended for white actors; however, those roles typically are action heroes, gritty detectives, and the like (e.g. the Will Smith vehicle *Hancock* originally had been linked to George Clooney, Ben Affleck, and others). Indeed, Glover himself jokes, "That shit [being a black nerd] was illegal until 2003" (*Comedy Central Presents*).

With this in mind, it is easy to understand how Bernardin's suggestion that Glover be considered for an audition for *Amazing Spider-Man* was found appealing by thousands of Glover's fans and even many comic book readers. Bernardin's article was followed by dozens of Glover/Spider-Man mash-ups, several Facebook fan pages pledging support (the most popular one exceeding 11,000 members), a Twitter hash tag that has continued a year later, and even a few YouTube videos of fans making a case for Glover as Spider-Man. Moreover, the campaign was quite diverse, receiving support from fans of varying racial and ethnic backgrounds.

Nonetheless, Glover — while engaging in clear hyperbole — makes a valid point when he suggests in a stand-up routine that the notion of him as Spider-Man triggered rather strong opposition as well: "That's when the world went crazy. And half the world was like, 'Donald Glover for Spider-Man! We're only going to watch the next Spider-Man movie if Donald Glover's playing Spider-Man!' And the other half was like, 'He's black! Kill him!" ("Donald Glover's Thoughts..."). Given the long history of resistance to racial and ethnic superheroes (particularly when they are assuming the role of a hero typically portrayed as white) and desires for fidelity and continuity by many comic book fans, this is not particularly surprising.

The Ensuing Firestorm: Resisting a Black Spider-Man

While the call for a Glover audition came about in the midst of a growing presence of black nerds in popular culture and the rapid development of Glover's acting and stand-up comedy career, it also came about during a wave of a comic book nostalgia that was often coupled with animosity towards racial and ethnic superheroes. Comics Alliance columnist Chris Sims (2010) effectively summarizes the impetus and results of this nostalgic trend:

> "The Good Old Days" have become a driving force in the comics industry.... [I]t's all built around a desire to recapture a feeling these creators got when they were kids.... [W]e're in an industry right now that wants to constantly reset itself, running on nostalgia rather than innovation, moving backwards instead of moving forwards, and while I complain about it both often and at length, it seems to be what the majority of comics readers want, no matter how wrongheaded I think it is. But there's an unintentional side-effect to all this regression that often goes ignored: The piece-by-piece white-washing of the DC Universe. (n.p.)

Sims is speaking particularly about the trend in DC Comics to revert heroes such as The Atom and Firestorm—who until recently had been Asian American Ryan Choi and African American Jason Rausch, respectively—back to their traditionally white alter egos of Ray Palmer and Ronnie Raymond, respectively. Sims notes that DC Comics relies far more on legacies than does Marvel, the publisher of *Amazing Spider-Man*, and that "the idea of a legacy character is being totally subverted. They're not roles that are passed down anymore [e.g. Barry Allen taking over the helm of The Flash from Jay Garrick], they're roles that are passed *back up*" (ibid., emphasis in original).

Sims is correct in implying that Marvel has not been burdened by legacy as much as its counterpart. However, that is not to suggest that Marvel has not had its problems. One need only look to the backlash that ensued after Robert Morales and Kyle Baker's *Truth: Red, White & Black* mini-series, which told the story of Isaiah Bradley, a black World War II soldier who was subjected to experiments intended to recreate the Super Soldier formula that produced Captain America. Current Marvel Editor-in-Chief Axel Alonso succinctly described the negative reactions to the mini-series: "There are the fanboy continuity purists who don't like Marvel messing with sacred cows; those who worry the series will somehow besmirch Steve Rogers' legacy; and 'outright racists who just don't like the idea of a black man in the Cap uniform'" (Sinclair, 2002: n.p.).

As a review of comments on prominent comic book and entertainment sites reveals, Alonso's summary of the reactions to *Truth* also encapsulate many of the responses to the campaign for a Glover audition. In fairness, much of the concern about Glover's casting was based on desires for authenticity, which occurs amongst avid comic book readers whenever any superhero film is made. Oftentimes, these concerns regarding fidelity are in regards to origins and powers. For instance, the first *Spider-Man* trilogy was panned by some comic book fans when it was revealed that the cinematic Spider-Man had organic web-shooters as opposed to the mechanical ones in the comic books. Though concerns about web-shooters seem relatively trivial in comparison to concerns about race, they put into perspective the importance of fidelity for comic book readers. Indeed, many of those who opposed a Glover casting couched their disagreement in these terms. For example, "Brad" posted the following comment on the popular comic book forum Newsrama:

> For myself I am something of a character purist. A given character portrayed in movies or on TV should look (more or less) the way that character is commonly depicted, end of story. Peter Parker and Clark Kent should be played by white actors, not from any racial issue but simply because

that is how the characters are depicted. For the same reasons Luke Cage and Storm should be played by black actors/actresses and Lady Shiva and the Mandarin should be played by asians [*sic*]: it is simply a part of who the characters are and have been since their creation. ("Community's Donald Glover 4 Spider-Man?!")

The tenor of Brad's comments reverberated throughout many sites covering the Glover campaign. In short, maintaining fidelity meant retaining the phenotypical appearance of the original Peter Parker. Like Brad, many commenters suggested that they would have the same concerns if a black character was replaced by a white character.

In fact, many of the responses rejecting a Glover audition — reasonable or otherwise — tended to draw equivalences between the possibilities of a black actor filling a traditionally white role and a white actor filling a traditionally black role. Frequently, commenters suggested that African Americans would be quite upset if, say, a white actor portrayed a black superhero such as Black Panther or Storm. Indeed, the other meme that emerged from the campaign was "Michael Cera 4 Shaft," which was based on a comment on one of the comic book forums (and later part of Glover's musings on the matter).

So the question becomes, outside of the phenotypical appearance of him in the comic books, is there anything demonstrably "white" about Peter Parker? Or, put another way, would Parker somehow be dramatically different had Glover successfully auditioned for the role? As indicated thus far, the answer seemingly would be no because of the all-encompassing nature of the nerd persona. Additionally, one must consider the increase in what media studies scholar Vincent Brook (2009) deems "convergent ethnicity." According to Brook, convergent ethnicity is the increased use of multiracial, multi-gendered casts largely as a response to "global economic forces, sociocultural changes, and media monitoring pressures" (331). Brook asserts that one of the outcomes of convergent ethnicity is the "dissolution of difference": "Colorblind casting may promise an end to 'othering,' but this potential benefit is compromised by a damaging cost: the dissolution of difference. The multiethnic members of the neo-platoon [ensemble cast television] shows may look different, but they tend to act the same. Historical and cultural distinctions, not to mention persistent ethno-racial inequities, are ignored for the most part, if not denied altogether" (348). While Brook is speaking primarily of post-millennium television shows, his findings also can be applied to post-millennium films. Though films still rely heavily on racial and ethnic stereotypes, difference is often downplayed in many films, particularly action films. Indeed, whether through the numerous "buddy" action films, such as the *Fast and the Furious* series in which black characters are portrayed quite similarly to their white counterparts, or the frequent interchangeability of black and white actors in the genre, action films long have attempted to mitigate or erode racial differences with varying degrees of success.

That said, oftentimes, when a black actor assumes a role previously intended for a white actor, changes are often made to accommodate the actor. A glaring example of this would be the character James West of *Wild Wild West* (1999), played by Will Smith. The role of James West, originally played by Robert Conrad in the television series upon which the film was based, was altered because Smith is African American. For instance, viewers learn that West was a former slave who once lead a settlement of freedmen in the fictional town of New Liberty, Illinois. In this instance, indeed, an iconic character was changed to fit Smith's racial background. This type of alteration seems to be a primary concern for many who opposed Glover's campaign. However, there is little likelihood that the makers of *Amazing Spider-Man* would dramatically alter Parker's character for any actor. After all, even with British actor Andrew Garfield assuming the role, Parker will not speak with a Cockney accent while swinging through the streets of London. While liberties are often taken with origins, powers, and other matters in superhero films, the protagonist typically adheres closely to how he or she is portrayed in the comics. Regardless of the actor playing the role, Bruce Wayne is always an eccentric philanthropist; Bruce Banner is always a troubled genius; and Parker is usually an awkward teen trying to come to terms with great powers and great responsibilities.

Much Ado About Nothing

The imbroglio over the campaign for a Glover audition is a bit moot as there was never much of a chance that Glover would be cast as Parker. First, there is little indication that Glover actually was genuinely interested in auditioning for the role. Though he is largely credited for leading the campaign, his initial response to fans clamoring for him to audition was in the form of a joke: "I'm putting myself in the running for the Spider-Man [sic] reboot. I'm actually quite interested to see how far this goes. If this happens, I'll buy each and every one of you a mini cooper [sic]" ("#donald4Spider-Man"). Later, during a stand-up performance, he insisted that his involvement in the campaign was merely "tongue-in-cheek" ("Donald Glover's Thoughts..."). Moreover, the die already had been cast by the time the campaign had been started, as the frontrunners for the position had already been named.

Nonetheless, while there was ever little likelihood that Glover would be cast as Parker and Spider-Man, the fans' willingness to see a black Spider-Man stands as a testament to both Glover's appeal and to the universality of the character. There is perhaps no better indication that Spider-Man could be portrayed by a non-white actor than co-creator Stan Lee's response to the Glover campaign: "[A]s far as I'm concerned ... *anybody* should have a chance to audition for the role. I certainly think [Glover] should have a chance to audition" (Marshall, 2010: n.p.). While not a ringing endorsement of Glover, Lee's emphasis on the term *anybody* is quite telling, for it reifies Lee's earlier musings that Parker was intended to represent "all young boys." Given Lee's intent for Parker to be a character identifiable and representative of all, then, it stands to reason that Donald Glover would make as fine a Spider-Man as Tobey Maguire or Andrew Garfield. For now, we can only speculate.

Works Cited

Bernardin, Marc. "Donald Glover for Spider-Man: The Evolution of A Meme." *io9*. June 1, 2010. Accessed 6/20/2011. http://io9.com/5552684/donald-glover-for-spider+man-why-the-hell-not.
Brook, Vincent. "Convergent Ethnicity and the Neo-Platoon Show: Recombining Difference in the Post-network Era." *Television & New Media* 10:4 (July 2009): 331–353.
DeMatteis, J.M. "The Story Behind The Hunt—Again." *J.M. DeMatteis' Creation Point*. 9/27/2010. Accessed 6/20/2011. http://www.jmdematteis.com/2010/09/story-behind-huntagain.html.
"Donald Glover's Thoughts on Donald 4 Spider-Man." *Facebook*. 3/7/2011. Accessed 6/23/2011. http://www.facebook.com/video/video.php?v=1837580668207&oid=130945906916984&comments.
Eglash, Ron. "Race, Sex, and Nerds: From Black Geeks to Asian American Hipsters." *Social Text* 71:20 (Summer 2002): 49–64.
Glover, Donald (performer). *Comedy Central Presents ... Donald Glover*. Comedy Central, 2010.
_____. "#donald4Spider-Man." *iamdonald*. 5/30/2010. Accessed 6/29/2011. http://www.iamdonald.com/post/647884473/donald4Spider-Man.
Jensen, Bill. "Donald Glover Is More Talented Than You." *Village Voice*. 4/13/2011. Accessed 6/21/2011. http://www.villagevoice.com/content/printVersion/2508381/.
Kendall, Lori. "Nerd Nation: Images of Nerds in US Popular Culture." *International Journal of Cultural Studies* 2:2 (1999): 260–283.
Kenney, Brian. "Stan Lee: Spider-Man's Alter Ego Based on Me." *School Library Journal*. 4/25/2007. Accessed 6/20/2011. http://www.schoollibraryjournal.com/article/CA6436085.html?rssid=190.

"The Last Thing Spider-Man Should Be Is Another White Guy." *Io9*. May 28, 2010. Accessed 6/20/2011. http://io9.com/5549613/the-last-thing-spider+man-should-be-is-another-white-guy.

Marshall, Rick. "What Stan Lee Thinks of Donald Glover's 'Spider-Man' Casting Campaign." *MTV Splash Page*. 6/9/2010. Accessed 6/20/2011. http://splashpage.mtv.com/2010/06/09/stan-lee-donald-glover-spider-man-casting-campaign/.

Sandhu, Sukhdev. "World Wide Web." *New York Magazine*. 5/21/2005. Accessed 6/20/2011. http://nymag.com/nymetro/arts/comics/9600/.

Siegel, Lucas. "Community's Donald Glover 4 Spider-Man?!" *Newsarama*. 5/31/2010. Accessed 6/20/2011. http://blog.newsarama.com/2010/05/31/communitys-donald-glover-4-spider-man.

Sims, Chris. "The Racial Politics of Regressive Storytelling." *Comics Alliance*. 5/6/2010. Accessed 6/21/2011. http://www.comicsalliance.com/2010/05/06/the-racial-politics-of-regressive-storytelling/.

Sinclair, Tom. "Black in Action." *Entertainment Weekly*. 11/22/2002. Accessed 6/21/2011. http://www.ew.com/ew/article/0,390672,00.html.

Have Great Power, Greatly Irresponsible: Intergenerational Conflict in 1960s *Amazing Spider-Man*

PETER LEE

When Spider-Man debuted in 1962, writer Stan Lee claimed that costumed heroes were "a dime a dozen! But, we think you may find our *Spider-Man* just a bit ... different!" (Lee, 1962: 1). In that issue, readers meet Peter Parker, a quiet, studious teenager, who becomes the famous wall-crawler. By the story's end, however, Parker has matured rapidly; the oft-told origin concludes with Parker learning that "with great power, there must also come great responsibility"—a motto that would follow him into the twenty-first century.

Although Parker continually endeavored to shoulder that power responsibly, Parker himself was an outcast. In early issues, Lee emphasized Parker's social rejection by contrasting him with frequent guest stars such as Johnny Storm—the Human Torch. As a member of the Fantastic Four, whose mission advanced scientific exploration, the Torch was endorsed by comic book New Yorkers as a teenage celebrity who handed out autographs. Conversely, as an outsider, Parker—and Spider-Man—serves as a commentator of the changing social milieu during the 1960s. His observations reflect his youthful audience's alienation toward the older generation's values and social standards, even though he was created by middle-aged men. Spider-Man became a platform for Lee and his readers to explore the intergenerational tension in the 1960s between the emerging counterculture and the "establishment." The "establishment" in Spider-Man stories eludes a specific definition; it merely signifies the elders who dominated social and political institutions. Although those adults had great power, in the eyes of Spider-Man, his creators, and the readers, they were greatly irresponsible.[1]

The Cast

The first issue of the *Amazing Spider-Man* already hinted at the intergenerational clash in the coming pages. J. Jonah Jameson is on the opening splash page, leading a bunch of suited gentlemen accusing Spider-Man of being a "freak" and a "public menace." On the next page, Jameson identifies himself as a media mogul who publishes *The Daily Bugle* and *Now Magazine*, appears on television, and travels lecture circuits. Unfortunately, Jameson's lectures play off his characterization as a loud-mouthed, closed-minded braggart. In the first issue, Jameson labels the costumed Spider-Man as "a bad influence on our youngsters! Children may try to imitate his fantastic feats! Think what would happen if they make a hero out of this lawless, inhuman monster!" In claiming to shield the city's youth from Spider-Man, Jameson bills himself as a protective authority figure. Indeed, Jameson proudly directs his viewers' attention toward his own son: "The youth of this nation must learn to respect real heroes — men such as my son, John Jameson, the test pilot!" (Lee, 1963, *1*: 5). The younger Jameson is likewise an "establishment" figure, being a military colonel. The younger Jameson doesn't share his father's extreme views, but Jonah Jameson nevertheless flaunts his patriarchal authority as a source of righteousness.

However, readers saw through Jameson's vociferous vehemence. In the comic's first letter column, fans rejected Jameson's justifications. One reader demanded, "How can the reading public believe what this guy writes?" (Jones, 1963, *3*: Letter). His question went unanswered, but Jameson's reputation spread: a few issues later, one letter announced that Marvel's "greatest super-villain is ... J. Jonah Jameson! Power? ... Power of the press!" (Nicholson, 1964, *3*: Letter). One fan even tried to redeem the publisher, believing that Jameson "is — or would be — a fine person if he'd only try" (Bradley, 1964, *17*: Letter).

Such attempts would prove abortive. Jameson reaffirmed his point of view, explaining his editorial policy: "I have only *one* real motive ... to make *money*! The more I attack Spider-Man, the more people read my papers! [...] Everybody is interested in him ... whether they *agree* with me or no doesn't matter ... Spider-Man *sells papers*!" (Lee, 1963, *5*: 8). Jameson's unwavering support of the free capitalist system didn't hold for long, however. By the tenth issue, Jameson privately muses that Spider-Man "risks his life day after day with no thought of reward! If a man like him is good — is a hero — than what am *I??* I can never *respect* myself while he lives!" He concludes that he is envious of the wall-crawler, and that "I, J. Jonah Jameson — millionaire, man of the world, civic leader — I'd give anything to be the man that *he* is!" (Lee, 1964, *10*: 22). Jameson saw himself as successful by American standards; but, according to those values, the result was less than the sum of the parts.

One fan took issue with Jameson's confessional soliloquy. John Bailey demanded, "I ask by what standards may J.J.J., a producer, be said to be less moral or even immoral in comparison with Spider-Man. How can J. Jonah Jameson, who has provided work for hundreds or thousands and news for millions, be said to be immoral?" In a defense of free enterprise, Bailey asked, "Why has a man that has amassed a fortune solely through providing the news faster, cheaper, more concisely, and more accurately than any other source accepted a standard of morality that holds his production, his virtue to be evil?"(Bailey, 1965, *21*: Letter). Lee responded that, as producers of a disposable product, Marvel was not "anti-money." Nevertheless, while Jameson's admission was indicative of flaws in American institutions, Jameson was too deeply ingrained in the establishment and he would never change.

Jameson was a symptom of the status quo that younger readers would later challenge. However, while the teenage and college-aged readers saw through Jameson's boldfaced editorials, the comic book New Yorkers were confined to a one-dimensional viewpoint in two-dimensional artwork. Early issues presented an informed citizen body sharing Jameson's views in a public forum:

> "Well, I see that *Spider-Man* captured that awful *Sandman*!"
> "According to the editorial, *Spider-Man* is just as bad as the other one!"
> "Jonah Jameson writes that *Spider-Man* has no business trying to catch criminals by himself!"
> "If you ask *me*, that's *right*! Who knows when *Spider-Man* may turn *against* society?"
> "What would make a guy wear a goofy costume and run around chasin' crooks?"
> "I dunno! He must be a *neurotic* of some sort! Probably has delusions of grandeur!" [Lee, 1963, *4*: 21].

Throughout the 1960s, Parker would be continually exposed to the clouded judgments of these well-meaning adults.

Similarly clouded is Parker's only living relation, Aunt May. In scripting May, Lee depicted her as the ignorant senior citizen unaware of the radical changes taking place in American society, but also in her own household, as she remained unaware of her nephew's alter ego. Instead, May frequently aired her views about the distasteful Spider-Man, while, at the same time, expressing admiration for J. Jonah Jameson. Worse, the villainous Otto Octavius charmed May; at one point, "Doc Ock" kidnaps the elderly woman, but May chooses to compliment his gentlemanly manners while he plots her death (Lee, 1964, *Annual*). Later, May would even take Octavius into her house as a boarder. May does exhibit some inner strength, at one point claiming, "even though I'm an old woman, I'm not a quitter! A person needs gumption ... the will to live ... to fight!" (Lee, 1964, *18*: 21). Unfortunately, the elderly Parker never employed such strength, as she was more often seen fainting or near death throughout the 1960s. May's later behavior, such as her attempts to learn 1960s slang—substituting "pussy-willow" for "pussycat"—confirmed her status as a kindly, but clueless old woman.

While May's attempts to join the younger crowds were played for laughs, many readers responded to May's presence with cries for her death. John Brant was among the more critical fans, speaking for the "I Hate Aunt May 'Cause She Is A Trouble-Making Nag Society." The title sums up the group's purpose. Brant provided several ideas: "Have Aunt May trip on her crutches, or choke on one of her beauty pills, or even have a heart attack after reading this great letter" (Brant, 1966, *35*: Letter). Lee repeatedly insists that May was popular with the older fans. In addition, May was a convenient plot device, since Parker continually needed to provide her with life-saving serums consisting of rare elements. However, in acquiescing to reader wishes, Lee later effectively writes May out by sending her on vacation in Florida or giving Peter Parker his own apartment. As Ora McWilliams points out later in this volume, her appearances would become more sporadic and increasingly multivalent.

Other adults figured into Spider-Man's early issues. Many of these stories cast the web-slinging outsider against middle-aged men in respectable positions. The afore-mentioned Octavius was an esteemed atomic scientist driven mad in an accident. Other researchers proved equally unscrupulous. For example, Spencer Smythe, funded by Jameson, would construct various mechanical "spider slayers." Farley Stillwell joins Jameson to create a super villain, the Scorpion. Stillwell sells his conscience for ten thousand dollars, but when the Scorpion goes on a rampage, Stillwell is killed trying to administer an antidote and Jameson ignores his own irresponsible use of power: "I know now that *anyone* with too much power is liable to turn into a menace sooner or layer! And *Spider-Man* is no exception! It's *still* my duty to fight him ... to expose ... and someday ... to destroy him!" (Lee, 1965, *20*: 20). Another researcher, Curt Connors, experiments with reptiles' regenerative properties to aid medical science. Unfortunately, an accident causes the good doctor to change into a Jekyll/Hyde humanoid lizard with grandiose dreams to mutate the human race into beings just like him.

An exception to this group of media moguls, scientists, and one confused old woman is George Stacy, a retired police captain and father of Parker's girlfriend. Stacy still maintains a commanding presence in New York civic affairs, and views Spider-Man with fascination. Liked by readers and respectful toward Parker, Stacy was a counterpoint to the relentless Jameson. Stacy's presence in Spider-Man comics lasted for thirty-four issues before his death, but his demise was fitting: he gives his life to save a youngster.

College-Aged Crises

As one reader stated, the increasing popularity of Spider-Man throughout the 1960s was indicative that Peter Parker "is a symbol of our generation" (Yablonka, 1969: Letter). In *Amazing Spider-Man 36*, Lee reprinted a column from *The National Observer*, concerning the rapid growth of Marvel's official fan club chapters on college campuses, explaining the company's new popularity with one word: "sophistication, both in the comics and the readers" (Bullpen Bulletins, 1966). Other scholars have observed the increasing affiliation between Marvel's characters and the college-aged crowds on over 225 campuses (Wright, 2001: 223–225). These club chapters offered a community spirit for like-minded, isolated fans beyond the comics themselves, complete with badges, slang, and assorted merchandise. Marvel's alliance with college crowds led many young adults to claim Spider-Man as representation against an unfriendly outside world.

However, a battle of words ignited in the letter pages over what that representation meant. Specifically, readers traded barbs as they contemplated whether Peter Parker should outlive their age group. One fan pondered the problem after Parker graduated high school, "desperately" hoping that Parker will "go through college and become the first intellectual, left-wing liberal super-hero, helping to stop wars, supporting [civil rights and youth groups] SNCC, CORE, and the NAACP" (Ravenson, 1966, *35*: Letter). Three issues later, another fan replied that Spider-Man should not "indoctrinate readers with any specific political credo. If you succeed in presenting democracy as superior to tyranny, courage to cowardice, and brotherhood to bigotry, then you will have accomplished all that can be expected" (Abernathy, 1966, *38*: Letter). Another reader rejected political labels for the hero, and wanted Parker to "develop into a super-hero with a mind and personality of his own!" (McBride, 1966, *39*: Letter). Lee wrote that "many fans seem to feel the way you do, [...] preferring Spidey to be a middle-of-the-roader"—a position that Marvel also tried to maintain.

A far more disturbed reader was Stephen Bowell, who empathically wrote, "No!—No! A zillion times no! Spider-Man must never grow up! [...] Spider-Man is a symbol of teenage youth—our energy, our arrogance, our idealism, our confusion, our harassments, our frustrations, our hidden desires." Instead, Bowell wanted to revert Parker "back to high school [and] keep him there! There's a new generation of teenagers coming right after us, and they deserve better than to have nobody represent their generation!" (1966, *43*: Letter). Lee later reported a vote of "about six to one to let ol' Web-head gradually age—albeit at a slower than normal rate." Another fan, Joe Malik, insisted that Spider-Man's representation for the Sixties generation should reach a full conclusion: "Spidey is a symbol of today's teenage youth and should grow up with today's teenagers. The fact that Marvel heroes age right along with their readers is one of the reasons why your mags are as great as they are" (1967, *46*: Letter).

Such lively debate over Spider-Man's symbolic status turned to Parker's—and Marvel's— stance on various rights revolutions against a static establishment. One historian had noted that the emergence of an active counterculture in the 1960s had, in part, stemmed from the escalating arms race and that "if the world was going to be there when they grew up, it was only because they had worked to change their present society" (Jacobs, 2010: 116). In 1967, Lee noted that many readers "have demanded that we take a more definitive stand on current problems such as Viet Nam, civil rights, and the increase in crime, to name a few." Lee resisted, claiming that the company's first purpose was to entertain rather than editorialize. "Of course, you've probably noticed that it's not too easy to keep our own convictions out of the soul-stirring sagas we toss at you—but, in our own bumbling fashion, we do try" (Lee,

1967, 53: Soapbox). A year later, Lee maintained that "we've received a zillion letters asking for the Bullpen's opinion about such diverse subjects as Viet Nam, civil rights, the war on poverty, and the upcoming [1968] election." However, he restated Marvel's neutrality "because we share the same diversity of opinion as Americans everywhere." However, Lee concluded, with a reference to the recently assassinated Dr. Martin Luther King, Jr., that people must judge "each fellow human on his own merit, regardless of race, creed, or color. That we agree on — and we'll never rest until it becomes a fact, rather than just a cherished dream!" (Lee, 1968, 65: Soapbox). The next issue, Lee consents to editorialize, citing the voluminous correspondence as a "magniloquent mandate to sock it to ya, and let the chips fall where they may" (Lee, 1968, 66: Soapbox).

The chips fell mainly on the liberal side. Lee's first storyline against the establishment took place in the form of a student protest. Lee had featured a student protest in *Amazing Spider-Man* nearly thirty issues earlier. Unfortunately, the scripted dialogue from that earlier episode showed the protesters in a less than flattering light and was irrelevant to the plot:

> PARKER: "Another student protest! What are they after *this* time?"
> OBSERVING STUDENT: "Didn't you *hear*? They're protesting tonight's protest meeting!"
> PARKER: "It figures!"
> [When asked to join in, Parker responds that he has nothing to protest.]
> STUDENT 1: "Nothing to *protest* about?? What *are* you — some kinda religious fanatic, or something?"
> STUDENT 2: "What 'smatter with you? Aren't you interested in saving the world?? Anyway, it's an excuse to cut classes!"
> STUDENT 1: "— and maybe you'll get your picture in *Newsweek*!"
> STUDENT 3: "C'mon Parker — if you join our protest meeting, we'll join one of *yours* some time!"
> STUDENT 4: "Sure! And, if you've nothing to protest, don't worry about it! *That* won't stop us!"
> [Lee, 1966, 38: 10].

The exchange ends with the protestors telling the "rosy-cheeked reactionary" Parker to go back to "Squaresville." Parker is hardly such, but the shallow name-calling from the demonstrators reveal their own lack of a coherent ideology.

One university student, Bill Fletcher, wrote that he was "disappointed at the way you dumped on the protest marchers." Conceding that there were "a number of clods and politically naïve schlemiels who frequent picket lines and social movements," Fletcher blamed Marvel for painting a "picture of student protest which focuses on the personalities of the picketers, not the reason for their picketing" (Fletcher, 1966, 41: Letter). Lee admitted his "blushing bullpen blunder," claiming that "we never in a million years thought anyone was gonna take our silly protest-marchers seriously! We just tossed it in for a little comedy relief — or so we thought!" Lee had treated the youths as misguided at best, shiftless at worse, but with a new mandate from readers to editorialize, Lee took student protests in full seriousness with depicting a new crisis on campus.

"Crisis on Campus," first published in 1969, was Lee's first full foray into the youth movement. However, now armed with a mandate from his readers to editorialize his views, Lee mixed student protesting with the civil rights movement. Leading up to the "Crisis on Campus," Lee laid "it right on the line. Bigotry and racism are among the deadliest social ills plaguing the world today." He labels the bigot as hating "people he's never seen — people he's never known — with equal intensity — with equal venom" (Lee, 1968, 67: Soapbox). Lee tempers his notice, saying that "we're not trying to say it's unreasonable for one human being to bug another. But, although anyone has the right to dislike another individual, it's totally irrational, patently insane to condemn an entire race — to despise an entire nation — to vilify an entire religion."

The presence of African Americans was not new to either comics or Spider-Man's New York. The first black individual to appear in *The Amazing Spider-Man* was a police officer in issue eighteen, and his ethnicity was inconsequential to the plot. However, the unnamed officer had greater significance. The issue, cover dated November 1964, came out shortly after the riots in Harlem-Bedford Stuyvesant that July. The immediate cause of the riots was an instance of police shooting a black teen, leading to three hundred "screaming youths" pelting the patrolman with rocks, *The New York Times* reported, followed by a wider-scale riot the following day (Jones, 1964: 1). Fittingly, the depiction of the first African-American in *Amazing Spider-Man* as a police officer symbolized an integrated police force; blacks had a share in the civil administration. Black characters were background characters in subsequent issues, but their appearances enticed no feedback. However, as readers began seeing more social significance in Spider-Man stories, concerns about civil rights inevitably became a major undercurrent. One soldier, Martin Rudow, who "was not colored," observed that Marvel seemed

> to be sensitive to the problems of our world and are trying to help solve them, at times, in your mags. In view of this, why don't you show Negro policemen? Your books are always full of cops doing their best, but they're always white. Surely you're aware that the presence of more Negro policemen would go a long way toward solving some of the unrest in our cities today. So how about helping the public get used to the idea? It would also add to the realism of your stories [Rudow, 1967, 55: Letter].

Lee responds that they "have shown Negro policemen in the past," but, by that point, Lee had already introduced the first major African American character in Spider-Man's canon: Jameson's city editor, Joe Robertson.

As a foil to J. Jonah Jameson, Joe Robertson played the moral, upright role model for Spider-Man's cast of characters. As city editor, Robertson was personable, fair, and was respected by the entire *Daily Bugle* staff. Artist John Romita remembers that, when designing Robertson he "was thinking of a prize fighter. [...] I gave him white hair and I wanted him to be a guy from a poor background who was a Golden Gloves champ. He worked his way up, educated himself and became a role model. Stan, of course, ignored almost everything that I told him" (DeFalco, 2004: 33). However, like the unnamed police officer, Lee's use of Robertson suggested that African-Americans had stakes in the establishment. One scholar, Janet L. Abu-Lughod, has noted that New York's mayoral office was "dedicated to defusing racial tensions and 'empowering' minority leaders by appointing blacks to higher offices and to civil service positions" in the city's longstanding political and social institutions (2007: 168). Abu-Lughod argues that, after the 1964 riot, such integration helped New York to avoid more aggressive race riots that broke out in other major cities during the 1960s.

Robertson would play a similar role in "Crisis on Campus." Lee also introduces Robertson's son, Randy, one of the student protestors who has doubts about the future. In contrast to Randy, Lee also scripts Josh, a black militant, whose last name is not given. Josh is also the first character in the book to express an ethnic awareness: while minority groups were presented in silence, Josh openly remarks about fellow "brothers" and "whiteys." As the story opens, Josh immediately asks Parker for his stance on the "exhibition hall" issue. Parker, like the readers, is unfamiliar with the controversy, so Josh fills everyone in: the College Board is using a low-rent dorm intended for students to house visiting alumni instead.

Parker remains uncommitted, but he later runs into another group of picketers. Unlike those in issue thirty-eight, this multi-ethnic crowd has a purpose: to march down to the hall in question and demand that hall not be turned "over to the *establishment* [because] it belongs to *us* ... and we *want* it!" Parker chooses not to participate, although his sympathies "are *all* with the *kids* down there." Meanwhile, Randy is accused of being "the son of an *Uncle Tom*," because his father is not "militant enough" (Lee, 1969, *68*: 10–11). A violent misunderstanding at the demonstration results in the students' arrest. Joe Robertson upholds the police, but says that he will stick by his son.

> RANDY: You're talking ... as though I did ... something *awful*! Don't you *see*? Can't you even *understand*? I *have* to be tougher ... I *have* to be more militant ... because of *you*! You've become part of the *establishment* ... the *white man's establishment*! I've gotta live that down!"
>
> ROBERTSON: But isn't this what we all *want* ... what we're all *fighting* for, boy? To make it on our own? To prove we're as good ... or better ... than anyone?
>
> RANDY: I dunno! I dunno *what* to think! [Lee, 1969, *69*: 5].²

In the end, the college dean sides with the students and Josh is victorious. But his triumph is hollow, since the dean says he was on Josh's side all along: he had "an uphill *fight* to convince the *trustees*!" Lee may have presented Parker as sympathetic with the activists, but his neutral ending suggested that the youth movements were more multifaceted than simple clashes between generations: the dean and Joe Robertson also share in the victory. Lee's liberalism also demonstrated more continuities than radicalism, as Josh soon disappears from future issues and Parker — whose wealthy roommate footed his living expenses — had no need of a low-rent dorm. Randy sums up the complexities of the rights movements: "Sometimes it isn't easy to tell ... who your *real* friends are!" Josh concurs to Randy's father that "even if you work for a *whitey* ... you're a *right cat* on my book!" (Lee, 1969, *70*: 9).

"Crisis on Campus" generated some buzz in the fan community. One reader, Charles Blackcrow, applauded that he was "happy to see that the demonstration of E.S.U. wasn't a Communist plot as the John Birch Society would have done if it wrote the story. I thought this would happen since Mr. Lee writes 'patriotic' stories" (1969, *72*: Letter). Lee asserted that he was hardly a conspiracy-monger and that "it will be a sad day, indeed, when the word 'patriotic' denotes a witch-hunting fervor to crush the crusade for the rights and opportunities of every man [and] that there are no clear-cut, fool-proof, 100% effective ways of labeling such events as we pictured on the campus as 'Communist,' 'right-wing,' or what-have-you!" In reply to Blackcrow, another fan was disturbed about the references to John Birch Society: "I don't like that fan tearing it down. Although some may think it 'square,' in my book, patriotism is something that will never go out of style as long as mankind endures" (Bassi, 1969, *76*: Letter). Lee, despite his liberal leanings, agreed with the fan's defending the John Birch Society, replying that "there's no one any prouder of our American freedoms (even with their limitations and imperfections) than we — and no one who thinks it less 'square' to be patriotic."

Lee's use of African-American characters also enticed some feedback. Steve Games comments on the changing storytelling format of *Spider-Man* from the first issue, stating that "we now have Mr. Robertson, his son Randy, and Josh, who might not have existed three years ago because of their color" (1969, *75*: Letter). However, Lee failed to utilize cultural references that would signified black activists' group identity that "black is beautiful" (Colburn and Pozzetta, 1996). One fan picked up on this, noting that "it seems to me that your Negroes are merely white people drawn by the artist with their skins darkened by the colors. I don't think Negroes who read Marvels and see token Negroes who live in luxury, popularity and good health are going to feel any better when they themselves may live in poverty and have vast racial pressure on them" (Stern, 1968, *59*: Letter). The only printed comment from the African American community came from Elaine Glover, who commended Lee "on the use of Negros in your mags" (1964, *64*: Letter). Glover didn't elaborate, but her letter shows that Lee's use of integration in Spider-Man stories met with approval from those he depicted.

The issue of race and its ties to the youth movement lingered long after the crisis on campus passed. Joe Robertson encourages his son to stay at ESU. Randy sees it differently, commenting, "I know you've got it made here in whitey's world! But what about the *other* brothers who played it your way ... who *got* their sheepskins ... and *still* can't make it on the outside?" Robertson replies that he wasn't promising utopia, and J. Jonah Jameson proves Robertson's point by barging in with his usual bluster. After Jameson leaves, the younger Robertson asks his father, "Why should you haveta take all that *bull* from a *racist* like him?" However, Robertson cautions his son not to use such language freely, because Jameson was no bigot: "He's a big blundering blowhard [...] But just 'cause he's *white* doesn't make him a *racist*. We'll never get *anywhere* till we recognize who our *real* enemies are!" (Lee, 1969, *73*: 13–14).

Such a real enemy appears shortly later. Black youngster Hobie Brown debuts as an inventor by day and window washer by night. Unlike Josh or Randy Robertson, Brown wants to join the establishment and find "some way to really do my thing." Brown's employer, Mr. Clark, has no intention of letting Brown do anything, informing him, "I've had it with your type!" However, J. Jonah Jameson — a client of Clark — intervenes and tells Clark to "shut your big *yap* or I'll do it *for* ya!" Jameson further tells the befuddled boss to leave because "all of a sudden, I don't like the *smell* around here;" his lit cigar notwithstanding (Lee, 1969, *78*: 14). Jameson, who has a mixed record when it comes to upholding the law, reveals a streak for social justice (see Andrew Smith's analysis of Jameson later in this volume). One reader was surprised, thinking it was "out of character for him to show signs of sympathy for anyone. I half way expected [Jameson] to offer [Brown] a job" (Cassello, 1970, *82*: Letter).

Brown's employer was the first instance of racism in Spider-Man's colorblind city. During "Crisis on Campus," Josh had utilized ethnic labels, but the main storyline avoided the civil rights movement. After the crisis dissipated, demonstrators found new causes to protest, including anti-war rallies (Lee, 1970, *88*) and environmental pollution (Lee, 1970, *89*). However, these struggles are preempted by Captain Stacy's death, which segues into a new storyline dealing with racism and corruption at the political level in the midst of an election.

Peter Parker had fought corrupt politicians before. In the short-lived *Spectacular Spider-Man* magazine, Spider-Man derailed the campaign of political candidate Richard Rudolph, a black-and-white villain who created monstrous menaces in his spare time. By the time of Stacy's demise, however, social tensions are a more compelling campaign issue than worldwide domination. The unsavory politician in the latter election is Sam Bullit, a hard-hitting contender with more realistic views than global governance.

Bullit's words speak for themselves: "society today is at *war*, do you hear? We're at *war* with the left-wing *anarchists* who are trying to *destroy* this great, proud *nation* of ours!" Bullit's anti-crime platform earns him *The Daily Bugle*'s endorsement. However, Joe Robertson cautions Jameson that Bullit's vision of a great society is not only crime-free, but also a racial whitewash. Robertson cautions that Bullit is reminiscent of fascists from the 1930s, echoing contemporary rhetoric comparing the perceived stifling of intellectual dissent in America with the politics of the master racists in the Third Reich (Brick, 2000).

Robertson forewarning bears fruit; Jameson soon rejects the candidate's plans to institute

Gestapo-like tactics in his war on crime (one reader applauded that "JJJ is as much or more of a man than most us [Ostapkovich, 1971, *96*: Letter]). John Romita uses a first-person perspective as Robertson confronts Bullit, as if the readers were pointing fingers at the political hack: "I *know* where your support comes from! I *know* about the lunatic *hate groups* who are backing you! [...] I *know* what you think of *minority groups*—and the *plans* you've got for them!" (Lee, 1971, *92*: 9). Bullit, accused of racial extremism, resorts to his criminal constituency, but Spider-Man stops him with the aid of Iceman, a youngster who is acutely aware of bigotry from another series (although Bullit seemed to be free of anti-mutant prejudice). Bullit is later arrested; the last panel shows the police hauling him off in handcuffs.

Bullit's arrest highlighted the establishment's capabilities to reign in their more radical representatives. Lee also pointed out that the "youth rebellion" contained undercurrents that threatened to sweep the more positive aspects away. One fan observes that "the big point is that more and more of your heroes are fighting the ills of society, rather than the superpowered clods with whom few can identify, if at all....They deal with robbery, murder, and host of others—except one. *Drugs,*" and cites his high school as an example of one overrun with drug abuse (Katten, 1971, *97*: Letter). Lee agreed that "the problem of drug abuse could not continue to be ignored. And so we had to deal with it, regardless of the repercussions from those who are not aware of the importance and scope of the drug problem in this country." Indeed, the letter appeared in an issue that was already attacking substance abuse. Furthermore, the illustrations of Parker's roommate popping pills led the comics to be rejected by the Comics Code, the industry's censorship body.

Despite Marvel's entrenchment in youth culture, the storyline's attack on the counterculture's flirtation with drugs met with overwhelming approval. As Randy Robertson notes, drugs had no racial or class boundaries. "It hurts us more than anyone else—'cause too many of us got no *hope*—so we're easier *pickin's* for the pushers. But it ain't just *our* problem! It's *yours*, too!" (Lee, 1971, *96*: 15). Joe Robertson echoes his son, urging Jameson to expose that drugs "hit the *rich*—same as the poor. It's *everyone's* problem!" (Lee, 1971, *98*: 9). Letters from readers agreed, as did Stan Lee, who took pride that the drug story rebelled against the industry's own establishment: "in those days, you couldn't be distributed and wouldn't go to heaven if you didn't have the Comics Code on your books." Nevertheless, Lee says he received "letters from parents and teachers and religious leaders who all commended us. It worked out very well" (DeFalco, 2004: 17 and 20).

Ironically, Lee's questioning of authority became a new trend in the industry. Even DC's Robin, the Boy Wonder, chafed at social institutions while attending college and Marvel expanded their rhetoric to others (Wright, 2001: 235–237). Given the complexities of the issues presented in the pulp pages, some readers felt that comics were capitalizing on the themes of youth rebellion. One anonymous naysayer claimed that Marvel was "trying to brainwash the public" and accused the company of "doing it because you think it's 'in' thing to do—and make a fast buck" (Lee, 1971: *96*: Soapbox). Lee justifies himself, adding that "at every college campus where I may speak, there's as much discussion of war and peace, civil rights, and the so-called youth rebellion as there is of our Marvel mags per se. None of us lives in a vacuum—none of us is untouched by the everyday events around us—events which shape our stories just as they shape our lives" (Lee, 1970, *83*: Soapbox).

The sociologist Daniel Well would posit that the 1960s counterculture "produced little culture and it countered nothing" (Patterson, 1996: 442). Indeed, throughout the decade, Spider-Man's sales never surpassed two characters who stressed conformity rather than confrontation: Archie, who affirmed small-town values in Riverdale; and Superman, whose conservative battle for "truth, justice, and the American Way" outsold the Web-slinger. The Man of Steel triumphed, as he always did (Miller, 2010). Nevertheless, Spider-Man's ascendancy signified a shift in the comic book-reading public as Marvel explored the fissures in American politics, media, and culture. With audience approval, Marvel set their superheroes against establishment figures that had great power, but were greatly irresponsible.

Notes

1. The term "establishment" had a more specific definition in the Cold War. The historian James T. Patterson identifies the "establishment" as "the leaders of America's [post World War II] foreign policy" (Patterson, 1996: 84).

2. The Robertsons' father/son bond is the strongest depiction of familial generational strife. Parker's parents are dead and disgraced as communist spies. Parker's roommate, Harry Osborn, has a neglectful father who is a super villain prone to hypnotic suggestions and flashbacks stemming from a split personality. Mary Jane Watson and Gwen Stacy have living older relations, but Lee did not address the women's movements. Watson is concerned primarily with boys and Stacy has her eye on Parker.

Works Cited

Abu-Lughod, Janet. *Race, Space, and Riots in Chicago, New York, and Los Angeles.* New York: Oxford University Press, 2007.
Brick, Howard. *Age of Contradiction: American thought and culture in the 1960s.* Ithaca, NY: Cornell University Press, 2000.
Colburn, David R., George E. Pozzetta. "Race, Ethnicity, and the Evolution of Political Legitimacy" in David Farber, ed. *The Sixties: From Memory to History.* Chapel Hill, NC: The University of North Carolina Press, 1994.
DeFalco, Tom. *Comic Creators on Spider-Man.* London: Titan Books, 2004.
Jones, Theodore. "Negro Boy Killed, 300 Harass Police." *The New York Times.* CXIII: 38, 891. (July 17, 1964): 1.
Jacobs, Robert A. *The Dragon's Tail: Americans Face the Atomic Age.* Boston: University of Massachusetts Press, 2010.
Lee, Stan, Steve Ditko, et al. *Amazing Fantasy 15.* New York: Marvel (August 1962).
_____, Steve Ditko, et al., *Amazing Spider-Man Annual 1.* New York: Marvel (1964).
_____, Steve Ditko, et al., *Amazing Spider-Man 1.* New York: Marvel (March 1963).
_____, Steve Ditko, et al., *Amazing Spider-Man 3.* New York: Marvel (July 1963).
_____, Steve Ditko, et al., *Amazing Spider-Man 4.* New York: Marvel (September 1963).
_____, Steve Ditko, et al., *Amazing Spider-Man 5.* New York: Marvel (October 1963).
_____, Steve Ditko, et al., *Amazing Spider-Man 10.* New York: Marvel (March 1964).
_____, Steve Ditko, et al., *Amazing Spider-Man 17.* New York: Marvel (October 1964).
_____, Steve Ditko, et al., *Amazing Spider-Man 18.* New York: Marvel (November 1964).
_____, Steve Ditko, et al., *Amazing Spider-Man 20.* New York: Marvel (January 1964).
_____, Steve Ditko, et al., *Amazing Spider-Man 21.* New York: Marvel (February 1965).
_____, Steve Ditko, et al., *Amazing Spider-Man 35.* New York: Marvel (April 1966).
_____, Steve Ditko, et al., *Amazing Spider-Man 36.* New York: Marvel (May 1966).
_____, Steve Ditko, et al., *Amazing Spider-Man 38.* New York: Marvel (July 1966).
_____, John Romita, Mike Esposito, et al., *Amazing Spider-Man 39.* New York: Marvel (August 1966).
_____, John Romita, Mike Esposito, et al., *Amazing Spider-Man 41.* New York: Marvel (October 1966).
_____, John Romita, et al., *Amazing Spider-Man 43.* New York: Marvel (December 1966).
_____, John Romita, et al., *Amazing Spider-Man 46.* New York: Marvel (March 1967).
_____, John Romita, Mike Esposito, et al., *Amazing Spider-Man 53.* New York: Marvel (October 1967).
_____, John Romita, Mike Esposito, et al., *Amazing Spider-Man 55.* New York: Marvel (December 1967).
_____, John Romita, Mike Esposito, et al., *Amazing Spider-Man 59.* New York: Marvel (April 1968).
_____, John Romita, Mike Esposito, et al., *Amazing Spider-Man 64.* New York: Marvel (September1968).
_____, John Romita, Jim Mooney, et al., *Amazing Spider-Man 65.* New York: Marvel (October 1968).
_____, John Romita, Mike Esposito, et al., *Amazing Spider-Man 66.* New York: Marvel (November 1968).
_____, John Romita, Jim Mooney, et al., *Amazing Spider-Man 67.* New York: Marvel (December 1968).
_____, John Romita, Jim Mooney, et al., *Amazing Spider-Man 70.* New York: Marvel (March 1969).
_____, John Buscema, John Romita, et al., *Amazing Spider-Man 72.* New York: Marvel (May 1969).

_____, John Buscema, John Romita, et al., *Amazing Spider-Man 73*. New York: Marvel (June1969).
_____, John Romita, et al. *Amazing Spider-Man 75*. New York: Marvel (August 1969).
_____, John Buscema, Jim Mooney, et al., *Amazing Spider-Man 76*. New York: Marvel (September 1969).
_____, John Buscema, Jim Mooney, et al., *Amazing Spider-Man 78*. New York: Marvel (November 1969).
_____, John Romita, Jim Mooney, et al., *Amazing Spider-Man 82*. New York: Marvel (March 1970).
_____, John Romita, Mike Esposito, et al., *Amazing Spider-Man 83*. New York: Marvel (April 1970).
_____, John Buscema, Jim Mooney, et al., *Amazing Spider-Man 88*. New York: Marvel (September 1970).
_____, Gil Kane, John Romita, et al., *Amazing Spider-Man 89*. New York (October 1970).
_____, Gil Kane, John Romita, et al., *Amazing Spider-Man 92*. New York (January 1971).
_____, Gil Kane, John Romita, et al., *Amazing Spider-Man 96*. New York (May 1971).
_____, Gil Kane, Frank Giacoia, et al., *Amazing Spider-Man 97*. New York: Marvel (June 1971).
_____, Gil Kane, Frank Giacoia, et al., *Amazing Spider-Man 98*. New York: Marvel (July 1971).
_____, John Romita, Jim Mooney, et al., *Spectacular Spider-Man 1*. New York: Marvel (July, 1968).
Miller, John Jackson. "1969 Comic Book Sales Figures." *The Comics Chronicle*. Accessed 10/25/10 http://www.comichron.com/yearlycomicssales/1960s/1969.html.
Patterson, James T. *Grand Expectations: The United States, 1945–1974*. New York: Oxford University Press, 1996.
Wright, Bradford W. *Comic Book Nation: The Transformation of Youth Culture in America*. Baltimore, MD: The Johns Hopkins University Press, 2001.

"Continually in the Making": Spider-Man's New York

MARTIN FLANAGAN

Introduction

The superhero narrative, already a culturally prominent trope in comic form but expanding to become a central component of Hollywood film and televisual production strategy around the late 1990s, tends to revolve around issues to do with growth, identity and the achievement of social agency. Frequently allied to this is a discourse around mobility and freedom that particularly links the superhero story to conceptions of the modern city as a place of dynamic movement and perpetual social and technological change; superheroes, as both subjects within and upholders of social arrangements, experience this dynamism as both exhilarating and entrapping (Bukatman, 2003: 191; Peaslee, 2007: 37–9). In superhero comics that utilize real cities as settings (notably, and distinctively, those published by Marvel Comics), substitutions of enhanced or even "hyperreal" locations—whereby the real physical logic of the city is replaced with a purely narrative geography—are commonplace. This is also true of the spectacular cities of blockbuster "event" films, many of which, whilst not direct adaptations of extant comic narratives, are inspired by superhero culture (most obviously, the *Matrix* films [Larry and Andy Wachowski, 1999–2003]).

Yet superheroes have other functions to fulfill that pull them back from this existence on a level of pure fantasy. Between the 1960s and early 1970s—the period known as the "Silver Age" of American comics and still the era most identified with the culturally influential "boomer" generation—the core thematic of much superhero culture was to do with exploring the relationship between an extraordinarily gifted or powerful hero and a "realistic" space inhabited by people with plausibly relevant social values (for instance, the X-Men and their campaign for tolerance of the different, or, in the early 1970s, the famous interventions of DC's Green Lantern and Green Arrow with drug pushers, Manson-like cult messiahs, and environmental problems such as over-population). Ever since, superhero cities have had to reconcile themselves with other extant discourses about the health of the body politic. In keeping with this tradition, Sam Raimi's three *Spider-Man* movies (2002, 2004 and 2007) have attempted to gauge the impact of the 9-11 World Trade Center attacks, particularly their impact upon New York City—although as we shall see, the approach taken is hardly direct. Underscoring the tendency of Spider-Man's New York to be reiterated in new versions that cross Marvel's various product lines, timestreams, and alternate continuities that ask the question "What If...?," Sony Pictures recently announced the departure of Raimi from the film series and the "rebooting" of the franchise under a new creative team led by director Marc Webb (Child, 2010). Rebooting in film business logic is a practice that roughly resembles the formation of a branching reality—often incorporating a new telling of the heroic origin, and/or a shift in how diegetic co-ordinates relate to external history—such as the *Ultimate* line, introduced by Marvel with *Ultimate Spider-Man* #1 (Bagley and Bendis, 2000).

In considering the relationship between New York and Spider-Man, its premier though certainly not singular fantasy hero, this chapter will move between the comic incarnation of the city and its transfer to film (nearing fifty years' worth of mythology associated with the character stretching across both forms). At a broad level of how the hero functions in relation to cultural concerns, the comic and its adaptations are fairly interchangeable; I am not interested in issues of adaptation *per se*, although I do believe there are important differences between the mediums, especially in terms of how each version deals with the traumatically charged context of American national identity after September 11, 2001. However, I feel that the best approach to define Spider-Man's New York "universe" will be to move relatively freely between the two forms, building towards an assessment of the part that fantasy narratives play both in raising fears of apocalypse, and providing mythic resolutions to those fears. To this end I will refer to a range of superhero cities, both in comic and film, whilst keeping in mind the broader, generic concept of the "spectacular city" that will be associated with recent CGI-enhanced event cinema.

Such cities are sometimes referentially "real" on some level, as in New York in *The Day After Tomorrow* (Roland Emmerich, 2004) or *Cloverfield* (Matt Reeves, 2008); but they may also be archetypal or composite, as with Gotham in *The Dark Knight* (Christopher Nolan, 2008), or various cities in the *Matrix* and *Lord of the Rings* (Peter Jackson, 2001–3) sagas. Occasionally they are somewhere in-between, as in the case of the titular city of Wolfgang Petersen's *Troy* (2004). Moving on to explore how superhero cities respond to the incorporation of the urban concept into discourses of "homeland security" (more strongly referenced in Marvel's comic output than Raimi's films), it will be argued that what all of these cities hold in common, across different sub-generic articulations of the adventure-fantasy spectrum, is their capacity to be spectacularly destroyed, with attendant implications both for audience pleasure, and anxiety.

The Superhero and Their Environment: Modes of Difference

In terms of concrete connections to real, lived-in cities, superheroes' home cities—not just the famous composite cities like Gotham or Metropolis but also Spider-Man's New York City—are undoubtedly abstract spaces, planned and built around the generic and narrative exigencies of action scenes and battles. These cities have to be pliable, spectacular backdrops to the hero's astonishing bodies and abilities, yet at the same time connect to real social spaces in a way that engages the spectator. Although Marvel's "realism" has frequently been seen as its chief differentiator from its main rival, DC Comics (Weiner, 2009: 464), this can be a difficult balance to strike in a textual environment that is notoriously liable to wholesale revision for the sake of continuity, which is zealously monitored by comic fan communities. To use Mikhail Bakhtin's term, the time/space context or "chronotope" inhabited by the superhero constitutes a perpetual present, an abstract, rolling "now" with a carefully controlled relationship to diegetic history (Bakhtin, 1994). In this way, the superhero city structurally resembles the worlds of other long-running but ageless fantasy heroes; in the cinema, James Bond — himself recently "rebooted" — is paradigmatic (Flanagan, 2009: 62–9).

The city thus cannot maintain a direct relationship with the history that transpires outside the comic's borders, hence the tendency of major comic publishers to co-ordinate distinct "universes," as mentioned earlier, as a tool for stabilizing continuity. This instability of the city in relation to the extra-textual "real" echoes the fluidity of identity that is implicitly connected with the superhero persona. As fans of Spider-Man, a hero whose civilian identity became controversially unfixed from its moorings in the mid-1990s (DeMatteis and Bagley, 2010), know only too well, identity is prone to be revised at any time; far from being limited to a simple binary structure of hero persona/civilian persona, identity is frequently multiple in nature as the mythology of the character grows and their universe expands. However, the default myth of identity for superheroes remains the Oedipal narrative, and it is within the specific parameters of this struggle that the forging of the hero's individual destiny takes place (Bukatman, 2003: 185; Peaslee, this volume). Oedipal trials became the hallmark of the flawed, neurotic "outsider heroes" created by Stan Lee and collaborators like Jack Kirby, Steve Ditko and Bill Everett at Marvel in the 1960s. As I have discussed elsewhere, Spider-Man, the Hulk, Daredevil and others were defined through their constant battling with various forms of repressive patriarchal authority, the publisher consciously offering them up as figures of identification for the counter-culture (Flanagan, 2007: 143). Yet even as the teenaged Spider-Man struggled to understand the older generation, he simultaneously sought the approval of attractive Oedipal mentor figures. The most important of these for Peter in the main Marvel comic continuity is arguably the kindly newspaper sub-editor Robbie Robertson, a foil for Peter's hostile employer J. Jonah Jameson; however, Raimi's films reduce Robertson's role in order to leave a gap in Peter's life whereby he can experience conflicting emotional ties with the older men who constitute his principal villains (Green Goblin/Norman Osborn; Otto Octavius/Dr Octopus).

Raimi's first installment conforms to the general tendency for superhero origin tales to employ a truncated Oedipal passage to spur the hero's quest for identity, which they eventually discover through their actions in selflessly defending society. Peter's opening voiceover question, "Who am I?," is thus answered by the body of the narrative wherein Peter finds the moral strength to measure up to the expectations of his late Uncle Ben (Cliff Robertson), slain early in the film as a tragic consequence of Peter's teenage selfishness and lack of adult definition. The film thus charts Peter's maturation process, framing this in the narrative doubling of Spider-Man's rise to New York celebrity — if not always appreciation — with Peter's civilian move to Manhattan, a sign of his independence after graduating high school (although Peter has grown up in Forest Hills, Queens, Spidey's true environment is undoubtedly a generous web-line across the East River).

Thomas Bender has written of the "unfinished" quality of New York, borne out of several factors including the historical tendency to resist centralization within the political order of the United States; the city's huge physical, cultural and ideological diversity and drive towards economic self-determination; and a unique value of metropolitanism not in thrall to the routes to modernity taken by other cities (Bender, 2002: xi). These factors result in a city determined to lead civic trends but always understanding each phase in its development as "temporary, subject to further change"; hence the essence of the city's character "is to be continually in the making" (2002: xi–xii).[1] It is this capacity for constant *revision* (particularly through waves of superhero-focused destruction and rebirth) that makes New York the quintessential "real world" superhero city, exploited so well in the adventures of the major Marvel heroes (Bainbridge, 2010 *passim*). In comics, what counts is that the superhero city — whether it is Superman's Metropolis, Green Lantern's Star City or the more concrete but still highly stylized Marvel Universe "take" on New York City — is a colorful, dynamic, playful space, a crucible of modern progress and sky-scraping movement. It is a place where *difference* is constantly in process, and this discourse of difference is mobilized in the fact that whenever Spider-Man wears his unique costume and exercises his unreal and utterly singular abilities, he commands the cityscape; however, when Peter tries to "blend in" as a civilian, to emphasize his desired normality and sameness, his problems — with girls, with his studies, with his job and lack of money — multiply. However much Peter desires anonymity amongst the "eight million stories" personified on New York streets (according to the television serial *Naked City* [1958–63], a text that concluded its run in the same year that Marvel published the initial issue of *The Amazing Spider-Man*), the comics and films go to great lengths to emphasize that that is not his lot in life.

Yet Spider-Man is no cosmically omniscient hero in the Superman mold: he is placed *within* the city as well as above it, defined by emotional ties to the city's populace that are frequently unrequited (the refusal of sections of the city's law enforcement and media establishment to embrace him). It is precisely his profound human empathy and underdog status that made the character available for counter-cultural identification in the late 1960s. His creators make Peter/Spider-Man seem connected to the city's population and the ebb and flow of its life even though his powers serve to separate him from "normality"; rejected by officialdom, he becomes a true folk hero (Raimi adapts this aspect of the character into a montage sequence in the first film, presenting a cross-section of New Yorkers in a television "vox pop" pastiche that reveals the view from "the street" and demonstrates popular support for Spidey as transcending race, gender and social class lines).

Moving on from the rash self-interest that tragically defines the outset of his super-heroic career (leading to Uncle Ben's death), Raimi uses the Oedipal tussle with Norman Osborn/Green Goblin (Willem Dafoe) to establish Peter's growing bond with his fellow city-dwellers and his level of comfort with a diverse citizenry. Among the rooftops, with Peter temporarily paralyzed by nerve gas, the villain proposes a Nietzchean team-up. Osborn argues that by exploiting their unique positions as "amazing creatures," he and Spider-Man could work together to elevate themselves above the city's "teeming masses" with a minimum of unnecessary bloodshed; Peter declines. In each of the first two movies, by opposing figures who embody the city's patrician elite — the unhinged CEO Norman Osborn, the brilliant but crazed scientist Dr. Otto Octavius (Alfred Molina) in *Spider-Man 2* — Peter shows that he cannot conceive of using his powers in a way that would definitively separate him from the people on the streets; hence, he will not entertain the Goblin's pact. In mainstream comic continuity, Osborn has become even more of an establishment figure, directing the powered wing of America's security forces from atop a gothic skyscraper in midtown Manhattan, until being deposed by the combined heroes in the events of *Siege* (Bendis and Coipel, 2010).

Mobility and Spectacle

What is the nature of Spider-Man's city? "Unfinished" as it is, the superhero city acts as an endlessly fresh catalyst for pulpy adventure. The representation of New York in Raimi's trilogy, despite the terror wrought by super-villains Osborn, Octavius and Venom/Eddie Brock (Topher Grace), is essentially utopian, emphasizing a sharp contrast with some significant representations of that city in recent "high" culture. Examples include, in the postmodern novel, the oppressive, metrical gridlock of Don DeLillo's *Cosmopolis* (2003),[2] or the patterns of obsessive urban life in Paul Auster's *New York Trilogy* (1988); in cinema, such texts find correlatives in the threatening, uncanny Manhattan dreamscape that entraps Tom Cruise's character in Stanley Kubrick's *Eyes Wide Shut* (1999). In its dominant characteristic as a locus of spectacle and movement, Spider-Man's ongoing New York narrative appears more akin to the utopian tradition of urban representation in the classical American film musical; movies like *42nd Street* (Lloyd Bacon, 1933) and *On the Town* (Stanley Donen/Gene Kelly, 1949) indulge in a similar "reconfiguration of the city as a delirious space of possibility and becoming" as do the hero's adventures (Bukatman, 2003: 158). Yet, in contemporary terms, if anything, Spider-Man's movie New York is perhaps closest in spirit to the romantic and emotional playground that Manhattan becomes in *Sex and the City* (1998–2004), that other long-running popular fiction where (sexual) adventure and personal growth via constant test and re-evaluation are presented as the twin poles defining the life of a New York celebrity.

While not the most tourist-friendly vision of New York ever beheld on screen (Raimi's landscape is no more iconic than many of Woody Allen's films, or *Sex and the City*), *Spider-Man* does present a familiar, condensed Manhattan environment, with few defining markers in its Queens sequences. However, Peter Parker's street-bound existence is clearly demarcated from the exhilarating sequences in Manhattan's heights where Spider-Man lives his life in perpetual motion (this tension is comically rendered in sequences that show Peter, in civilian guise, either as an un-coordinated klutz [*Spider-Man 2*] or — possessed by an alien symbiote — an overconfident buffoon [*Spider-Man 3*]). The films build on a sense that Spider-Man never quite seems himself as a truly "street level" character, despite Marvel's attempts to position him as such in crime sagas like the 2010 mini-series *Shadowland*, which transpires in and around Daredevil's turf of Hell's Kitchen (Diggle and Tan, 2010). Raimi's scenes of sheer vertical momentum, of web-swinging above traffic-packed avenues, provide the necessary spectacle to balance the slow-burning classicism of the first film's patient build-up, which is all about acquainting audiences with Peter's family and romantic life. In achieving this balance, Raimi understands that what counts in a superhero story is the way the protagonist navigates their way around the city; not only how they interact with people but how they incorporate an intimate knowledge of urban space to their advantage (and how the city facilitates their omnipotence). The superhero enacts what Scott Bukatman, invoking the architect Rem Koolhaas, calls a "dynamic negotiation" with the city space (2003: 189). It is the very quality of dynamism associated with the hero's exploitation of city space that marks out *Spider-Man*'s playful New York from the static, nightmarish repetitions of DeLillo or Kubrick.

Bukatman's "dynamic negotiation" plays out physically in the superhero's soaring or leaping around the city but also incorporates a negotiation of identity. Cities permit a "slippery sense of self" and offer a place of "rebirth" to individuals, according to Bukatman (2003: 212); such room to maneuver through layers of social mobility — connected to the expansion and movement of capital — exploded nineteenth century hierarchies within cities, at least at the level of fantasy (in filmic terms, this is the case with the 1930s gangster tale or backstage musical narrative as much as the superhero). And superheroes *move*, of course; it is their reason to exist, that which connects them to the vibrant essence of a perpetually unfolding city that "declines any notion of completeness" (Bender, 2002: xi). If, as David Bordwell (2008) notes, the new techno-architecture of movie theatres and home entertainment systems demands immersive "yawning landscapes" filled with adventure and motion, surely the city-based superhero satisfies the zeitgeist.

Sequential art has evolved its own graphic conventions to represent heroes in all their kinetic glory. When a hero is in full flight the city becomes a trail of lines in the background; when we see the fastest heroes (say, Superman or the Flash) from the point of view of ordinary people on the street, the heroes themselves become a blur to the reader's eyes. The superhero moves with such awesome speed and power that the city warps around them, an effect exploited recurrently in the depiction of Neo (Keanu Reeves), superhero of *The Matrix* films. The two-dimensional comic-book city in this sense is a true antecedent of the computer generated "spectacular city" of the contemporary event film; the fluid and mercurial urban environments created for *The Matrix*, *Dark City* (Alex Proyas, 1998) and *Inception* (Christopher Nolan, 2010) filter physical principles through the spatial logic of comics and animation.

The moral function of the superhero is also connected to mobility and freedom: to enforce a fair and equal *distribution* of space — essentially "reclaiming" the streets from crime in the interests of ordinary citizens, while rescinding the right to move of villains. The villains, of course, are always locked up, almost never killed; no matter how advanced the penal technology, they always escape, perpetuating the cycle whereby "nothing really changes through [the hero's] actions," keeping the macro-narrative open (Bukatman, 2003: 186)[3] — another sense in which the "unfinished" takes precedence. The superhero's dazzling sense of freedom, expressed as untrammeled movement through the city space, is marked as a significant source of audience pleasure in the extended "web-swinging" sequences that end the first two films by showing Spider-Man depart for his next adventure (and, simultaneously, confirm the inevitable sequel promise). These scenes — like identical ones in *Daredevil* (Mark Steven Johnson, 2003), *Fantastic Four* (Tim Story, 2005), *Superman Returns* (Bryan Singer, 2006), *Iron Man* (Jon Favreau, 2008) and *The Matrix Reloaded* (2003) — are realized through sophisticated CGI effects that deliver Spidey's impossible vantage point on the city to us. However, as noted by Koh (2009: 743), the two Raimi films also privilege a spectatorial engagement with character that gives the storytelling apparatus a more deliberate classical feel; the first character seen in close-up in Raimi's saga is Mary Jane Watson (Kirsten Dunst), with Peter's voiceover emphasizing her central role in the narrative and serving to embed the film's spectacle in a careful relationship with crucial emotional/developmental subplots in a manner that blatantly broadens the film's address beyond the stereotypical young male moviegoer.

Raimi's handling of the delicate equation of spectacle and narrative — following the comic book tone set by Stan Lee's definition of the Spider-Man character, which always devoted as much time to the ongoing "soap opera" of Peter's life as to Spidey's battles (Wright, 2003: 212) — positions the series (at least until the messier, less coherent third installment) at a certain remove from trends in spectacle "event" cinema. What is meant here is that which Neil Bather, developing a phrase coined by Thomas Schatz (1993), calls "purposeful incoherence": "This 'incoherence' [...] to be found within the spectacle of the film, was designed so that possible meanings within the film were placed in a state of flux in order to attract the widest possible audience" (Bather, 2004: 42).

Bather expounds this notion with specific reference to the narratively slender spectacle films of "high concept" producer Jerry Bruckheimer; while expressing several of the traits of a high concept production,[4] Raimi's *Spider-Man* generally eschews the hyperactivity of contemporary action editing styles (the presence of which is noted with dismay by Bordwell [2008] in Nolan's *The Dark Knight*), and uses a far more character-driven approach to narrative identification, making the idea of a designed "incoherence" rather more difficult to apply. In recent attempts to theorize popular cinema affect in the digital age, the discussion of spectacle films can become loaded with pessimistic assumptions about denuded texts and fragmented audiences; Yvonne Tasker notes that "critics repeatedly single out for comment the exaggeration or stylization, the sheer *excess* of spectacle as the defining feature of contemporary action [...f]or some, the narrative of contemporary action is all but subsumed within the spectacular staging of action sequences, employing star bodies, special effects, artful editing and percussive music" (2004: 6). Clearly, though, if one looks at the success that both comics and comic-derived spectacle films have had in transferring between cinema and videogame (recently in Marvel/Activision's *Spider-Man: Shattered Dimensions* [2010]), questions about the nature of identification and narrative "coherence" can be raised. Furthermore, the urban concept seems especially linked to the discussion of the film and the videogame as sorts of narrative/identificatory experience, as work by Greg Singh (2005) on the *Grand Theft Auto: San Andreas* (Rockstar Games, 2004) game has shown. One gratuitously pleasurable "spectacle" sequence in *Spider-Man* unites various elements of this debate with a particular take on the representation of New York.

The location of the Green Goblin's first public attack and battle with Spider-Man is a "World Unity" festival taking place in a Disney-fied and family-filled Times Square. This area of midtown Manhattan is often seen as the chief symbolic space of New York regeneration, and consequently has been the focus of much criticism of the city's encroaching corporatization and homogeneity (see Comella, 2003). This is illustrated in Thomas Bender's contention that "[I]f twenty years ago many New Yorkers avoided Times Square because it was dangerous, they do now because it is an alien intrusion of the culture of sameness" into the city's natural state of diversity (2002: 196). Yet the choice of Times Square for Raimi's sequence also looks back to previous fictional incarnations of the area where 42nd Street and Broadway converge, returning us to the comparison between Spider-Man's New York and the movie musical. Just as Raimi's film strives to keep narrative and spectacle in check, the narrative "frame" into which exuberant musical numbers were planted in films like *42nd Street* and *Swing Time* (George Stevens, 1936) served a function of formally bracketing a joyous "aesthetic liberation" (Bukatman, 2003: 165). The presentation of a version of Times Square as an unparalleled site of leisure, pleasure and carnivalesque festivity in many musicals fed a popular image of New York as "amusement park" (2003: 165–6) that is consciously echoed and updated in *Spider-Man*'s spectacle sequence (with the obvious complication that while as audiences we are positioned to enjoy the Goblin's attack, for the New Yorkers depicted it is an experience of terror). There is still further ambiguity in the musical's deployment of Manhattan as a generalized locus of urban pleasure; as James Sanders points out, while classical genres such as the musical depended on New York as *signifier* of urbanity and sophisticated leisure, they rarely actually *used* New York locations in their soundstage-bound productions. Indeed, between the introduction of sound and the late 1940s, the high period of classical American film, feature production activity in New York locations was scarce at best (Sanders, 2002: 327–330), a situation that only changed when figures like screenwriter Malvin Wald pitched projects that would borrow their distinctiveness from using city locations, such as his *The Naked City* (Jules Dassin, 1948), progenitor of the previously mentioned television show. The slipperiness of the correlation between New York as fantasy symbol and its actual civic and social history are well adumbrated by Sanders, and some of this ambiguity carries across into Spidey's confrontation in the revamped and rebranded Times Square: representing a debatable unity, it becomes a dangerous place for a superhero.

Historicizing Spider-Man's New York

Spider-Man comics, making a virtue of their long and expansive history, admit a degree more of the "real" New York into their narratives than Raimi's films, for understandable reasons, could ever hope to. Although drawing on a number of key moments from the character's four decades worth of publishing history, the movie cycle cannot achieve the depth and complexity of the various Spider-Man comic books' engagement with New York history from 1963. To cope with this intimidatingly expansive catalogue of events, Raimi employed a typically postmodern *bricolage* strategy, blending elements of real New York history with highlights from four decades of Spider-Man's comic existence, creating an incarnation of the city that is both comforting and dangerous, at once contemporary and retro-styled, with reference points that blur the extra-textual and purely fictional in the style of other Marvel publications dedicated to "mapping" New York (Gruenwald, et al., 2006: 19; Sanderson, 2007).

"Bronze Age" comics featuring Spider-Man attempted to keep pace with representations of the city available in other forms of culture, particularly cinema, which at the time focused real anxieties in their audience and America at large. It could be said that Spider-Man has always been a mild variety of vigilante, despite attempts in early 1990s comics (partly in response to the 1980s multimedia reinvention of Batman as a dark avenger) to stress his ruthless streak. During the 1970s, however, the iniquities and dangers of big cities both real and imagined were explored against an increasingly grim urban template as superheroes took a vengeful turn, emulating the violent revenge cinema of the period. While cinema audiences were being challenged and fascinated by the dystopian presentation of New York in films like *The French Connection* (William Friedkin, 1972) and *Serpico* (Sidney Lumet, 1973), Marvel's narratives similarly portrayed urban America on the edge, with the containment of socially divisive impulses in post–1960s politics and culture presenting problems that confounded its heroes. As Peter Lee notes above, an uncaring, Nixon-esque capitalism is embodied in comics of the time by right-wing authoritarians (sometimes within the police, sometimes disguised as cult leaders in order to stoke racial or social conflicts), or cynical slum landlords. These hostile and morally fraught conditions became reflected in Marvel's increasingly guilt-wracked heroes, with Spider-Man and even, unthinkably, Captain America finding themselves caught between a natural inclination to support the official word of law and order and a growing realization that their moral positions are laughably simplistic (Wright, 2003: 238–9; 244–5). With heroes like Cap too inherently moderate (and, with Steve Rogers' irreconcilable generational difference from Peter Parker, too *square*) to grasp the true problems of being forced into an outsider position by the status quo, more radical Black heroes arose to combat these problems, notably in the inner-city New York adventures of Harlem's "Hero For Hire" Luke Cage, introduced in 1972 in the wake of Blaxploitation cinema (Wright, 2003: 247).

Rather like the recovering, auteur-infused mainstream American cinema of the late 1960s and early 1970s, Marvel's strategy at this time was to court a young, hip readership through social engagement, achieved by casting the city in a dystopian light. Many of Spider-Man's epochal storylines come from this period (including, in 1974, the introduction of the Punisher, a Vietnam-scarred Dirty Harry equivalent operating outside of the law). Coming three decades after the peak of this trend, and presented with the considerable challenge of compressing Spider-Man's expansive comic history into a few hours of screen time, Raimi's films faced the problem of generating their own New York City with regard to very different internal and global perceptions. Mostly, Raimi delivers a socially healthy, multicultural city, populated by individuals that, with a gesture towards a post–9-11 unified citizenry, are as heroic in their own way as Spider-Man, and who more than once unite to come to his aid. The New York of the movies seems to have largely resolved many of the problems in the cultural fabric that made the task of Spider-Man's 1970s comic incarnation so difficult, processing civic history as expressed in crime rates, personal safety and the rebranding of the city. In *Celluloid Skyline*,

James Sanders discusses the revisionist treatments of New York City in films across the 1990s. Mayor Rudolph Giuliani's era, although beginning in controversy and unpopularity, came to be defined by the gentrification of certain notorious parts of the city, economic recovery and a dramatic reversal of crime trends that had soared upwards in the 1970s and 1980s, for which Giuliani gladly took credit (although the amount of credit actually due to him was much disputed). Sanders identifies a corresponding change in New York fictions, noting the transformation from the "horror city" of violent urban crime films such as the mythic *The Warriors* (Walter Hill, 1979), *Escape from New York* (John Carpenter, 1981) and *Fort Apache: The Bronx* (Daniel Petrie, 1981), to a New York coded as "a city physically reshaped around security, safety and the *fear* of crime," if not the act itself (Sanders, 2002: 383). The reordered, post–Giuliani city is essentially that of *Spider-Man* and *Sex and the City*. However, the fear mentioned in Sanders' phrase evokes larger anxieties that with strange predictive force began to manifest in visions of the city as a site of apocalypse in 1990s movies.

Spider-Man After 9-11

Comic book fantasies, like spectacle films, have long incorporated scenes of mass devastation. After September 11, however, even the previously innocent phrase "Look, up in the sky! It's a bird! It's a plane!" came to sound "different; its awe [...] replaced by shock and revulsion" (Wilonsky, cited in Wright, 2003: 288). In moving towards a conclusion, I would like to address how the representation of New York in the three Spider-Man films can be read in relation to the events of 9-11. I will then briefly comment on the implications this response has for the discourse of heroism within both movie and comic incarnations of the character of Spider-Man, for I believe these implications highlight a thread that can be seen to weave through heroic representations in popular media since the attacks.

Despite widespread predictions in the immediate aftermath of the 9-11 attacks that the production of Hollywood action and disaster movies would be rendered ethically and aesthetically impossible, popular cinema has continued to produce images of major American cities in apocalyptic scenarios (Prince, 2009 *passim*). Indeed, an argument could be made that the depiction of New York City as a locus of large-scale disaster merely went on a brief hiatus with respect to post–9-11 sensitivities, with films like *The Day After Tomorrow* quickly resuming the trajectory established as far back as *King Kong* (Ernest B. Schoedsack/Merian C. Cooper, 1933). To underline the pervasive iconicism of destructive fantasies based around New York, the meteor attack suffered by the city in the quintessentially "incoherent" spectacle movie *Armageddon* (Michael Bay, 1998) is cited by Bather as an exemplary "high concept" amalgamation of technology, production value and spectacle (2004: 44). Considering that, as a formula for mass appeal filmmaking, "high concept" is itself frequently referred to as the pre-eminent mode of production in contemporary Hollywood (Gross, 2000), it seems logical to propose a significant link between the destruction of New York — or a city closely modeled upon it — and the essence of spectacle cinema. Indeed, the list of post-classical Hollywood films imagining New York in the throes of terrorist, criminal, or environmental destruction grows, with an article in the *New York Times* noting the tendency in anticipation of the release of *Cloverfield*, even as the similarly destructive *I Am Legend* (Francis Lawrence, 2007) still attracted theatrical audiences (Chan, 2007).

It is widely known and often mentioned that Raimi's *Spider-Man* was still in production during September 2001. The hero's adventures take place in a New York visibly shaped not only by the Giuliani period of regeneration discussed earlier, but one still more radically altered in terms of audiences' emotional perceptions of its populace and symbolic global position. 9-11 can be construed as introducing a sensibility of censorship to the Spider-Man movie project, famously manifested in the removal of World Trade Center images from the initial summer 2001 teaser trailer, but also at a thematic and tonal level. The need to present a *reassuring* vision of New York and New Yorkers — one that nevertheless allows for spectacular action and the threat of mass destruction (from city "insiders" like Osborn, no less) — poses a challenge to the traditional superhero narrative dynamic, which tends to revolve around a city in crisis that can be redeemed by the hero's utopian will and physical grace. Standard arguments about popular films replaying cultural anxieties in a mythical register undoubtedly apply here, but more complex variations of this process are imaginable. In his book on the symbolic impact of 9-11, Slavoj Žižek inverts that reading to argue that in this case, the real attack acts out the fantasy of spectacular destruction dreamed of for years in movies; in other words, "America got what it fantasized about," a horrible, tragic reality confirming the potency of the fantasy (2002: 15–20). It is true that a series of films that drown, blow up, or otherwise bring New York to the edge of calamity or beyond appeared in the half-decade running up to the attacks; one of these was a superhero film, *X-Men* (Bryan Singer, 2000).

The *Spider-Man* films avoid direct reference to 9-11, and thus sidestep the more overt analysis of discourses of national security and anti-terrorism policy articulated in recent comic arcs involving Spider-Man (the Norman Osborn-led "Dark Reign," "American Son" and "Siege" storylines, spanning 2008–10 in a series of Marvel titles). The state's responsibility to organize superheroes in a way that can vouchsafe a secure society receives some attention in *Iron Man* and its sequel (Jon Favreau, 2010), and forms the thematic core of Nolan's *Dark Knight*, which, similarly to Marvel's "Dark Reign," explores the sanctioning of super-powered individuals who "cross the line" to defeat terror tactics (with critical readings of Nolan's film disputing the ideological results — see Ip, 2010 and McGowan, 2009). Perhaps justified by the character's traditional "soap opera" basis, Raimi's films instead situate Peter Parker in a strangely quasi-contemporary world: one that features WWF wrestling but few computers; a quaint approach to celebrity culture and media saturation; and where fashions, youth culture and featured musical cues from Chubby Checker and James Brown (in the third film) pay homage to the venerated 1960s of the comics' initial boomer-generation audience (see Koh, 2009: 736–8). Through production design and art direction, the diegetic world seems designed to resemble the distinctive graphic style of Steve Ditko art, a "look" indelibly associated with his Silver Age residency on *Amazing Spider-Man* and serving to situate the present of the narrative some time before the world-changing events of 9-11; this, even as the discourse of heroism that runs through all three installments places Spider-Man squarely in a post–September 11 world (the films go out of their way to include emotionally loaded scenes where the support of "ordinary" New Yorkers inspires the hero to new heights of selflessness). More ambiguously, the pressure of heroic expectation reverberates at a level that invokes a crisis in the American self-image. When Peter Parker tries to walk away from his powers in *Spider-Man 2* — a treasured but, quite honestly, oft-repeated device since its first use in the comics in 1967 — he is placed in a series of post–September 11 reluctant heroes in movies ranging from *National Treasure* (Jon Turteltaub, 2004) to *Troy*, and, prototypically, Mel Gibson's *The Passion of the Christ* — all of which were released in 2004. The trope of problematic heroic destiny was also incisively played out in Pixar's *The Incredibles* (Brad Bird, 2004), a superhero pastiche that posits an era when heroes have been effectively outlawed after a litigious society makes their existence financially unsustainable.

Max Page has suggested that New York's global pre-eminence is reinforced the more it is depicted as a target in apocalyptic imaginings (cited in Chan, 2007). If, since the 2001 attacks, American popular cinema has tried to re-examine and retool its own attitude to violence and disaster, while finding it hard to fully kick the habit, the concept of heroism has at least been opened up to a more problematic treatment. In all of the above narratives, of course, the hero ultimately accepts their destiny within the terms of the social contract; similarly, as events in Spider-Man comics and other Marvel events over the past decade have repeatedly testified, however much society's view of superheroes deteriorates, they are always ultimately welcomed back as protectors. Yet the new American hero bears that mantle as both a "gift and a curse," as Peter Parker reflects on his own powers in Raimi's first film. Interestingly, Marvel's *Amazing Spider-Man* comic also explored the nature of the heroic burden in the wake of September 11, but faced the event head-on, producing a dedicated 9-11 narrative barely two months after the attacks. The story, self-consciously presented as a so-called "Special Bulletin" interrupting normal continuity (and thus, unusually, drawing attention to its boundaries), takes the angle of commencing with Spidey arriving at Ground Zero moments after the devastation and realizing his essential powerlessness. This device, along with the pseudo-news format styling, acknowledges the thin but unassailable line separating fact from fiction (rebutting Žižek, the destruction of the World Trade Center and environs is an excess of "the real" in the comic, and the fictional superhero merely a personification of the nation's distress). Spider-Man materializes in Manhattan too late to do anything but provide inspiration to the real heroes, the police and fire department, whom we see him working alongside. In broad terms, both films and comic stress that the crisis galvanizes a visibly multi-faith and multicultural citizenry (Straczynski and Romita, Jr., 2001: 33); however, this unification of hope and intent is rendered more easily as a symbolic moment outside "normal continuity," with its frame-breaking connotations, than in the clumsier "World Unity festival" of Raimi's Times Square.

What do New York City and Spider-Man mean to each other? The explosion of viewpoints ("eight million stories...") that made New York the ultimate modern city, and which helped to structure the form of sequential art in the late nineteenth century (Becker, 2010: 273), provides a paradoxical unity that grounds the character across increasingly diffuse textual incarnations. Ultimately, the metafictional resonances of *Amazing Spider-Man* #36 befit the dense narrative of Spider-Man's comic world and can only incompletely cross over into cinema; generic necessities that bind the films into the logic of high concept spectacle production demand spectacular individual agency. Yet, as Spider-Man prepares to emerge in full 3D in Sony's 2012 reboot, the fact of being "continually in the making," as Bender has it, identifies Spider-Man with his city.

Notes

1. More ambiguously, this unfinished quality is inscribed in *Spider-Man 3* as a threat to the New York citizenry. Separate incidents show a crane go out of control, necessitating the spectacular rescue of Gwen Stacy (Bryce Dallas Howard), and the villains Venom and Sandman (Thomas Hayden Church) selecting an unfinished high-rise development to stage their last stand against Spider-Man.
2. A David Cronenberg adaptation of the DeLillo novel has been announced for cinema release in 2012.
3. Yet, without the hero's interventions the streets would be as threatening as the gothic mazes of Batman's filmic universe, particularly in Tim Burton's installments (*Batman*, 1989; *Batman Returns*, 1992), and Christopher Nolan's. In Nolan's *Batman Begins*, the moment when Bruce Wayne's father (Linus Roache) is murdered in a dark alley is shocking despite its signposting as Oedipal catalyst of Batman's heroic journey. The murder shocks because the character's idealistic moral rectitude has been established in his benevolent planning and building of a monorail for Gotham City, which democratically links the towers of the city's prosperous classes

with the so-called "Narrows," where the poorest and most wretched live. Batman's legacy from his father, the film suggests, is to facilitate safe passage around the city for the weakest of its inhabitants, just as Peter Parker's defining sense of responsibility derives from his experience of seeing his Uncle Ben slain in an act of criminal violence (on the Fifth Avenue sidewalk in front of the New York Public Library, according to Raimi).

4. The notion of "high concept" refers to the mode of production of modern blockbuster cinema that introduces the "package" mentality of Hollywood deal-making into film aesthetics. Such films are thought to exhibit "modular" narratives whose structure is organized around the promotion of ancillary products (toys or soundtrack albums) and the fetishistic presentation of production value (star or special effects), with "coherency" of plot or consistency of character relegated to minor concerns. Studios prize high concept film proposals that exploit narratives with pre-existing popular recognition (sequels, remakes, topical news items, book or video game adaptations); comic-to-film adaptations inarguably emerge within this scope. Indeed, *Superman* (Richard Donner, 1978) is cited as exemplary in Justin Wyatt's 1994 book, still the classic scholarly elucidation of the high concept approach.

WORKS CITED

Bagley, Mark and Bendis, Brian Michael et al. *Ultimate Spider-Man 1*. New York: Marvel Comics (October 2000).
Bakhtin, Mikhail. "Forms of Time and of the Chronotope in the Novel." in Michael Holquist ed., trans. by Caryl Emerson and Michael Holquist. *The Dialogic Imagination: Four Essays*, Austin: University of Texas Press, 1994: 84–258.
Bendis, Brian Michael and Oliver Coipel et al., *Siege 1*. New York: Marvel Comics (March 2010).
Bather, Neil. "Big Rocks, Big Bangs, Big Bucks: The Spectacle of Evil in the Popular Cinema of Jerry Bruckheimer." *New Review of Film and Television Studies*, 2:1 (2004): 37–60.
Bender, Thomas. *The Unfinished City*. New York: The New Press, 2002.
Bordwell, David. "Observations on Film Art: Superheroes for Sale." www.DavidBordwell.net. 8/16/2008. Accessed 11/27/10. http://www.davidbordwell.net/blog/?p=2713.
Bukatman, Scott. *Matters of Gravity: Special Effects and Supermen in the Twentieth Century*. Durham: Duke University Press, 2003.
Chan, Sewell. "The Irresistible Urge to Destroy New York on Screen." *The New York Times City Room*. 12/26/2007. Accessed 11/28/10. http://cityroom.blogs.nytimes.com/2007/12/26/the-irresistible-urge-to-destroy-new-york-on-screen/.
Child, Ben. "Spider-Man Loses Sam Raimi and Tobey Maguire." *The Guardian*. 1/12/2010. Accessed 11/28/10. http://www.guardian.co.uk/film/2010/jan/12/spider-man-loses-sam-raimi.
Comella, Lynn. "Re-inventing Times Square: Cultural Value and Images of Citizen Disney" in Justin Lewis and Toby Miller eds., *Critical Cultural Policy Studies: A Reader*. Oxford: Blackwell, 2003: 316–26.
Corrigan, Timothy. "Auteurs and the New Hollywood." in Jon Lewis ed., *The New American Cinema*. Durham: Duke University Press, 1998: 38–63.
DeMatteis, J. M. and Bagley, Mark et al. *The Complete Clone Saga Epic: Volume One*. New York: Marvel Comics, 2010.
Diggle, Andy and Tan, Billy et al. *Shadowland 1*. New York: Marvel Comics (September 2010).
Flanagan, Martin. *Bakhtin and the Movies: New Ways of Understanding Hollywood Film*. Basingstoke: Palgrave Macmillan, 2009.
____. "Teen Trajectories in *Spider-Man* and *Ghost World*" in Ian Gordon, Mark Jancovich and Matthew McAllister eds., *Film and Comic Books*. Jackson: University of Mississippi Press, 2007: 137–59.
Gross, Larry. "Big and Loud." in José Arroyo ed., *Action/Spectacle Cinema: A Sight and Sound Reader*. London: BFI, 2000: 3–9.
Gruenwald, Mark, Howard Mackie, John Byrne, et al. *Essential Official Handbook of the Marvel Universe: Deluxe Edition, Volume 2*. New York: Marvel Publishing, 2006.
Ip, John. "The Dark Knight's War on Terrorism." *Ohio State Journal of Criminal Law*. Working Paper Series (April 19th 2010). Accessed: 11/28/10 http://papers.ssrn.com/sol3/papers.cfm?abstract_id=1574539.
Koh, Wilson. "Everything Old is Good Again: Myth and Nostalgia in *Spider-Man*." *Continuum* 23:5 (October 2009): 735–47.
McGowan, Todd. "The Exceptional Darkness of *The Dark Knight*." *Jump Cut* 51 (Spring, 2009). Accessed 11/28/10. http://www.ejumpcut.org/archive/jc51.2009/darkKnightKant/index.html.
Peaslee, Robert M. "Superheroes, Moral Economy and the 'Iron Cage': Morality, Alienation and the Super-Individual" in Wendy Haslem, Angela Ndalianis and Chris Mackie eds. *Super/heroes: From Hercules to Superman*. Washington, D.C.: New Academia Publishing, 2007: 37–50.
Prince, Stephen. *Firestorm: American Film in the Age of Terrorism*. New York: Columbia University Press, 2009.

Sanders, James. *Celluloid Skyline: New York and the Movies.* London: Bloomsbury, 2002.
Sanderson, Peter. *The Marvel Comics Guide to New York City.* New York: Simon and Schuster, 2007.
Schatz, Thomas. "The New Hollywood" in Jim Collins, Hilary Radner and Ava Preacher Collins eds. *Film Theory Goes to the Movies.* London: Routledge, 1993. 8–36.
Singh, Greg. "*San Andreas*: Agency, Movement, and Containment; or, How the West is (Frequently) Won." *The Aesthetics of Play Online Proceedings.* 2005. Accessed 11/27/10. http://www.aestheticsofplay.org/singh.php.
Straczynski, J. Michael and John Romita, Jr., et al. *Amazing Spider-Man 36.* New York: Marvel Comics (November 2001).
Tasker, Yvonne. "Introduction: Action and Adventure Cinema" in Yvonne Tasker ed., *Action and Adventure Cinema.* London: Routledge, 2004. 1–13.
Weiner, Robert G. "Sequential Art and Reality: Yes, Virginia, there is a Spider-Man." *International Journal of Comic Art* 11:1 (Spring 2009): 257–77.
Wright, Bradford W. *Comic Book Nation: The Transformation of Youth Culture in America.* Baltimore: Johns Hopkins, 2003.
Wyatt, Justin. *High Concept: Movies and Marketing in Hollywood.* Austin: University of Texas Press, 1994.
Žižek, Slavoj. *Welcome to the Desert of the Real.* London: Verso, 2002.

Hegemonic Implications of Science in Popular Media: Science Narratives and Representations of Physics in the *Spider-Man* Film Trilogy

Lisa Holderman

> ...when the producer of the movie *Spider-Man* says during an interview that his movie is very accurate scientifically, our duty is not to stare back at him in disbelief, but to take that sentiment and try to understand the cultural framework that enables him not just to say this with a straight face, but to mean it.
>
> —Frank, 2003: 427

For centuries, the general public has been misled about, denied access to, or in some way made apathetic or hostile toward scientific truths. There is little doubt that religious, political, social, and economic forces worked — either by direct, planned actions or as by-products of the existing ideology — to maintain public ignorance about science and, more generally, critical thinking. Given that scholarship suggests that many, if not most, people gain knowledge of science through popular culture (Apple and Apple, 1993; Basalla, 1976; LaFollette, 1990; Mains, 2008; Van Riper, 2003; Vílchez-González and Palacios, 2006), I propose that representations of science in popular media are one contemporary parallel to some of the forces that distanced, misled, and disinterested the public from science throughout history. That is, I contend that popular media, including (and perhaps, especially) high-budget Hollywood science-fiction films rife with riveting special effects, compelling stories about science, and scientific inaccuracies, contribute to a denigration of science in the public sphere, and by extension, to a general anti-intellectualism that has hegemonic implications.

The *Spider-Man* film trilogy (Raimi 2002, 2004, 2007) serves as an example of an ideal vehicle for dispensing science narratives and scientific misinformation. Since the character's introduction in the comics in 1962 (Trushell, 2004), Spider-Man has been a popular American icon; yet the recent films brought the character to life in a way that audiences had never before experienced. Blending riveting superhero science-fiction plots with superb cinematography and effects, all three *Spider-Man* films were phenomenal box-office successes, both in the United States and worldwide[1] and, as such, I contend they function as important cultural artifacts and storytellers that, ultimately, reflect a popular anti-science ideology.

I am certainly not the first to examine public apathy or antagonism toward science; indeed I am only able to provide a very cursory review of this scholarship here. Circumstances wherein the public are denied access to scientific thought and evidence are plentiful, usually when the science conflicts with preferred belief— religious or otherwise (Brody, 2007). However, while clashes between science and religion still exist (see Gieryn, Bevins, and Zehr, 1985; Williams, 1983), the antagonism toward science is now less religious and mostly secular (Coulter, 1920)—a phenomenon Shils (1976) suggests to be relatively new.

Clearly, the mechanisms through which apathy and antagonism are constructed are complex. Seventy years ago, Merton (1938) argued that "hostility toward science may arise under at least two sets of conditions, although the concrete systems of values — humanitarian, economic, political, religious — upon which it is based may vary considerably" (322). One explanation, he contends, is the "logical" idea that science is contrary to "the satisfaction of certain values," while the other, "non-logical" idea suggests that scientific ethos and ethos in other institutions conflict. And, although it is clear that the concept of "the public" as a unified mass is simplistic (Etzioni and Nunn, 1976), many scholars agree that the "laity" are indifferent toward and disinterested in science (Shils, 1979), that scientific literacy among the public is too low (Prewitt, 1982), and that the American public's appreciation of science has declined.

In many ways, the *Spider-Man* films represent a cultural antagonism toward science. As Burge (2002) notes, movies are important because they "have become a repository of myths about ourselves. We measure the significant action of our lives — loving, fighting, failing, succeeding — against the repertory of dramatic scenes from the shared experience of cinema" (166). Although mass media are not the only channels through which ideas about science are communicated (Perlman, 1976), they are clearly important ones. It has been suggested that the public's desire for and assessment of certain types of knowledge may be explained, at least in part, by their portrayals in popular fictional media (Kahlenberg, 2008). Numerous scientists and media scholars believe that popular media are "at least partially responsible and are a significant source of the public's misunderstanding and faulty knowledge of science" (Efthimiou and Llewellyn, 2003: 1). In this analysis of the *Spider-Man* trilogy, I focus on three general areas of representation in the films: the narratives of science as dangerous, uncontrollable, and corrupted, the constructions of scientists as powerless and victimized, and the inaccurate representations of the laws of physics.

I am not suggesting, however, that media-makers deliberately attempt to confuse, mislead, or otherwise keep the public in the dark. On the contrary, it has become fairly commonplace to employ science consultants on big budget films to ensure as much scientific accuracy as possible (Kirby 2003a, 2003b; Frank, 2003; Goldman, 1998; Smith, 2006). Representations of science in popular media reflect deeper, pre-existing, ideological issues regarding science and intellectuality. As Gerbner (1987) states in his analysis of scientists on popular television:

> Television did not invent the negative image of science. It only streamlines the image, puts it on the assembly line, and delivers it into every home. The image of science on television is only part of a broader problem: the skewed image television presents to the world [115].

The popularization of science, however, may be more complex than might seem at first glance.

Hilgartner (1990) suggests that the dominant view of the ways in which science is popularized is problematic in its simplicity. The commonly-held belief about the process is that scientists develop knowledge, which "popularizers" (usually journalists) then oversimplify and/or misrepresent to the public. He contends that such a view has political uses for scientists in that they can use it to their favor, citing problematic reporting when it fits their needs and giving them exclusive rights to "genuine knowledge." The underlying notion here, however, is that scientific knowledge needs to be disseminated accurately in order to keep the public informed. The social and political uses of representations of science in popular media, of which the *Spider-Man* trilogy is an example, differ from science journalism in that most viewers treat the films' content as "pure entertainment" and may not care about accuracy. This creates a situation in which viewers are uncritical about the images and narratives on the screen — an ideal situation, some might argue, for introducing, reproducing, and instilling certain ideologies.

It seems almost trite to issue a caveat about the issue of "realism" in an analysis of films within the science-fiction genre; however, I feel a brief disclaimer is necessary. The *Spider-Man* films are, of course, fictional and, while audience members may have varied motivations for viewing these films, there is little doubt that they approach them with a willingness to suspend disbelief and to accept the impossible. That being said, my goal is not simply to show how the filmmakers "got it wrong" (although my discussion of the misrepresentation of physics in the films does lay this out), but also to explore the meaning and implications of the media constructions. Kirby (2003a, 2003b) suggests that popular film serves as an important conduit through which masses of people "virtually witness" science. He states:

> The narrative framework in film is designed to highlight the representation's "reality" and to make opaque its construction. This blurring is especially evident for natural phenomena that have never actually been "directly" witnessed (e.g., dinosaurs) [Kirby, 2003a: 54].

Therefore, both the narrative framework and the state-of-the-art special effects create a reality that allows audiences to experience science in various manifestations, be they dinosaurs, comets, or, perhaps, a spider-man.

The Dangerous and Uncontrollable Science of *Spider-Man*

Unquestionably, one of the most effective methods of keeping people distanced from or antagonistic toward something is to make them fearful of it. Clearly interconnected with the constructions of scientists (as I detail in the next section), patterned portrayals of science in popular media are, more often than not, negative. Most science-fiction narratives focus on both science and intelligence and systematic analyses reveal them to be de-valued in such narratives (Thomas and Holderman, 2008). Goldman (1989) suggests that science in popular films is often represented as inherently dangerous: scientific knowledge is regularly shown as corrupted through exploitation and these types of knowledge are "intrinsically corrosive of human well-being, that they inevitably precipitate personal or social disasters regardless of human attempts to control them for society's benefit" (286). In this section, I explore some of the ways the *Spider-Man* films depict science as problematic in this manner.

All three *Spider-Man* films portray science as disastrous, corrupted, and exploited, despite scientists' generally good intentions. The well-known catalyst of all *Spider-Man* stories — the incident that turns an everyday young man into a "Spider-Man" — is a scientific experiment gone awry. In the first film, high-school student Peter Parker visits Columbia University's science department and is bitten by a genetically-engineered "super-spider" that has somehow escaped captivity. Clearly, a narrative of this sort (in any medium — comic book, animated television program, or Hollywood film) needs an explanation of how Spider-Man came to be, and yet, of all the explanations possible in these science-fiction genres, the one that persists is that of science as uncontainable and dangerous. No good reason is given for genetically engineering the spiders in the first place and, despite seemingly good efforts to contain the spiders, one manages to escape. Hence, the entire *Spider-Man* narrative is predicated on the idea that science is dangerous and uncontrollable.

Science fiction films, like those of the *Spider-Man* series, are ideal sites to dissect popular and prevalent ideas about science because they "articulate possible worlds"; their reference worlds are neither representative of the actual world, nor are they wholly imaginary worlds, but they make the unfeasible seem feasible (Buckland, 1999: 177). Moreover, these worlds do more than simply amaze audiences with special effects. Booker (2006) states:

> Science fiction is very much a genre of ideas. As one might expect, SF films have provided the popular imagination with some of its most compelling visions of both the possibilities and the dangers of a future increasingly dominated by advanced technologies. Perhaps more importantly, such films, despite being widely regarded as mere entertainment, have often provided serious and thoughtful explorations of important contemporary social and political issues [266].

Spider-Man 2 introduces a reference world in which the possibilities and, more prominently, the dangers of scientific progress are negotiated.

Represented primarily by the character Dr. Otto Octavius, an earnest scientist working on fusion research, the fundamental lesson of *Spider-Man 2* is that even the most sincere science can turn catastrophic and deadly. Octavius, who eventually is transformed into villain "Doc Ock," is initially constructed as a well-meaning scientist (Peaslee, 2005). In a conversation with Peter Parker, Octavius states, "Being brilliant's not enough, young man. You have to work hard. Intelligence is not a privilege, it's a gift and you use it for the good of mankind." Despite Octavius' aspiration to use fusion to better mankind, his public reaction turns deadly when a containment breach kills his wife and fuses four mechanical arms to his body.

Paralleling the second film, a scientific accident is the sole cause of the creation of the Sandman villain in *Spider-Man 3* as well. Here, escaped convict Flint Marko runs from the authorities to a particle physics test facility, falls into a large testing container, and is accidentally "de-molecularized." Once again, well-meaning science spins quickly out of control resulting in disaster both for Marko personally and for the society at large as he uses his new powers to inflict havoc on the city.

In addition to being dangerous and out-of-control, the science of the *Spider-Man* films is also shown to be corrupted and exploited. Goldman (1989) suggests that some negative depictions of science in popular films represent socio-cultural anxieties over the corporate and political domination of scientific and technological research. Such corruption and exploitation of science is evident throughout the *Spider-Man* film trilogy, most specifically in the Oscorp Corporation, which appears as an integral part of each of the three films. The first film presents greed as a motive for hastily testing a new drug on humans, which ultimately leads to death and destruction. Dr. Norman Osborn, the president of Oscorp, a corporation developing "Human Performance Enhancers," ignores warnings of potential serious side effects (such as aggression, violence, and insanity) and insists on testing in order to retain military funding. In an argument with his lead scientist he exclaims, "Don't be a coward, risks are part of laboratory science!" He decides to test the drug on himself, which results in his transformation into the murderous Green Goblin.

In *Spider-Man 2*, Dr. Otto Octavius, despite his intentions to provide a cheap and clean source of electricity for the world, is ultimately working for Oscorp. During the fusion reaction demonstration, Dr. Octavius makes his reliance on Oscorp very clear:

> OCTAVIUS: Precious tridium is the fuel that makes this project go. There's only 25 pounds of it on the whole planet. I would like to thank Harry Osborn and Oscorp Industries for providing it.
>
> HARRY: Happy to pay the bills, Otto.

Even well-intentioned, Octavius' research is tainted by the corporation's ultimate goal to profit from it, which may have contributed to his decision to continue with the fusion experiment even when it became clear that something was amiss.

And while the presence of Oscorp is more subtle in *Spider-Man 3*, its existence hangs over the film as Harry, the son of the now-deceased Norman Osborn, uses Oscorp's science to avenge his father's death. In essence, although to different degrees, Oscorp's presence is threaded throughout the series and is the basis for most of the science-related problems. The use of science for profit turned Osborn into the Green Goblin, transformed Otto into Doc Ock, and turned Harry superhuman in order to get revenge on Spider-Man.

The Scientists of *Spider-Man*: Powerless, Victimized and Occasionally Mad

Another way to ensure apathy or hostility toward science is to construct scientists and/or people interested in science in a negative light. Scholarship shows us that media-constructed images of scientists vary, but are most often negative and unflattering (Gladstone, 1980); research indicates that scientists in popular culture are often portrayed as evil, deranged villains (Basalla, 1976), heartless (Goldman, 1989), unsociable, odd, and peculiar (Gerbner, 1987), and, of course, "mad" (Skal, 1998; Smith, 2006; Toumey, 1992). Basalla (1976) suggests that, among other things, scientists are portrayed the way they are in popular culture because of a more general bias against scientists as intellectuals — as individuals who are suspect because they don't have the same tastes of everyday people. And while Skal (1998) is careful to point out that the mad scientist image is complex and should not be attributed solely to "knee-jerk anti-intellectualism," he goes on to say that "a puritanical suspicion of the intellect is still deeply ingrained in the American characters; ideas, like sex (not to mention ideas about sex), are still regarded in many quarters as a slippery slope to hell" (25).

The scientists in the *Spider-Man* series are not uniformly characterized or categorized; while Otto Octavius eventually is transformed into a mad scientist, most are portrayed as well-intentioned but careless, powerless, easily-duped, and/or victimized. *Spider-Man* creator Stan Lee's scientist characters are often constructed as having a propensity for mental instability and social irresponsibility; those who are not evil are often shown as easily manipulated and flawed (Basalla, 1976). These representations, however, are not unique to the *Spider-Man* films — Goldman (1989) finds that scientists in popular films are sometimes shown as powerless servants of corporations or political/military institutions, which he sees as being rooted in "high-culture antagonism to technology" (278).

The scientists in the *Spider-Man* films are generally careless, easily fooled, or clueless; they tend to be so mired in the world of science that they are mostly unaware of or powerless to fight the outside forces imposed upon them. Before his transformation, Peter Parker is portrayed as the quintessential science geek. In the opening scenes of *Spider-Man*, he is clearly set up as both a science genius and a social outcast. Although the Peter-as-nerd narrative is threaded throughout the three films, his real-life geeky-ness is, of course, balanced by his super alter-ego — one that is super because he was bitten by a spider, not because he is scientifically intelligent. Science may be to blame (or to be thanked) for Peter's powers, but his knowledge of science doesn't contribute much to his greatness. Characters whose primary asset is scientific brilliance are often punished, such as the head scientist working for Norman Osborn in the first *Spider-Man* film. This character is portrayed as both book smart and ethical, but weak as he is unable to navigate the corporate world in which he works and is powerless against Osborn. Despite his strong objections, he bows to Osborn's desire to test the Human Performance Enhancer on himself and is eventually murdered by the transformed Osborn.

In *Spider-Man 2*, Otto Octavius is introduced as a well-meaning scientist who hopes to use his discoveries to better the world, but his science turns on him and, despite glimpses of the well-meaning man, he becomes a villain, obsessed only with bringing his idea to fruition once again. The de-molecularization experiment scene in *Spider-Man 3* constructs a slightly different image of science researchers, essentially one of scientists as careless and set on a plan from which they cannot deviate. As the experiment begins, the scientists realize there is an anomaly:

SCIENTIST 1: "We got a little fluctuation on one."
SCIENTIST 2: "There's a change in the silicon mass."
SCIENTIST 3: "It's probably a bird. It will fly away when we fire it up."
SCIENTIST 4: "Initiating de-molecularization."

The scene is brief; in fewer than 10 seconds the scientists consider and then discount a possible problem in the testing site, which results in fusing Marko's DNA with the sand in the experiment site and ultimately creates a powerful villain.

While the images of scientists are meaningful, the representations of the science itself are equally so. I now turn to a discussion of the ways in which physics is incorrectly represented in the *Spider-Man* films.[2]

Physics-Schmysics

A third way to keep people distanced from, hostile toward, or, perhaps most importantly, ignorant about something is to misrepresent it. Much of the science of the *Spider-Man* films, the physics in particular, is, altered, exaggerated, and in most cases, simply incorrect. Of course, it is not at all unusual for science to conflict with a movie script (Bowman, 1998) and violating the laws of physics is fairly common in science-fiction films (Koerner, 1998) — as I state above, most viewers clearly understand the fictional nature of a film that features a man who can spin webs at will, scale tall structures with no tools, and swing from building-to-building. But, *physics* (whether it is represented by a falling apple or a swinging spider-man) has well-known and widely-accepted laws that popular media can choose to obey or not. More often than not, the *Spider-Man* films represent the laws of physics incorrectly and if, as Kirby (2003b) suggests, fictional films can act as virtual witnessing technologies because the images appear to be "real," then these inaccurate representations have a socio-cultural significance that goes beyond simple Hollywood fun.

Efthimiou and Llewellyn (2007) contend that the ways in which Hollywood blockbusters break the laws of physics contributes to science illiteracy. They write: "The inconsistencies of the Hollywood products with science may come as a surprise to many people who simply accept what they see as realistic or, at worst, slightly modified from reality." (1). Consolmagno (1996) suggests that science fiction film "colors" the way viewers of popular culture understand astronomy and Burge (2002) states that films about science often break the laws of nature in order to produce a better story. He writes:

> There is even a genre which exists for the sole purpose of flouting them. Superhero films, of which "Spider-Man" is the latest example, fashion their plots out of the physically impossible. The genetically modified spider that turns Peter Parker into Spider-man is, like the nerve gas

which turns Norman Osborn into the Green Goblin, a simple magic potion which owes nothing to science. These movies represent the triumph of digital effects over three hundred years of scientific rationalism (Burge, 2002: 167).

Accurate science, it seems, doesn't fare well in Hollywood films. While there are myriad incorrect representations of scientific properties in the *Spider-Man* films, I will detail just a few examples here.

Many of the problematic representations of physics in all three films involve wind and air resistance, the suspension of gravity, and inaccuracies with acceleration and deceleration. For example, there are several problems with the representation of wind and air resistance in Scene 13 of the first *Spider-Man* film, wherein the newly-costumed Peter Parker chases the man he assumes has murdered his uncle. The representations in this scene are inconsistent. Although Parker is shown to be traveling at high rates of speed (his shirt flaps dramatically in the breeze) he then jumps with absolutely no regard to air resistance from one car to another, over bridges, and onto the top of a truck. If, as indicated, there is significant air resistance, then Parker's motion through the air would be impeded considerably from his shown course. In a subsequent scene, the acceleration due to gravity is portrayed very poorly as Spider-Man attempts to save Mary Jane after she falls from a tall building. Although she seems to not accelerate at all, Spider-Man dives after her, catches up in mid-air, and grabs hold of her from above—all of which is scientifically incorrect.

In *Spider-Man 2*, Spider-Man's attempt to stop an out-of-control train filled with innocent passengers also goes against accepted laws of physics. While trains are often used in physics to demonstrate inertial reference frames (non-accelerating frames in which Newton's laws are obeyed), most of Newton's laws are violated in this representation. First, there appears to be little or no wind while standing atop the roaring train. Second, the movements of Spider-Man above the train are not consistent with an inertial reference frame, as this scene contains several examples of people being thrown from the train and then "caught" by Spider-Man and tossed into a safety web. There are references in the literature (see Kakalios, 2005) to an incident in the original comic book in which Spider-Man's girlfriend, Gwen Stacy, is killed during a fall from the George Washington Bridge. Although Spider-Man is able to catch her just before she hits the ground, she is killed from the shock (or sudden acceleration) of the catch. This reaction is ignored repeatedly, however, in the *Spider-Man* films. Finally, the biggest problem with the train-stopping scene is the way in which the train is finally brought to rest. A train without brakes could not be stopped simply by slowing down the front car, as it would derail or buckle in the middle. Moreover, even though Spider-Man warns the people on the train to brace themselves, they do not appear to decelerate at all, in fact they just stand there in an upright position and watch.

Spider-Man 2 also violates several scientific properties in, among others, its representations of Otto Octavius' fusion demonstration and the disaster that follows. First, the actions performed by the arms of the actuator apparatus are not represented correctly because the torque produced by their actions is not balanced by the motion of an opposing arm. In some shots, one or more of the arms is somehow attached to the ground in order to give the motion some basis, but in other shots they are not. Second, the demonstration indicates that the apparatus is rigidly attached to Octavius' body, yet its violent movements would surely result in his destruction. Finally, the scene in which doctors attempt to remove the mechanical arms that have become fused to Otto's body is the worst offender in terms of unbalanced torques in the mechanism. While on his back on an operating table, the arms are able to throw and swing heavy objects with no movement of the other parts—a representation that violates the real-world laws of physics.

The fusion reaction itself is also problematic. Although the reaction is quoted to be producing enormous amounts of energy, the energy is not observed as either heat or radiation in the room — although the plasma may play a part in confining the reaction, the energy needs to be accounted for. Moreover, the magnetic field appears to attract non-ferrous objects as well as ferrous ones, which is not consistent with magnetic fields. Finally, the idea that a fusion reactor could slowly become unstable is unrealistic; nuclear reactions typically spiral out of control in nanoseconds, not in minutes. Normally there is not enough time to warn the people in a room with an unstable nuclear reaction to take cover, not that taking cover would make any difference anyway.

In *Spider-Man 3*, the Sandman character is problematic in terms of the representation of weight and rigidity. In terms of weight, he appears very heavy at times, but at other times, for example when he is standing on the top of the moving armored car, he appears almost weightless. It makes little scientific sense that the driver would not notice the impact of the weight by changes in the performance of the car when Sandman landed. As for his rigidity, when Spider-Man strikes Sandman in the stomach, his hand goes through the abdomen because there is little resistance to the punch, yet when Sandman throws a punch, his arm remains inconsistently rigid.

The above examples are just a sample of a much larger set of problematic depictions of scientific properties in the *Spider-Man* films. In his analysis of scientific misrepresentations in *Armageddon* and *Deep Impact*, Goldman (1998) notes that even though viewers know the film is fiction, "the more realistic the story seems to be, the more enjoyable it is ... artistic license is often taken to make a movie more enjoyable ... but it mustn't go beyond the point of insulting viewers' intelligence or the spell will be broken" (29, 30). Although, as I note above, it is far too simplistic to view "the public" as a mass of people who interpret depictions of science in approximately the same way, the representations of physics in the *Spider-Man* films are problematic in that they *are realistic* enough for most viewers to lose themselves in the action and the narrative.

Conclusion

Overall, my analysis of the *Spider-Man* films shows narratives of science as dangerous, uncontrollable, and corrupted, constructions of scientists as powerless and victimized, and the laws of physics inaccurately represented. I suggest that these films serve as just one example of a cultural antagonism toward science, and by extension, toward critical thinking and intellectuality.

These films, which make up one small part of a broader gestalt of popular anti-intellectualism, have hegemonic implications as they reinforce an ideology that ultimately keeps the public fearful of and/or disinterested in science and critical thinking. By wrapping up anti-science narratives in captivating, special-effected, science-fiction packages, audiences are immersed in a world that is both realistic and fantasy — a world for which critical viewing seems unreasonable and unnecessary and one that serves as an ideal conduit for dispensing and dramatically reinforcing familiar (and quite negative) accepted wisdom about science. The *Spider-Man* films exemplify an underlying ideology that is deeply-rooted and resonates with audiences of popular communication: avoid intelligence and inquiry as they bring nothing but trouble.

Notes

1. *Spider-Man* and *Spider-Man 3* were the top-grossing films of their release years in the United States (grossing $403,706,375 and $336,530,303 respectively), while *Spider-Man 2* was second only to *Shrek 2*, with a gross of $373,585,825. The first two films were nominated for Academy Awards in both visual effects and sound, with the second film winning the award in the sound category.
2. Many thanks to Kevin Warner for his helpful explanations of the laws of physics.

Works Cited

Apple, Rima D., Michael W. Apple. "Screening Science." *Isis* 84:4 (1993): 750–754.
Basalla, George. "Pop Science: The Depiction of Science in Popular Culture" in Gerald Holton, and William Blanpeid eds., *Science and Its Public: The Changing Relationship*. Boston: D. Reidel Publishing Company, 1976.
Booker, M. Keith. *Alternate Americas: Science Fiction Film and American Culture*. Westport, CT: Praeger, 2006.
Bowman, Lee. "Smashing an Asteroid Harder Than in Movies." *Chicago Sun-Times*. (June 1998): 39.
Brody, William R. Johns Hopkins Commencement Address, 2007.
Buckland, Warren. "Between Science Fact and Science Fiction: Spielberg's Digital Dinosaurs, Possible Worlds, and the New Aesthetic Realism." *Screen*. 40:2 (1999): 77–192.
Bukatman, Scott. *Matters of Gravity: Special Effects and Supermen in the 20th Century*. Durham, NC: Duke University Press, 2002.
Burge, Jim. "In Search of Science on the Big Screen." *Interdisciplinary Science Reviews*. 27:3 (2002): 165–168.
Consolmagno, Guy. J. "Astronomy, Science Fiction and Popular Culture: 1277 to 2001 (and Beyond)." *Leonardo*. 29:2 (1996): 127–132.
Coulter, John Merle. "Science and Religion: 1. The Methods and Results of Science." *The Biblical World*. 54:4 (1920): 339–347.
Efthimiou, Costas, Ralph Llewellyn. "Cinema as a Tool for Science Literacy." *Eprint arXiv:physics*/0404078 v1, 2004.
_____. "Hollywood Blockbusters: Unlimited Fun but Limited Science Literacy." *Eprint arXiv*:0707.1167v1 [*physics.soc-ph*] July 9, 2007.
_____. "Physical Science: A Revitalization of The Traditional Course by Avatars of Hollywood in The Physics Classroom." Retrieved from http://www.arXiv.org/physics/0303005, 2003.
Etzioni, Amitai, Clyde Nunn. "The Public Appreciation of Science in Contemporary America" in Gerald Holton, and William Blanpeid eds., *Science and Its Public: The Changing Relationship*. Boston: D. Reidel Publishing Company, 1976.
Frank, Scott. "Reel Reality: Science Consultants in Hollywood." *Science as Culture*. 12:4 (2003): 427–469.
Gerbner, George. "Science on Television: How it Affects Public Conceptions." *Issues in Science and Technology*. 3 (1987): 109–115.
Gieryn, Thomas. F., George M. Bevins, Stephen C. Zehr. "Professionalization of American Scientists: Public Science in The Creation/Evolution Trials." *American Sociological Review*. 50:3 (1985): 392–409.
Gladstone, Josephine. "Commentary: Remarks on the Portrayal of Scientists." *Science, Technology, & Human Values*. 5:32 (1980): 4–9.
Goldman, Stuart J. "The Science of Hollywood." *Sky and Telescope*. 95:6 (1998): 28–31.
Goldman, Steven L. "Images of Technology in Popular Films: Discussion and Filmography." *Science, Technology, & Human Values*. 14:3 (1989): 275–301.
Hilgartner, Stephen. "The Dominant View of Popularization: Conceptual Problems, Political Uses." *Social Studies of Science*, 20 (1990): 519–539.
Kahlenberg, Susan. G. "Book, Street, and Techno Smarts: The Representation of Intelligence on Prime-Time Television" in Lisa Holderman, ed., *Common Sense: Intelligence as Presented on Popular Television*. Lanham, MD: Lexington Books, 2008.
Kakalios, James. *The Physics of Superheroes*. New York: Gotham Books, 2005.
Kallick-Wakker, Ingrid. "Science Icons: The Visualization of Scientific Truths." *Leonardo*. 27:4 (1994): 309–315.
Kirby, David A. "Science Advisors, Representation, and Hollywood Films." *Molecular Interventions*. 3 (2003a): 54–60.
_____. "Science Consultants, Fictional Films, and Scientific Practice." *Social Studies of Science*. 33:2 (2003b): 231–268.

Koerner, Brendan. I. "Reel Gaffes." *US News and World Report*. 124 (1998, June 29): 1
LaFollette, Marcel C. *Making Science Our Own: Public Images of Science 1910–1955*. Chicago: University of Chicago Press, 1990.
Landon, Brooks. "Synthespians, Virtual Humans, and Hypermedia: Emerging Contours of Post-SF Film" in Veronica Hollinger and Joan Gordon eds., *Edging into the Future: Science Fiction and Contemporary Cultural Transformation*. Philadelphia: University of Pennsylvania Press, 2002.
Locke, Simon. "Fantastically Reasonable: Ambivalence in The Representation of Science and Technology in Super-Hero Comics." *Public Understanding of Science*. 14 (2005): 25–46.
Mains, Christine. "Brains in Service of Brawn: The Scientist/Soldier Dynamic in Science Fiction Television" in Lisa Holderman, ed., *Common Sense: Intelligence as Presented on Popular Television*. Lanham, MD: Lexington Books, 2008.
Mellor, Felicity. "Between Fact and Fiction: Demarcating Science From Non-Science in Popular Physics Books." *Social Studies of Science*. 33:4 (2003): 509–538.
Merton, Robert. K. "Science and the Social Order." *Philosophy of Science*. 5:3 (1938): 321–337.
Peaslee, Robert Moses. "With Great Power Comes Great Responsibility": Central Psychoanalytic Motifs in *Spider-Man* and *Spider-Man 2*." *PSYART: An Online Journal for the Psychological Study of the Arts*, Article 050720. http://www.clas.ufl.edu/ipsa/journal/2005_peaslee01.shtml, 2005
Perlman, David. "Science and the Mass Media." in Gerald Holton, and William Blanpeid eds., *Science and Its Public: The Changing Relationship*. Boston: D. Reidel Publishing Company, 1976.
Prewitt, Kenneth. "The Public and Science Policy." *Science, Technology, & Human Values*. 7:39 (1982): 5–14.
Richardson, Niall. "The Gospel According to *Spider-Man*." *The Journal of Popular Culture*. 37:4 (2004): 694–703.
Shils, Edward. "Faith, Utility, and the Legitimacy of Science." in Gerald Holton, and William Blanpeid eds., *Science and Its Public: The Changing Relationship*. Boston: D. Reidel Publishing Company, 1976.
Skal, David. J. *Screams of Reason: Mad Science and Modern Culture*. New York: W.W. Norton & Company, 1998.
Smith, Deborah. "The Science of Fiction." *Sydney Morning Herald*. (October 28th 2006): 13.
Telotte, J. P. *Science Fiction Film*. New York: Cambridge University Press, 2001.
Thomas, Sari, Lisa Holderman. "The Social Construction of Modern Intelligence." in Lisa Holderman, ed., *Common Sense: Intelligence as Presented on Popular Television*. Lanham, MD: Lexington Books, 2008.
Toumey, Christopher P. "The Moral Character of Mad Scientists: A Cultural Critique of Science." *Science, Technology, & Human Values*. 17:4 (1992): 411–437.
Trushell, John M. "American Dreams of Mutants: The X-Men—"Pulp Fiction, Science Fiction, and Superheroes." *Journal of Popular Culture*. 38:1 (2004): 149–168.
Van Riper, A. Bowdoin. "What the Public Thinks It Knows About Science." *European Molecular Biology Organization*. 4:12 (2003): 1104–1107.
Vílchez-González, Jose Miguel, Javier Perales Palacios. "Image of Science in Cartoons and Its Relationship with Image in Comics." *Physics Education, 41*:3 (2006): 240–249.
Williams, Robert Charles. "Scientific Creationism: An Exegesis for a Religious Doctrine." *American Anthropologist*. 85:1 (1983): 92–102.

Teaching Peter Parker's Ghosts of Milton: Anxiety of Influence, the Trace, and Platonic Knowing in *Ultimate Spider-Man Volume 1*

James Bucky Carter

Harold Bloom is known to have formed a poor opinion of Jacques Derrida. For example, in an interview with *The Atlantic*, Bloom laments that his work once lead him to a situation in which he "suddenly found [him]self fighting the Deconstructionists." He considers most of these people friends, he says, "Except for one—I don't talk to Derrida anymore, for all sorts of complicated personal reasons that I wouldn't want to bring up." Yet, in my junior-level "Contemporary Trends and Issues in the Graphic Novel" course, Bloom works seamlessly alongside the deceased Derrida to help students explore multiple themes.

Well, some of their ideas work together, anyway; specifically, Bloom's concept of the anxiety of influence and Derrida's talk of absent presences and trace theory. Who could bring these two powerhouse theorists back together arm-in-arm? Gayatri Spivak? Mihaly Csikszentmihalyi? Gunther Kress? Julia Kristeva? No. The mediator in this case in none other than Peter Parker—with a little help from Socrates.

After being exposed to what I call my textus/praxis theory of textuality, in which I express to my students my firm belief that a text is anything that can be interpreted, communicated and understood through discourse, students get a crash course in the basics of comics composition and study through Scott McCloud's *Understanding Comics*. Once this background information is covered, the first graphic novel they encounter is *Ultimate Spider-Man Volume 1: Power and Responsibility*. My class is arranged as an examination of several intersecting and rolling themes. These themes include "Pop Art"—based on the phrase Art Spiegelman uses to describe the father-son dynamic inherent in *Maus* and other examples from his milieu (Spiegelman, 2006)—family and identity, social issues, deconstruction, and making/breaking canons. Through these themes, several graphic novels, and some additional scholarly readings, we form opinions about how important ideas running throughout salient graphic novels form a sense of contemporary living and also see how salient ideas of Western thought and critical theory are represented in comics and help situate them in larger literary traditions.

In introducing students to *Ultimate Spider-Man Volume 1*, I review several Western notions concerning truth, being, knowing, and the influence of knowledge. We read and discuss Jeremy Barris' "Plato, Spider-Man and the Meaning of Life" for specific background knowledge, and I pull from this essay in the lecture leading up to reading the graphic novel.

Plato, I inform them, saw "truth" in embracing the world's natural conditions and contradictions, its boundaries, potentials, and limitations. As Barris says, "the meaning of life is to be found ... in appreciating what already surrounds us" (2005:63).

As well, for Plato, there are degrees of separation regarding reality: objects, thoughts, and ultimate truths. "For Plato, the true reality to which images, including everything we immediately experience, are inadequate, is found in the eternal, unified, self consistent 'separate forms.' This is the famous Platonic ideal reality," states Barris (2005:81).

Objects, for Plato, were man's representations of thought about forms, and the thoughts or conceptions of those forms were supposedly closer to the thing itself than tangible objects. "The thing itself" is one more degree of separation from the thought of the thing itself, according to Plato. Or, from a top-down perspective, the real thinglyness of anything can't be known, fully and truly. It can be thought, but not in its purest state, which is beyond human conceptualization. Humans make things to represent the thoughts that are close but flawed approximations of the things themselves, which exist in a sort of over-thought.

While admittedly it is unfair to pass over so many great thinkers, after explaining this concept of knowing, I move out of the 300s B.C. into the 20th century. I mention Bloom's concept of the anxiety of influence, in which he suggests that poets often experience angst over their place and the quality of their works in relation to other poets and their achievements. The Ghost of Milton is presented as a force bearing over the work of Romantic poets, for example. Students and I enjoy visualizing a poet at a typewriter in the middle of the night, too anxious to hit another key, as a spectral John Milton seems to whisper in his ear, "You'll never be as good as me! Why bother?"

To help get at the answer to that question, I introduce Jacques Derrida's concepts of absent presences and traces. I sum up Derrida's big ideas by telling students that, in Derridian theory, we are what we are by recognizing what we think we are *and* what we aren't. We can't escape this defining middle ground or liminal condition. So, in a basic sense, existence is in the contradictions for Derrida, a statement that seems to echo Plato's notions of the natural world. Furthermore, every instance of being for Derrida exists in a contemporary moment of novelty but is also situated in an over-arching historicity of influence and repeating events: "The present therefore is always complicated by non-presence. Derrida calls this minimal repeatability found in every experience 'the trace'" (*Stanford Encyclopedia of Philosophy*, 2006). Not only is our existence defined by who and what is around us, but by past presences and experiences relative to the human condition. These absent presences, or traces of things past and present, influence our lives' meaning and our identity formation. They may go relatively unnoticed or can produce in humans, among other things, inspiration, meaning, or anxiety.

While an explanation of trace theory and absent presences is important to our critical underpinning for reading this specific graphic novel, the bigger question still remains: is anxiety always crippling? Can it also be freeing, especially when one sees life and existence as Derrida has explained them as the natural order of things? An acceptance of Derridian precepts, among them being the idea that we are defined by forces tangible and intangible, past and present, suggests that one can't escape anxieties of influence; indeed, to live a decent life, one might need to embrace them.

To illustrate how these ideas from Plato, Bloom and Derrida can intersect, I finish my lecture with a quote from Robert Browning's 19th century poem, "Andrea del Sarto": "Ah, but a man's reach should exceed his grasp/Or what's a heaven for?" I do so to suggest that anxieties of influence, traces and absent presences do not have to have negative connotations towards humanity's contemporary existence. For Browning as it is for Plato, the living is in the struggle, the constant striving to attain unattainable truth, self-knowledge and meaning, while simultaneously knowing it will never fully be captured. In terms of educational psychology parlance, the zone of proximal development is ever-evolving and can never be closed. We can be crushed by the anxieties of other presences, or we can accept the anxieties as the defining condition of being, part of appreciating what surrounds us. It is this connection between antiquity and New Criticism and Deconstruction and Postmodern thinking that we take into our reading of *Ultimate Spider-Man Volume 1*.

In *Ultimate Spider-Man Volume 1: Power and Responsibility*, students find an adolescent male on the cusp of adulthood living out the tensions and ties among these poets, philosophers and critical theorists: Peter Parker. The *Ultimate Spider-Man* series ran from 2000 to 2009 and was conceived as a way of updating the Spider-Man brand and mythos for new, younger readers and those traditional Spider-Man readers seeking a reality free of the continuity the original series and its spin-offs had accumulated after forty years of publishing. The first seven issues comprise a retelling of the basic origin story and reset the Spider-Man mythos. Much remains the same as in the original: Parker, who is being raised by his Aunt May and Uncle Ben in a working-class New York neighborhood (Queens), is a teen with a love of science who is bitten by a spider and thereby gains new abilities. He has the chance to stop a thief shortly after gaining his new powers, but he doesn't. The thief later kills Uncle Ben and forces the youngster to consider the connections between power and responsibility. These first seven issues are available in graphic novel/trade paperback form in *Ultimate Spider-Man Volume 1: Power and Responsibility*. It is through this book and this iteration of Parker that students can see a character not much younger than themselves striving to live in a world full of contradictions and in conditions that include his own Ghosts of Milton.

The ghosts/traces/absent presences that most influence Peter and cause him anxiety in the first volume of *Ultimate Spider-Man* are not as much those of Uncle Ben, as they are in the series originating in the 1960s, as they are connected to Peter's conceptualization of his long-dead father and their relationship. Students now know to key in on instances where this tension is braided throughout the text, and the Barris article, which only addresses the original Spider-Man ethos, helps them connect what they are reading to its source material. When they see Peter staring at a chalkboard bearing a formula that his father was working on before his death, they see image-text evidence of the trace and how Peter deals with this particular anxiety of influence from a somewhat absent presence (his father is there via the formula but not there in actual physicality): Peter seeks to complete the equation. The last panel of this sequence shows Peter alone in the dark, mulling over the chalk lines, spending time bonding with as much of his father as he has left. Much later in the text, Peter resolves the formula and reveals that its presence represents an anxiety regarding a son's desire for pride and approval in his father's eyes. "We did it, Dad," he says, "I've been staring at your formula for the molecular adhesive you were working on since before I could read. And I could never finish it for you. But tonight ... I figured it out, Dad!" He then tells his dad that with a little tweaking to the compound, he has created web fluid. "And Dad — Look — Spider-man has ... Webs!" (Bendis, 2004). This suggests Peter's understanding of his relationship with the trace of his father is one based on togetherness, desired connectivity, and the longing to perform in ways he feels his father would approve. In short, making the sticky web fluid is for Peter a quite literal bonding experience. While anxiety over lack of an actual fatherly presence clearly exists, it comes to some resolution when we see that Peter has kept the trace of his father with him through positive means and positive anxieties that strengthen his familial ties to this paternal absent presence.

Between these episodes, and after the spider bite seems to have spring-loaded a sort of super-powered puberty (Carter, 2007) for Peter, involving more conflict than usual with his aunt and uncle, Ben attempts to rein in the rebellious youth. Ben references Peter's father when trying to reach out to the confused youngster, telling Peter that his father had a particular philosophy of life:

> He believed that if there were things in this world that you had to offer, things that you did well — better than anyone else — things that you could do that helped people or made people feel better about themselves.... Well, he believed that it wasn't just a good idea to do those things.... He believed it was your responsibility to do those things.
>
> Don't try to be something else. Don't try to be less. Great things are going to happen to you and your life, Peter. Great things. And with that will come great responsibility.
>
> Do you understand?
>
> Great responsibility [Bendis, 2004].

Here the words do not inspire Peter, but they do reveal another facet of Peter's relationship with his absent present father. Peter begins to cry, runs off, and screams, "If he knew so much.... Then where the #$@? Is he?!" He later chastises himself, saying in thought, "The one person who would know what to do was my dad. My dad would have known what to make of all this — my powers — what they mean" (Bendis, 2004). It is certainly understandable that the boy would miss his father, but he wants him around for very specific reasons in these instance: to help him make sense of the changes to his body and mind and to help guide him in his use of his new powers. He is the seeker without a sage at this point, at least in his own mind, and the lack of his father in this specific moment of his development is rife with angst. The existential problem for Peter Parker here is again wrapped up in family dynamics and critical theory: The trace may linger, but it can't touch. Sometimes, absent presences aren't enough.

Of course, anxiety and angst as they are related to existentialism can be resolved through choice, and after this bit of self-inspection, Peter decides to tell his aunt and uncle of his recent developments. He gets no such resolve through his agency, however, as Ben has been murdered while Peter was out. When Peter hunts down the gunman later that night, he sees the face of man he let escape with stolen spoils during another spell of introspection while walking New York's streets. Now he speaks to another influence, recently become trace, and Peter flashes back to the discussion of will and responsibility, already laced with the trace of his father, now layered with the presence of another ghost.

"You told me — You told me," he says, now speaking to the absent presence of Ben. He relives Ben's words — "Do you understand?" — and says aloud to no one but himself/the ghost of Ben, "I do now." Here we see the development of Peter's new anxiety of influence, that of possibly forgetting his uncle's/father's words and their meaning to him, thereby living a flawed, self-serving but directionless life. This new anxiety will be different than the one defining his relationship with his father, as guilt will be a primary element rather than pride: "I was selfish. So selfish — and you paid the price.... I will never forgive myself for that. I will never forget that I could have stopped it." Peter continues to speak to Ben's disembodies presence: "I see the world clearly now.... With power comes responsibility.... I will never let you down again, Uncle Ben" (Bendis, 2004).

In *Amazing Fantasy* #15, the origin story of the original Spider-Man, what would become the Spider-man mantra, "With great power comes great responsibility," comes from a much more disembodied, detached presence, that of the narrator who proclaims, "And a lean, silent figure fades into the darkness, aware at last that in this world, with great power there must also come — great responsibility!" Ben wouldn't be attributed these words until further into the series. This fact allows Barris to wrap up his thoughts on Plato and Spider-Man as such:

> The evident unreality of Plato's dialogues and Spider-Man comics, then, their presence as made up of here and now, is part of the sense of reality we need if we are to relate the truth of reality [2005:83].

Ultimate Spider-Man Volume 1, however, situates the iconic phrase squarely in relation to Peter Parker's family and contemporary moment and thereby crafts an alternative reality. To live a life appreciating what is already around Ultimate Peter Parker, he will continue to acknowledge the absent presences, now grown by one, occupying his schema for father-son relationships, and the traces of Ben and his father will always be with him, contradictions in their being there but being absent. It's not the happiest way to leave Plato, Bloom, Browning and Derrida — and throughout subsequent volumes in the series Peter's desires to connect with living, breathing father figures continually open up new troubles — but that is where *Power and Responsibility* leaves readers.

Students respond to reading the text through these lenses and with these terms with a sense of awe. I intentionally use a super-hero comic as our first graphic novel to play with their preconceived notions of literary merit and worth and what they may see as comics' other perceived limitations. I know that when they read the Barris essay and see my overhead that some smirk and feel that I'm just another academic reading into things that aren't there. But, upon reading the text looking for these elements, they find their thematic presence/absent presence and importance undeniable. Furthermore, students attend to each additional graphic novel we read in class, regardless of genre, cognizant to textual detail and with an aim of considering how every graphic novel reveals important elements of human thought and contemporary theories of living and knowing.

I admit that teaching this text this way relies on Western ideologies at the expense of other philosophies. Further, I know that for some it is apparent that I do not give Bloom or Derrida full justice in my treatment of them regarding this text, and focusing on their similar ideas belies their many differences. I do not go out of my way to discuss Derrida's *difference* and *differance* at this point in the semester, though the terms clearly connect to trace theory. That comes later, once the class is more familiar with the concepts I have discussed and I feel I can build upon them. Certainly they will see more absent presences and traces and family/daddy issues/Pop art in other texts we read, such as *Jimmy Corrigan, Unstable Molecules, Ghost World, Planetary* and *Watchmen*, all texts that challenge them to consider comics as literature or canon-worthy.

I also can readily share that my students mention a certain synergy with my class and their critical theory class, if they are required to take one, and I have even had that class's instructor mention how well prepared for her class my students seem to be. I am also cognizant of Geoff Klock's seminal *How to Read Superhero Comics and Why* (2006) in which he situates many of Bloom's concepts, including the anxiety of influence, and some of Derrida's as quintessential to the super-hero genre. So, my particular angle is not without theoretical grounding in comics scholarship. As well, students who want to examine Klock's ideas on Bloom, Derrida and comics can do so via selecting the text for another assignment for the course: a review of an important text from comics scholarship. In other words, I have arranged the class with built-in opportunities for further examination based on growing knowledge and individual interest and thereby do not feel particularly irresponsible in my whole-class treatment of the theories mentioned herein.

I also do not apologize for what some might see as a confusion of anxiety of influence/trace/and absent presence with simple memory. Memory is a tricky thing, and no longer do we define it as the absolute re-imaging of truth, but as what we perceive to be truth. Plato's ideas now wring stronger than ever via considerations of memory: a memory is not necessarily what happened, but as close an approximation as we can muster, wrapped in its own moment but connected to many other essences of import to us at the time and throughout our lives. But, memories are real in their influence on us. Their trace lingers. Indeed, a student in my first-ever session of "Contemporary Trends and Issues in the Graphic Novel" eventually became a secondary school teacher and used *Ultimate Spider-Man* as a springboard into conversations about memory as absent presence. She informed me that her high school students, reluctant readers everyone, not only enjoyed the text and the concepts but "got it." They used the concept of absent presences to talk about influences that they constantly feel on their own lives, whether or not the person embodying that influence is always with them physically. An end result with young people reading and considering Derrida in a public school? That's a pretty strong example of power, will and responsibility to humanity for which I feel neither I nor Peter Parker need apologize. Indeed, I think Uncle Ben would be proud.

Works Cited

Barris, Jeremy. "Plato, Spider-Man and the Meaning of Life" in Jeff McLaughlin ed., *Comics as Philosophy*. Jackson: University of Mississippi Press, 2007.
Bendis, Brian Michael et al., *Ultimate Spider-Man Volume 1: Power and Responsibility*. New York: Marvel, 2004.
Carter, James Bucky. "*Ultimate* Spider-*Man* and Student-Generated Classics." In James Bucky Carter ed. *Building Literature Connections with Graphic Novels: Page by Page, Panel by Panel*. Urbana, IL: NCTE, 2007.
Gritz, Jennie Rothenberg. "Ranting Against Cant." *The Atlantic*. 7/16/2003. Accessed 10/15/10. http://www.theatlantic.com/magazine/archive/2003/07/ranting-against-cant/3095/.
Klock, Geoff. *How to Read Superhero Comics and Why*. New York: Continuum, 2006.
Lee, Stan, et al. *Amazing Fantasy 15*. New York: Marvel (1963).
Spiegelman, Art. "The Origins of *Maus*." *The Virginia Quarterly Review*. 82.4 (Fall 2006): 30–43.
Stanford Encyclopedia of Philosophy. "Jacques Derrida." 11/22/2006. Accessed 10/15/10. http://plato.stanford.edu/entries/derrida/.

II. Considering Specific Graphic Novels

Weaving Webs and True Lies: Revisiting *Kraven's Last Hunt* Through the Lens of *Brooklyn Dreams*

David Walton

Marvel bills *Kraven's Last Hunt* (*KLH*) as "the ultimate revenge narrative," which is accurate only insofar as the same could be said of *Moby Dick*. Both texts are elevated by metaphysical concerns. Ahab and Kraven eventually come to understand their respective obsessions, the White Whale and Spider-Man, as attempts to put a face on intangible forces. Thus Kraven's stake in Spider-Man's life feeds into his much broader claim to "see into things, beyond things" (54, 73).

The focus of Kraven's vision is the mystical entity known only as "the Spider." He traces its influence as far back as his parents' exile during the Russian Revolution. The Spider is an agent of Chaos that takes on various forms, including Trotsky, Lenin, Gorbachev, Reagan, and most notably, Spider-Man (40). Kraven's Spider construct carries natural, psychological, and religious implications, all of which he acknowledges. Is the Spider a drug-induced hallucination? Did he invent the Spider to nurse his wounded pride? Has he tapped into the spiritual plane and discovered another level of reality (45)? DeMatteis leaves room for interpretation, but textual clues complicate a strictly natural or psychological reading of the Spider. Delirium alone fails to account for Kraven's psychic link with Spider-Man and Vermin. The first evidence of this link is Peter's nightmare of spiders crawling all over him, an experience that parallels Kraven's drug-laced spider-consumption ritual (16–17). From there Peter goes out as Spider-Man, almost as though being called; it "feels like someone's playing jungle drums" (18) inside his head, and senses something waiting for him (19). This notably occurs before Kraven drugs him (20), which only intensifies his impression of jungle drums (23). Later Vermin hears a voice calling to him from the surface world (43), Kraven calls on Spider-Man to exit his grave (78), and somehow knows when he does so (90). Peter's encounter with "the Spider" is perhaps even more compelling evidence of supernatural forces in play. Kraven's drugs can account for Peter's hallucination, but not for its content. Since Kraven never articulates his construct to Spider-Man, any prompting would need to occur telepathically, as when he calls Spider-Man back to the surface (78). Regardless of whether the Spider is the result of similar prompting, or Peter actually encounters a mystical entity, something not strictly natural occurs.

Kraven views the natural, psychological, and religious aspects of this mental link more like dimensions than competing explanations. He has "widened [his] consciousness with herbs and roots," or natural means. His mind has "penetrated" Spider-Man's "essence," that is to say his psychology. And in a ritual invoking imagery similar to Communion, Kraven has "immersed" himself in Spider-Man's "being" and "eaten" of his "flesh" (21). Kraven's intricate philosophy illustrates the perils of confusing single-mindedness with small-mindedness. While his self-destructive tendencies tend to eclipse his complex worldview, insanity and insight are not mutually exclusive. This raises an interesting question. Is there a critical standard by which we can gauge the significance of Kraven's alleged insight? I believe such a standard exists in the form of DeMatteis' *Brooklyn Dreams* (*BD*).

BD was first published in 1994 as a serial by Paradox Press, a DC Comics imprint, and collected in 2003. It is DeMatteis' thinly-veiled autobiography, narrated through the filter of Carl Vincent Santini. More than a distancing mechanism, Santini is the incarnation of a philosophy he personally articulates in the opening sequence of *BD*:

> Now, everything I'm about to tell you is true, I swear it. But the problem is — I don't really believe that there's any such thing as a "true story." Perception is limited. Memory is faulty. I think the moment the words come out of our mouths, we create something wholly different from the truth we're trying to communicate. A shadow-show of reality. A waking dream, if you will ... so sit back, relax, give me a small chunk of your time — and I'll weave you some lies about my life. Who knows? With a little luck — they just might turn out to be true [2003, Ch. 1: n.p.].

Because a strictly "factual" representation is not equipped to express spiritual reality, Santini takes on the roles of "true lie" and "true liar."

Santini's focus is his arrest for drug possession in high school. He comes to see this experience as a metaphor for the metaphysical prison he has been trapped in his entire life. His search for a way out culminates with a fateful, acid-laced walk through the city where all his questions about life come to a head. In the midst of his disillusion over the apparent meaninglessness of life, Santini has a revelation. He sees a "quality" in each passerby likened to beauty but more intense, one that "shone out, not from the body, but the soul." Here Santini discovers the key to his prison and the universe, "a love without time or space" that is God and God in him (ibid., Ch. 4).

The next morning, Santini's ex-girlfriend apologizes for giving him bogus acid, which as it turns out, was nothing more than food coloring. There are conflicting clues in the text as to whether Santini's acid trip was legitimate. He treats it as though it were earlier when he wonders whether it was as hot as he thought that day, if the acid tainted his perceptions, or raised his physical temperature. But the news he receives of the bogus acid is treated just as earnestly, if not more so. Whether Santini is exaggerating a bogus acid trip, undermining a legitimate one, or knows with any certainty is irrelevant to the reality of his experience. Two things are certain: Santini never used drugs again, and he continued to build his relationship with God.

Thus DeMatteis transforms his experiences into "moments that remain true under any classification" (ibid., Ch. 1) through the medium of "true lies," or storytelling. If Brooklyn is actually "a little dark and grey and depressing," Santini muses, "why should I go back to that when it's so much more vibrant in my head?" (ibid., Ch. 4). This is more than selective memory. Santini argues the larger universe is reflected in our own "personal universes." If so, "the missing puzzle piece that holds the key to God's universe" has its parallel in the human mind. Storytelling brings that parallel to light (ibid.).

DeMatteis alluded to something like "true lies" early in his career. *Greenberg the Vampire* is the story of a reclusive horror writer muted by his vampirism. Forced to hide from the press and suffering from writer's block, Oscar Greenberg struggles to write his autobiography. Unfortunately, he cannot get over his ambivalence about the format. His attempts at fiction fare no better, suffering from what he feels is a lack of honesty. Greenberg's search for his voice comes to a head in the mythical Lilith, who sees his talent as a vehicle to seduce mankind. Greenberg believes he is susceptible to her charms because his previous work ultimately fell short of his ideals. Greenberg's subsequent commitment to "stop looking for nightmares and start looking for miracles" (DeMatteis, et al., 1986: 68) reflects the young DeMatteis' concerns with violence in mainstream comics and pop culture.

There is another parallel. In a literary manifesto that could just as easily be DeMatteis,' Greenberg explains why fantasy is so well equipped to express truth:

> The reason so many writers turn to fantasy is because life itself is so utterly fantastic, so bewilderingly surreal, that one of the few ways to fully do justice to it is to tell surreal *stories* filled with witches and wizards and monsters and Martians. So Baum creates an Oz, Bradbury creates a Mars — and by *distorting* reality, they're actually able to see it more clearly; certainly more so than those oh-so-serious novelists who think that what's in front of their faces is all there is to life.... And Brooklyn is Oz ... if only we would see it! [ibid.].

We can see the first hints of the idea behind *BD*'s Carl Vincent Santini here. If Brooklyn is Oz, fiction might be autobiography, too — and perhaps already was.

When *Greenberg* was published, DeMatteis was about midway through his fantasy maxi-series, *Moonshadow*. Like *BD*, *Moonshadow* is narrated by a man looking back at his formative years. This would seem to be where any surface comparisons end, but DeMatteis would later see the less fantastical *BD* as its flipside. "In an odd way," he says of *BD*, "it's the same story as the one I told in *Moonshadow*, only it's not presented as a fairy tale set in the far reaches of space" (DeMatteis, email communication). *BD* might be said to have brought DeMatteis' philosophy of autobiography full circle. If fiction can be autobiography, the reverse is true, too.

Greenberg, *Moonshadow*, and *BD* are all connected by this concern with autobiography, and the first two by a chronological overlap. This is not surprising since DeMatteis says the idea that became *BD* first formed when he was writing what he calls "the Brooklyn sections" of *Moonshadow*. Using his timeline, we can make a third connection. DeMatteis believes the writing of *Moonshadow* and *KLH* overlapped for a few months during the fall of 1986 (ibid.).

Greenberg, *Moonshadow*, and *KLH* arguably represent different faces of the religious/autobiographical experience that would manifest as *BD*. *Greenberg* is the search for a voice, *Moonshadow* a story, and *KLH* an author. Kraven's struggle over authorship is three-dimensional. He seeks to find the author of his family's humiliation (the Spider), confront the author (via the host Spider-Man), and by doing so take authorship of his own life *as* the Spider. Kraven notably uses the phrase "I am" at least thirty times throughout the course of the narrative. Yet he never does so after Spider-Man's resurrection, presumably because he believes he has exorcised his authorship concerns through a scapegoat ritual.

I believe Kraven's struggle for authorship leads him to a revelation at least partially consonant with DeMatteis/Santini's worldview. By this token, the relationship between DeMatteis and Santini is comparable to that of Kraven and the Spider. Kraven sees himself as an author, labeling others as "magnificent actors in a play of my creation" (DeMatteis, et al., 2006: 56). And like DeMatteis/Santini, Kraven frequently blurs the line where he ends and the Spider begins. He seeks to "shatter ... Kravenness — and let Spiderness in" (ibid., 39). This breakdown between author and text points to a Hindu concept called Maya. DeMatteis defines Maya as "the fact that this world's nothing but a dream, floating around in the divine unconscious ... an illusion: God's greatest trick" (DeMatteis, et al., 2003: n.p., Ch. 2). DeMatteis recently expanded that thought on his personal website:

The Hindus believe that all the gods are reflections of the One God that we all are. I see them as thought forms ... created as much by the soul of man as the whim of the Divine. But (and here's the paradox), I also see humankind as thought forms dreamed into being by the gods/God. In the end, it's all One Infinite Being and all of this separation is just a beautiful shadow play [DeMatteis, 2010: n.p.].

Viewing *KLH* through this lens of Mayan interconnectedness gives us a credible explanation for Kraven's psychic connection with Spider-Man and Vermin. Maya also gives us insight into the Spider's true nature. We can arguably see the Spider as just such a thought-form created by Kraven.

If Kraven's worldview is consonant with DeMatteis', one might ask, why do their insights lead down such different paths? I would argue Kraven's reaction is inverted. If DeMatteis sees Santini as a surrender to grace, Kraven perceives only "victims" and "victors" (DeMatteis, et al., 2006: 54, 73). Where DeMatteis understands Santini as the living embodiment of his inner reality, Kraven treats the Spider like an independent agent he must internalize.

Peter Parker gives us an intriguing middle ground between DeMatteis and Kraven's worldview. Where DeMatteis and Kraven seek, he reacts. Peter's "Spider" is the manifestation of his personal fears, but he does not come to see himself as author and/or text. Yet he does achieve enlightenment when he sheds the Spider and acknowledges his humanity. DeMatteis recognizes the human as the divine, Peter seeks to be a man, and Kraven tries to be the One God at the expense of humanity.

One key component of Santini's insight is his conviction that the universe isn't composed of "opposites fighting for ascendancy ... but equal elements in a continuum" (DeMatteis, et al., 2003: n.p., Ch. 2). Kraven grasps this Mayan unity at work in the universe, but sees it as a tool to exert his will over others. He uses this connection to call Spider-Man to his staged death and Vermin to his capture. Even when he reaches the point of enlightenment, Kraven cannot transcend his struggle with the Spider and the world around him.

This continuing struggle culminates in the manner of Kraven's death. Although Kraven claims to be at peace with his suicide, DeMatteis had this to say about the text:

> ... the one thing I feel strongly about is that Kraven's death *wasn't noble in the least*. I don't think it was even noble in his own mind. His last words were "They said my mother was insane." The unsaid part of that is "And I am, as well." Then he pulls the trigger. I think the deepest part of Kraven knows that he's gone completely off the rails. That suicide is both a mad and cowardly act. But some other part of him is desperately trying to cling to the illusion of nobility [Email interview].

Kraven's "triumph" is really his failure to cope with his father's humiliation; his suicide, to come to terms with his mother's insanity. Kraven fails because he trades his true lie — and ultimately his life — for an empty one.

Works Cited

DeMatteis, J.M. *Email interview*. Oct. 8, 2009-May 5 2010.
_____. (2010). "A Halloween Scare." J.M. DeMatteis' Creation Point. Available online: http://www.jmdematteis.com/2010/10/halloween-scare.html#comments. Accessed 5/ 31/11.
_____. (2009). "Top to Bottom." J.M. DeMatteis' Creation Point. Available online: http://www.jmdematteis.com/2009/12/top-to-bottom.html. Accessed 5/31/11.
_____, Glenn Barr, Bob Lappan, et al., *Brooklyn Dreams*. New York: DC 2003.
_____, Jon J. Muth, Kent Williams, et al., *The Compleat Moonshadow*. New York: DC 1988.
_____, Mark Badger, Joe Rosen, et al., *Greenberg the Vampire*. New York: Marvel 1986.
_____, Mike Zeck, Bob McLeod, et al., *Kraven's Last Hunt*. New York: Marvel 2006.

The Hermeneutics of Spider-Man: What Is Peter Parker Doing in Elizabethan England?

Christina C. Angel

Hermes, in Greek Mythology, is the messenger of the gods. On his winged feet, his purpose was to deliver the word of the gods to human beings, to demystify and translate the incomprehensible for mere mortals. As the patron of travelers — and, thus, boundaries — Hermes is associated both with poets and thieves alike, and is often depicted as a trickster, particularly because his business has to do with making the abstract literal (which leaves rather a lot of space for mischief). It is from his name we get the term *hermeneutics*, which is about "'interpretation' or even 'translation,' and especially the interpretation of sacred texts" and represents "the most fundamental ways in which we perceive the world, think, and understand" (Jasper, 2004). Furthermore, such a definition is itself tricky as it relates to the comprehension of a text, because texts are themselves unstable, always changing in meaning, just as we are always changing what we bring to a text every time we read it. And let us not forget the very issue of defining *text* to begin with; for now, let us assume that what I mean by *text* is words, images, and concepts that can be *read* to some degree or another.

What interests me in the scope of hermeneutical inquiry here is the way in which a literary character can be read in various backdrops, seen through a host of lenses, or even be entirely rewritten and still maintain the essence, or core, of the original character. For example, Jon C. Stott, in his 2007 article "Will the Real Dragon Please Stand Up?," discusses literary convention and the concept of what a dragon is and/or represents. He states: "No one has ever seen a dragon; yet everyone has a general idea of what dragons look like and what they do. Dragons do exist, but only in one place: in stories" (803). Furthermore, in an experiment with my adult students in a Children's Literature course, I have often asked them to describe the general appearance and demeanor of a dragon. They can all answer readily and come up with the same basic set of criteria: dragons are scaly, reptilian, and winged; they have nasty tempers, jealously guarded hoards of treasure, and are able to breathe fire. When I ask them "how do you know these things?" they are immediately silent. What we know about dragons is, in fact, what we have heard in stories *about* them; what is curious is that we all know about them *regardless* of the kinds of stories we like or have heard. Thus it stands that dragons come to us via hermeneutics — we have translated and informed what a dragon is by our repeated, collective experience with the text of "dragon." True, the 21st century has done its best to debunk the traditional dragon by way of parody and satire (think Disney's 2009 *How to Train Your Dragon*), but such things have done little to alter the general perception of what a dragon is and how it might behave. What proves interesting about such a phenomenon is not what happens in the text itself when characters (or concepts, in the case of the dragon) get reformulated; it is that all efforts to re-envision a popular figure seem to have little overall bearing on the popular perception of that character.

Given these immediate definitions and examples, I hope to make what might seem a huge leap, and use them to explore a particular text of one of Marvel Comics' most enduringly popular characters: Peter Parker/Spider-Man. He is at once Peter Parker, the shy, studious boy who has no luck with girls, and Spider-Man, the enigmatic masked hero who swings from one building to the next on a perpetual quest to rescue the city from the latest villain. Even when placed into a new landscape, the lore of Spidey transcends the backdrop; he can appear nearly anywhere, have an evil twin, become a zombie, or serve Queen Elizabeth, and still remain exactly who he is (yet oddly, like the dragon, he is a fictional construct). O'Rourke and Rodrigues (2007) call this Spider-Man's "mediated myth," and it is, but it is also something else. The primary example I hope to explore is Neil Gaiman's *Marvel 1602*, in which Spider-Man does not even make an appearance — only Peter Parker (Parquagh) does, yet Spider-Man is still clearly present in ways which will be discussed anon. In this vein, the question posed in the title is not entirely about what Peter Parker is doing in Renaissance England; it includes a necessary query about what the rest of the Marvel superheroes are doing there as well. For our purposes, however, we will examine the question via hermeneutic inquiry of the character Peter Parquagh, and the rest will follow.

Marvel 1602 represents the intersection of what comic books can accomplish in the world of story. The brief series — only eight parts written by Neil Gaiman, though there were later sequels by others — at once tackles not only a powerfully intense historical moment known by early modern scholars as "The Wonderful Year," but also manages to address Elizabethan/Jacobean politics and religion using quintessentially American and famous Marvel comic characters from the 20th century. Thus the book stands not only as a critically-acclaimed comic series, but as a crossroads of interpretive values, not the least of which is how these two disparate chronotopes (Renaissance England and 20th century America) can be in dialogue with one another in meaningful ways. "The Wonderful Year" is technically 1603 and an ironic title, as there was nothing at all wonderful about it in the modern sense of the word; it was in fact full of "wonders," but the events of said year were not considered positive. The so-called Wonderful Year references a pamphlet written by the playwright Thomas Dekker, in which he chronicles the public reaction to the death of Elizabeth I (which was dramatic and mourned at great lengths) and the unpopular ascension of James I. During that year[1] London saw not only the death of her mostly-loved, long-sitting Queen and the death of a long-held royal house (the Tudors), but one of the worst bouts of plague in recent memory. Because Elizabeth had no heir, a great deal of anxiety surrounded her impending death, and when the fictional Elizabeth asks on the opening page of Part One of *1602*, "Is the *world* truly *ending*?" she echoes the fears of the people living in England during that year, and also sets a general tone for the book. There were widespread fears of the end of the world, but these were not uncommon during resurgences of the Plague, which, as its name suggests, implies judgment from an angry God. Therefore, Elizabethan England provides a compelling backdrop against which to portray chronologically displaced superheroes, particularly when comic book heroes have arrived 400 years too soon.

One of the stated reasons for Gaiman's writing the book, as noted by Peter Sanderson in the introduction to the collected *1602*, is that "people think of the super hero as a creation of the 20th century, but it is really a modern guise for character archetypes that have endured throughout the history of literature.... Gaiman shows us what remains the same about each character in such different circumstances." This proves plausible, as we see Marvel characters operating in the space of Renaissance England: Nick Fury appears as Sir Nicholas, servant to the Queen, Dr. Strange is her adviser, and many others from X-Men to Fantastic Four, make appearances and are easily identified by their particular powers (explained in the text by the Renaissance phobic term of "witchbreed"). But something is clearly absent from this narrative: one of the most popular and famous Marvel figures, Spider-Man. In the Marvel Universe, Spider-Man dominates, and one must wonder why he does not figure into a story that appears to be reasonably inclusive of the major Marvel icons. Present, however, is Peter Parker (Parquagh) and the choice of his remaining fully human throughout the series has its own interpretive implications. Why leave one of the most widely recognizable heroes out of this comic? The obvious answer is that Gaiman made a conscious choice to leave Spider-Man out, perhaps for fear of overshadowing others, or perhaps for reasons upon which we cannot begin to speculate. But whatever the reason, it is clear that Parquagh is Parker, assistant to Sir Nicholas, who is perpetually depicted as fascinated with spiders and is often the butt of in-jokes directed at his inability to be Spider-Man at this particular moment. The first time we meet Peter in the comic is in Part One, when he encounters "A *spider*, sir. And such an *interesting* beast it is." Peter is dismayed when the spider is thoughtlessly smashed on the table before him, and at a later point in the story, he is saved a Black Widow bite. At various other moments, he is seen staring at a spider web, dreaming of swinging through trees whilst in the Tower of London in Part Seven, and being mocked at not being able to "climb a wall."

Something is at work here, however, beyond Gaiman merely being playful with Parquagh. The presence of Peter alone (*sans* Spider-Man) represents something that is *about* to happen. The audience knows that Peter *will be* bitten eventually and will in fact become Spider-Man, even if it doesn't necessarily happen in the story being read, and this is what makes the jokes and the almost-bites work. Symbolically speaking, this fact works to represent the tension and anxiety of the events of the story as it unfolds. Because *1602* opens with fears of the world ending, some kind of "weapon" on its way from Jerusalem (a clear reference to the Yeats poem "The Second Coming"), the machinations of the Inquisition, and the too-soon arrival of superheroes, Peter's lack of transformation makes perfect sense. Everything about his remaining Peter is a metaphor of that which has yet to manifest; after all, Spider-Man, unlike the other comic characters present here, is innately *scientific*, more than mutants/witchbreed are. Parquagh's character in *1602* is also of a different ilk: he is obedient but questioning, and his sense of moral quandary at not being able to kill Nick Fury at the end of the series echoes the famous moral problem in Spider-Man lore about great power and great responsibility. The fact that this incident with Fury happens in the "New World" is indicative of a different kind of meaning associated with Peter. One of the main fears of the English Renaissance is the notion of discovery and science, and this story takes place in a time *just before* a great deal of scientific discovery and the birth of the New World in a solid sense. The only English colony at play in *1602* (both the year and the book) is Roanoke, which history tells us was a disaster wrapped in mystery — most of the colonists died and it is suspected that any remaining members of that colony "went native" and were never heard from again. Thus, Gaiman's perpetual teasing of the audience with Peter's near misses at becoming Spider-Man speaks thematically to the thwarting of potential in the major movements of the plot. Yet there is a sense in these plot points, as represented most poignantly in Parquagh, that the prevention of something happening is only temporary: James I cannot get rid of witchbreed — he can only damage their ranks. The Inquisition cannot be successful for the same reason; the impending doom of the colony can only be at best postponed. In this vein, then, Peter not becoming Spider-Man is equally temporary, particularly since in the final frames of the series, a green-glowing spider in fact bites him. Just as we know he is about to *become*, so too are all of the other historical and literary concerns of the text.

What proves compelling, however, is that despite the obvious absence of Spider-Man throughout, he *is* present in the *Marvel 1602* series by way of Parquagh; the two cannot be ultimately separated from their collected mythologies. And here's where it gets interesting: there is a clear paradox at work in that Peter Parker is different from Spider-Man, but they are still one and the same. Parker alone represents angst, frustration, and unrealized potential, while Spider-Man activates the loss of that innocence and the gaining of superficial freedom (because that freedom to swing around the city unencumbered carries with it a crushing responsibility). Despite this clear difference, they still manage to operate as a single unit. I assert that Peter Parker/Spider-Man can in fact appear anywhere at any time (whether he is spinning webs or not) and we accept him as such. It matters not whether he is costumed, or not-yet-Spider-Man; his history and mythology precede him. Furthermore, as readers, we are not persuaded to change our interpretation of this complex character, regardless of his situation and story. Thus, if Peter Parker is in a story, so is Spider-Man, and vice versa. How can this be? The answer is not so simple as "they are the same person," either. It does, however, have everything to do with *hermeneutics*.

Before we make our way back to hermeneutics, however, it is necessary to examine the ways in which scholars have attempted to address these concerns of Spider-Man as concept. Much has been made about the links between superheroes and the Bible, or superheroes and the Christ figure, and this vein of discussion is useful to our purposes. Niall Richardson (2004), in the article "The Gospel According to *Spider-Man*," makes the central claim that "*Spider-Man* is a metaphor for Christian shame, shame for longings of the flesh and an attempt to transcribe this shame into more manageable guilt" (696). Richardson goes to great lengths to explain the connection between the story of Spider-Man and Christian ideas via shame and guilt, and ultimately surmises that "superhero narratives are often crude allegories of the Bible's stories" (695). This is perhaps correct, but such a statement does not go far enough to account for *why* this may be true, or how the interpretation of Spider-Man into film might play upon concepts reaching further afield than just the Bible. I assert that superhero narratives transcend "crude allegory" of Bible stories because the Bible and Christianity themselves transcend this measure. Superhero narratives mimic the Bible because the Bible itself mimics the stories of oral and written traditions emerging many centuries before its first composition.

It is fairly well assumed that many comic superheroes, particularly those of the Marvel Universe, have much in common with modern Christianity. Stan Lee himself notes this in the Foreword to *The Gospel According to Superheroes*: "I wasn't consciously trying to inject religious themes into my stories, but the chapters in this book will clearly demonstrate how religious and mythological themes are often dramatically intertwined in comic books" (xii). Furthermore, in the same book, editor B.J. Oropeza notes that "while the characters [in comic books] themselves might not always speak outwardly about religion and the Gospel, their storylines make implicit, and sometimes explicit, points about theology" (21). Again, the issue here is that such views, while they take into account the larger scope of a superhero's role in a society, continually leave it at the door of Christianity without looking beyond. The missed opportunity of such a narrow focus is that it leaves out the possibilities that hermeneutic inquiry might afford.

In a related vein, Kozlovic (2006) equally misses the point when he states that "Spider-

Man is an Everyman superhero not a cosmic superhero, and certainly no Christ-figure superstar like Superman" (35). Palumbo (1983), meanwhile, suggests that Spider-Man's creators "think of him as something of a Christ-symbol; but like other unlikely existential Christ-figures ... it is his social role of outcast and scapegoat ... that connects him with Christ" (74). I do not suggest that these types of discussions are meaningless, but I am curious about the continued comparisons of Spider-Man to Christ. For a hero to be Christ-like, there is a necessary component not just of persecution but also crucifixion and resurrection. So, is Spider-Man Christ-like? Actually, no. In many ways his character is self-sacrificing, like many heroes, but neither he nor Superman (mentioned above) fit the bill of crucifixion and resurrection. It is true that they have both "died" in various stories and have been "brought back to life" in others, but this is clearly not a direct analogue to Christ. The question then becomes what superheroes, and in this case Spider-Man *have to do with* Christ, which is a far more pressing question. Spider-Man is not so much Christ-like as he is *like* Christ (a fine but important distinction), from a hermeneutical perspective.

While this seems like a digression, hermeneutic inquiry is not only an apparatus for discussing Spider-Man as a concept, but the form itself is applicable from the standpoint of Renaissance discourse and certainly to the comic form, both of which are essential to *Marvel 1602*. As a practice, hermeneutics is about interpretation and translation, primarily with regard to the gospels of the Bible, and is first and foremost about questions rather than answers. It focuses on the idea that composers of sacred texts, in this case, the writers of the gospels, clearly had read other "gospels" and stories of Christ before they wrote their versions. That is, the writers who created the character Jesus Christ in the Bible did so based on other texts that may or may not still exist, and by the time the famous gospel writers (Matthew, Mark, Luke, and John) write about Jesus, they do so well after the fact of his life and based on their various interpretations of who he was. Furthermore, the writers of the gospels also wrote interpretable material based on varied perceived audiences. In using Jesus Christ in this example, we can say that *as a character* in a story, he is always an amalgamation, always a site of interpretability, and this is abundantly clear when one consults the contemporary bases of most major religions in the world. What proves fascinating about this interpretability is that beliefs about the role, existence, and divinity (or lack thereof) of Christ vary from group to group but remain absolutely solid within and among that group of believers, despite any evidence or textual support that may contradict those beliefs. In other words, once a person believes a certain doctrine about Christ, it is unlikely that such a belief can be altered, even when weighed against varying texts or scholarly interpretation and discovery. According to David Jasper (2004), such a phenomenon is the result of the dialectic of a hermeneutic circle; he states that "a certain belief dictates how we read the Bible, and reading the Bible in this way confirms that this belief is true or at least legitimate" (19). This type of circular reasoning is true not just of the Bible, but of any text we encounter, including comic books.

In light of the above discussion, the same might be said about how superheroes function in popular culture, and literature in particular, in ways similar to Christ. More specifically, the myth and popularity of Spider-Man as a concept can be explained in a quite similar fashion. Even though he is a creation of Stan Lee and Steve Ditko, Spider-Man has both transcended his original formation *and* maintained his original characteristics. While the previous statement is clearly contradictory, consider this: the Peter Parker/Spider-Man story has been told and retold in so many formats and places — comics, cartoons, films, and video games — and by so many different voices that one could argue that he has no stability of character whatsoever; yet any fan of Spider-Man, just like the students I asked about dragons, will be able to outline more or less the same set of defining characteristics. The hermeneutic circle concept comes into play here, and with direct regard to *Marvel 1602*. Spider-Man can be present in the story without being present because as readers, we find that which we already know about Peter Parker and assign him the role of Spider-Man, even if he has not yet been bitten by that spider. We *read into* the story what we already believe to be true about this character, which is why it often has little to no effect on public perception to remove him to a different century or setting.

Fictional characters — that is, those of the traditional short story, play, novel, or film — are, more often than not, creations of their authors. Particularly since the advent of "the author" and notions of copyright, a character is solely the intellectual property of its creator — an extension of that creator — a real person or at least personality that lives beyond the pages in which s/he is written. Robert Weiner similarly observes that "once a character is created, it sometimes becomes bigger through its dissemination in sequential art narratives, movies, novels, toys, and video games, and through its visibility in various places throughout popular culture" (457). In short, characters become "real" to writers and readers alike. Take Harry Potter for example (who is, incidentally, an *actual* Christ figure): JK Rowling created him, put him into stories, and gave him an entire existence and mythology that is largely unchallenged in terms of his stability as an established person (whether or not he is fictional is no longer important). But comic book characters, and particularly those of the mainstream superhero ilk, are entirely different in this regard. They are in fact "created" by an individual who thought them up and put them into stories, and maybe the creator even drew them and colored them too, but figures such as Spider-Man (or Batman, or Captain America, or Superman for that matter) live far beyond the scope of their origination. They are taken up by other artists, other writers, other forms of media, and transformed. It could be argued of course that Harry Potter is rewritten in fan fiction and so forth, but this is clearly not the same thing. One could not write Harry Potter into Elizabethan England without the certainty of an eight-figure lawsuit. Spider-Man translates into a host of potential textual interpretations, from his location in history, to the cultural milieu at the time of his variable reemergence, and thus he enters the mythic realm because he is two people at once, and because he is both the sum of all the stories told about him as well as something that transcends all of that. He remains an interpretable site of discourse, always ready to be written upon and created and recreated.

Notes

1. The year is chronologically questionable since the calendars of the time changed over to the next year in a different month than they do now, and sometimes Elizabeth's death is noted as 1602 and others, 1603.

Works Cited

Gaiman, Neil, Andy Kubert et al. *Marvel 1602*. New York: Marvel, 2003.
Jasper, David. *A Short Introduction to Hermeneutics*. London: Westminster John Knox Press, 2004.
Kozlovic, Anton Karl. "Spider-Man, Superman — What's the Difference?" *Kritikos: An International and Interdisciplinary Journal of Postmodern Cultural Sound, Text and Image*. Electronic resource. 3 (July 2006): 38 pp. Accessed 6/28/2011. http://intertheory.org/Spider-Man-superman.htm.
Lee, Stan. "Foreword." in B.J. Oropeza ed., *The Gospel According to Superheroes: Religion and Pop Culture*. NY: Peter Lang Pub., Inc., 2005.
Oropeza, B.J. "Introduction: Superhero Myth and the Restoration of Paradise." in B.J. Oropeza ed., *The Gospel According to Superheroes: Religion and Pop Culture*. NY: Peter Lang Pub., Inc., 2005. 1–24.
O'Rourke, Dan, and Pravin A. Rodrigues. "The 'Transcreation' of a Mediated Myth: Spider-Man in India." in Terrence Wandtke, ed., *The Amazing Transforming Superhero! Essay on the Revision of Characters in Comic Books, Film and Television*. Jefferson, NC: McFarland & Co., Inc., 2007. 112–28.

Palumbo, Donald. "The Marvel Comics Group's Spider-Man is an Existential Super-Hero: or 'Life Has no Meaning Without My Latest Marvels!'" *The Journal of Popular Culture.* 17:2 (Fall 1983): 67–82.

Richardson, Niall. "The Gospel According to *Spider-Man.*" *The Journal of Popular Culture.* 37:4 (2004): 694–703.

Stott, Jon C. "Will the Real Dragon Please Stand Up? Convention and Parody in Children's Stories." in J.D. Stahl, Tina L. Hanlon, and Elizabeth Lennox Keyser eds. *Crosscurrent of Children's Literature: An Anthology of Texts and* Criticism. NY: Oxford University Press, 2007: 800–805.

Weiner, Robert G. "Sequential Art and Reality: Yes, Virginia, There is a Spider-Man." *International Journal of Comic Art.* 11.1 (Spring 2009): 457–477.

Strategies of Narration in Jeph Loeb and Tim Sale's *Spider-Man: Blue*[1]

Derek Parker Royal

Historically, most Marvel comics have maintained a fairly consistent point-of-view, a heterodiegetic omniscient narrator whose focal perspective is unlimited, that is, not restricted by geographic or temporal space. Often this narrative voice is linked to the comic book title's editor (e.g., Stan Lee, Danny Fingeroth, or Ralph Macchio) who updates readers on contexts and events in past issues and does so through a familiar tone that assumes shared knowledge and interests. The only access we have to a character's interior is what this omniscient narrator chooses to reveal, and often these thoughts are nothing more than reflective commentary that illustrate the hero's actions. As a result, the superheroes in these traditional Marvel comics are presented in a more objective and detached manner, viewed as central figures performing within the larger "stage" of the paneled pages. This has been the case with most Spider-Man comics.

However, in Jeph Loeb and Tim Sale's *Spider-Man: Blue* (2003)[2], there is a significant shift in the narrative strategy, one that allows us a personal and more immediate association with the hero. Loeb and Sale's take on the webslinger is unique, not only because of the inclusion of Spider-Man in their "color" limited-series for Marvel—e.g., *Daredevil: Yellow* (2002), *Hulk: Grey* (2004), and *Captain America: White* (2008)—but because they allow us to see the hero from an interior perspective. The entire *Spider-Man: Blue* run, serialized between July 2002 and April 2003, is focalized through Peter Parker himself, and without any supplemental commentary provided by a heterodiegetic narrator. What is more, the narrative is epistolary in nature, presented as a "love letter" from Parker to a dead Gwen Stacy and dictated onto a tape recorder. In their comic, Loeb and Sale transform our understanding of Spider-Man through this more intimate narrative strategy, foregoing the kind of detached, god/editor-like perspective that was common in most Marvel comics. The team not only accomplishes this through dialogue, but through the visuals as well. The composition of the images within the panels—in essence, how we see things through Parker's perspective complement the interiority of Loeb and Sale's text. As a result, the creators of *Spider-Man: Blue* were able to effect an empathic and more personal narrative tone, presenting a more private storyworld than that found in any of the Spider-Man comics that came before, and doing so without compromising on the fast-paced adventure and heroism that have traditionally defined Spider-Man titles.

While significant in its own right, *Spider-Man: Blue* is not the writing team's only notable contribution to the superhero or fantastic genres. Indeed, Loeb and Sale have a rich tradition in taking well-established characters and teams and transforming them into something singular.

The two first worked together on a revival of Jack Kirby and Dave Wood's *Challengers of the Unknown*, an eight-issue mini-series that ran from March to October 1991 (and later collected in the trade paperback, *Challengers of the Unknown Must Die!* [2004]). They next worked on a string of critically acclaimed *Batman* titles, including the collections *Batman: Haunted Knight* (1996), *Batman: The Long Halloween* (1998), and *Batman: Dark Victory* (2001).[3] In addition to two other collaborations in the DC Universe—the Eisner Award-winning *Superman: A Man for All Seasons* (1999) and *Catwoman: When in Rome* (2005)[4]—Loeb and Sale produced a series of titles for Marvel. Although their first graphic novel for the publisher was *Wolverine/Gambit: Victims* (1996), they are perhaps best known at Marvel for their various "color" series: *Daredevil: Yellow*, *Spider-Man: Blue*, *Hulk: Grey*, and *Captain America: White*.[5] In the three completed graphic novels, Loeb and Sale differentiate their versions of the Marvel characters by privileging affection and interiority, presenting their stories through first-person narrators, each of whom is in conversation with another. Daredevil/Matt Murdock addresses his story to his and Foggy Nelson's former secretary, Karen Page, and Bruce Banner speaks directly to his friend and psychiatrist, Dr. Leonard Sampson. What distinguishes Spider-Man's narrative, and what makes it so significant for the present study, is the context of Peter Parker's addressee. The person with whom he appears to be speaking, Gwen Stacy, is dead. And given this fact, one cannot help but wonder if Parker himself is the subject of his own ruminations, holding a conversation with himself in ways that make *Spider-Man: Blue* one of Marvel's most intimate narratives to date.

What underscores this intimacy—not only for Peter Parker, but for readers as well—is the place and significance of Gwen Stacy in the Spider-Man's, and Marvel Comics,' world. She was Parker's first love, and, according to the *Marvel Universe Wiki*, after the death of Peter's Uncle Ben, "no death has weighed as heavily upon Spider-Man's shoulders as [Gwen's] passing." We can see this in the original death story and in the sheer number of comics in which Gwen, in some form or another, has appeared. Her death at the hands of the Green Goblin, and Spider-Man's part in and reaction to that event, occurred in *The Amazing Spider-Man*, issues #121 and #122 (June and July 1973).[6] Of particular significance are the details surrounding the very moment of Gwen's death, specifically the infamous "snap!" sound effect that accompanies Spider-Man's rescue attempts after she is thrown off of the George Washington Bridge (26/4). Many readers have interpreted that sound as Gwen's point of death, her neck breaking as a result of Spider-Man's webbing suddenly stopping her high-velocity fall. This raises the question, one that has haunted Peter Parker ever since: was Gwen dead before being thrown from the bridge, or did the hero's attempted rescue cause her demise? Regardless of the ambiguity surrounding this major comic-book event, and despite any ultimate resolution readers may find for themselves, the fact remains that Gwen's death remains a watershed in the Spider-Man series, an event that has reverberated throughout Spider-Man franchise.[7] The reality of her death has remained a catalyst in a variety of Spider-Man narratives, including the 1970s and 1990s Clone Sagas, the "Sins Past" and "Sins Remembered" story arcs, as well as taking center stage in the alternate universe *Ultimate Spider-Man* series.[8] Indeed, no better series of images captures the impact of (and near-obsession over) Gwen Stacy's death than does Peter's mirror hallucination scene in *The Amazing Spider-Man* #147 (Aug. 1975), part of the original Clone Saga storyline (14/1–3). In the top three panels of that page, Spider-Man looks into a mirror and sees running toward him an almost endless series of Gwen images, one following the other. (These panels are reminiscent of the famous scene in Orson Welles's *Citizen Kane*, when an aging Kane walks between two mirrors facing one another, projecting multiple images of himself that seem to recede into infinity.) Some have even maintained that the resonance of Gwen's death extends well beyond Marvel comics, that its brutality brings a close to the more "innocent" or idealistic Silver Age of comics and sets the stage for the more violent and ambiguous Bronze Age.[9] To argue that Gwen's passing is a linchpin in the Marvel Universe would be an egregious understatement.

Yet, the significance of Loeb and Sale's *Spider-Man: Blue* rests not so much on its subject matter — still another Spider-Man arc centered around the death of Gwen Stacy — as much as it does on the way that the story is told. Like the other "color" series Loeb and Sale wrote for Marvel, their representation of Peter Parker's personal world is made most effective in its manner of narration. This more subjective, first-person point-of-view is made evident through both word and image. What is more, it stands out from the more common modes of narration found in the vast majority of Marvel comics. Historically, Marvel's various titles, including those surrounding *Spider-Man*, have been narrated in a relatively straightforward and traditional manner. Overshadowing the action (both physical and speech-related) that makes up the core of the story is an extradiegetic heterodiegetic narrator, someone who is on a "higher" level of narration and completely outside of the events unfolding, and at the same time someone who never takes part in any of the action he narrates.[10] In other words, the storyteller of most Spider-Man comics is a (mostly) faceless, detached, third-person omniscient narrator, a god-like figure who sets up and contextualizes the various events as they unfold, panel to panel.

This kind of narrator functions in several ways. First, he introduces the particular story we are about to read and provides a context that assists in the exposition, such as that found in the opening panel of *The Amazing Spider-Man*, issue #7, where the webslinger encounters the Vulture for the second time and the narrator describes their history in issue #2 (2/1). This type of narration becomes a crucial element of serialized comics, where an awareness of the events in a previous issue is indispensable for our understanding of the comic we are currently reading. The narrator fills us in, or reminds us, of the actions from the previous month's issue(s) so that we can pick up where that issue — or where several previous issues — left off. Another function of the traditional Marvel narrator concerns levels of dramatic knowledge. In this instance, the extradiegetic heterodiegetic narrator reveals information that a character (Spider-Man himself or some other) does not have, thereby creating suspense. Such a strategy is used in *The Amazing Spider-Man*, issue #29, when the narrator fills us in on consequences of which Spider-Man is currently unaware: "Thus, though he doesn't suspect it at the time, Spidey's plan actually backfires against him..." (6/4). Goaded by questions such as "Who knows what?," "What doesn't a character know?," and "When will they find out?," the reader feels him- or herself propelled through the story through sheer anticipation and continues to turn the pages. A third purpose behind this kind of point-of-view is clarification through editorial aside. In these instances, a character's words inside a speech balloon will contain an asterisk, and accompanying that will be very brief mentioning of an event that occurred one or more issues back. Sometimes the reference will be to an action that took place in the same comic-book series, but just as many references will be to completely different Marvel titles that nonetheless elucidate the current storyline. Often these narrative asides are informal in tone, even humorous, and they are almost always signed by the Marvel title's editor (e.g., "*The Scarlet Spider was buried beneath fall rubble last issue, remember?— Eric [Fein]," "*See *Web of Spider-Man* #121— Danny [Fingeroth]," and "*Way back in the semi-classic issue #182 — Semi-classic Ralf [Macchio]."). In this way, these editorial contexts are less faceless and more chummy, creating a kind of "insider knowledge" and a sense of pop cultural exclusivity commonly found with fans of Marvel comics. This is similar to still another function of the Marvel omniscient narrator: to create a feeling of shared experience that will secure and sustain a reading audience. Such narrative posturing, often playfully exaggerated, was especially common to Marvel comics in the 1960s and 1970s (like that found in the concluding panel of *The Amazing Spider-Man*, issue #31, where the narrator implores the reader to pick up the next issue, and that "[b]ecause you're *our* kind of reader, we offer this admonishment — you must *not miss* it! *'Nuff said!*" [20/9]) and it was an appeal to the "true believers" that they were in on something special, which thereby made them special readers. Yet regardless of its function (exposition, level of knowledge, editorial aside, or shared community) this kind of extradiegetic heterodiegetic narrative voice is always detached and marked by zero focalization, that is, a non-locatable and indeterminate perceptual position. If there is any "personality" to the narration, its goal for immediacy is between the author/editor and reader, not between the character (i.e., Peter Parker) and the reader.

Yet, while more recent *Spider-Man* comics may not rely on the exact same kinds of narrative strategies commonly found in older pre-Modern Age titles, they nonetheless privilege a third-person omniscient narrator of some sort, usually marked by the absence of a direct voice, but whose presence is evident through a zero focalization when it comes to the narrative's presentation.[11] Such is not the case with *Spider-Man: Blue*. In this work, Loeb and Sale forego any external, non-engaged narration and place that task solely in the hands, or the voice, of the protagonist. What is more, the art complements Peter Parker's verbal directness to create a comic that is much more immediate and personal than almost anything found in the Spider-Man universe. Loeb and Sale are able to effect this kind of readerly engagement through at least five different aspects of their narrative strategy: Parker's role as the only narrating voice, the context of his narration, his function as the narrative's focalizer, the frequency of visual close-ups, and the angle and perspective of the comic panels.

Over the entire six-issue run, Peter Parker functions as the sole external, or extradiegetic, narrator. Outside of the voices that are heard within the narrative itself, the intradiegetic speech events that make up the story proper (i.e., the first narrative level), Parker's is the only perspective we have outside of the first-narrative actions, guiding us through the story. His is a retrospective voice, relating events that are years in the past (thus, a largely analeptic narrative) and visualized through the blue-tinted dialogue boxes that are present in the text. Indeed, the blue of the dialogue boxes not only corresponds to the color theme of the text, but, more significantly, it underscores the somber tone of the book and helps to enhance the closeness we as readers feel for Parker as narrator.[12] He is a homodiegetic narrator throughout, but only in the last three pages does Peter Parker relinquish his role as a narrator separated by temporal distance. There we see the present-day Parker who has been telling us his story of Gwen Stacy, and the mood of the narrative — the distance between events and the narrating of them — shifts from one of diegesis, or one of telling, to mimesis, that which is shown. Here we find a solitary Peter Parker, alone in his attic talking into a tape recorder to a former lover who is now dead. And although Mary Jane arrives on the scene to lend support to her somber husband, the panel framing on these last pages denies Peter any intimacy. Outside of a close-up of his and Mary Jane's fingers touching on the penultimate page of the story, Peter is never presented in frame with the person to whom he is now the closest. He is always presented as an isolated figure, sharing panel space with no one. If, before this elucidating moment, we had not fully realized the melancholy and highly personal tone produced by the comic's narrating presence, in the last three pages of *Spider-Man: Blue* Loeb and Sale drive that point home. Parker's role as the book's first-person narrator, and only narrator, is highlighted by the overriding solitariness of his situation. And it is this sense of aloneness that helps produce the intimacy generated by the text.

Another way in which Loeb and Sale engender reader empathy is through the context of Parker's narration. It is Valentine's Day, and he is speaking to Gwen Stacy, a figure that he refers to in the past tense. And we learn relatively early on that he is talking into a tape recorder. Not only are there sound effect clues that suggest as much — the "whrrr" and "klik" that appear at the beginning and end of almost all six chapters[13] — but he states directly at the very beginning of the second chapter, "So here I am with this tape recorder." The sadness of this situation, a lone figure speaking into a tape recorder to a person who is now dead, is enough to bind readers to the protagonist through sympathy and sentimentality. This emotional pull is further enhanced by the ramifications of Parker's narrating speech act. Since Gwen is now dead and can no longer receive or respond to his words, the only logical audience for Peter's recorded musings is Peter himself. In other words, the narrating frame of *Spider-Man: Blue* is a man talking with himself, using the story of Gwen Stacy — or, as Parker states it in the opening pages of the book, "the story of how we fell in love. Or more appropriately, how we almost didn't fall in love" — as a form of therapy to better understand his own psyche. This is the kind of reader-protagonist closeness that could not easily be generated through the kind of omniscient narrative practices found in the vast majority of Marvel comics.

Focalization is a third way in which Loeb and Sale particularize their narrative. Given the fact that Peter Parker is the book's homodiegetic intradiegetic narrator, it only makes sense that he is the primary focalizer. Indeed almost every bit of information that we receive in the book is filtered through Peter's consciousness, and every image framed within the panels is something that he would have seen. The apparent exceptions to this (e.g., Mary Jane talking with Aunt May at the end of Chapter 1, the Rhino breaking out of his enclosure in Chapter 2, Blackie's fight with the Vulture in Chapter 4, and Kraven's stalking in Chapters 5 and 6) occur outside of Parker's awareness. However, if Parker's retrospective narration functions on an extra-diegetic level — that is, outside of the first narrative level, which is the story of his relationship with Gwen — then he would certainly have been able go back and fill in the gaps of his past knowledge and in his present narration, the story he is currently telling, provide the information as if he had experienced it at the time of its occurrence. In other words, Peter as reflective narrator has the luxury of going back, before the current telling, to find the various pieces of his story and put them together in a coherent and presentable whole. So even the events that are seemingly outside of his awareness become plausible representations of his skills both as a crime fighter (finding the clues and missing pieces) and as a narrator (pulling together all of his information, regardless of first-hand experience, into a series of interlinked sequential events).

Yet, Peter's verbal reconstruction is not the only component of the book's unique approach to narration. The art of *Spider-Man: Blue* also suggests a first-person point-of-view and as such, contributes to its rather familiar tone. One way that Sale accomplishes this is through an abundance of close-ups. Much more so than in other Spider-Man comics, the frequency of tight shots (that is, images that frame individuals from a short distance at least from the chest up), as well as objects that are shown consuming the entire panel. Almost every page in the comic contains at least one close-up or an extreme close-up of a head, a facial feature, a hand or fist, a visual glance, or an item that is the subject of that glance. By populating his pages with such paneling, Sale emphasizes the closeness of the text, a strategy that works hand-in-hand with the story's intimate first-person narration.

The artwork's visual line and angle of presentation function similarly. Throughout the text, the composition and perspective within the panels — the placement of the comic's "camera eye" in relation to its subjects and the angle at which it is positioned — complements the empathy generated by Peter's words and the closeness we as readers feel to the narrator. There are many panels where characters are looking directly out at the reader, as if the reader were a stand-in for Peter Parker as he experiences the events. These can be seen, for example, during the first appearance of the Green Goblin in Chapter 1, Gwen Stacy's coy glance at Peter toward the end of that same chapter, the Lizard crawling toward Spider-Man in Chapter 3, Harry Osborne answering the door at the beginning of Chapter 5, and Kraven crashing through the apartment window in the final chapter of the book. This kind of visual presentation prompts identification with the narrator, allowing us to more easily slip into his skin, so to speak, thereby underscoring Loeb and Sale's first-person approach. Nowhere does this visual narrative strategy become more evident than on the last page of Chapter 2, where Peter meets Mary Jane for the first time. This image is presented as a full-page panel, with Mary Jane voluptuously consuming the entire spread, looking directly into the reader's (and thus, Peter's) eyes and uttering her now-famous line, "Face it, Tiger, you just hit the jackpot!" It is as if she says this directly to the readers, suggesting for us some kind of identification or rapport with Peter Parker. The full effect of this visual, and the significance of Loeb and Sale's approach to narration, becomes even more evident when compared to the original scene to which they are alluding. The very first meeting of Peter and Mary Jane took place in *The Amazing Spider-Man* #42 (20/6), and the way that John Romita drew that encounter is strikingly different from that found in *Spider-Man: Blue*. In contrast to Sale's head-on and direct staging of Mary Jane, Romita has the character looking off to the side, addressing a Peter whose face we actually see on the left edge of the panel. Whereas the earlier visualization of this first-time encounter is highly effective in its own way — we get the speechlessness of Peter in the presence of the red-haired beauty — its composition is of a kind with the Marvel narrative style of old: a more omniscient and detached presentation. (What is more, by including Parker in the frame, Romita's art works against any direct identification with the protagonist since we see him as part of the paneled landscape.) Sale's revisualization of this scene, on the other hand, ensures more of an affinity with Peter Parker, thereby supplementing the direct homodiegetic presentation of the narrative, which in this case includes both Peter's words and the tape recorder sound effects.

In all, Loeb and Sale's various narrative strategies provide a Spider-Man story that is significantly different from the many comics that had come before, and that have appeared since. Their choice to present *Spider-Man: Blue* from Peter Parker's perspective, a homodiegetic intradiegetic narrator, creates a sense of empathy that is not as evident in the more traditional Marvel comics. Instead of relying on a detached, god-like narrator who hovers over all of the events, Loeb and Sale opt for a more engaged viewpoint that places the reader at the center of the action. They accomplish this not only through the actual story that Parker tells, and the manner and context in which he tells it, but through the visuals that he would have been encountered as he had lived the experiences. The reader sees many things that Spider-Man/Parker would have, thereby accentuating the direct and participatory effect of the diegesis. In presenting their narrative in this way, Jeph Loeb and Tim Sale have created a Spider-Man story that, while focusing on a series of events that had been told several times before, comes across as fresh and unique, introducing us to a storyworld that we many not really have known before.

Notes

1. The citation style in this essay is based on the website, "Comic Art in Scholarly Writing: A Citation Guide," produced by the Popular Culture Association's Comic Art and Comics Area (http://www.comicsresearch.org/CAC/cite.html). As such, writers (w) are distinguished from artists (a) in the Works Cited, and

references to specific comic book passages are made parenthetically within the text, citing both the page number and the panel number, separated by a slash.

2. Unless otherwise noted, all references to *Spider-Man: Blue will* be to the collected edition, not the six individual comic books that originally composed the mini-series.

3. *Batman: Haunted Knight* was originally published in separate issues of *Batman: Legends of the Dark Knight Halloween Special* (1993), *Batman: Madness: Legends of the Dark Knight Special* (1994), and *Batman: Ghosts: Legends of the Dark Knight Special* (1995). *Batman: The Long Halloween* was first published as a thirteen-issue limited series that ran from January 1997 to January 1998, and *Batman: Dark Victory* also originated as a limited series, thirteen issues published between December 1999 and December 2000 (with a issue #0 prequel published in September 1999). *The Long Halloween* won Eisner Awards for the Best Limited Series in 1998 and the Best Reprint Graphic Album in 1999. *Dark Victory* won the award in 2002 for Best Reprint Graphic Album.

4. *Superman: A Man for All Seasons* was originally a four-issue series published between July and October 1998. *Catwoman: When in Rome* first ran as a six-issue series, published between November 2004 and August 2005.

5. *Daredevil: Yellow*, *Spider-Man: Blue*, and *Hulk: Gray* were all originally six-issue mini-series published, respectively, between August 2001 and January 2002, July 2002 and April 2003, and December 2003 and April 2004. Although Marvel released *Captain America: White* issue #0 in September 2005, the series ceased publication after that and remains incomplete to this day.

6. These two issues were later collected in a larger volume, *Spider-Man Death of the Stacys* (2007), where Gwen's death is placed alongside that of her father, Captain George Stacy, at the hands of Doctor Octopus (*The Amazing Spider-Man*, issues #88–92, Sept. 1970-Jan. 1971), making for a broader context that establishes greater tensions between Gwen and the webslinger.

7. Gwen's death remains an open question, and the evidence for and against Parker's culpability is conflicting. For example, in Kurt Busiek and Alex Ross's *Marvels* (1994, originally serialized January-August 1994), news photographer Phil Sheldon says after witnessing the death of Gwen Stacy, "I read later that it was the shock of the fall that killed her." On the other hand, in one of the *Civil War* event titles, *Iron Man, Captain America: Casualties of War* (2007), Iron Man urges for the necessity of superhero registration, and cites as an example Gwen's death: "If [Spider-Man] had been properly trained, maybe he could have broken her fall without breaking her neck." However, the same year as Iron Man's speculations, the author of the Gwen Stacy death story, Gerry Conway, stated the uncertainty of his original intentions: "Did I add the 'snap' sound effect at the last minute, or did I always plan to raise questions about our hero's contribution to his loved one's final fate? [That is a question] that can't really be answered(because [it depends] on some very human memories of events long past, and memory, as any psychologist will tell you, is self-deceiving. Truth is ambiguous" (5). And in his book, *The Physics of Superheroes*, James Kakalios argues that the physics surrounding the incident suggest that her neck was indeed broken when Spider-Man suddenly stopped her fall. Still, no one has adequately answered the question of whether or not Gwen was dead before the fall and if her broken neck occurred post-mortem. Regardless, since that moment on the bridge, Peter blames himself for Gwen's demise, and his obsession over this fact has been a component of innumerable *Spider-Man* comics.

8. The 1970s clone storyline has been collected in *The Amazing Spider-Man: The Original Clone Saga* (2011), the later (and much longer) clone saga issues of the 1990s make up the five-volume *Spider-Man: The Clone Saga Epic* (2010–2011), "Sins Past" was collected in *The Amazing Spider-Man, Vol. 8: Sins Past* (2005), and "Sins Remembered" was published as a volume in *The Spectacular Spider-Man, Vol. 5: Sins Remembered* (2005). Gwen's death becomes another major event in *Ultimate Spider-Man* #62 (Sept. 2004), this time at the hands of Carnage, and, similar to the regular *Spider-Man* event, she also plays a major role in the title's subsequent clone saga (issues #97–105, Sept. 2006-April 2007).

9. See, for example, Arnold T. Blumberg's reading of Gwen's death as a transitional event between the optimism found in 1960s comics and the more gritty, world-conscious characters and stories beginning in the early 1970s.

10. For fuller descriptions of these and other narratological terms used in this essay, see Gérard Genette's *Narrative Discourse: An Essay in Method* (1980) and *Narrative Discourse Revisited* (1988).

11. There are exceptions to this, of course, such as *The Spectacular Spider-Man* #8 and *The Web of Spider-Man* #122, where the protagonist is the book's narrator. However, these deviations from the standard Marvel omniscience are a rarity.

12. None of Loeb and Sale's other "color" books for Marvel bears the same characteristic. The colors of the first-person dialogue boxes in *Daredevil: Yellow*, *Hulk: Gray*, and *Captain America: White* have no overt connection to the theme of their respective texts.

13. There are no sound effects at the end of Chapter 1. Other than that, these sounds open and close each installment.

Works Cited

Blumberg, Arnold T. "'The Night Gwen Stacy Died': The End of Innocence and the Birth of the Bronze Age." *Reconstruction* 3:4 (2003). Accessed 8/28/2011 http://reconstruction.eserver.org.
Brevoort, Tom, et al., *Spider-Man: Funeral for an Octopus 3*. New York: Marvel Comics (May 1995).
Busiek, Kurt and Alex Ross. *Marvels*. New York: Marvel Comics, 2004.
Conway, Gerry. "Introduction." *Spider-Man: Death of the Stacys*. New York: Marvel Comics, 2007: 4–5.
_____, Ross Andru et al. *The Amazing Spider-Man 147* New York: Marvel Comics (August 1975).
_____, Sal Buscema et al. *The Spectacular Spider-Man Annual 8*. New York: Marvel Comics (1988).
DeMatteis, J. M., Steven Butler et al. *The Web of Spider-Man 122*. New York: Marvel Comics (March 1995).
Gage, Christos N. et al. *Iron Man, Captain America: Casualties of War 1*. New York: Marvel Comics (Feb 2007).
Genette Gérard. *Narrative Discourse: An Essay in Method*. Trans. Jane E. Lewin. Ithaca: Cornell University Press, 1980.
_____, *Narrative Discourse Revisited*. Trans. Jane E. Lewin. Ithaca: Cornell University Press, 1988.
Kakalios, James. *The Physics of Superheroes*. New York: Gotham Books, 2005.
Lee, Stan, Steve Ditko et al. *The Amazing Spider-Man 7*. New York: Marvel Comics (Dec 1963).
_____, Steve Ditko et al. *The Amazing Spider-Man 29*. New York: Marvel Comics (Oct 1965).
_____, Steve Ditko et al. *The Amazing Spider-Man 31*. New York: Marvel Comics (Dec 1965).
_____, John Romita et al. *The Amazing Spider-Man 42*. New York: Marvel Comics (Nov 1966).
Lee, Stan (w), et al. *Spider-Man: Death of the Stacys*. New York: Marvel Comics, 2007.
Loeb, Jeph, and Tim Sale et al. *Spider-Man: Blue*. New York: Marvel Comics, 2008.
"Stacy, Gwen." *Marvel Universe Wiki*. Marvel Comics, n. d. Accessed 9/1/2011. http://marvel.com/universe.

III. The J. Jonah Jameson Problem

Spider-Man: MENACE!!! Stan Lee, Censorship and the 100-Issue Revolution

Aaron Drucker

> "'I knew how to keep it simple,' said Stan Lee, who revived Marvel Comics in the sixties by developing a new batch of hypertrophied costumed heroes. 'We wanted to give kids a good time and give them something positive to enjoy. We didn't want to change the world'"
>
> —*Hajdu, 2008: 330*

Thus marks the end of David Hajdu's case against the Comics Magazine Association of America and its Comics Code in *The Ten-Cent Plague: The Great Comic-Book Scare and How It Changed America*. True comics of the "Golden Age" died and gave way to the final triumph of the super-hero in the transition to the (somehow) less authentic and far more commercial "Silver Age." Subversion shifted to the youth sub-culture of the 1960s and that was that. Comic books "became specialty items for adolescent boys and collectors" (330). One of the few survivors of the comic book industry collapse after 1955, Stan Lee went on writing in the vein of "hypertrophied costumed heroes," creating the Hulk, the Fantastic Four, the Silver Surfer, and a score of other iconic heroes. Resurrecting Marvel Comics, he brought back the Human Torch and Namor and Captain America. He also created Spider-Man, bringing him to life with his partner, illustrator Steve Ditko. Super hero comics are still dismissed by many "hard core" comic enthusiasts as boring or predictable. Nothing changes; nothing challenges; nothing surprises. These do-gooders go through their "freak of the week" adventures seeking to entertain children or the small-minded. Echoes of the great pre-Code days whisper rhapsodically in the hallowed halls of comic shops as DC challenges conceptions with their Vertigo line, or some new, nominally interesting, and invariably short-lived independent book. Spider-Man, a character openly crafted to appeal to the audience of teenagers and misfit young adults who avidly read anything in primary colors, is easy to dismiss. But Stan Lee's *The Amazing Spider-Man* is "just a bit ... different!" (*Amazing Spider-Man 1*, 1964: 1).

Introduced in the final issue of *Amazing Fantasy*, Spider-Man is a "science nerd" who gets bitten by a radioactive spider, and gaining the proportionate strength and speed, becomes a superhero. The origin story is familiar thanks to the many representations of the character, but often overlooked during Peter Parker's tragic transformation into hero is his initial success at self-promotion. "In the days that follow [Spider-Man's first public appearance], the Spider-Man becomes the sensation of the nation" (*AF 15*, 1962: 9). Ditko frames Stan Lee's caption with a sheaf of newspapers sporting triumphant headlines: "Spider-Man Slated for New TV Series!; Spider-Man Wins Showbiz Award!; Spider-Man Plays to Packed House!; Who Is

Spider-Man?" The world wants to know more about this new sensation. But Spider-Man's publicity blitz is short-lived, as (out of frame) Uncle Ben is killed in a botched home invasion and Spider-Man learns first hand, "With great power there must also come — great responsibility!" (11). Between the frames, a story takes shape. A new super-powered character appears on the scene. He realizes that such powers can generate a great deal of wealth and personal gain, so he utilizes them to showboat. The media are immediately taken with the brash showman. The costume is great. His powers are spectacular. He plays to the camera. The popular culture is thrilled to have a new sensation. Everyone loves him, except J. Jonah Jameson, who stews in his boiling outrage at this mysterious usurper. *Amazing Spider-Man* #1 (1964) opens with a splash page: "FREAK! PUBLIC MENACE!" It announces this with pointed fingers and a violently shouting Jameson thrusting towards an awkwardly stunned Spider-Man (1). A brief summary of the origin follows and ends with the title of Jameson's first editorial in 48-point type across the front page of the *Daily Bugle*: "SPIDER-MAN / MENACE" (5).

In the video interview with Kevin Smith, *Stan Lee's Mutants, Monsters & Marvels,* Lee claims that Jameson is "the version that so many people had of me": irritable, demanding, irascible, but genuine in his conviction and not really a bad man or a villain. The character's prejudices and predilections coalesced nicely to create the dramatic tension for Parker (the *Daily Bugle*'s freelance photographer) and Spider-Man (the target of the *Bugle*'s incessant accusations). Lee wrote knowingly about the "bigot" that "everybody knows," who "hates Spider-Man ... but he always wants pictures of Spider-Man because it sells papers" and he "hates teenagers because to Jameson, every teenager was a long-haired, Commie, pervert, hippie!" (Zakarin, 2002). As a plot device, Jameson is a central foil for the struggling Peter Parker: a real-life nemesis with whom the protagonist must negotiate rather than defeat. In developing the internal narrative, Jameson and the *Bugle* are inspired devices. Throughout the history and continuity of Spider-Man, they faithfully serve their narrative function. For decades, the motivation of Lee's characterization of Jameson has perplexed critics and fellow artists alike. Roy Thomas, Lee's successor in writing *Amazing Spider-Man,* interviewed him in 1998. Thomas asks: "You started right off joking about super-heroes being 'long underwear characters,' so it [*Amazing Spider-*Man] had a different tone at the very beginning. It was obvious that there was lot of thought going into it" (*SMRB*, 1998). Yet even to his close associates, Lee remains coy about his motivations: "I don't know if there was that much thought, or if I was just uninhibited when I wrote it" (*SMRB*, 1998). When asked if he ever wanted to challenge the Comics Code Authority directly, he evades the question: "I never thought about the Code when I was writing a story, because basically I never wanted to do anything that was to my mind too violent or too sexy. I was aware that young people were reading these books, and had there not been a Code, I don't think that I would have done the stories any differently" (*SMRB*, 1998). Critically, however, the opposition between Jameson and Spider-Man operates within three parallel frameworks of interpretation. The first is simple narrative, the useful antagonist to the intrepid but troubled hero. The second offers a subtle but persistent antagonism within the industry itself. Finally, as new creative teams pick up the threads Lee leaves for them, he offers a template to critique the power and the flaws of media.

Page 5 of *Amazing Spider-Man* #1 is framed, top left and bottom right, with the *Bugle* headline, but it reads as a prop and is easy to push into the background. Jameson's monologue dominates the page as he rants about the dangers Spider-Man poses. But "menace" reverberates with allusion. In the mid-1950s, comic books proliferated with stories that ranged from the innocuous to the mostly innocuous. But as with "rock-n'-roll," the devil was thought to be in those pages, giving idle hands less than idle thoughts. "As our work went on [researching the effects of comic books on young children]," Dr. Fredric Wertham notes in *Seduction of the Innocent*, "we established the basic ingredients of the most numerous and widely read comic books: violence; sadism and cruelty; the superman philosophy" (15). While Dr. Wertham's famous treatise offered no formal evidence of a viable trend, the uproar it stirred lead to the establishment of a Congressional commission on comics in 1954 that was followed up by the formation of the Comics Magazine Association of America, which created and enforced the Comics Code Authority. Stan Lee was an editor at Atlas Comics at the time, and among his many responsibilities, he was the writer and publisher of a title called: *Menace*. Depicting tales of horror and dark science fiction, often with a "twist" ending, Lee wrote to the delight of teens and young children throughout the country. With a circulation in the hundreds-of-thousands, Lee's popular book was one of five cut from the Atlas line when the CCA purge began in 1955 (comics.org). The stories remind the reader of riffs on noir or Universal horror themes: familiar and undistinguished fare of the kind young readers thoroughly enjoy and still might find surprising despite their formulaic nature. But such "horror" comics were purged from the industry. The crusade to purify the medium — embodied in lectures such as Dr. Wertham's traveling series "Comic books, the menace to American childhood" (Wertham, 1954: 15–16) — would attempt to thoroughly cleanse the evils of "illiteracy ... cruelty and deceit ... temptation ... unwholesome fantasies ... criminal or sexually abnormal ideas ... rationalizations [for the above] ... forms of a delinquent impulse [that supplies] details of techniques ... [and] maladjustment or delinquency" (Wertham, 1954: 118). EC, publisher of the most famous of the horror and crime comics, restructured to produce only *MAD Magazine*, Atlas folded into Marvel Comics, and many other comic publishers either collapsed, went bankrupt, or submitted to censorship. Stan Lee brought Timely, Marvel, Atlas, and a handful of other ailing publishers together under the umbrella of the re-launched Marvel Comics in 1960, establishing a new "safe" environment for that stable of creators and properties. Following the censorship of the CCA, comics were forced into the pose of innocent, even sycophantic, pabulum. Lee's super-heroes started by being shaped around the CCA restrictions, with family friendly fare like *The Fantastic Four*, his first Marvel super-hero comic. Establishing his credibility and playing under the new, rigorously enforced self-censorship rules, Lee developed a series of new super-heroes that made Marvel a player in the comic book industry. From the success of the *FF*, Lee shifted into a slightly more rebellious mode with the anti-hero figure of *The Hulk*. Lee's publisher at the time thought, as Lee notes, he "could do no wrong" (Zakarin, 2002). *Captain America*, *Thor*, and *Iron Man*, among several others, established Lee's legacy of writing inspired new characters for a burgeoning, post-Code comic book universe. In 1963, however, Lee pitched a concept that was met with considerable skepticism: a teenager, given great power, turns into a superhero, and the book follows the young fellow through his troubles both as a hero and a misfit adolescent. Lee remembers his publisher's objections: "People hate spiders! You can't do a book called *Spider-Man*. And you want him to be a teenager? Teenagers can only be sidekicks" (Zakarin, 2002). As Kevin Smith follows up, other heroes "didn't even have real life identities" at the time. But Lee got the origin story published in the final issue of *Amazing Fantasy* nonetheless, and it was met with overwhelming demand for more. Only nine months later, the first full issue of *Amazing Spider-Man* was released to the public.

Unburdened by the constraints of an already completed origin story, Lee delves into the world of Peter Parker, extraordinary teenager and super-hero. But from the very first page, Stan Lee's Spider-Man is truly something different: Spider-Man, Menace. When the character initially confronts the headline of *The Daily Bugle*, Spider-Man gets blackballed by his agent, while Jameson is on television, honing his philippic on masked heroes, particularly the scene-stealing Spider-Man. The diatribe appeals to the lawful, the parental, patriotic. Spider-Man is a vigilante, taking the law into his own hands. He represents a moral hazard to children, as they may imitate his feats of daring. He misrepresents heroism, this Über-mench standing in for real heroes (like his astronaut son, John). By the end of the page, Spider-Man is the unmasked teenager Peter Parker, again rendered unable to make a difference in the adult world. "Oh, no! [Aunt May]'s pawning her jewelry ... for me! ... I've got to earn some money — somehow!" he cries as he literally pounds his fists against a wall (*ASM 1*, 1964: 6). Thus positioned, Spider-Man must choose between impudence and impotence. At first, he tries to gain the good will of Jameson through an act of all-American heroism, saving Jameson's own son from a technical failure during a space-module descent. Jameson's reaction is to call for the arrest and prosecution of Spider-Man. "Spider-Man is a MENACE to America!" Jameson declares to his audience. And public reaction follows: "Spider-Man oughtta be run out of the country," intones one newspaper reader. "And how!" his associate replies (14). The story ends: "And so, a lonely boy sits and broods, with the fate of society at stake! What will his decision be? What will Spider-Man do next?? Only time will tell!" (14). With *Amazing Spider-Man*, Lee hit upon a strategy that would contest the strictures of comics as a censored medium and slowly construct a critical apparatus for his readers and fellow artists to entrench in capital letters.

In the fourteen pages of the first arc in *Amazing Spider-Man #1*, Stan Lee writes a manifesto as metaphor. Lee's demurring notwithstanding, the construction of the first issue reveals a sublime rebellion. Some ten years earlier, Lee wrote a short piece in *Suspense #29* (1953). In it, a troubled, vindictive man attacks a comics editor, demanding the cessation of all comics publications. "But I don't like your stories!! You can't make me like them!!" he growls. The man gets taken away, and the reasonable editor goes home to tell his young daughter about the time someone stormed the offices to try to stop publishing fairy tales. Like *Amazing Fantasy #15*, it was a last-issue throw-away, but the story establishes the depth of Lee's feeling and experience in the comic industry. Lee recollects his thoughts on the issue: "In the story, I was the headman at a [comic book publishing] company when suddenly, some nutcase, raving maniac came crashing in to [scream at me] about the evils [of comic books] ... The executive whom I portrayed lashed back with some of the usual arguments plus a new one or two.... Naturally, those points were so powerful in that story that the raving maniac slunk off in utter defeat. But that was fiction. I wish we could have dismissed Dr. Fredric Wertham as easily" (Gitlin, 2010). Stan Lee's *Amazing Spider-Man #1* breaks his silence over the Code crackdown. J. Jonah Jameson figures as the purveyor of decency and exhibits the sensibility of a conservative, morally self-righteous, repressive, and reactionary demagogue. He may have the best of intentions, but his rhetoric is both inflammatory and counterfactual. Significantly, Jameson's argument parallels Dr. Wertham's seminal *pseudo*-scientific diatribe against comic books, *Seduction of the Innocent*.

Jameson's excerpted television editorial is, by the nature of the medium, highly compressed. Comprising four panels on page 5 of *Amazing Spider-Man #1*, Lee abbreviates Wertham's major themes. "He is a bad influence on our youngsters," Jameson begins, pointing to Spider-Man stopping a criminal *in medias res*. The frame highlights Spider-Man, who has webbed the crook's hand, stopped the gun, and has just punched the man unconscious. Beneath the still are three upstanding, older members of the community. The reiteration of one of Wertham's major themes (and most affective arguments of moral decay) couldn't be more direct. Wertham's description of a similar scene explicates the message of violence as the only effective resolution: "He bangs their heads together and exclaims: 'You always have to slug 'em! Remember that!' This is the elementary lesson of crime comics." (18). The essential thesis of *Seduction of the Innocent* is that comic books influence the choices of children. That influence is universally negative. While Wertham's diatribe is extensive and wide-ranging, his argument rests on just a few points. The first is imitation. Time after time, Wertham tells troubling stories of tragic youth. From suicides to sexual victimization to homicides, several children (all of whom happened to read comic books) made terrible choices. He begins with the story of a young child convicted of manslaughter; the child claims to have fired a gun no one ever found into a crowd at a baseball field, much like something that happened on the cover of one issue of one series. Wertham claims: "Slowly, and at first reluctantly, I have come to the conclusion that this chronic stimulation, temptation and seduction by comic books, both their content and their alluring advertisements of knives and guns, are contributing factors to many children's maladjustment" (10). In short, kids imitate what they see in comics. Lee picks up Wertham's reactionary stance as a critical foundation for Jameson's character. Through Jameson's visage, Lee echoes Wertham using Spider-Man as his incendiary illustration: "Children may try to imitate his fantastic feats! Think what would happen if they make a hero out of this lawless, inhuman monster!" (*ASM* 1: 5). In unison with his inspiration, Jameson howls: "We must not permit it!"

Fears of imitation give way to fears of vigilantism. Jameson intones: "I say that Spider-Man must be outlawed! There is no place for such a dangerous creature in our fair city!" (5). Wertham's treatise contains the explanatory reasoning for Jameson's more condensed diatribe: "The form in which this distrust for democratic law and the morality of taking punishment — or rather vengeance — into one's own hands has done the most harm to the ethical development of young people is the superman conceit" (96). Super-powered beings as objects of imitation also become objects of morality. If Spider-Man fights against criminals, it is only in order to aggrandize his own self-worth. He must be "greater than." He must be "superman." He must be Über-mensch. Jameson follows Wertham's logic to the letter. The appearance of a "super man," a man whose abilities far exceed the ordinary person, is "psychologically most unhygienic. The would-be supermen compensate for some kind of inferiority, real or imagined, by the fantasy of the superior being who is a law unto himself" (Wertham, 1954: 97). Subsequently, Spider-Man is both a threat and a lesser being ripe for ridicule and accusation. Moreover, since he is Nietzschian, he is also the Nazi ideal. This slide to the radically un–American, unpatriotic nature of an unknown other at first appears quite a leap, especially as Jameson accuses Spider-Man of intentionally undermining the respect of "real heroes — men such as my son, [astronaut] John Jameson, test pilot!" (*ASM* 1: 5). Eliding the two would be a significant jump in logic for Lee if not for Wertham's own slippage: "In these children there is an exact parallel to the blunting of sensibilities in the direction of cruelty that has characterized a whole generation of central European youth fed on the Nietzsche-Nazi myth of the exceptional man who is beyond good and evil. It is an ethical confusion.... The very children for whose unruly behavior I would want to prescribe psychotherapy in an anti-superman direction, have been nourished (or rather poisoned) by the endless repetition of Superman stories" (Wertham, 1954: 97). Being super-powered, then, is *de facto* un-American. Telling such stories is, by definition, to be against American "values," as defined by Jameson and Wertham.

Set in opposition to this is a blindsided wall-crawler. Spider-Man reads and witnesses this with apprehension and bewilderment: "But why? What have they got against me? What have I done?" (*ASM* 1, 1964: 5). He wonders why more public figures whose influence seems the same or greater don't have the same virulent pitch thrown at them, and the newspaper vendor notes: "Bah! I don't even believe that there **is** a Spider-Man! It's all a publicity stunt!" (5). In the wake of HUAC and the Red Scare, in the lull between the anti-Communist fervor and the rise of the counterculture sixties, no one really even believes that comics "exist," which is to say they are of no cultural value or significance to the adult masses. Whether Lee is pointing to the contemporary spate of contemporary, sub-par comic lines or the suppressed books of the pre-Code days might be an interesting question, but ultimately it applies to both. The mere existence of comics is a menace, like the mere appearance of Spider-Man menaces Jameson. Paralleling Spider-Man's constant struggle to do the right thing despite the vilification of the hounding media, Lee appeals to the better nature of the industry. After the (largely baseless) attacks by Wertham, the comic book industry instituted the Comic Code Authority that listed a series of stringent rules for comic publication. Unlike the previous Association of Comics Magazine Publishers code, this was strictly enforced. Even when Lee's Atlas line conformed to the new authority, the loss in sales and revenue were so severe that the business folded. In attempting to do right by his critics, like Spider-Man's brave if ostentatious save of John Jameson's free-falling space capsule (10–13), Lee was only met with repudiation and further accusation, largely by twisting the truth. Jameson takes one instance and generalizes it into Spider-Man's "criminal activity," as Wertham takes individual, rare, cherry-picked cases of troubled youth and defines an industry by the uncommon negative outliers. It is difficult not to hear Lee's experience echo in Peter Parker's frustration: "It's all his fault! Because of him, I can't perform as the Spider-Man! But I can't give up! I've got to earn some money — somehow!" (6).

Spider-Man. *Menace.* Lee's establishing issue creates the unmistakable intertwining of the character and the antecedent comic, and through Jameson's libelous accusations of Spider-Man's activities, Lee begins an argument that would take nearly 100 issues to resolve. Jameson represents the amalgamated world of anti-comic hysterics anthropomorphized into a loud-mouthed publisher and editor (not coincidentally, much like those in charge of the CCA). Spider-Man stands alone, the single person who is not just a "hypertrophied costumed hero," but a "regular guy" tethered with extraordinary gifts. With the Comic Code Authority rules and the Wertham ideology transcendent, comics often found themselves the victims of a crusade. Spider-Man is tried in the court of public opinion similarly. "The Spider-Man Menace!: A New Series by J. Jonah Jameson" splashes across a billboard in *Amazing Spider-Man #4* (2), reflecting and referencing Wertham's "Comic Books, the Menace to American Childhood" lectures and the televised Senate Subcommittee on Juvenile Delinquency hearings of 1954.

In a brief aside in *Amazing Spider-Man #5* (1964), Lee gives voice to the public interest, and (perhaps inadvertently) sheds light on his position. Peter Parker's teenage friends are listening to Jameson's new series. One friend remarks: "Boy, imagine Jameson sponsoring his own program, just to attack Spider-Man!" Flash Thompson adds: "Yeah! Personally I think that Spider-Man's the coolest!" Peter, not wanting to look as if he supports his alter ego, offers a feeble rejoinder: "You can't tell! Jameson may be right! Nobody really knows Spider-Man!" Peter is then invited to leave, with Flash noting, "You're in the wrong place, anyhow! This is a bowling alley, not a knitting parlor!" (*ASM* 5, 1964: 2). Lee's apparent acquiescence to the CCA and prevailing censorship of the time gave him the appearance of being "slightly daft" and mainstream, utterly complacent and appeasing. Comic books were vilified by the mainstream press, and in reaction to mounting public calls for censorship, comic creators had to reinvent themselves as goody-two-shoes. Lee notes of the period just before Marvel: "I wanted to quit at that time [around 1961]. I was really so bored and really too old to be doing these stupid comic books; I wanted to quit. I was also frustrated because I wanted to do comic books that were — even though this seems like a contradiction in terms — I wanted to do a more realistic fantasy. Martin [Marvel's first publisher] wouldn't let me and had wanted the stories done the way they had always been done, with very young children in mind. That was it" (*SMRB*, 1998). The success of the *Fantastic Four* allowed Lee a greater canvas and kept him in the industry, but Lee's fight was bigger and more complex, demanding what amounted to a secret, "nerd" identity.

By *Amazing Spider-Man* #50, Lee's narrative opposition between Spider-Man and Jameson reached a boiling point. If, from issues 1 to 49, Spider-Man was figuratively a "Menace" and represented the other comics cancelled by the purges of the mid-1950s, in issue *#50*, Spider-Man was Lee himself. The plot, in brief, begins with a harangue by Jameson that accuses Spider-Man of a classic Wertham aspersion: "Do we want our youngsters to make an idol of a mentally-disturbed menace??" (6). Spider-Man begins to question himself. Jameson's case is constantly in the echo-chamber of his world. Jameson's reach in the media is comprehensive. "Perhaps ... only a madman would do what I do ... taking the risks ... accepting the dangers ... and for what??" (7). Like Lee, Spider-Man questions his motives, his need to commit to his choices. And like Lee, he makes up his mind to quit. *Amazing Spider-Ma*n #50 reads like a dream version of Lee's professional crisis of conscience. Peter Parker sets down the mask and the suit and leaves the trouble to others. Jameson finds the suit and hangs it in a glass case, declaring, "everything's coming up roses!" (9). He does the media rounds, talks the talk shows, and makes bigger headlines. But Peter's fantasy of a "normal life" requires the abdication of responsibility. Lee projects into this narrative the difficulty of living with the CCA restrictions after the 1950s "comics scare." Moving away from creating comics after the suppression of 1955 is the easy choice. Staying was drudgery and boredom. Like Peter Parker's milestone story, when Lee was about to quit, an opportunity presented itself and it was the necessity to act that compelled him: "My wife Joan said to me, 'You know, Stan, if they asked you to do a new book about a new group of super-heroes, why don't you do 'em the way that you feel you'd like to do a book? If you want to quit anyway, the worst that could happen is that he'll fire you, and so what? You want to quit.' I figured, hey, maybe she's right.... I wanted to create a new group and do them the way I had always wanted to do a comic book" (*SMRB*, 1998). As Lee weaves his turmoil into his writing, Spider-Man's struggle takes on an autobiographical tone. Parker, passing a guard being assaulted on a roof, saved the guard and realized, "That was the turning point — That's when I became Spider-Man — for real!!" (*ASM 50*, 1967: 11–12). Lee's investment in the critical dynamic of *The Amazing Spider-Man* shifts from the fouled memories of Wertham's crusade and the beloved *Menace* to the reality of publishing comics in the contemporary environment of the Code and its authoritarian censorship on artistic creativity. In the following two issues, Spider-Man quite literally saves Jameson from drowning, and Jameson's repayment is to throw Spider-Man under the bus as an accomplice of the Kingpin (*ASM 52*, 1967). The economic metaphor could not be more pronounced. *Amazing Spider*-Man was one of the top selling books of the time, and Lee's Marvel comics was second to none in the era. Monthly, Marvel was, quite literally, saving comics from being drowned out by television, video games, and the other forms of modern distractions that continue to gain ground over the once dominant medium. But this was not a war of attrition. For Lee to win would require an overt rejection of the authority of the CCA, and Lee waited for just the right moment.

Over the following years, Jameson's crusade against Spider-Man neither progresses nor relents. Jameson attacks in the same vein, portraying Spider-Man as a criminal influence and villainous role model, while Spider-Man continues to be the hero the world never sees, one save at a time. Lee carefully balances the story, continually critiquing the vitriolic media engaged in constant character assassination with satirical representations, but never letting Spider-Man succeed in the public eye, no matter how much his hero achieves. Jameson's continued vilification of Spider-Man, constantly rebuffed by the hero's success, parallels the stalemate between Wertham's libel and the CCA's draconian censorship of Lee's medium. His *coup d'état* awaits its time. He recounts the story:

> I got this letter—I don't remember the exact wording—and [the Department of Health, Education, and Welfare] were concerned about drug use among kids. Since Marvel had such a great influence with young people, they thought it would be very commendable if we were to put out some sort of anti-drug message in our books.
> I felt that the only way to do it was to make it a part of the story, and we made that three-parter of Spider-Man. I remember it contained one scene where a kid was going to jump off a roof and thought he could fly. My problem is that I know less about drugs than any living human being! I didn't know what kind of drug it was that would make you think you could fly! I don't think I named anything; I just said that he had "done" something [*SMRB*, 1998].

He reminisces to Kevin Smith in a later interview: "Who was I to deny the will of the HEW?" (Zakarin, 2002). Lee's typical lightly toned delivery belies the seriousness of context. The Comic Code Authority's list of rules offers the short-list of plots for *The Amazing Spider-Man*, though to chronicle Lee's issue-by-issue slipping and sliding around the General Standards (especially Part A) would be too extensive for this paper. By placing Spider-Man in the dubious position of being portrayed as a criminal, though not actually being one, Lee constantly blurred the lines between the Code's censorship and what he could get away with—until the letter arrived from the government. The general plot of issues *96–98* is an encounter with the Green Goblin, during which Spider-Man fights against his merciless foe. In the first issue in the arc, an unnamed character stands precariously on the roof: "I got here just in time," Spider-Man thinks. "The poor guy's stoned right out of his mind" (10). The man teeters precariously on the roof, then falls, though Spider-Man catches him and brings him to the ground safely. However, the man has suffered some sort of attack and is no longer breathing. Risking arrest (Spider-Man is a suspect in the accidental death of Captain Stacy [*ASM 90–91*, 1970]), Spider-Man leaves him with the police, who perform CPR and resuscitate him. Spidey swings off with the drug abuser on his way to the hospital. This story, clearly depicting the negative effects of drug abuse in the most colorfully drawn lines possible, was rejected as "immoral" by the CCA. The issue went to press without the Code's seal of approval.

Then Stan Lee did something rather extraordinary. With the CCA stamp denied, he went forward and wrote two more issues dealing with the dangers of drug abuse. In the second and third issues, Harry Osborn—son of Norman Osborn, the Green Goblin, and Peter Parker's friend—overdoses on an unknown drug that, the dealer promises: "Just try a few—and nothing's gonna bother you" (*ASM 96*, 1971: 12). He takes a few, then a few more. Lee's depiction of Harry's overdose is somewhat short on subtlety. The center panel on page 19 features a cornucopia of scattered pills surrounding a hallucinogenic series of close-ups as Harry exclaims: "It's like—I'm drowning—falling—dying inside! Nothing seems real—nothing hangs together—The pills! It—must be—the pills—They're driving me—out of my mind!" He collapses on the bed. Fortunately, Peter returns just in time, though the Green Goblin hovers threateningly outside. Parker does get Harry to the hospital, and the plot is resolved through Spider-Man's realization that seeing Harry in mortal danger would snap the Goblin back to reality, and his positive persona, Norman Osborn. Lee's message is unquestionably anti-drug.

It chronicles three cases in which illicit drug use causes insanity and near-death experiences. Under the influence, the first youngster is driven to jump off a building. The second is the overdose of Harry Osborn, who survived through timely medical help and now battles pill addiction. The last is the psychotic break brought on by the Goblin formula, a form of steroids that enhances strength but also aggression to the point of madness, from which sanity can only be recovered through an encounter with radical loss. According to *The Amazing Spider-Man*, use — any use — of illegal drugs is bad.

Stan Lee could have chosen to put a story dealing with drug use in any of the several books Marvel published at the time. At the time, *The Amazing Spider-Man* was by far Marvel Comics' best-selling title. Using *The Amazing Spider-Man* for this forum was a tremendous risk, and one that could have backfired catastrophically. As one reader noted: "This was the first time I had seen any company put their magazine in jeopardy rather than cut out something which they felt was right, and was needed" (*ASM 100*, 1971: 31). To get a sense of the risk involved, in 1971 (the year the series was printed), *The Amazing Spider-Man* circulated 307,550 copies. At 12 issues a year, that's an average 25,630 copies per issue. Risking the publication of a comic without the CCA approval risked the possibility of pulping an entire run. To run a single issue represented a loss of thousands of dollars in an industry with razor thin margins. But Lee and his publisher ran three, which could have put the Spider-Man title at risk, and possibly Marvel Comics itself. As the Lawrence van Gelder of the *New York Times* notes, "Consistent violation of the code could mean expulsion from membership in the Comics Magazine Association, accompanied by notification of news dealers, many of whom presumably would decline to handle the publisher's wares" (1971: 37). In other words, three issues could shutter Marvel Comics. As it turns out, that's not what happened. Dealers and fans alike loved the story.

Looking at the numbers for the year, 1971 represented the only downtick in the percentage of issue returns in the 1970s. Like most comics, *The Amazing Spider-Man* was losing readership to television and other media that attracted the younger generation, but issues 96–98 were — by all accounts — tremendously successful (Wright, 2001: 239). *The Amazing Spider-Man* gained a reputation as "groundbreaking." Its cultural capital soared. Stan was, from then on, "the man." The CCA drew a line in the sand; Lee inked it, colored it, and published it. The effect was almost immediate. The Comic Code Authority revised its stringent rules to allow depiction of criminality, the death of law-enforcement officers, seduction, and permit supernatural characters (Thompson, 1971). Further liberalization followed, including stories about drug use, so long as it was shown to be harmful and immoral. The stringent self-censorship instigated by Wertham and the anti-comic hysteria of the 1950s was eroded (and eventually erased) by the heroic acts of *The Amazing Spider-Man*.

Once the sales numbers for issue 96 came in, Stan Lee signed off as the writer of *ASM*. Issue 100 was his last, leaving Peter Parker and cast in the hands of Roy Thomas. In his 1998 interview with Lee, Thomas expresses his surprise: "You wrote up to [*Amazing*] *Spider-Man #100*, which you ended by giving him four extra arms and tossed it to me, saying, 'Take it, Roy.' ...You were still involved editorially though, because this was right after the Code was liberalized, and you told us you wanted Spidey to fight a vampire" (*Stan the man, Roy the Boy*, 1998). But issue 98 foreshadows Lee's intent. In an aside with Robbie Robertson, J. Jonah Jameson expresses his concerns about printing the Harry Osborn story: "That kid's father is one of our biggest advertisers! He's not gonna like us printing this story." Robertson is outraged that Jameson might consider covering up a story over advertising revenue. Jameson corrects him: it's about how they approach the story. Robertson says, "I'm showing that drugs aren't just a ghetto hangup! They hit the rich — same as the poor" (9). Jameson immediately approves the story. For the first time in the series, J. Jonah Jameson is the newspaper editor of *The Daily Bugle*. As a reader notes in the letters page: "The conversation, concerning drugs, served as food for thought.... I see Jameson as an honest man, and more importantly, an honest editor" (*ASM 102*, 1971: 36). The dialogue Lee features announces the accomplishment: Jameson no longer needs to be the amalgamated censors; he no longer needs to be the harping voice of pure censorship hysteria. By succeeding without the CCA's approval, Lee showed the Code was ineffectual. Issue *100* marks the final issue of Lee's metaphor, as he returns Spider-Man to being purely a comic book character. The title of the story is: "The Spider or the Man?" In the end, Lee gives him six arms: a very amusing nod to the idea that Spider-Man's real-world war with censorship is over. The book can return to its roots: a monster story of transformation, mystery, and confusion, one not entirely unlike the lead feature in *Menace #4* (June 1953), which contains the story of the four-armed man.

Lee's departure from *The Amazing Spider-Man* precipitated a four-month leave of absence (*SMRB*, 1998), after which he returned to work as editor-in-chief of Marvel Comics (and occasional writer in any number of Marvel comics). He left the book in the hands of a capable creative team of Thomas and Gil Kane, and since September 1971, many talents have written, drawn, and collaboratively crafted the mythos of Spider-Man. While Jameson continues to be a thorn in Spider-Man's side, and on more than a few occasions throughout the series, he accuses Spider-Man of several heinous things, the story of *Amazing Spider-Man #96–98* opens the reader to the possibility that Jameson is more than just an egomaniacal, hot-headed, insecure, blow-hard. The conversation portrayed between Robertson and Jameson fundamentally alters the dynamic of Jameson's character from a pure antagonistic foil and single-issue critic to a powerful voice in the media generally. Lee offers a model for cultural critique and opens the door for later writers to criticize, lampoon, and castigate the polemical media of their day. From the work of Roy Thomas to Frank Miller to J. Michael Straczynski, Mark Waid, and the rest of the Marvel bullpen, the framework Stan Lee constructed in his 100-issue run as writer of *The Amazing Spider-Man* serves to expose, dissect, and deconstruct the raving maniacs who would scream and yell the loudest. In *The Amazing Spider-Man #1*, Stan Lee writes: "Unfortunately, if something is shouted loud enough, there are always those who will believe it..." (14). Changing minds takes time. It takes strength of character, fortitude, patience, knowledge, and understanding. For him, Jameson's crusade was the voice of Wertham's baseless but effective ramblings about the evils comics represent. Lee's nearly twenty-year battle with conservative critics and censors, his war of art and words, changed the perception of comics both in and out of the community of collectors. *The Amazing Spider-Man* transformed comics from pop-culture iconography to agents of cultural criticism. The writers that followed picked up the mantel and continually took to task the failures of the media. From Dennis O'Neil and Frank Miller's *Amazing Spider-Man Annual* 15 (1981), which chronicles the news cycle's rise and fall and rise again of Jameson's editorial: "Spider-Man: Threat or Menace!?" and ends in a morose newsstand clerk unable to move the libelous issues, to J. Michael Straczynski's silent tale of Aunt May, resigning her subscriptions to *The Daily Bugle* and a handful of other biased dailies and suggesting that "beneath that mask there is a good person, a kind person, a good face ... who could profit from the exposure this would provide to set the record straight" (*ASM 39 (480)*, 2002: 16), *The Amazing Spider-Man* continues to deal directly with Lee's critical legacy. With the rise of right-wing media dominance in political discourse and tabloid-style one-source reporting overwhelming traditional news journalism, *The Amazing Spider-Man* continues its crusade against baseless, one-sided assaults on common sense, reason, and the evidence of our own eyes. The stories serve as lessons, like fairy tales, and Lee identifies the real nefarious villain of all art and culture: "Once upon a time an excited little man, with nothing more important on his mind, ran into an editor's office to complain about some magazines..." (*Suspense 29, 1953*: 19). Here comes the Spider-Man.

Works Cited

David, Peter, Todd Nauck, et al. *Friendly Neighborhood Spider-Man 23*. New York: Marvel (October 2007).
Gitlin, Marty. *Stan Lee: Comic Book Superhero*. New York: ABDO Publishing, 2010.
Hajdu, David. *The Ten-Cent Plague: The Great Comic-Book Scare and How It Changed America*. New York: Picador (2008).
Lee, Stan, Joe Maneely, et al. *Suspense 29*. New York: Atlas Comics (April 1953).
_____, Steve Dikto, et al. *Amazing Fantasy 15*. New York: Marvel (December 1963).
_____, Steve Dikto, et al. *Amazing Spider-Man 1*. New York: Marvel (March 1964).
_____, Steve Dikto, et al. *Amazing Spider-Man 4*. New York: Marvel (September 1964).
_____, Steve Dikto, et al. *Amazing Spider-Man 5*. New York: Marvel (October 1964).
_____, Gil Kane, et al. *Amazing Spider-Man 90*. New York: Marvel (November 1970).
_____, Gil Kane, et al. *Amazing Spider-Man 91*. New York: Marvel (December 1970).
_____, Gil Kane, John Romita, et al. *Amazing Spider-Man 96*. New York: Marvel (May 1971).
_____, Gil Kane, et al. *Amazing Spider-Man 97*. New York: Marvel (June 1971).
_____, Gil Kane, et al. *Amazing Spider-Man 98*. New York: Marvel (July 1971).
_____, Gil Kane, et al. *Amazing Spider-Man 100*. New York: Marvel (September 1971).
_____, John Romita, et al. *Amazing Spider-Man 50*. New York: Marvel (July 1967).
_____, John Romita, et al. *Amazing Spider-Man 51*. New York: Marvel (August 1967).
_____, John Romita, et al. *Amazing Spider-Man 52*. New York: Marvel (September 1967).
Miller, John Jackson. "Amazing Spider-Man Sales Figures." *The Comics Chronicles: A Resource for Comics Research*. Accessed 11/30/10 http://www.comichron/titlespotlights/amazingSpider-Man.html.
O'Neil, Dennis, Frank Miller, et al. *Amazing Spider-Man Annual 15*. New York: Marvel, 1981.
Straczynski, J. Michael, John Romita, Jr., et al. *Amazing Spider-Man, Vol. 2, 39 (480)*. New York: Marvel (March 2002).
Thomas, Roy. "Stan the Man & Roy the Boy: A Conversation Between Stan Lee and Roy Thomas." *Comic Book Artist #2*, 1998. Accessed 11/30/10 http://twomorrows.com/comicbookartist/articles/02stanroy.html.
Thomas, Roy, Gil Kane, et al. *Amazing Spider-Man 102*. New York: Marvel (November 1971).
Thompson, Don, Maggie Thompson. "Crack in the Code." *Newfangles* 44 (February 1971): 1.
Van Gelder, Lawrence. "A Comics Magazine Defies Code Ban on Drug Stories." *The New York Times*. Feb 4, 1971: 37, 44.
Wertham, Fredric, M.D. *Seduction of the Innocent*. Clarke, Irwin & Company, Ltd.: Toronto and New York, 1954.
Wright, Bradford. *Comic Book Nation*. Johns Hopkins Press: Baltimore (2001).
Wymann, Adrian. "Bring on the Bad Guy: The Day Stan Lee Met Fredric Wertham — in the Pages of *Suspense #29*." *Panelology.info*. 6/9/2010. Accessed 11/30/10. http://www.panelology.info/RavingManiac.html.
Zakarin, Scott (director), Kevin Smith, Stan Lee, et al. *Stan Lee's Mutants, Monsters & Marvels*. Sony Pictures, 2002.

J. Jonah Jameson — Hero or Villain?
Spider-Man's Nemesis Hard to Pigeonhole

ANDREW A. SMITH

J. Jonah Jameson, publisher and editor of the *Daily Bugle* newspaper (and, when convenient to the plot, *Now* and *Woman* magazines), debuted in *Amazing Spider-Man* 1 (1963). He began as a contradictory and controversial figure, and remains one still, half a century later.

In several instances in that first issue, Jameson is depicted using his newspaper and public appearances to vilify an innocent person: Spider-Man, secretly high school student Peter Parker. This proves to be just the first of Jameson's many faults. As issue after issue demonstrates, Jameson is vain, cowardly, stubborn, miserly, envious, cruel, thoughtless, and overbearing. He's also unprofessional; his willingness to twist the news to serve a personal agenda would get him fired from any newspaper he didn't own.

But Jameson is vast; he contains multitudes. That is to say, he occasionally exhibits virtues. For example, he frequently stands up to bigotry. He's pro-active against crime. He's often astoundingly good at being a newspaperman (where it doesn't involve Spider-Man). And his worst excesses are couched in the rhetoric of a heroic crusader for the public good (which he may be delusional enough to believe).

So he is sometimes admirable, sometimes not — and sometimes it's just hard to tell. Who is the real J. Jonah Jameson?

The Awesome Origin of Editor-Man!

"Jonah is pompous, narrow-minded, bigoted, and egotistical — and those are his good qualities," joked Stan Lee in his biography, *Excelsior* (Lee and Mair, 2002: 136). And he ought to know: Lee, who co-created Jameson (with artist Steve Ditko), wrote the character for the first 100 consecutive issues of *Amazing Spider-Man*, plus six annuals. Before any other writers tackled *Amazing Spider-Man* (beginning with Roy Thomas in October 1971), and before the Wall-Crawler branched out into multiple titles every month (beginning with *Marvel Team-Up* in March 1972), Lee was the only writer to handle Jameson monthly for eight years, establishing the character so strongly that there has been little variation since. In the compendium *Stan Lee Conversations,* Lee is quoted as saying "I don't really know where I got him ... maybe a combination of everybody I've ever known" (Pitts, 2007: 97).

Gerry Conway, the first long-term writer on *Amazing Spider-Man* after Lee, said he picked up the character without changing a single hair of his flattop. "(There were) no instructions regarding JJJ's portrayal," Conway said in an unpublished interview with this author. "He was/is such a well-delineated character it wasn't necessary." Conway said of his approach to Jameson, "On a subconscious level ... I admit I probably patterned him a little after Stan. Not in the bluster and temper, but in the lack of self-awareness, matched by self-importance."

Ditko, who co-plotted and drew Spidey's adventures from his first appearance in *Amazing Fantasy* #15 through *Amazing Spider-Man* #38, was equally important in defining Jameson as a character. In his book *Strange and Stranger: The World of Steve Ditko*, Blake Bell said Ditko deliberately drew Jameson ugly, as a "grinning hyena." The artist delighted in reader complaints that Jameson was "physically grotesque," Blake said, because Ditko felt that reaction validated how he had "grounded the character in reality" (Bell, 2008: 60).

"Something tells me that subconsciously, Stan also patterned JJ after himself," said Conway, now the story editor on *Law & Order*, in the interview. "Or maybe [publisher] Martin Goodman? I guess whenever we write a boss character we use the opportunity to lovingly lampoon our own bosses." Lampoon or not, Jameson wasn't originally meant to be permanent. "When I first wrote him into the series, he was just a minor throwaway character," Lee said in the "Introduction" to *Marvel Masterworks Vol. 5* (1988), which reprinted *Amazing Spider-Man* #11–20. "Then y'know what happened? The irascible ol' curmudgeon became one of the mainstays of the entire series" (Lee, 1988).

J. Jonah Jameson: Threat or Menace?

Whatever stray synapses gave Jameson birth, he certainly makes his presence known dramatically in *Amazing Spider-Man* 1. Characteristically, his first words are a smear. "When I'm thru (sic) with this article, Spider-Man will be run out of town!" he says in his very first panel, an angry figure hunched over a typewriter (Lee, 1963: 4).

Jameson single-handedly ends Spider-Man's show business career with his first editorial (headlined with typical hyperbole "Spider-Man Menace"), consigning Parker to eternal financial embarrassment. Jameson goes beyond the printed word, sponsoring a television show to attack Spider-Man, and delivering anti-Spider-Man lectures around New York City:

> We cannot allow that masked menace to take the law into his own hands! He is a bad influence on our youngsters! Children may try to imitate his fantastic feats! Think what would happen if they make a hero out of this lawless, inhuman monster! We must not permit it. I say that Spider-Man must be **outlawed**! There is no place for such a dangerous creature in our fair city. The youth of this nation must learn to respect **real** heroes — men such as my son, John Jameson, the test pilot! Not selfish freaks such as Spider-Man — a masked menace who refuses to even let us know his true identity! [Lee, 1963: 5].

And that's only the first issue! During Lee's 100-issue run, Jameson appears in almost every book, haranguing the Web-Spinner verbally, in print, on billboards, on the sides of trucks — any forum available. The television show in the first issue becomes an ongoing platform, and in *Amazing Spider-Man* 50 Jameson unleashes a rant so vile, so vicious, so vituperative that a shocked Parker begins second-guessing himself and briefly quits being Spider-Man:

> ...he's really an egomaniac ... a neurotic trouble-maker, flaunting his power, before the ordinary citizens whom he despises! For all we know, he himself provokes the criminals he later seems to defeat! Do we want our youngsters to make an idol of a mentally-disturbed menace?? I say no!!

We must find him ... unmask him ... and then ... destroy him! As publisher of the Daily Bugle, I offer one thousand dollars for the capture and conviction of that web-slinging mockery of a man....

Jameson's tactics progress. In *Amazing Spider-Man* 24 he attempts a ploy familiar to today's audiences, the verbal equivalent of a push poll. He sends a reporter out on the streets with a tape recorder to gin up negative comments on Spider-Man, so that Jameson can print "other people's opinions on why they hate [Spider-Man]"— even if they didn't. In *Amazing Spider-Man* 9 Jameson crosses a more serious ethical line — and possibly a legal one — when he runs a story attesting that Spider-Man is masquerading as a new super-villain, without any evidence to support, or even suggest, the allegation. In journalism terms, this surpasses the "actual malice" standard, where even celebrities — well, those without masks — can sue and win.

It gets worse. Three issues later (*Amazing Spider-Man* 12), Jameson crosses another line by printing a challenge to Spider-Man in the *Daily Bugle* from Dr. Octopus — and fails to tell the police. After Dr. Octopus escapes, a furious policeman says, "Jameson, next time you withhold information from us, it will go hard with you. If you had told us of this, we would have set a trap for Dr. Octopus and caught him by now. But you thought more of an exclusive story than anything else" (Lee, 1964: 9).

Jameson goes even farther in the next issue (*Amazing Spider-Man* 13), where he not only prints a challenge from Mysterio — a new "hero" who publicly announces his plan to illegally assault Spider-Man — but makes a shady deal with him. At a news conference, Jameson crows, "Once Mysterio has defeated Spider-Man for good, he will reveal his true identity exclusively to my newspaper! It'll be the scoop of the century for me! Right, Mysterio?" To which Mysterio responds, "Right! Just so long as you remember the money you promised me!" (Lee, 1964: 13). Is this checkbook journalism, or is Jameson actually hiring a knee-breaker? It would take a New York jury to sort out whether this is illegal, but it is certainly both unethical and immoral.

Jameson is aware he is flirting with felonies. When he tries to bribe Kraven the Hunter for an exclusive interview two issues later (*Amazing Spider-Man* 15), the legendary tracker announces his plans to hunt Spider-Man like an animal. "I can't say it isn't an intriguing idea, Mr. Kraven!" Jameson says. "But you know there are laws against things like that! You can't just track down a human being in this country." But Jameson does agree to it, with the caveat, "Remember — it has to be perfectly legal! Much as I hate Spider-Man, I won't stand for anything that violates the law!" (Lee, 1964: 6, 15). Given that everything the pair discuss is manifestly illegal — by Jameson's own admission — it seems obvious the newsman is rationalizing.

But it is in January 1965 when Jameson finally, inarguably commits a crime, funding a scientist to create a super-villain called Scorpion. In *Amazing Spider-Man* 20, it is revealed that Jameson has been paying a private detective named Mac Gargan to follow Parker and discover how he gets his photos (which alone is probably illegal). He relieves Gargan of that duty, and pays him $10,000 to be the guinea pig in Dr. Farley Stillwell's experiment to give a man the powers of a scorpion. Jameson also gives the scientist $10,000, and promises more: "Stillwell, if this works, I'll make you rich ... famous! I'll become your patron! ... For the world must be rid of Spider-Man! And at last we've been given the tools to do the job!" (Lee, 1965: 7). While it could be argued that Jameson intends something relatively benign, like a citizen's arrest, in the end his language leaves little doubt as to his intentions. For one thing, he doesn't care that the experiment is dangerous for Gargan — he wants someone who could "beat that blasted Spider-Man! That's all I want!." And later, he urges Scorpion to "smash" Spider-Man (Lee, 1965:6, 9).

By the end of the story, Jameson seems to understand how far he's gone: "Nobody knows it, but it's all my fault! ... Just to satisfy my own personal hatred, I tried to destroy Spider-Man! And, in so doing, I've unleashed a far worse menace upon the world! A menace I can no longer control! A menace which no one can control!" (Lee, 1965: 15). He is just self-aware enough to worry he'll get caught, but nothing has really changed. He publishes a story that omits his connection to the Scorpion, invents heroism on his own part, and relegates Spider-Man's role to that of—as one *Daily Bugle* reader says—someone who "showed up when it was almost over!" (Lee, 1965: 20). He vows to continue his crusade against the Wall-Crawler with a flimsy justification:

> I know now that anyone with too much power is liable to turn into a menace sooner or later! And Spider-Man is no exception! It's still my duty to fight him ... to expose him ... and someday ... to destroy him! And I will ... if it takes the rest of my life, I will!

Consorting with (or creating) super-villains would prove to be something of a pattern for Jameson over the years. In *Amazing Spider-Man* 25, he funds the creation of a robot with the ominous name "Spider-Slayer," built to capture Spider-Man. In *Amazing Spider-Man* 82, he pays the super-villain Electro $5,000 to attack Spider-Man on national television. In *Amazing Spider-Man Annual* 10, he repeats the Scorpion fiasco, resulting in another super-villain, the Human Fly.

Why is Jameson so obsessed? In 1964, at the end of *Amazing Spider-Man* 10, the editor explains his obsession with a soliloquy. "Am I always to be thwarted, embarrassed, frustrated by Spider-Man??" says Jameson, alone in his office. "I hate that costumed freak more than I've ever hated anyone before! I'll never be contented while he's free!" Then comes the speech for which readers had been waiting—an explanation for all the vicious attacks. Bell said Ditko set the scene in such a way as to "dramatically [cast] the envious publisher in darkened shadows, left to his own despair and shame" (Bell, 2008: 64):

> All my life I've been interested in only one thing—making money! And yet, Spider-Man risks his life day after day with no thought of reward! If a man like him is good—is a hero—then what am I?? I can never respect myself while he lives! Spider-Man represents everything that I'm not! He's brave, powerful, and unselfish! The truth is, I envy him! I, J. Jonah Jameson—millionaire, man of the world, civic leader—I'd give everything I won to be the man he is! But I can never climb to his level! So all that remains for me is—to try to tear him down—because, heaven help me—I'm jealous of him! [Lee, 1964: 22].

Jameson never admits his envy publicly, but few are fooled. Secretary Betty Brant raises the issue of jealousy in *Amazing Spider-Man* 5. In *Amazing Spider-Man* 66, City Editor Joe "Robbie" Robertson refers to Jameson's "almost psychotic" hatred of Spider-Man (Lee, 1968: 11). In *Amazing Spider-Man* 4, a policeman says, "You can print what you want in your papers, but sooner or later people will realize you're just airing a private grudge of your own!" (Lee, 1963: 19). And in *Amazing Spider-Man* 42, Jameson's heroic astronaut son John asks his father if he's "really being fair" to the Web-Spinner (Lee, 1966: 4).

Not even criminals are fooled. Crime reporter Frederick Foswell, who is once captured by Spider-Man when he tries to become a criminal kingpin, asks Jameson in *Amazing Spider-Man* 34, "What have you got against that guy, anyway, boss?" (Lee, 1966: 19). Smythe, the creator of the Spider-Slayer, calls Jameson a "neurotic nut" in *Amazing Spider-Man* 58 and says, "Don't talk to me about motives, you pious hypocrite! You've lied about [Spider-Man] in your paper for years!" (Lee, 1968: 17–19).

Jameson's news-twisting isn't his only ethical problem. He also makes a deal with Parker rife with potential conflict of interest. When Parker first brings in exclusive photos in *Amazing*

Spider-Man 2, Jameson agrees to buy them — and all future Parker photos — without knowing their source. As if that wasn't red flag enough, Parker asks to have his name redacted! That last part didn't endure. But not verifying the source of content is a serious violation of journalism ethics.

Among Jameson's other character flaws is a distinct lack of personal courage. Even the Vulture, a super-villain, tells Jameson — in disgust — to "stop blubbering like a coward" (*Amazing Spider-Man* 7) when being robbed (Lee, 1963: 13). In "The Coming of the Scorpion!," Jameson says to his own threatening creation, "I-I'll pay any price ... but don't hurt me...!" (Lee, 1965: 17). In the second Scorpion story in *Amazing Spider-Man* 29, he tells the revenge-minded Gargan, "No! You can't get me! ... You mustn't! Get Spider-Man instead!" Even the murderous super-villain is appalled: "You'd throw anyone to me in order to save yourself, wouldn't you?" (Lee, 1965: 11). In *Amazing Spider-Man* 52, Jameson freezes when Spider-Man tries to rescue him from underworld boss The Kingpin, and goes into a fugue state: "He's almost petrified with fright!" thinks Spider-Man, who has to threaten him to provoke a response (Lee, 1967: 9).

And yet, Jameson remains delusionally convinced of his own innate heroism and altruism. When he agrees to print Mysterio's challenge to Spider-Man in the paper, he says, "If it means the end of Spider-Man, I'll become a hero to this city!" (Lee, 1964: 8). As noted, when Spider-Man and the Scorpion battle it out in the *Bugle* newsroom, Jameson prints the story as if he were the victor over both. When Spider-Man and Scorpion battle in the newsroom again in "Never Step on a Scorpion!," Jameson stages a photo shoot of himself in the "ruins of battle" after the super-powered pair are gone. "It'll make a great front-page story!" he gloats. "'Fearless, courageous publisher saves his employees from deadly costumed killers.' I'll be a hero! Make sure these pictures do me justice! Get my courageous expression ... my determined, fighting stance ... my iron fists, clenched and ready!" Later, he says to Parker, "You missed a chance to photograph me in action, heroically defeating Spider-Man and the Scorpion!" Parker thinks, "Wow! Now he's convinced that he really beat us!" (Lee, 1965: 13, 18).

Jameson is also arrogant and vain. In "The Man Called Electro!," he yells at a bank employee, "Nobody keeps J. Jonah Jameson waiting! I want those figures, and I want them now! ... When I give an order, I expect people to hop!!" (Lee, 1964: 6). In "Unmasked by Dr. Octopus!" when Doc Ock has Jameson and Parker pinned to a wall, the publisher's ego trumps his cowardice: "Don't just dangle there, Parker! Tell him who I am!" (Lee, 1964: 6). After the aforementioned second Scorpion battle (*Amazing Spider-Man* 29), he writes, "Jonah Jameson proved himself to be as brave as he is handsome!" because, he says, "I don't believe in false modesty!" ("Or any other kind," thinks Parker) (Lee, 1965: 19).

He is completely self-certain. In the first issue of *Spectacular Spider-Man* magazine, Jameson says of a mayoral candidate: "Facts? What facts? I know all I need to know about the man" (Lee, 1968: 32). Amusingly, retired police Captain George Stacy says of Jameson's judgment, "Since you never question it, perhaps someone should" (Lee, 1968: 27). Jameson also routinely takes credit for the work of others. In response to a suggestion by Parker in "Captured by J. Jonah Jameson!," he says, "It's a good thing I thought of that angle! Another typical Jameson brainstorm!" (Lee, 1965: 3). After Foswell (and Spider-Man) crack the Crime-Master case in *Amazing Spider-Man* 26, Jameson tells the men at the Midtown Business Executives Club, "Foswell? He was just a cog in the wheel! I was the master planner! The entire capture of the Crime-Master took place under my personal direction! But my natural modesty prevents me from bragging about it!" (Lee, 1965: 17).

Jameson is also a notorious cheapskate. In "Nothing Can Stop.... The Sandman!," when

Parker doesn't have time to develop film before turning it in, Jameson said he'll "take the cost of developing out of [Parker's] pay!" (Lee, 1963: 19). When a trip with Parker to Florida to track down the Lizard fails in *Amazing Spider-Man* 6, he stiffs Parker on his paycheck and says, "The way I figure it, you owe me for your plane fare down here and half of the hotel bill!" (Lee, 1963: 21). In *Amazing Spider-Man* 88, he tells his son, "nothing's more important than making money, boy! Remember that!" (Lee, 1970: 9). Occasionally Parker asks for financial help for his ailing Aunt May, and Jameson is routinely unsympathetic. "An advance??! Are you kidding?" he says in the fourth issue. "What do you do with money, eat it?? Look — this is a business, not a charity! ... You teen-agers are all alike — you think the world owes you a living!" (Lee, 1963: 9). That sets the pattern, and in ensuing issues readers see Jameson routinely and callously shoot Parker down despite his great need. Jameson is so stingy, it even outweighs his cowardice. When the Vulture tries to rob the *Bugle* payroll in *Amazing Spider-Man* 7, Jameson stalls, negotiates, and begs: "No! No! You can't rob my payroll! You mustn't! It's all I've got! It would put me out of business! ... Have you no conscience? No feelings? Y-you're as bad as Spider-Man! ... I've spent years building up this business ... it means everything to me! You can't.... Look — maybe we can make a deal? I can give you publicity..." Parker thinks, "Jameson is such a skinflint, he'd probably rather get shot than part with his dough!" (Lee, 1963:13). He routinely takes financial advantage of Parker, but feels fully justified in doing so. "I'm robbing him!" he thinks in "The Man Called Electro!." "I'll make a fortune with his pictures! But I deserve it — 'cause he's a fool!" (Lee, 1964: 8). Again, this was the start of a pattern.

His behavior is particularly egregious given that Jameson is under no illusions about how good Parker is. In the second issue of *Amazing Spider-Man*, when Parker first begins selling photos to Jameson, the publisher says, "Tell me, Parker, are you a magician? How does a teen-ager like you manage to get pictures that our best staff photogs would give their eyeteeth for?" (Lee, 1963: 14). More grudging compliments follow in *Amazing Spider-Man* 3 (July 1963), *Amazing Spider-Man* 11 (April 1964), and *Amazing Spider-Man* 13, once again establishing a pattern. Later, in "The Birth of a Super Hero!" Jameson reminds a reporter that, while the *Bugle* has plenty of other photographers, "none are as good as that lazy lowlife" Parker (Lee, 1966: 2). Jameson values Parker so much that he sends the freelancer on numerous out-of-town trips that would normally be the province of staff photographers. As noted, he takes Parker to Florida to search for the Lizard as early as the sixth issue. He sends Parker to the filming of Spider-Man movies in New Mexico (*Amazing Spider-Man* 14, July 1964) and in Los Angeles (*Amazing Spider-Man Annual* 4). He also takes Parker to the "Savage Land" under Antarctica where dinosaurs dwell (*Amazing Spider-Man* 103), and sends him to Canada to photograph the Hulk (*Amazing Spider-Man* 119).

Despite Parker's value, Jameson remains routinely abusive to him. "Out, Parker!" Jameson barks in "Unmasked by Dr. Octopus!," when Parker comes by to pick up secretary Betty Brant for a date. "This is an office, not a social club! You can come in here whenever you have a set of exclusive news photos for me, and not before! Now get!" (Lee, 1964: 2). This is a representative greeting from Jameson, who reminds Parker in other issues that he doesn't keep him around for his "looks" (Lee, 1964: 12, *Amazing Spider-Man* 10) or his "personality" (Lee, 1964: 6, *Amazing Spider-Man* 16). He routinely reminds Parker of other things the newsroom is not: "This is an office, not an arena!" (Lee, 1965: 6, *Amazing Spider-Man* 25). It is also not "a campus hang-out" (Lee, 1966: 14, *Amazing Spider-Man* 39), a "lonely hearts club" (Lee, 1965: 5, *Amazing Spider-Man* 23) or a "hangout for loafers!" (Lee, 1967: 10, *Amazing Spider-Man* 51). If nothing else, he is consistent when bawling out subordinates.

Jameson hates Parker in those early days, Lee said in *Excelsior*, because Parker is "a teenager, and to Jolly Jonah all teenagers were useless, good-for-nothing, long-haired hippies. The fact that Parker had short hair cut no ice with the intractable Mr. Jameson" (Lee and Mair, 2002: 136). In fact, Jameson says in *Amazing Spider-Man* 95, "Next to Spider-Man, I hate loud-mouthed students the most. I even hate 'em when they're quiet" (Lee, 1971: 3). But Jameson is "an equal-opportunity hater," according to *Excelsior* (Lee and Mair, 2002: 136), and treats all of his staff poorly. "Can't anyone think for himself here?" he shouts in *Amazing Spider-Man* 19, "am I surrounded by incompetents?" (Lee, 1964: 4). Coffee breaks were a favored target, such as in *Amazing Spider-Man* 45 and *Amazing Spider-Man* 47.

The sentiment is surely returned by staffers. "I quit! Nobody could work for a tyrant like you!" says a fill-in employee in *Amazing Spider-Man* 12, "you don't need a secretary, you need a psychiatrist!" (Lee, 1964: 2). Two years later, Jameson has to go through other temporary secretaries, with similar results. "Holy smoke!" thinks Parker in *Amazing Spider-Man* 38, "has old Jameson got another new secretary? She must be the third this week! And today's only Tuesday!" Said the secretary in question: "I quit! I won't work for that old skinflint another second! ... No wonder he can't keep a secretary! A man with a temper like his ought to be in a cage!" (Lee, 1966: 3). When Jameson gloats over one particular victory in *Amazing Spider-Man* 18, one reporter thinks, "Jameson's liable to crack his face wide open with that phony smile of his!" Another thinks, "He reminds me of a tiger who's just made a kill!" (Lee, 1964: 7). Brant thinks of him as "nasty" (Lee, 1965: 19, *Amazing Spider-Man* 22) and an "old hypocrite" (Lee, 1965: 14, *Amazing Spider-Man* 31). Parker thinks of him as an "old phony" (Lee, 1965: 5, *Amazing Spider-Man* 23) who is "selfish — stingy — and hot-tempered! He's jealous of Spider-Man — and of anyone who's more glamorous than he is!" (Lee, 1964: 13, *Amazing Spider-Man* 10).

Perhaps the character who puts it best is George Stacy, father of Parker's erstwhile girlfriend Gwen, who says in *Amazing Spider-Man* 42: "I've known men like Jonah Jameson before! Iron-willed, vain, and unwilling to ever change their minds!" (Lee, 1968: 4). Or maybe we should credit the Tarzan-like Ka-Zar, who says in *Amazing Spider-Man* 57, "The man Jameson reminds me of a human jackal!" (Lee, 1968: 10).

And Lo! There Shall Come a Hero!

Lee said in the Introduction to a collection reprinting *Amazing Spider-Man* 11–20, however, that Jameson is not a villain, but simply a "perfect foil" for Spider-Man. "JJJ has come to represent the most conservative, strait-laced members of society, the self-righteous know-it-alls who dislike and distrust anyone who looks, acts, or thinks differently than they do," he said. "He just marches to the beat of a different drummer. Just like Captain Queeg in *The Caine Mutiny*, Jonah and his ilk are part of the fabric of America. We may not want to party with them, but life would surely be a whole lot duller if they weren't around" (Lee, 1988).

Lee elaborated on those assertions in the book *Stan Lee Conversations*: "He's very reactionary, he thought the last good times we had in America were when Herbert Hoover was president, he hates teenagers, he hated hippies, he hated long hair, he hated guitars. I thought it would be funny to get a guy like that and show he isn't really a villain" (Pitts, 2007: 97). It is politics, Lee argues, not villainy. "He's not a bad guy. He just represents that segment of society that is very arch conservative" (Pitts, 2007: 97).

Some would even argue that there is heart buried somewhere beneath all that greed, self-absorption, and vanity. For example, he is noted in New York for philanthropy, although, to be fair, it often comes with strings attached. In "The Clown and His Masters of Menace!" (March 1965), he sponsors an art exhibit, saying "I believe it's my civic duty to bring art appreciation to the masses! I love nothing better than helping my fellow man!"—although he thinks, "And if I can make a nice, healthy profit as well, it doesn't exactly break my heart, either!" (Lee, 1965: 5). And he co-signs for Parker's motorcycle in *Amazing Spider-Man* 41, which could be interpreted as generous, though his thought balloon reads, "If he has a debt to pay off, he'd have to sell me more pictures—and I can buy 'em cheaper than ever from him" (Lee, 1966: 2).

These examples may be taken at face value as proof Jameson cynically plays the part of the philanthropist, or the decent boss, solely for his own advantage. One could also argue, however, that in both cases he was actually being generous, but must excuse his own "weakness" with rationalizations. He re-hires crime reporter Frederick Foswell, for example, after Foswell is released on parole in 1965 after his arrest for being The Big Man in 1964. Sometimes he explains this cynically. In *Amazing Spider-Man* 23 he regards this act of charity as "good for my public relations! It'll build up my image as a loveable do-gooder!" (Lee, 1965: 5). In *Amazing Spider-Man* 26 he explains to his colleagues at the Executives Club that he re-hired Foswell because he "works like a dog!" (Lee, 1965: 8). But at other times this generosity seems genuine. For example, in "The Goblin and the Gangsters" (April 1965) he compliments Foswell on exposing a crime ring for no obvious reason aside from encouraging an employee. And when Spider-Man accuses the crime reporter of secretly being the Crime-Master or the Green Goblin in *Amazing Spider-Man* 27, Foswell appeals to Jameson: "Look, do I haveta answer questions from him, Mister Jameson?" "Of course not!" Jameson roars in defense. "Now get back to work—I trust you!" (Lee, 1965: 12).

Jameson can be charming, especially to old ladies. While the students at Midtown High razz the speech he gives at Parker's graduation in *Amazing Spider-Man* 28, he impresses Parker's elderly Aunt May and her equally elderly friend, Anna Watson. "Such a charming, sincere, warm-hearted man!" enthuses Aunt May. "To know him must be to love him!" (Lee, 1965: 20). Some of the members of Jameson's Executives Club believe him to be "mighty generous" for re-hiring Foswell (Lee, 1965: 6, *Amazing Spider-Man* 23). His philanthropy goes over well with elderly rich women, too, like the one at the art exhibit who exclaims in *Amazing Spider-Man* 22, "You dear man! To be so successful and have such taste in art, too! How I admire you!" (Lee, 1965: 5).

Surprisingly for a character Lee describes as conservative, Jameson has a liberal attitude toward race relations. For example, Jameson defends a black window washer from his racist white supervisor in the *Bugle* building in *Amazing Spider-Man* 78, complaining about "the smell" of the bigot's presence (Lee, 1969: 14). In *Amazing Spider-Man* 92 (January 1971), he drops support for mayoral candidate Sam Bullit when Robertson's investigation shows funding from hate groups. When the candidate calls the black Robertson "Sambo," Jameson throws him out of his office: "Get out, Bullit! You're turning my stomach!" (Lee, 1971: 9). In *Amazing Spider-Man* 105, Jameson tells civil rights marchers in front of his building, "The *Bugle's* been fighting for civil rights since before you were born!" (Lee, 1972, 4).

As further proof, there is the very existence of Robertson, who became Jameson's second-in-command in 1967. "As a counterpoint to Jameson, I created the character of Robbie Robertson, the clear-thinking, impartial, black editor of the *Daily Bugle*," Lee explained in *Excelsior* (Lee and Mair, 2002: 137). His role appears to be that of Jiminy Cricket, fearlessly correcting Jameson's unethical and irrational impulses. It's strange that Jameson would tolerate that, given what we know of his ego; stranger still, Robertson is African-American. The fact that a cranky, old, white conservative like Jameson respects anyone enough to let that person correct him — let alone a black man in 1967 — says a lot about the *Bugle* editor's character. As Robertson tells his son Randy in *Amazing Spider-Man* 73, "Jameson is no more a racist than Little Eva!" (Lee, 1969: 14).

Jameson can also be an impressive newspaperman, when the topic is not costumed vigilantes. In *Amazing Spider-Man* 9, he swings into action when news breaks: "Stop the presses! Prepare to reprint Page One! Send all department heads in here on the double! We're going to put out an extra!" (Lee, 1964: 22). This is just one occasion among many where readers see Jameson shout "Stop the presses!" and efficiently wield the machinery of a big newspaper.

Jameson is depicted as very hands-on in the war against crime, with early issues showing the *Bugle* in pursuit of the Cat, the Master Planner, Crime-Master, and the Green Goblin. In 1967 Jameson goes after a new underworld mastermind so effectively that The Kingpin moves to have him silenced. But when The Kingpin orders Jameson in *Amazing Spider-Man* 51 to "stop steaming up the public about the so-called crime wave in the city!" the publisher's cowardice is superseded by his pride: "In a pig's eye! Nobody tells me what to write in my paper!" Even The Kingpin is impressed: "Excellent! Spoken like the true crusader that you are! I applaud your obvious courage ... but alas ... you will not live to regret it!" (Lee, 1967: 9). Of course, he does — thanks to Spider-Man's interference, which Jameson couldn't have expected when he defied the most dangerous man in the city.

Jameson shows an ethical side when he is blackmailed by a super-villain named the Hobgoblin for funding the creation of the Scorpion — and resigns. "I love this newspaper," he tells a flabbergasted Web-Spinner in *Amazing Spider-Man* 251. "I won't see its journalistic integrity questioned because of my mistake — so I'm stepping down as editor-in-chief!" (Stern, 1984: 16). It isn't long before the status quo is restored, but Jameson's act is nonetheless surprisingly noble. On another occasion, Jameson gives an impressive motivational speech to reporter Ben Urich when an agent of The Kingpin breaks the fingers on Urich's right hand and frightens him off a story. "Listen, Urich, there are things that just don't happen in this racket," he says gruffly in *Daredevil* 230. "Number one is you never get scared away from a story. Not while you've got the most powerful weapon in the world on your side." Brandishing a newspaper, Jameson continues: "This is five million readers' worth of power. It can destroy presidents. And it's been due to get aimed at The Kingpin for years now. But it takes you to do it" (Miller, 1985: 10).

In *The Pulse* 2, a new reporter describes Jameson as a lion rampant in the newsroom. "He's got his sleeves rolled up and ink all over his shirt and he's running around in everyone's face," she says in wonder, "rewriting copy, setting headlines, dictating assignments, enforcing policy ... he's everywhere!" (Bendis: 2004: 4). In that same story, Jameson shows flexibility by introducing a supplement on the superheroes he hates to increase circulation "before we all bleed to death here" (Bendis, 2004: 12). When one of his reporters is killed in *The Pulse* 3, Jameson heroically marshals the paper's resources to find the killer. And when Urich discovers that Norman Osborn is the probable murderer, Jameson decides to pursue the story — even though Osborn once nearly sued the paper out of business when the *Bugle* (correctly) identified him as the mass-murdering Green Goblin, and this new story would likely be called a vendetta.

Currently, the *Daily Bugle* is owned by a man named Dexter Bennett, who has since turned it into a tabloid called *The DB!*—complete with exclamation point — filled with sensationalized, gossipy content. Bennett pulls a boardroom coup to get majority ownership of the *Bugle* when Jameson is in the hospital after a heart attack, unable to mount a defense. But

Jameson is admired enough in New York that he wins a special election for mayor when the occupant resigns in *Amazing Spider-Man* 591. Of course, this being comic books, it is likely the status quo, with Jameson at the head of a reconstituted *Bugle*, will someday return. In the meantime, though, Jameson is revealed in *World War Hulk: Front Line* 6 to be secretly bankrolling the *Front Line*, a newspaper founded by two reporters (one of them Urich) with the intention of maintaining high ethics — another example of Jameson's dedication to good journalism (Jenkins, 2007).

Portrait of the Newsman as a Middle-Aged Crank

So who is J. Jonah Jameson? I think it's safe to say: "He's a jerk." Despite Jameson's virtuous qualities, they are far outnumbered by his negative ones. While we can nod in approval at his occasional foray into generosity, bravery, or professionalism, those moments are far outweighed by the decades of misery through which he's unfairly put Peter Parker — in both of his identities. Or the browbeating he delivers to his staff on a daily basis. Or, really, the abuse he heaps on anyone with whom he comes in contact. "I hate to sound disloyal," says secretary Betty Brant in *Amazing Spider-Man* 83, "but nobody ever leaves Mr. Jameson's office with a smile."

In criminal cases, however, intent is often an important part of the indictment. And Jameson, despite the occasional moment of self-revelation, firmly believes himself to be the hero of the story. When robot-builder Spencer Smythe returns in "To Kill a Spider-Man!" to "slay the Web-Slinger without mercy," Jameson replies, "now wait a minute! Nobody's talking about murdering him! I just want him captured, see! I want him behind bars ... forever!" (Lee, 1968: 8). It is evident here, in his earlier conversation with Kraven, and in dozens of other examples, that Jameson deludes himself into thinking his vendetta is somehow heroic. For example, when offering the Lord of the Savage Land $10,000 to capture Spider-Man in "The Coming of Ka-Zar!," he says, possibly sincerely, "you'd be ridding the world of a dangerous, deadly menace" (Lee, 1968: 7). This is the same rhetoric he uses in regard to deadly, criminal sociopaths like The Kingpin and the Green Goblin — and, in Jameson's mind, Spider-Man may be much the same.

So for all of his shortcomings — and, yea, verily, they are legion — Jameson is on occasion the heroic, civic-minded, crusading editor he thinks he is. That contradictory behavior makes it impossible to label him neatly as hero or villain, black hat or white hat, despite the title of this essay. Fortunately, real life does not often present such Manichean choices, and in trying to reflect life, neither does Stan Lee. "It should be abundantly clear that I've always tried to make our characters as realistic as possible," Lee said in *Excelsior*, "given the fact that they were living in a world of fantasy" (Lee and Mair, 2002: 137). And the result of his efforts is characters in shades of gray, who are neither all hero nor all villain. That makes multidimensional characters like Jameson interesting — far more so than if he were simply one thing or another. Which perhaps explains why a character that started out as a throwaway ended up being a critical — and successful — part of the Spider-Man franchise. Regardless of what we think of J. Jonah Jameson, he will likely be with us as long as the Wall-Crawler is. For, as Lee said in the Introduction to *Marvel Masterworks Vol. 16* (1991), "Spidey without Jonah would be like rock without roll!"

Works Cited

Bell, Blake. *Strange and Stranger: The World of Steve Ditko.* Seattle, WA: Fantagraphics, 2008.
Bendis, Brian Michael, Mark Bagley, Scott Hanna, et al. *The Pulse 2.* New York: Marvel (May 2004).
_____, Mark Bagley, Scott Hanna, et al. *The Pulse 3.* New York: Marvel (July 2004).
Conway, Gerry, John Romita, Tony Mortellaro, et al. *Amazing Spider-Man 119.* New York: Marvel (April 1973).
Jenkins, Paul, Ramon Bachs, Matt Milla, et al. *World War Hulk: Front Line 6.* New York: Marvel (December 2007).
Lee, Stan, George Mair. *Excelsior: The Amazing Life of Stan Lee.* New York: Fireside, 2002.
_____, Gil Kane, Frank Giacoia, et al. *Amazing Spider-Man 105.* New York: Marvel (February 1972).
_____, Gil Kane, John Romita, et al. *Amazing Spider-Man 92.* New York: Marvel (January 1971).
_____, "Introduction." *Marvel Masterworks Vol. 5: The Amazing Spider-Man Nos. 11–20.* New York: Marvel Comics, 1988.
_____, "Introduction." *Marvel Masterworks Vol. 16: The Amazing Spider-Man Nos. 31–40 and Annual No. 2.* New York: Marvel Comics, 1991.
_____, John Buscema, Jim Mooney, et al. *Amazing Spider-Man 78.* New York: Marvel (November 1969).
_____, John Buscema, John Romita, et al. *Amazing Spider-Man 73.* New York: Marvel (June 1969).
_____, John Romita, Don Heck, et al. *Amazing Spider-Man 57.* New York: Marvel (February 1968).
_____, John Romita, Don Heck, et al. *Amazing Spider-Man 58.* New York: Marvel (March 1968).
_____, John Romita, Don Heck, et al. *Amazing Spider-Man 66.* New York: Marvel (November 1968).
_____, John Romita, Jim Mooney, et al. *Amazing Spider-Man 82.* New York: Marvel (March 1970).
_____, John Romita, Jim Mooney, et al. *Amazing Spider-Man 88.* New York: Marvel (September 1970).
_____, John Romita, Jim Mooney, et al. *The Spectacular Spider-Man 1.* New York: Marvel (July 1968).
_____, John Romita, John Buscema, et al. *Amazing Spider-Man 83.* New York: Marvel (April 1970).
_____, John Romita, Mickey Demeo, et al. *Amazing Spider-Man 39.* New York: Marvel (August 1966).
_____, John Romita, Mickey Demeo, et al. *Amazing Spider-Man 41.* New York: Marvel (October 1966).
_____, John Romita, Mickey Demeo, et al. *Amazing Spider-Man 50.* New York: Marvel (July 1967).
_____, John Romita, Mickey Demeo, et al. *Amazing Spider-Man 51.* New York: Marvel (August 1967).
_____, John Romita, Mickey Demeo, et al. *Amazing Spider-Man 52.* New York: Marvel (September 1967).
_____, John Romita, Sal Buscema, et al. *Amazing Spider-Man 95.* New York: Marvel (April 1971).
_____, John Romita, Sam Rosen, et al. *Amazing Spider-Man 42.* New York: Marvel (November 1966).
_____, John Romita, Sam Rosen, et al. *Amazing Spider-Man 45.* New York: Marvel (February 1967).
_____, John Romita, Sam Rosen, et al. *Amazing Spider-Man 47.* New York: Marvel (April 1967).
_____, Larry Lieber, Mickey Demeo, et al. *Amazing Spider-Man Annual 4.* New York: Marvel (Summer 1967).
_____, Steve Ditko, et al. *Amazing Spider-Man 4.* New York: Marvel (September 1963).
_____, Steve Ditko, Art Simek, et al. *Amazing Spider-Man 6.* New York: Marvel (November 1963).
_____, Steve Ditko, Art Simek, et al. *Amazing Spider-Man 7.* New York: Marvel (December 1963).
_____, Steve Ditko, Art Simek, et al. *Amazing Spider-Man 9.* New York: Marvel (February 1964).
_____, Steve Ditko, Art Simek, et al. *Amazing Spider-Man 12.* New York: Marvel (May 1964).
_____, Steve Ditko, Art Simek, et al. *Amazing Spider-Man 13.* New York: Marvel (June 1964).
_____, Steve Ditko, Art Simek, et al. *Amazing Spider-Man 14.* New York: Marvel (July 1964).
_____, Steve Ditko, Art Simek, et al. *Amazing Spider-Man 15.* New York: Marvel (August 1964).
_____, Steve Ditko, Art Simek, et al. *Amazing Spider-Man 22.* New York: Marvel (March 1965).
_____, Steve Ditko, Art Simek, et al. *Amazing Spider-Man 23.* New York: Marvel (April 1965).
_____, Steve Ditko, Art Simek, et al. *Amazing Spider-Man 27.* New York: Marvel (August 1965).
_____, Steve Ditko, Art Simek, et al. *Amazing Spider-Man 38.* New York: Marvel (July 1966).
_____, Steve Ditko, John Duffy, et al. *Amazing Spider-Man 2.* New York: Marvel (May 1963).
_____, Steve Ditko, John Duffy, et al. *Amazing Spider-Man 3.* New York: Marvel (July 1963).
_____, Steve Ditko, Johnny Dee, et al. *Amazing Spider-Man 1.* New York: Marvel (March 1963).
_____, Steve Ditko, Sam Rosen, et al. *Amazing Spider-Man 5.* New York: Marvel (October 1963).
_____, Steve Ditko, Sam Rosen, et al. *Amazing Spider-Man 10.* New York: Marvel (March 1964).
_____, Steve Ditko, Sam Rosen, et al. *Amazing Spider-Man 11.* New York: Marvel (April 1964).
_____, Steve Ditko, Sam Rosen, et al. *Amazing Spider-Man 16.* New York: Marvel (September 1964).
_____, Steve Ditko, Sam Rosen, et al. *Amazing Spider-Man 18.* New York: Marvel (November 1964).
_____, Steve Ditko, Sam Rosen, et al. *Amazing Spider-Man 19.* New York: Marvel (December 1964).
_____, Steve Ditko, Sam Rosen, et al. *Amazing Spider-Man 20.* New York: Marvel. (January 1965).
_____, Steve Ditko, Sam Rosen, et al. *Amazing Spider-Man 25.* New York: Marvel (June 1965).

———, Steve Ditko, Sam Rosen, et al. *Amazing Spider-Man 24*. New York: Marvel (May 1965).
———, Steve Ditko, Sam Rosen, et al. *Amazing Spider-Man 26*. New York: Marvel (July 1965).
———, Steve Ditko, Sam Rosen, et al. *Amazing Spider-Man 28*. New York: Marvel (September 1965).
———, Steve Ditko, Sam Rosen, et al. *Amazing Spider-Man 29*. New York: Marvel (October 1965).
———, Steve Ditko, Sam Rosen, et al. *Amazing Spider-Man 31*. New York: Marvel, (December 1965).
———, Steve Ditko, Sam Rosen, et al. *Amazing Spider-Man 34*. New York: Marvel (March 1966).
Miller, Frank, David Mazzucchelli, Max Scheele, et al. *Daredevil 230*. New York: Marvel (May 1985).
Pitts, Leonard, Jr. "An Interview with Stan Lee." *Stan Lee Conversations*. Jeff McLaughlin ed. Jackson, MS: University of Mississippi Press, 2007.
Slott, Dan, Barry Kitson, Jesse Delperdang, et al. *Amazing Spider-Man 591*. New York: Marvel (June 2009).
Society of Professional Journalists. "SPJ Code of Ethics." Accessed 6/26/2010. http://www.spj.org/ethicscode.asp.
Stern, Roger, Tom DeFalco, Ron Frenz, et al. *Amazing Spider-Man 251*. New York: Marvel (April 1984).
Thomas, Roy, Gil Kane, Frank Giacoia, et al. *Amazing Spider-Man 103*. New York: Marvel (December 1971).
Wein, Lein, Bill Mantlo, Gil Kane, et al. *Amazing Spider-Man Annual 10*. New York: Marvel (Summer 1976).

Spider-Management: A Critical Examination of the Business World of Spider-Man

MATTHEW MCGOWAN *and* JEREMY SHORT

One of the most intriguing elements of the comic narrative is that of the context in which these epic tales take place. Considering the dynamic, outlandish, and often unbelievable qualities of many of the heroes and villains of these tales, it is perhaps surprising that the settings in which many of the most famous comic icons such as Batman, Superman, and — the subject of our essay — Spider-Man, operate are not far away mythical galaxies, but large cities and major metropolitan areas (Ahrens and Meteling, 2010; Flanagan, this volume).

We approach this essay by exploring the world of the famous Webslinger through our own vocational backgrounds and biases. Specifically, one of us is a working newspaper reporter — familiar with the daily routine often glamorized and sensationalized by the work and antics of Peter Parker (aka Spider-Man). The other author is a professor of management, who studies applied psychology, organizational behavior, and decision processes in an attempt to better understand how and why individuals act in certain ways within their workplace environments. Together, we hope our backgrounds allow us to provide a unique lens to examine the working world in which Spider-Man interacts.

To provide a framework for examining the workplace environment in Spider-Man, we organize our thoughts based on the key elements that encompass the field of management. Specifically, these elements — common to most management textbooks — involve planning, organizing, leading, and controlling (e.g., Carpenter, Bauer, and Erdogan, 2009). Application of all of these management processes can be found in the adventures of Spider-Man. Consequently, we use these general concepts to provide a critical perspective on the similarities and differences between the workplace environment found in Spider-Man, and the realities of the modern workplace — especially with regard to the newspaper publishing industry.

Planning at *The Daily Bugle*

The publishing world surrounding Peter Parker bears some resemblance to its real-world counterpart. Many of his experiences in the comics hew to the broader professional and ethical context of today's press. Parker often works under time pressures to meet deadlines, and as a freelance worker lacks the financial security to plan his future far in advance.

Particularly instructive in understanding the business world of Spidey are the actions and motivations of J. Jonah Jameson, editor and publisher of *The Daily Bugle* and Parker's boss. Jameson has played a central role in Spider-Man's universe since the superhero's beginnings in the 1960s, when Parker took his first gig as a freelance photographer at the newspaper. This inveterate newsman has been portrayed as a slave driver, a staunch critic of Spider-Man and, at least in a more recent edition, a beacon of journalistic integrity. He's been both villain and unlikely ally to Spider-Man. But most would probably recognize him from one simple phrase: "Get me more photos of Spider-Man."

Jameson bellows at Parker every time the teenager's alter ego makes headlines. Here is a fiercely competitive editor desperate for exclusive and "sensational" content for his beloved *Bugle*. Who can blame him? He's a businessman, and Spider-Man sells. Out here in the more mundane real world, so do teen starlets, accused criminals and political scandals. Any of these things pop up on any given news day, and it's not long before an editor like Jameson steps in and starts assigning stories.

How often do these drop-what-you're-doing stories spring up? The answer to this question depends on the size and location of the paper. But, for most mid-sized dailies scattered across the country, these sorts of events occur maybe a few times a week, so it's not as if the average newsroom revolves around individuals like Jameson demanding a particular scoop. Most of the stories readers see in their newspapers each morning have been scheduled days, weeks or even months in advance. Crime stories, which occur without warning, make for one notable exception, though even crime beat writers have longer-term projects such as evaluating crime trends or in-depth features about, say, a local community struggling to secure itself from a vandalizing troop of bored teenagers.

The process for these lengthier projects most often begins with beat reporters who stumble upon a story idea and then pitch it to their immediate editor. These aren't the Jamesons of the world who call for Spider-Man's capture or insist he steps in to catch the crook *du jour*. No, these section editors are the folks in the background, choreographing a story's coverage from a coffee-stained desk with no bylines and no glory. Unless it is a particularly small daily paper, these mid-level editors oversee particular sections like metro, features or entertainment. Usually reporters don't bring the story directly to the paper's editor in chief, and almost never to the paper's publisher, who is more focused on the broader picture.

Once cleared by a section editor, the reporter decides how long it will take to get a particular piece together. Timeliness certainly plays a factor here. For instance, if a particular holiday or some other community event looms on the calendar, the story will appear on the budget on or before that particular occasion. Other stories are "evergreen," to use newsroom parlance, meaning they can go to print at just about any time of year.

When something more unexpected occurs, like a bank robbery, the immediate impact of the news takes precedence, and a team of editors makes room for the breaking news stories during their twice-daily meetings about the next day's issue. The formula makes sense for obvious reasons. Who wants to read initial reports of an event a month later? Plus, in today's news business defined by the immediacy of the Internet, competition reigns.

Jameson may tell Parker, "Get me photos of Spider-Man," but a real news editor is more likely to tell a photographer to get out to the scene and get some "art" before turning to a reporter and saying, "And get me a few (para)graphs online." Never let the other guy's online time stamp precede yours. The financial decline of many American newspapers serves as a stark reminder of how much the Information Age has redefined the concept of "timely." By the time readers see a story in their morning paper, chances are they've already read all about it on their smart phone or laptop.

Paper and ink? No. Today's readers are increasingly seeking their news online, so the medium has changed. The core mission, however, has stood the test of time and technology. Newspapers still serve a pivotal role in depth and analysis, which takes time to compile and effectively disseminate.

Peter Parker, of course, began his freelance career during the newspaper's Golden Age in the mid–20th century, when newsrooms were smoke-filled and frantic in advance of tomorrow's edition. Today they're smokeless, downsized and digital in advance of now's edition. A modern Jameson might hustle up to a reporter and say, "We've been told Spider-Man is chasing down Doc Octopus downtown. Call Parker's cell phone and tell him to get over there. Also, get me something online immediately. Call your guy over at metro police and see if we can get a copy of the police report to supplement tomorrow's Web package. Oh, and when you get to the scene, bring a point-and-shoot digital camera in case a photographer takes too long. Make sure you get something up today on the Daily Bugle's Twitter and Facebook feeds, too."

Despite notable deviations from reality offered in the day-to-day workings of *The Daily Bugle*, it does seem that Jameson does practice in a planning technique known as SMART goal-setting (Drucker, 1954). This idea of this managerial tool is that the most effective goals are specific, measurable, aggressive, realistic, and timely. When viewed in light of these metrics, the call to procure Spider-Man pictures is not so far from the coverage requested by so many editors that help bring to life newspapers across the country.

Organizing the Ideal Job

J. Jonah Jameson would fit right in as a television news pundit. He's an opinionated sensationalist who never hesitates to speak up about what he insists is the best thing for the local or national community. This is exactly the sort of turgid character one might find on MSNBC or Fox News, finger-pointing and foaming at the mouth alongside Keith Olbermann, Bill O'Reilly or, especially, Nancy Grace.

Strangely enough, he doesn't quite fit the newspaper mold. Sure, newspaper editors and publishers regularly write editorials endorsing this or chastising that, but not many American newspapers today would run a headline on the top of its front page — a "power head" or "banner"— that reads "This Newspaper Demands That Spider-Man (or Bernie Madoff, or Osama bin Laden, etc.) be Arrested and Prosecuted!" A columnist, publisher or editor may say so in the editorial section within the paper, but the front page is typically reserved for the harder, more objective news pieces. Jameson's one-sided McCarthy-esque pillorying in the Spider-Man comics takes the punditry game to a level that one might find on cable news. Such tactics don't appear in the average American newspaper — at least not yet.

In one way, Jameson's job is made easy due to the characteristics endemic to most journalists. In the 1970s, an ideal job characteristics model was developed with the hope of increasing the motivational properties of specific vocations (Hackman and Oldham, 1975). In this model, jobs that are higher in skill variety (the ability to do lots of different things in contrast to a single monotonous task), task identity (the ability to see how individual input contributes to a final good or service), task significance (the ability to see that your work is important to others), autonomy (the freedom to decide how to complete your task), and feedback (you receive information regarding the quality of your work so that you can improve over time) lead to healthier psychological states and desirable work outcomes such as increased motivation, higher job satisfaction and performance, and lower levels of absenteeism and turnover. While the job of Spider-Man encompasses all of these characteristics, the job of a reporter (and freelance photographer) also scores high on a number of these dimensions.

Leading by (Bad?) Example

Such tactics by Jameson also bode poorly for other facets of a newsroom's organization because they suggest a sort of unilateral, iron-fisted approach to publishing. Any editor who routinely puts his own personal opinions on the front page — above and before all of the hard-sought, objective pieces written by a staff of journalists — may soon find a newsroom in mutiny.

Reporters tend to be deeply skeptical, independent, and highly ideological folks with their own reputations at stake. Also, they're not afraid to speak their mind. Unlike a worker's production in other industries, reporters' widely distributed works are tied directly to their names. Their names are written in bold lettering above their pieces and in association with the publication. They have a stake in the perception of the paper, because its reputation is, by affiliation, their reputation.

Given these dynamics of the newspaper industry, it is perhaps not surprising that Jameson's leadership style is best described in management as KITA (Kick In The Ass). Despite the enduring popularity of this style, Frederick Herzberg's (1959) classic book, *The Motivation to Work*, would suggest that Jameson's style leads much to be desired as KITA factors (company policy, managerial supervision, salary, work conditions, relationship with boss) are only effective in terms of creating dissatisfaction with a particular job. In contrast, the potential for achievement, recognition, and increased responsibility are much greater motivators. If his goal is to more effectively manage his workforce at *The Daily Bugle*, Jameson might consider, assuming his relationship with Parker is characteristics of his general style, increasing his carrot to stick ratio.

Controlling Your Employees

The final core element associated with management relates to control aspects that ensure that performance is held to a standard, and that corrective action is taken when necessary. The ethical onus, however, is not solely on publishers like Jameson. Reporters and photographers must maintain a high standard of practice. There's a saying in the news world: "If you're mother tells you she loves you, get a second source to confirm it." Accuracy and authenticity are the backbone of all good journalism. At stake, beyond the obvious legal repercussions accompanying libel, is the public's trust in the paper and its individual reporters.

Peter Parker learned this firsthand recently when he came under fire for a redemptive photo he submitted to the *Front Line* newspaper. The photo made headlines. The only problem was that Parker used photo-editing software to doctor it. The whole debacle would later cost him his job. The events leading up to Parker's firing unfold in issues *The Amazing Spider-Man 623–624* (both May 2010), after one of Spider-Man's nemeses, the Vulture, escapes from a psychiatric facility and goes on a revenge-fueled rampage through New York City. He seeks those responsible for his condition, which has given him wings, a deranged mental state and a somewhat ghastly superpower to spew acidic vomit at his foes. In other words, he's a hideous, disturbed mutant: not exactly popular with the ladies.

Readers later learn that several New York mafia bosses are responsible for turning a former foot soldier, Jimmy, into the freakish villain. They double-crossed him years earlier and wiped his memory clean before setting him loose on the city as a super-thug. But the Vulture goes rogue and eventually lands in the psychiatric ward, thanks to a little help from Spider-Man. He escapes, of course, and corners a crime boss identified as Francis who was, in fact, one of the men behind his condition. Fearing for his life, Francis declares his innocence and casts blame on Jameson, now the city's mayor. The Vulture takes the bait and swoops off to take out Jameson.

When word leaks to the press, the public cries for Jameson's head on a stake. The caustic former publisher turned mayor now finds himself in a fight for his political survival. Then the Vulture shows up at Jameson's office — where Parker now works — and nearly kills him before Spider-Man swoops in, as usual, to begrudgingly save Jameson. Spider-Man is by no means fond of Jameson, but in typical caped-crusader fashion, he values justice over his personal tiffs. That's when he decides to doctor photos of Jameson fighting the Vulture in his office.

Now, the events depicted in the photo did actually occur, but Parker didn't get the shot. He was, after all, a bit busy saving his boss' life. Parker decides to follow in the footsteps of disgraced New York Times journalist Jayson Blair, who fabricated large chunks of stories before resigning in 2003. The young City Hall staffer uses the Marvel equivalent of Photoshop. This makes for a refreshingly contemporary perspective of the increasingly digital news industry. It also raises the question: Is an altered photo unethical, even if its depictions are largely true? The answer is an unequivocal, absolute and resounding yes.

Misleading a reader in any way is a blatant violation of one of the profession's bedrock ethical standards: Thou shalt not tailor a story or photo to serve the interest of any party, regardless of motive. Or, to use the more official wording from *The Society of Professional Journalists' Code of Ethics*, a short but vital 85-year-old ethical bedrock of American journalism: "Never distort the content of news photos or video. Image enhancement for technical clarity is always permissible. Label montages and photo illustrations." One would have resort to funhouse-mirror logic to paint Parker's actions as anything but distortion.

Perhaps "fabrication" is a better word. Again, the SPJ Code of Ethics (1996) has a clear proscription against that, too, in the very next rule: "Avoid misleading re-enactments or staged news events. If re-enactment is necessary to tell a story, label it."

The photo appears on the May 12, 2010, edition of the fictional *Front Line* newspaper under the headline "The Photo that Saved a Mayor" from *Amazing Spider-Man 624*. Parker's coworkers greet him that morning with thunderous applause. They praised him for saving the administration, and their jobs. A smitten Parker walks into Jameson's office expecting more adulation. Instead, he finds an irate mayor on his way to a press conference. "Press conference?" Parker says. "What are we doing here? Look, Jonah, I don't need a public thank you.... Just renaming a street after me will suffice." Then, to Parker's shock, Jameson shows a redeeming dedication to truth reminiscent of his newsman roots.

"I was a newspaperman," he tells the press. "I devoted my life to truth. But this photo was faked. And I cannot support a lie, not even to save my own skin. Parker's intentions may have been good ... but his ethics are deplorable" (Waid, 2010: np). Then he publicly fires Parker and tells the media to blacklist the young photographer. He's right to do so. If it becomes known a reporter intentionally falsified even the smallest detail in a story or, in this case, a photo, they will almost surely lose their job. Few editors in the United States would not punish such behavior, and that includes Jameson. It's hard to believe this is the same man who, when the series was in its infancy, printed churlish and one-sided columns vilifying Spider-Man on the front page. This shows that although Jameson has never been a poster boy of journalistic integrity, he understands one of the industry's fundamental rules. Perhaps he did it for his own personal reasons. It could certainly be construed as a coy political maneuver, not some highfalutin adherence to ethical standards. But, either way, Jameson's firing of Parker and voluntary disclosure of the photo's falsity puts him back in the driver's seat and reinstates his control of the whole Vulture debacle.

The idea of matching the "fit" of an individual within a particular careers is one of the cornerstones of modern human resource practice. One particular model, known as the ASA framework, argues that firms will have a predictable organizational culture since individuals will tend to be attracted to particular vocations and environments, which will then select others similar to their culture, resulting in attrition from folks who do not fit into group and organizational norms (Schneider, 1987). This framework is valuable for demonstrating why some organizations such as General Electric have been able to establish a culture of excellence in innovation over time through their careful selection of excellent employees. At the same time, this framework also demonstrates the danger when a culture exists where generating outcomes by any means becomes an accepted organizational norm. Unfortunately, Spider-Man's story of falsifying information can be viewed much more as a commentary on the dubious decisions made leading to the current economic crises rather than an outlandish example to which few of us can relate. Overall, it demonstrates that even in the world of Spider-Man there is an explicit knowledge that fudging facts is the work of television and sensational magazines, but not reputable news outlets such as *The Daily Bugle*.

Conclusion

When Stan Lee and Steve Ditko created Spider-Man, one of their key contributions was injecting a relatable teenage character into the comic landscape. With the passage of hundreds of Spider-Man chronicles, we now have hundreds of epic battles between the web slinger and potential evil-doers that have inspired cartoon, television, and big screen sagas for generations. At the same time, we also have a number of more relatable battles between Peter Parker and his struggle to meet deadlines, manage the expectations of superiors, and simply survive in an increasingly competitive economic landscape.

While Parker's nemeses may not always be relatable, his workplace encounters are perhaps too realistic at times. One of the most lasting lines of the Spider-Man saga warns us that "with great power comes great responsibility." While Peter Parker took these words to heart as he heard them from his uncle, they also provide a timely reminder of the abused power harnessed by practicing managers on a daily basis. While few of us will have the strength, world-class speed, or access to superior technology available to Spider-Man, we all have the power to provide inspiration in the workplace. As such, we have even more reason to carefully harness our management "toolkits" for the powers of good, perhaps in spite of so many examples to the contrary in the world of Spider-Man — or the world in which we engage daily.

Works Cited

Ahrens, Jorn, and Aron Meteling. *Comics in the City: Urban Space in Print, Picture, and Space*. New York: The Continuum International Publishing Group Inc., 2010.
Carpenter, Mason, Talya Bauer, T. and Berrin Erdogan. *Principles of Management*. Nyack, NY: Flat World Knowledge, 2009.
Drucker, Peter. *The Practice of Management*. New York: Collins, 1954.
Hackman, J. Richard. and Oldham, Greg. R. "Development of the Job Diagnostic Survey." *Journal of Applied Psychology*, 60 (April 1975): 159–170.
Herzberg, Frederick. *The Motivation to Work*. New York: John Wiley and Sons, 1959.
Schneider, Benjamin. "The People Make the Place." *Personnel Psychology*. 40: 3 (September 1987): 437–453.
Society of Professional Journalists. *SPJ Code of Ethics*. (1996). Accessed 6/30/11. http://www.spj.org/pdf/ethicscode.pdf.
Waid, Mark, Tom Peyer, Paul Azaceta et al., *Amazing Spider-Man 623–624*. New York: Marvel (May 2010).

IV. Spider-Man and Other Sequential Art Characters

Anti-Heroes: Spider-Man and the Punisher

Cord A. Scott

> Punisher: "Jeez! You two wanna get a room?"
> Spider-Man: "What's up honey? You jealous?"
> —*Civil War #6 (2007)*

Two of the most popular characters in the Marvel line-up are Spider-Man and the Punisher. Both exude confidence and terrorize those who would wrong society, and yet both take opposite approaches to justice. But are Spider-Man (created in '62) and the Punisher (created originally as a villain in a Spider-Man story in 1974) really so far apart in their methods and manners? Both were born of their own idealism, even when it may not have been what was popular in society. They both believe in their righteousness towards their cause, albeit through an encroaching cynicism, and have experienced the cold realities of life. That cynicism has also changed their world outlook, and even today, with the offshoots and somewhat unpopular variations, they still have great followings of fans.

This essay looks at how the two characters developed, how they morphed into more nuanced characters, and how they became symbols of a dystopic America that dealt with corruption following the Vietnam War. Both characters have dealt with the loss of their hero/mentor, Captain America. The loss of Cap seemingly solidified both Spidey and Punisher's cynicism toward America, and the corruption of American society, especially in the post 9/11 world. The conflict and friendship of the two has even changed over years to the point that their interaction has become the central point of an apocalyptic form of biological warfare (*The Marvel Universe Vs. The Punisher*, 2010).

To date, there has been very little written comparing the two characters, their relationship, or their significance on the wider aspect of comic book characters in American history. While they have not been used in many combined issues featuring the two simultaneously, they have still been significant as well as popular characters for the Marvel comic book lines. Their actions have also been a reflection of the wider world of American society in the last 37 years.

Origins

Throughout history, the rebel that plays by his own rules has appealed to readers. To be a person who defies convention and does what he feels is right for society is a secret fantasy of many people, especially during times of strife and conflict. When one looks at the history of comic books, the tainted, socially conflicted character that struggles with their inner demons was often the purview of Marvel comics. By the start of the 1960s, comic book readers had gone from pre-teen to adolescence, and while DC superheroes had no real qualms about what was right or wrong, Marvel characters tended to struggle with what they should do versus what was expected. No "superhero" exemplified that struggle more than Spider-Man (Pustz, 1999; Wright, 2000). Spider-Man has been popular since his creation because the character often emulates the emotional aspects of the reader. He, like the reader, has doubts about his abilities and talents; both character and audience may be unpopular and trying to find their feet. The way in which Parker doubts his skills makes him "real" or human for the reader, unlike other heroes like Superman, who seems to exhibit insecurities neither about his duties to humanity nor his ability to see them through.

The character created by Stan Lee and Steve Ditko came in 1962, during the time when Lee wished to either mold characters and stories in ways that he wished or leave the comic book industry altogether. Enter Peter Parker, whose teen issues often mirrored what readers themselves were going through: awkwardness in school, troubles with the opposite sex and the usual attempt to state their independence. What is also important to understand was that Spider-Man came about in the 1962 when people were still enamored with America and its possibilities through a young, vibrant President in John Kennedy. Both the fictional character and the real president were youthful, seemingly well-meaning, and willing to take on the evils around them for the betterment of society. With Kennedy's assassination in November 1963, however, the tide of cynicism crept into the American mindset, and this distrust only grew during the Vietnam War.

As the character was developed in *Amazing Fantasy #15* (Aug. 1962), and then later in the *Amazing Spider-Man*, readers learned that Parker had to deal with the adult pressures of life, even when it was quite unpleasant. By the time readers learned that Peter was in a way responsible for his beloved Uncle Ben's death, he had taken on the mantle of the dutiful relative who must care for his Aunt May. It also paralleled the loss of the President soon after the creation of the series, as JFK was assassinated in the fall of 1963. The death of Uncle Ben served as a driving force for Peter: a way to continue fighting for the legacy of World War II veterans and their sacrifices for the betterment of American society during the Cold War. To that end, the drive for Spider-Man to better society through crime fighting is akin to JFK inspiring Americans to join the Peace Corps or in other ways serve their country. It was in part that spirit of global assistance that spurred the increase of military forces in Vietnam, and subsequently gave rise to the creation of the Punisher. The overall story of Spider-Man was intriguing, and the readers purchased the *Amazing Spider-man*, making it a fresh idea that ultimately saved Marvel.

Therefore it was not entirely surprising that *Amazing Spider-Man* would eventually give rise to another character who often acted in what he felt was the best interests of America. In 1974, in *Amazing Spider-Man #129*, the Punisher character was introduced to the American comic book reader. Created by writer Gerry Conway and artist John Romita, the Punisher has a clarity of purpose (take out any threat to society) that Spider-Man doesn't easily exhibit. Was he a villain or something else? As we learned through the back-story, he suffered a loss as great as Parker: his family was killed in a Mob hit in Central Park. What made the Punisher's introduction significant was that he was created as the U.S. was coming to terms with the end of the Vietnam War. While Spider-Man was not yet cynical towards the realities of the real world, Frank Castle was a Vietnam veteran, and was therefore far more jaundiced towards the "system." He saw men die horrible, seemingly purposeless deaths in a land far from the U.S.

As we shall see, these two characters' stories and mannerisms say much about their creators and about attitudes within American society in the last 40 years. The characters are important enough that their introductory issues now command hundreds (in the case of the Punisher) or tens of thousands of dollars ($50,000 for a mint *Amazing Fantasy #15*), and consistently rank in the top one hundred greatest comic books. The characters continue to spawn new titles, mini-series and are strong sellers. But their appeal to the reader is much deeper.

Both characters are idealists. For Parker, the idealism was instilled by his relatives and the belief that they reared him properly. After the death of his uncle, Peter had to demonstrate a concept of doing what was right — stopping criminals from destroying society and hurting innocent people. It was this drive that became a cornerstone of his mentality and actions. It is interesting to note that in so many of the storylines, Spider-Man could easily use violence to not only capture but maim or even kill those who threaten society, yet he does not. His maturity shows through at a time when many of that age (mid to late teens) would not show such restraint or logic towards taking a life.

Frank Castle came to his idealism through a different manner; his ideal was embodied in the concept of America, specifically through the armed forces. It was a faith and idealism that led him to join the military, especially at a time when many opted to gain deferment from military service in Vietnam. His idealism is further illustrated by the fact that he joined the Marine Corps, which required a 13-month tour of duty in Vietnam, as opposed to a standard tour of 12 months. Castle, in the early stories, even showed a trust that the system would serve justice on the mobsters that killed his family in such a brazen attack. When that didn't happen, he returned to his idealism in his training and purpose. Castle's training and ideology is influenced by the Old Testament notion of "an eye for an eye." In his worldview, the U.S. governmental and judicial systems have been corrupted by bureaucracy and less than honorable people, and his actions are merely streamlining the process of bringing justice to those who truly deserve it. In this regard, he is, much like contemporary cinematic characters such as "Dirty" Harry Callahan and Paul Kersey, acting out on the revenge fantasies that many people have about quickly punishing those who are evil.

Both also show a system of righteousness towards their cause. Spidey could simply step away from the world that seemingly overwhelmed him at times, and go on in life as a student and reporter. Yet his mindset of doing what is needed, as well as a sense of egoism, propels him on when others might have given up. For the Punisher, it is his righteousness, which finally sets in when he starts his assassination of those who bring pain and corruption to the system. Interestingly, even at a time in American history when police departments were seen as perpetuating the old system of inflexibility and corruption, both characters made a point of not harming police, even if it put them in danger.

Finally, both characters display a lack of confidence in the system in general. For Spidey, it's often through his hatred of his boss, managing editor J. Jonah Jameson, who seems to have an Ahab-like goal of bringing Spider-Man to justice for crimes against society. Spidey's cynicism also comes through in the constant quips he offers during the capture of his enemy. It is often a typical teenage way of displaying confidence, especially when one is good at their craft. For the Punisher, cynicism is embodied in his belief that the system of justice simply will not work. Given the conditions under which Castle lived in Vietnam, at a time of actual reports of "fragging" of officers due to general incompetence in the field against the enemy, as well as the observation that the system allows those with money and power to buy their way out of jail (as many mobsters seem to do), it isn't surprising that Castle gained a veneer of cynicism towards the system.

Both characters also relied on their training and background to see them through difficult times, both physically and mentally. For Parker, the strength to become Spider-Man came through analytical skills and the scientific method. His back-story was one of a gifted student in the sciences. This background fit well into the education outlines proposed by President Eisenhower in the 1950s, which stated that America needed to create more scientists to compete with the Soviets. So while Parker was the social outcast in a high school setting, he was inspiring, albeit in a roundabout manner, to the pursuit of science in high school.

The back-story on Castle was far more complex. His school years, aside from a parochial setting, were never established, but it was quite apparent as the Punisher stories developed that he was a gifted tactician with notable skills in warfare. As was illustrated in the Punisher stories in the late 80s and early 90s, Castle had once studied for the priesthood, and it was this moral grounding that tied into his Old Testament concept of punishment for the wicked and evil of society. It was also his training in the U.S. military system that prepared him for combat both in the Jungles of Vietnam and on the mean streets of urban America.

So while the two characters were created 12 years apart, they show a similar nature in their approach to the system. As Robert Peaslee (2006) noted in his look at the "moral economy" of superheroes, both characters exhibit aspects of breaking away from philosopher Max Weber's "iron cage" of bureaucracy. The Punisher goes one step further and not only tries to be pre-emptive in preventing crime, but is also trying to eliminate the bureaucratic aspects of legal manipulation. Both heroic characters are seen by society as a threat (vigilantism), yet are assisted by authority figures; they are, after all, willing to circumvent the system only for the expeditious greater good of "the innocent." Where the differences come in is how they have operated in society over the years. While Spidey has maintained an innocence of sorts, and hasn't been marred by overly negative opinions, the Punisher became a "Dirty Harry"-like character that took on a CIA-style attitude and punished those who opposed American society — or at times external threats to America — as he teamed up with Captain America in the early 1990s.

Methods Alike, Methods Different

Regardless of the origins, the two characters served as foils to one another early on. By 1974, in *Amazing Spider-Man #129*, Peter Parker (and his alter ego Spider-Man) had been well established in his wisecracking, honest element of doing right by the people of New York. It was into this milieu that the Punisher was introduced. Interestingly enough, he was established as a villainous character. He was working in the first issues for a Spidey nemesis called the Jackal.

The Jackal was using the Punisher to propel the agenda of violence against the city, as the vast majority of comic villains do, but the Punisher was acting out against Spidey for his own reasons. Castle felt that Spider-Man was a greater threat within the criminal system than without it. Castle sees Spidey as the worst sort of undisciplined vigilante in America. Castle was presented in the story as a former Marine who served in Vietnam. His personal life and back-story was a microcosm of what Americans were looking at in 1974: urban violence and the breakdown of law and order, either in the cities through urban decay and crime, or by the national distrust of government. This distrust was only amplified by the resignation of Nixon and the revelations of continued government obfuscation concerning U.S. actions around the world. Finally there was the distrust and shame associated with returning Vietnam War veterans. Some Americans felt that these veterans were either drug addled or had "lost" the war due to unpatriotic attitudes. Making Castle a veteran as well as a quasi-villain captured the confusion of the early 1970s in America.

One of the problems with the early Punisher character is that he seems rather emotional and therefore careless on the urban battlefield. This characterization of the Punisher seems quite at odds with the later character that is known for his ruthless, proficient pursuit of all manner of scum. But early on he seems to be a person immersed in an intense grief and easily manipulated by others, in this case an established villain.

Needless to say, despite these character flaws, Gerry Conway had hit (no pun intended) upon a character that was able to do what many people only fantasized: the Punisher could act outside the law to obtain justice for those who had suffered at the hands of evil. It was noted in one of Conway's stories that Parker had also lost the first love of his life, Gwen Stacy, at the hands of a murderer in the *Amazing Spider-Man #121*. But the Punisher shows no sense of remorse in using all manner of fighting to gain victory. While Spidey may beat a criminal, the Punisher saw capture as a chance for the criminal to again work their way out of the legal trap, and eventually roam free. To Castle, the only way to obtain justice was to kill the criminal.

As 1974 unfolded, the political atmosphere in the U.S. soured even further. Nixon resigned in disgrace before he could be formally impeached, and therefore escaped justice. Further frustrating the American populous was the fact that his successor Gerald Ford pardoned Nixon, preventing further prosecution. Again, the American people saw how those with power and influence manipulated the system. This further increased the appeal of a character like the Punisher.

Parker dealt with all manner of criminals throughout the years, and the Punisher character would make guest appearances in the Spider-Man books to help thwart greater villainy while at the same time confounding Spidey's efforts to stop crime. One story arc involved a Latin American assassin/revolutionary called the Tarantula. When various NY transit systems are threatened, specifically a ferry, again the Punisher appears at the wrong time to attempt to kill Spidey. Only after various near misses between the two did the Punisher and Spidey come to realize that they were allies in the same war against criminals (*Amazing Spider-Man #134*).

As the two characters were utilized in additional storylines, the villains became more ethnically or nationally diverse as well. For example, in *Giant Size Spider-Man #4* from April, 1975, Spidey and the Punisher collaborated against private companies who developed and tested bio-chemical weapons on people in South America, which hearkened back to Nazi experiments. It was in the late 1970s that the concentration camp experiments came back into the news due to the reported death of Dr. Joseph Mengele in Brazil. The story took the two heroes to South America where they fought to free American citizens who had been kidnapped and transported to the camp in the Amazon jungle. In the end, the head of the unscrupulous company dies by his own weapon — toxic gas shot by the Punisher while in Spidey's presence. When Spidey asked if the Punisher shot knowing the gas was in the canister, the Punisher didn't answer. This showed that while allies were important, for the Punisher the mission was first and foremost, echoing philosophical differences between the two.

While the appearances of the Punisher were limited in the 1970s, they often tied into some of the more successful Marvel comic book characters. The Punisher was featured in the *Amazing Spider-Man*, *Spectacular Spider-Man*, *Daredevil*, and *Captain America*. While he was a significant fan favorite, he was actually not given his own series until 1986. By that time, Reagan-era policies had driven most to fantasize about punishing evil. While Spider-Man may have kept his wit and sense of humor while fighting evil, Castle unleashed his rage on the enemies of society with limited language but a lot of firepower. His techniques were often far more severe than Spider-Man's, and the results far more permanent: death. While some superheroes (and politicians by extension) may have wanted to rehabilitate criminals or merely capture them, the Punisher embodied the fantasy of doing away with the criminal courts and simply killing those who were not worthy of salvation.

Changes of Character in the Post–9/11 Era

The events of 9/11 precipitated storylines illustrating how comic book characters of every stripe coped with the violence of the attacks. From the interior art of the *Amazing Spider-Man* #36 to the characters that attempted to cope with the destruction, creators and characters alike were afforded outlets for their grief and anger. While the two characters explored in this essay didn't interact directly at this time, they did figure into the aftermath.

The 2003 American invasion of Iraq (Operation Iraqi Freedom) alarmed some, who felt that the true struggle was in Afghanistan. The protests against the war were worldwide and the comic book companies used this as fodder for new stories. One of the most ambitious was the maxi-series *Civil War*. This series of interconnected stories, plus specific *Civil War* titles, split the superhero community as it did American society. The crux of the series concerned the use and regulation of superheroes. If they are not regulated, they may not be stopped in the long run. The two key groups from the series were those who followed Captain America (and felt that the passage of such legislation was a greater risk) and those who followed Iron Man and Reed Richards of the Fantastic Four.

Spidey actually proved to be a pivotal series figure in several ways. Initially, he was in favor of the registration act, and even revealed his identity so that he was seen as an approachable person willing to expose himself. For a while, it worked. He, along with the new Superhero response teams, looked to bring in (or down) any rogue superheroes and super-villains. But as the new society grew in scope, and rogue superheroes were being thrown into gulag-like prisons, Spider-Man had a change of heart. He saw how things were evolving and he didn't like it. After being confronted by Iron Man, Spidey broke away and went rogue himself.

As the story developed, one of the issues of tracking down those who did not wish to register was that super-villains were now incorporated into the Iron-Man agenda. Two villains, the Jester and Jack-O-Lantern, were used to track down Spider-Man when he left behind the ideals of Iron Man. Spider-Man was attacked, and The Punisher struck the two villains down with bullets to the head. After bringing Spider-Man to the anti-registration headquarters, the Punisher announced that he was helping Captain America. Iron Man had compromised the system by using known thieves and killers.

After an episode in which the villains mention their split allegiances (some joining the pro-registration forces, while former villains are used to capture anti-registration superheroes and villains), it is Spidey who is attacked and the Punisher who rescues him. This was a reversal of the characters first meeting in 1974, where the Punisher was attacked and Spidey came to the rescue. As the series progressed, both characters looked to a third person, Captain America, to guide them. The imagery in the *Civil War* series was interesting in that the Punisher has to gain access by hanging from wires to hack into a computer system (like Spider-Man), and Spidey often shows his emotion in a far more deadly way (like the Punisher). After the Punisher assassinated two more super-villains, Goldbug and Diamondback, as they attempted to join Captain America's forces, Cap beats the Punisher. After a series of blows taken undefended by the Punisher, Spider-Man is asked why the Punisher doesn't fight back. Spidey replies, "Are you kidding me? Cap's probably the reason he (Punisher) went to

Vietnam. Same guy, different war." While Cap certainly didn't agree with the assessment, the observation was telling as it showed that conviction to a cause can be both enlightening and blinding.

Finally, after Captain America's assassination, both Spidey and the Punisher end up taking on aspects of Cap. Both have their issues: For Spider-Man it is his absolute belief in the righteousness of the Initiative and the registration act. Only after he sees those closest to him die does he change from the system, becoming an outlaw of sorts. For the Punisher, the entire structure is difficult as it allows people to manipulate the system to become "good." He is angry that those like Hobgoblin could simply switch sides, and so he redoubles his efforts to punish the guilty.

Both come to realize towards the end of the series that that they have been manipulated for various reasons, and that ultimately they were pawns of a larger entity. Both grieve the loss of a mentor and even take on the concepts of the lost Captain America. For Spider-Man, it's the sense of justice tempered with the need to respect the higher concept of America, even if it means doing what is not popular. For the Punisher, it was the need to keep up the fight, even if it was to be in the shoes of the one man he would not and could not strike a blow against. In the end, the world benefited from their mutual trust. For both, their in-fighting and the death of Captain America symbolized the death of American ideals in the age of the PATRIOT act. The key here is that the Punisher represents an aspect of America that is akin to what has been erroneously associated with George Orwell: the "Rough Man" theory, in which rough men stand ready to do violence on another's behalf. While Captain America was a symbol of the most honorable aspects of American society, and was above "fighting dirty," the Punisher looks to use all aspects of fighting to win, even if it circumvents the law. Portions of the USA PATRIOT act passed in the weeks following the 2001 terrorist attacks on the United States are in the same vein, in that the government can act outside of the law for the "greater good."

The latest incarnation of the Spider-Man–Punisher stories took on the Punisher's need to "clean house." In 2010, Marvel launched the four-issue mini-series *The Marvel Universe Vs. The Punisher*. In the story line, a bio-weapon was inadvertently released into the atmosphere of New York when Punisher took out a Russian arms/mob deal. The first person affected by this deadly strain was "patient zero," later revealed to be none other than Spider-Man. While the story eventually blamed the Kingpin as the true enemy to what was left of civilization, the two principle characters had their own struggle over what to do. Kill off all humanity, since it has sown the seeds of its own destruction? Or make a deal with the enemy you know, versus the larger, unseen foe? It is these sorts of struggles that have been the cornerstone of the interaction between the Punisher and Spider-Man, so it was apt that the story should center on these issues.

As the series progressed, the Punisher becomes the de facto salvation of mankind, killing infected enemies while searching for uninfected people. The series eventually culminates with the plot twist that has overtures to any significant piece of literature wherein the tortured man overcomes nature, man, and others but ultimately sees himself as unredeemable. The new evil Spider-Man/Patient Zero (who is a substitute for the Devil) informs the Punisher that Spider-Man's wife, Mary Jane, is pregnant, and that she and presumably the unborn infant are uninfected. A deal is struck between the two: rescue Mary Jane from the King of Death, as the Kingpin is known in this post-Apocalyptic universe, and return her to Spidey, and the other uninfected people are handed over to the Punisher unharmed. The Punisher succeeds in his task, but in the end kills Spider-Man anyway. When asked by a priest why the Punisher broke the agreement, the Punisher stated, "I don't make deals with monsters." The priest responds: "I see only one monster here."

So What Can Be Learned?

Throughout their respective "lives" both Spider-Man and the Punisher have remained fan favorites. Their constant banter of playing off one another reads like competitive siblings who berate each other, while striving to improve their own skills. In the case of these two characters their skills mean literally the lives of innocent people.

Any attempts to alter the main characters have met with protest, perhaps unnecessarily. Still the original characters have continued. Whether in some symbiotic form (like Venom for Spider-Man) or a Frankenstein-like character driven to still avenge those wronged (Franken-Castle), the permutations still fall back to the basic principles that made the characters popular in the first place. They still resonate with a readership that wants strength from the characters while reading about superheroes that privately struggle with their inner demons. To that end, Spider-Man and the Punisher will continue in the war to assist mankind, especially in times of uncertainty in America.

WORKS CITED

Conway, Gerry, et al., *Essential Punisher*, vol. 1. New York: Marvel Comics, 2004. (Compiles all early Punisher appearances, including *Amazing Spider-Man* 129, *Amazing Spider-Man* 137 and *Giant Size Spider-Man* #4).
Maberry, Jonathan, Goran Parlov, and Lee Loughridge. *Marvel Universe vs. the Punisher*. New York: Marvel Comics, 2010.
Millar, Mark, Steve McNiven, Dexter Vines and John Dell. *Civil War*. New York: Marvel Comics, 2007.
Peaslee, Robert M. "Superheroes, Moral Economy, and the Iron Cage: Morality, Alienation and the Super-Individual." In Angela Ndalianis & Wendy Haslem eds. *Super/Heroes: Myth and Meaning*. Melbourne, Australia: New Academia, 2006.
Pustz, Matthew. *Comic Book Culture: Fanboys and True Believers*. Jackson, MS: University of Mississippi Press, 1999.
Straczynski, J. Michael and John Romita et al. *The Amazing Spider-Man* 36. New York: Marvel Publications, 2001.
Weiner, Robert, Ed. *Captain America and the Struggle of the Superhero*. Jefferson, NC: McFarland Publishing, 2009.
Weist, Jerry. *100 Greatest Comic Books*. Atlanta, GA: Whitman Publishing, 2004.
Wright, Bradford. *Comic Book Nation: The Transformation of Youth Culture in America*. Baltimore, MD: Johns Hopkins University Press, 2000.

The Sinister Six: Anti-Villains in an Anti-Heroic Narrative

Rick Hudson

The popularity of Spider-Man has often been attributed to the "believability" of the character: as a superhero he is very much presented as an "ordinary" guy with whom the audience can identify. Spider-Man's frailties and foibles could well be as responsible for his appeal as his ability to climb walls and shoot webs at his foes. We may even consider Spider-Man to be an anti-hero, as he has throughout his history succumbed to the weaknesses in his character, errors of judgment and plain bad luck. Whereas we *know* Superman will always save Lois Lane, the death of Gwen Stacy — as crucial a component of the Spider-Man mythos as the death of Ben Parker — established the precedent that Spider-Man will *not* always triumph. This paper elaborates on this position by suggesting that it is the "ordinary guy" quality and equivocal nature of all the characters in the Spider-Man universe — epitomized by J. Jonah Jameson — that have contributed to the success of this narrative. Importantly, unlike the somewhat "gothic" or perhaps even "operatic" villains of the Batman comics, the villains Spider-Man faces show qualities similar to the hero and supporting characters. Spider-Man's opponents — such as the Lizard and the Green Goblin — are in many ways "ordinary guys" living in a fantastical world where extraordinary things happen. This paper examines how the flawed likeability of Spidey's principal enemies has been instrumental in the continuing popularity of his adventures.

The success of Spider-Man as a character can be attributed in many ways not only to his "cool power" and his status as a superhero, but also in his persona and qualities as an individual. Constructed by Stan Lee and Steve Ditko in 1962 in response to increasing teenage demand for comic books, Spider-Man was aimed to draw this teenage readership by means of identification and empathy: Parker — Spidey's alter-ego — was presented as a "normal" teenager with "normal" problems. The Spider-Man comic books are as much — if not more so — Parker's as they are the adventures of Spider-Man. Indeed, it could be said that whilst the alter egos of Batman and Superman are mere plot devices or trimmings on these heroes, Spider-Man *really is* Parker and never stops being Parker even when he is fulfilling his heroic role. Spider-Man is still Parker under the mask. From his initial appearance in *Amazing Fantasy* #15 (August 1962) Spider-Man / Parker not only had to battle with super-villains, but also had to deal with girl trouble, high school bullying, completing college assignments and caring for elderly relatives. Importantly, until the appearance of Spider-Man the teenager had been limited to the role of sidekick in the superhero comic book (for example Robin in *Batman* and Bucky in *Captain America*). These preceding characters provided teenagers with a point of identification within the respective narratives, but cast them as the eager protégés of the central character. Parker, on the other hand, is thrown into the deep end of the superhero business with no mentor to guide or advise him: a metaphor perhaps for the teenager stumbling awkwardly into the realities of adult life.

The plausibility of Spider-Man / Parker is central to his commercial and aesthetic success; however, this paper aims to suggest that the plausibility of all the characters contribute to this success. One of the great strengths of the Spider-Man comic book is that although it portrays a fantastical world populated by great heroes and terrible villains, these bizarre individuals are eminently credible in terms of their personalities and dispositions. This is also true of the ancillary characters in the text and exemplified by Parker's place of work, *The Daily Bugle*. In many ways *The Bugle* is a parodic inversion of the worthy *Daily Planet* in the Superman stories: the *Planet*'s kindly and paternal editor Perry White is replaced by the *Bugle*'s tyrannical and bullying J. Jonah Jameson (superbly portrayed by J.K. Simmonds in Sam Raimi's 2002 film *Spider-Man* and its sequels); the doting Lois Lane is substituted by the acerbic and sarcastic Betty Brandt and the devoted Jimmy Olsen is supplanted by the frankly vile and devious Edward Brock. Furthermore, whereas the *Planet* practically worships Superman, one of the great ironies of the Spider-Man tales is that not only does the *Bugle* castigate Spider-Man, but Parker collaborates with his own defamation by providing photographs of Spider-Man to illustrate the very reports that slander his name. Crucially, however, the *Bugle* staff is not universally despicable; each demonstrates likeable qualities. For example, the horrific Jameson is so obnoxious he is entertaining; but he also demonstrates great strength of character and even a sense of honor when the reader least expects it (again, demonstrated in Raimi's film). The very fact that both Spider-Man and his supporting cast demonstrate ambiguity and contradiction contributes to both their believability and attraction. These same qualities are present in this comic book's villains.

One might argue that one feature of the Spider-Man story line that undermines the believability of the text is that the heroes and villains emerge from a very small world: the Green Goblin 'just happens' to be Norman Osborn, the father of Parker's best friend, and the Lizard 'just happens' to be Curt Connors, one of Peter's professors. Although we may claim that these coincidences stretch plausibility too far, we could argue that in dramatic terms this narrative closeness *adds* to the realism of the text. That is to say, because Norman Osborn and Curt Connors regularly inhabit Parker's world, we see the effects of their villainy upon their everyday lives and the lives of those around them. We not only see the Lizard on the Rampage, but we see the kindly Curt Connors trapped in the horror of his situation. We not only see the malicious acts of the Green Goblin, but also the breakdown and eventual death of Norman Osborn—and the effect this has upon his son. Consequently we empathize with these villains more and, on an emotional level at least, the narrative becomes *more realistic* rather than more implausible. I would maintain that regardless of their wrongdoing the villains in *Spider-Man* all demonstrate empathic and likeable qualities, even if this likeableness results from a certain degree of ineptitude. If Spider-Man himself constitutes an anti-hero (he is flawed, peevish, frequently the victim of his own personality, despised by the press and the police, and *can* fail on a spectacular level—see the death of Gwen Stacy in *Amazing Spider-Man #125*, June 1973), then the villains he opposes constitute what I shall term anti-villains. To explore this issue further, I know turn my attention to that hexahedral harem of hate: The Sinister Six.

The Sinister Six first appeared in *Amazing Spider-Man Annual #1* (1964), the plot of which essentially runs like this: following a series of defeats at the hands of Spider-Man, Dr.

Octopus contacts other villains who have a grudge against our web-slinging friend with a view to joining forces to defeat Spidey once and for all. Doc Ock is rebuffed or ignored by many villains (such as Dr Doom, the Chameleon and Green Goblin) and only five super-villains join him: Electro, the Vulture, the Sandman, Mysterio and Kraven. Doubtlessly, when Lee and Ditko conceived the Sinister Six, they assembled them out of the villains that they had available and which they thought would make the most interesting combination for this first Spider-Man annual. But in narrative terms this rather shoddy origin indicates the spirit of the Sinister Six: rather than being presented to us as the team of "ultimate villains," they are portrayed as a ramshackle collection of adversaries who are either preoccupied by resentment or don't have any profitable evil schemes of their own. The Six's ineptitude is compounded by their infighting and division: there is a split between the intellectuals (Dr Octopus, Kraven and Mysterio) and the working-class hoodlums (Vulture, Sandman and Electro). If that isn't enough, the efficiency of the Sinister Six is hindered by an egotistical rivalry between Dr. Octopus and Kraven, and the Sandman is subject to treacherous manipulation by Electro.

Interestingly, not only is the Sinister Six a dysfunctional unit, but its individual members are a rather sorry bunch of misfits. Dr. Octopus (Otto Octavius, first appearance *Amazing Spider-Man #3*, July 1963) follows the mad genius / scientist archetype (Holderman, this volume) but is also presented as an inversion of this character type — he is by no means a "cool" genius in the vein of Lex Luthor or numerous Bond villains. Rather he is a physically unattractive, bespectacled and socially dysfunctional individual: the bullied nerd gone bad. Although capable of terrible cruelty, he is at heart the unliked, bullied kid (a dark reflection of Parker perhaps?). The Vulture (Adrian Toomes, first appearance *Amazing Spider-Man #2*, May 1963) is an elderly, bitter and resentful man haunted by his own mortality and failure, a failed electrical engineer who believes he has been cheated of success that he deserves. The Vulture is an indignant "man for whom it never happened." Electro (Max Dillon, first appearance *Amazing Spider-Man #9*, February 1964), like many Spider-Man villains, is portrayed as a man whose circumstances have driven him to crime, (another thwarted engineer) plagued by low intelligence and an inferiority complex cultivated by a stifling mother. Electro is desperate for recognition and craves to be seen as a "big man." As such his escapades are often showy displays of his power rather than well thought-through criminal schemes.

The Sandman (William Baker / Flint Marko, first appearance *Amazing Spider-Man # 4*, Sept 1963) is perhaps the most subtly drawn villain in the Spider-Man mythos. Again, this villain is shown to be the victim of impoverished circumstances which have criminalized him. Even before his transformation into the Sandman, Baker / Marko is depicted as a potentially good man who is caught in a descending spiral of criminality which, despite his numerous attempts, he is incapable of escaping. Perhaps the most sympathetic and underestimatedly complex of the Spidey villains, the Sandman is unusual in that he has attempted to "go straight," eventually jumping ships to become a superhero and make amends for his past. These attempts have always failed, however, due to manipulation by other members of the Sinister Six. Interestingly, the Sandman's depression has become the focus of stories in recent years, and these tales qualify as some of the most intriguing studies of mental illness in the medium. Kraven (Sergei Kravinoff, first appearance *Amazing Spider-Man #15*, August 1964) stands out amongst the Sinister Six in that he is not a career criminal like the other five, but rather an adventurer driven by his own sense of honor to hunt down Spidey as the ultimate game. Although Kraven's sense of honor is decidedly warped, he is charismatic and empathic; on a number of occasions he has been the voice of ecological issues, and his nobility and principals have, very occasionally, led Kraven to ally himself with Spider-Man against other villains.

The killing off of Kraven in *Kraven's Last Hunt* (1987) was not only a very moving story in itself, but also explored Kraven's obsessive need to best Spider-Man. In doing so *Last Hunt* not only qualified as an interesting study of compulsive behavior, but also a compelling document of Kravinoff's decent into madness and death (see Walton, this volume).

Mysterio (Quentin Beck, first appearance *Amazing Spider-Man # 13*, June 1964) is the "poor relation" of the other super-villains; although he has one of the coolest and most sinister costumes in the genre, in terms of superpowers he is limited and in narrative terms — as a deceiver he has to act remotely — he is dramatically disappointing. However, in terms of character he is as interesting as his comrades in the Sinister Six. Again, in Mysterio we see the figure of the "failed man" of talent whose skills have not been recognized. Like the Vulture, Electro, Ben Parker and even to a degree Norman Osborn and Parker, he is a man of ability neglected by the inhuman corporate world. Some succeed, like Norman Osborn and Parker, while others — like Quentin Beck — fail. Beck starts his adult life as a special effects expert: he has a remarkable gift in this field but soon realizes that it is a dead end job and his skills, whilst feeding the bank accounts of movie executives, provide him with little financial reward. Beck decides to turn his skills to crime and creates the identity of Mysterio, the master of illusion. In this role he demonstrates a theatrical bent, not unlike Electro, and craves to be recognized as a great showman. Nevertheless, Mysterio repeatedly fails in his criminal career and suffers a string of defeats at the hands of Spider-Man that not only see him incarcerated but humiliated. On gaining his freedom Mysterio embarks on one final campaign of vengeance that is particularly cruel and spiteful in nature. Mysterio is confronted by Spider-Man's friend and ally, Daredevil, who defeats the master of illusion in a bitter battle. Mysterio is not only physically beaten — but mentally destroyed by Daredevil. The "great showman" expects Daredevil to kill him, and sees this as his grand stage exit; however Daredevil refuses to oblige, choosing instead to berate and mock Mysterio for his lack of originality and predictability. Robbed of his spectacular finale, a distraught Mysterio shoots himself. Mysterio perhaps best embodies the spirit of the Sinister Six, in that behind the persona of the great evil villain there is a little man lost in the big world. Like his allies, he is a man of talent whose legitimate ambitions have been thwarted and who has become entwined in the descending helix of criminality, resentment, hubris, obsession and madness.

Collectively the Sinister Six provide us with an interesting collection of villains who contrast with those of the Batman and Superman mythopoeias: they are not great evil masterminds, but flawed individuals: "dead beats" who have turned to crime out of frustration and failure. Indeed, the lone man of humble beginnings but great aptitude, desperately struggling to make his way in the world, is a character type returned to again and again in the pages of Spider-Man (perhaps emblematic of Stan Lee's own career experiences in publishing?). Super-villainy is a means through which the Six seek to gain the status, wealth and recognition that has eluded them. If Spider-Man is attractive because of his flaws, then so too are his adversaries both attractive and more terrible because of their weaknesses. Whereas Superman and Batman's adversaries are attractive because they are "cool" (such as the Joker and Lex Luthor), it is the pitiful nature of the Spider-Man's enemies that adds to their attraction and interest. The Spider-Man villains also function very differently on a narrative level to those of other comic book villains. I have detailed the role of the Joker in Batman comics elsewhere in great detail (Hudson, 2010), but to summarize we can claim that the Joker acts as a gothic, or even operatic, figure who provides a foil for the hero's somber and serious nature. Furthermore the Joker's "madness" does not correlate with any actual mental condition; rather it is a narrative device through which he can act as "holy fool" and critique the assumptions of the heroic narrative, the attitudes and beliefs of the hero and his world. Indeed, the Joker's "madness" allows him to dissect the character and motivation of Batman. For example in Alan Moore's *Killing Joke* (1988) he states:

> I've demonstrated that there's no difference between me and everyone else! All it takes is one bad day to reduce the sanest man alive to lunacy. You had a bad day once, am I right? I know I am. I can tell. You had one bad day and everything changed. Why else would you dress up like a flying rat? You had a bad day and it drove you as crazy as everybody else ... only you won't admit it! You have to keep pretending that everything makes sense, that there's some point to all this struggling! God, you make me want to puke. I mean what is it with you? What made you what you are? Girlfriend killed by the mob, maybe? Brother carved up like some mugger? Something like that, I bet. Something like that [n.p.].

Moreover, in Grant Morrison's *Arkham Asylum: A Serious House on Serious Earth* (1989) the Joker's function to tell the "laughing truth" is expanded to the point that it is suggested by one of the medical staff at the Arkham Asylum that his "madness" is in fact a state of total sanity in a frenzied post-modern world:

> The Joker's a special case. Some of us feel he may be beyond treatment. In fact, we're not even sure if he can properly defined as insane. His latest claim is that he's possessed by the voodoo loa, Baron Ghede. We're beginning to think of a neurological disorder similar to Tourette's syndrome. It's quite possible we may actually be looking at some kind of super-sanity here. A brilliant new modification of human perception more suited to urban life at the end of the Twentieth Century. Unlike you and I, the Joker seems to have no control over the sensory information he's receiving from the outside world. He can only cope with that chaotic barrage of input by going with the flow. That's why some days he's a mischievous clown, others a psychotic killer. He has no real personality. He creates himself each day. He sees himself as the Lord of Misrule, and the world as a theatre of the absurd [n.p.].

Morrison extends this literary, or aesthetic understanding and presentation of "madness" to other villains. Two Face's monologue demonstrates a poetic and mythic representation of insanity that acts to critique the delusions of the supposedly sane world:

Mr Apollo	Mr Dionysus
I am a lawyer	I am a liar
Yes	No
We the people of the United States	We the acid-scarred victims of history
In order to form a more perfect union	Of evil and hypocrisy
Establish justice	Exalt criminals to office
Insure domestic tranquility	Vietnam El Salvador Chile
Provide for the common defense	With lovely missiles and roaring bombs
Promote the general welfare	Of the rich, the white and the pious
And secure the blessings of liberty	And burn children and torture women
To ourselves and our posterity	Forever and ever amen (n.p.)

Conversely, in *Spider-Man* mental illness is presented less romantically: insanity is not a state of "alternative consciousness" that bestows an unorthodox vision of the world and society, but a debilitating condition that causes grief and suffering to its victims and their friends, families and enemies. The mental illness of Mysterio, for example, not only causes him to commit atrocious acts of cruelty, but also his own death. Norman Osborn's mental decline not only causes him to become a fiendish super-villain, but also causes misery in the lives of his own son and the Parker family. Curt Connors' life is torn apart by his mental torture; he is not heroically mad in the sense that the Joker is. I would argue that it demonstrates a far more sensitive understanding of such conditions and the impact they have upon the sufferer and the individuals who love and care for them.

The Spider-Man storyline also differs greatly from both the Batman and Superman storylines in terms of its attitudes towards death. In Batman's world death is, by and large, a rather temporary condition: we may be led to believe that the Joker has been killed, but we *know* that he will return because he is vital to the ongoing narrative. He is too great a villain to lose. However, in *Spider-Man* dead means dead: Peter's parents, Ben Parker, Captain Stacy and Gwen Stacy are all gone for good and their deaths have a resonance in the ongoing story. Likewise, when villains die we know they aren't coming back—sure, there might be a new Mysterio or a new Kraven or new Green Goblin; but Quentin Beck, Sergei Kravinoff and Norman Osborn are dead. And these deaths are felt deeply by Spider-Man. Though he must defeat his foes, Spidey feels great regret for their deaths and guilt for his culpability in their demise.

The representation of the villains in *Spider-Man* is crucial to the tone and theme of the comic book. Yes, we are reading adventures about super-powered fantastical characters in a fantastical world—but at the very same time we are reading about the people under the masks: individuals with strengths and frailties and flaws of character who make good and disastrous judgments. When we read Spider-Man we are reading a hugely exciting, frightening and funny superhero comic book; but also a hugely empathic narrative in which the heroes and villains must contend—alongside the mythic struggles that form the backbone of the narrative—with the mundane disasters and tragedies we all face. And that's why we love Spidey, and J.J.J. and Gwen Stacy and also Doc Ock and Electro and the rest of the crew. We are not in Metropolis. We are not in Gotham. We are in New York. And these are ordinary guys.

Works Cited

Hudson, Rick. "The Derelict Fairground: a Bakhtinian Analysis of the Graphic Novel Medium." *CEA Critic.* 72:3 (Spring-Summer 2010): 33–47.
Lee, Stan, Steve Ditko et al. *Amazing Fantasy 15.* New York: Marvel (August 1962).
_____, Steve Ditko, et al. *Amazing Spider-Man* issues *1–125.* New York: Marvel (1963–1973).
_____, Steve Ditko, et al. *Amazing Spider-Man Annual 1.* New York: Marvel (1964).
Moore, Alan, Brian Bolland. *Batman: The Killing Joke.* New York: DC Comics 1988.
Morrison, Grant, Dave McKean. *Arkham Asylum: a Serious House on Serious Earth.* New York: DC Comics 1989.

Spider-Man and Batman, Disordered Minds: Friendship Through Difference

Phillip Bevin

Introduction

The comic book *Spider-Man and Batman: Disordered Minds* presents an unusual opportunity to study a story that features both Batman and Spider-Man. Although superheroes often encounter other superheroes that are owned by the same company in crossover comics, characters from Marvel comics, such as Spider-Man, rarely interact with those from DC Comics, such as Batman, and the result is that comparisons have only infrequently been drawn between the characters of Spider-Man and Batman. It is a worthwhile endeavor to compare Spider-Man to a character that he is not normally partnered with because such a comparison may lead to a new perspective on the web-slinging superhero. This essay will attempt to reveal something about the nature of Spider-Man's character by offsetting him against the seemingly very different Batman in order to draw conclusions regarding how and why their outlooks, whether differing or in agreement, relate to each other. This essay will also compare the two characters in order to figure out why Spider-Man is able to work comfortably alongside Batman in *Spider-Man and Batman: Disordered Minds*. In order to pursue this goal, this essay will utilize the theories of Judith Butler, which offer some insight about the formation of personal identity. The essay will begin with a discussion of these theories in order to establish a firm theoretical foundation from which to build a deep analysis of the two superheroes.

Gender and the Formation of Identity

It is possible understand why the death of the young Bruce Wayne's parents, specifically his father, triggered the character's psychological transformation into a man who identifies himself as Batman by studying the theories that Freud expressed about the Oedipus complex. Judith Butler elaborates upon these theories in her work, *Gender Trouble* (1991). Here, specific attention must be paid to Butler's description of how the social norms that feed the "heterosexual" cultural hegemony are established with the formation of a patriarchal "paternal law" (Butler, 2008: 94). Butler notes that "in the experience of losing another human being whom one has loved, Freud argues, the ego is said to incorporate that other into the very structure of the ego, taking on attributes of the other and "sustaining" the other through magical acts of imitation" (Butler, 2008: 78). Butler then goes on to outline how sexual identity is formed by a prohibition of love for a desired object or "other" individual. The desired "object" is refused by the ego of the forming individual, a refusal which manifests itself as a "loss." According to Butler, a "refusal" (79) of "homosexual" desire must take place in order for the unformed individual to manifest desire "heterosexually." In other words, in order for the oedipal relationship that results in the prohibition against the incestuous desires that the "male" child harbors for his mother (through fear of reprisal and castration by his father) and the formation of the ego and the superego, as well as the consequent displacement of the male child's "heterosexual" desire for the mother onto other women, to occur, the child must first be operating according to "heterosexual" norms. In order to be operating under "heterosexual" norms the child must have already renounced any "homosexual" or "bisexual" desires that they might have had for the father through a prior act of prohibition. Due to the fact that, according to Freud, the "loss" of a loved one as an object of desire results in their incorporation into the child's psyche it would be fair to assume that the identity of the young Bruce Wayne was formed by the incorporation of his father's personality, which was prompted by the initial loss of his father as an object of desire (Butler, 2008). To understand how this might result in the formation of the characters of Bruce Wayne and Batman it is important to understand how the incorporated "lost object" influences the ego. According to Butler,

> Freud conceptualizes the ego in the perpetual company of the ego ideal which acts as a moral agency of various kinds. The internalised [sic] losses of the ego are re-established as part of this agency of moral scrutiny, the internalisation of anger and blame originally felt by the object in its external mode. In the act of internalisation, that anger and blame, inevitably heightened by the loss itself, are turned inward and sustained; the ego changes place with the internalised object, thereby investing this internalised externality with moral power. Thus, the ego forfeits its anger and efficacy to the ego ideal which turns against the very ego by which it is sustained; in other words the ego constructs a way to turn against itself [Butler, 2008: 84].

In the "heterosexual" boy, as in the young Bruce Wayne's case, it is the father who has been "internalised" as the lost love object and it is the characteristics of the internalized father that act as part of the superego (Butler, 2008), which regulates young Bruce's thoughts and character. Bruce's father, or the internalized characteristics that are representative of Bruce's father's behavioral norms, function as both the foundation for young Bruce's ego identity and part of the superego which regulates that ego identity, Bruce Wayne's own self. The difficulty with having an identity that is notionally immutable but conceived through the internalization of behavioral codes that are identified with the role of either the mother or, in this case, the father, both of which are identities based upon the concept of gender, is that gender is itself a product of normative codes of cultural practice. Butler explains this through the elucidation of the idea that the "bisexuality and homosexuality" that "are taken to be" the "primary" libidinal "dispositions" (Butler, 2008: 99) that supposedly exist "before," outside and prior to the ego and the superego, are actually "constructions" formed from "within the terms" of the "constitutive discourse" that brings the concepts of the ego and superego into being (Butler, 2008: 105). It is therefore the "constitutive discourse" which creates the individual subject's sense of identity, a discourse which has its origins in social culture. Gender identities, which are apparently formed through the repression of the "primary libidinal dispositions" and upon which the whole of patriarchal discourse and "heterosexual" "male" identity is based, are therefore suggested by Butler to be a product of the discourse that they supposedly enable and create.

Butler also refers to the need for the power relationships that are derived from the concept of differentiated genders to be repeated "incessantly" (Butler, 2008: 152) in order to consolidate and propagate the notion that the concept of binary opposed "male" and "female" genders, upon which so many power relationships and identities in patriarchal society are built, is natural. Therefore, this repetition occurs in order to disguise the reality that the concept of binary gender is a contingent fiction. In the penultimate chapter of *Gender Trouble*, entitled "subversive bodily acts," Butler outlines theories about the nature and function of this repetition, as well as how it could lead to the subversion of the gender norms that contribute to the formation of identity and which give power to certain types of gender identity — namely "masculinity" and the hegemonic patriarchal discourse through which the masculine gender identity comes into being, generating and consolidating its own dominant authority. She posits the question: "Is 'the body' or 'the sexed body' the firm foundation on which gender and systems of compulsory sexuality operate? Or is 'the body' itself shaped by political forces with strategic interests in keeping that body bounded and constituted by the markers of sex?" (Butler, 2008: 175). By asking this question, Butler is suggesting that the body as "sexed," that is, divided into the two separate binary groupings of "male" and "female," is, like the supposedly concrete notions of gender, a product of a hegemonic, patriarchal system of meanings that only ascribes agency to individuals who can be categorized according to an identity that has already been conferred by the system itself, a system which recognizes gender roles as the primary foundation for identity and the self. Butler is therefore arguing that the biological separation between the "male" and "female" sexes, which supposedly gives scientific weight to the practice of ascribing behavioral characteristics to people according to gender identities, which are, in turn, supposedly derived from "sexed," "bodily" identities, is a product of the normative gender ideals themselves; that is, the artificially, discursively generated notions of "masculinity" and "femininity," which retroactively dictate that bodies must be separated according to apparent differences in "sex." This is done in order to consolidate the hegemonic dominance of patriarchal discourse, which is sustained by the production of distinct "male" and "female" identities. If the "outer body" is a social construct, so must be the notion of the "inner" psychological domain that is contained within the "outer" shell. Any signification of the nature of the "inner self" must itself therefore be a construct of patriarchal social discourse.

Butler once again supports this idea with her theories: "The function of the interior soul understood as 'within the body' is signified through its inscription *on* the body, even though its primary mode of signification is through its very absence, its potent invisibility.... The re-description of intra-psychic processes in terms of the surface politics of the body implies a corollary re-description of gender as the disciplinary production of the figures of fantasy through play of presence and absence on the body's surface, the construction of the gendered body through a series of exclusions and denials, signifying absences" (Butler, 2008: 184). Gender as a concept is manifested and reinforced by the actions of individual subjects which serve to dramatize that concept in bodily performances that are "intended" to demonstrate that a concrete coherence exists between the "inner," supposedly identity-constitutive characteristics of an individual's immutably gendered "self" and the external behavior of an individual's body, which supposedly conforms to the individual's "inner" identity but which is, in fact, what actually constitutes that "inner" identity. Butler defines these actions as "performative" (Butler, 2008: 34). "Performative," as Butler defines it, denotes a performance of a given role that is enacted unconsciously and with absolute faith in the reality of the identity traits being performed on the part of the "performer."

Batman: The Normative Ideal

This analysis will utilize Butler's understanding of "performativity," as well as her other theories about identity, to demonstrate that both Batman and Spider-Man are defined by their awareness and fear of the fact that the characteristics and personality traits that constitute their own senses of self are contingent, and by their efforts to make these character traits appear to themselves as fixed and immutable in order to prevent their own identities from being lost. This relates to Bruce Wayne's adoption of the Batman identity as a replacement of his lost boyhood identity as "Bruce Wayne," because it is the disintegration of the correspondence between the "inner" immutably gendered self and the "outward," "performative," "bodily" behavior of his father that creates a recognition within Bruce Wayne's mind that the traditionally conceived notions of identity are a contingent and arbitrary product of discursively instituted social norms. It is this realization that results in the crisis that causes young Bruce Wayne's loss of faith in, and dissolution of his own self, later to be replaced by the persona of Batman.

The exact cause of this crisis can be examined in more depth by a close analysis of the sequence in *Spider-Man and Batman: Disordered Minds* that depicts the deaths of Bruce Wayne's parents, with particular reference to the "performative" behavior displayed by Bruce Wayne's father within this sequence. The panels that are placed across the top of the page focus on the expressions of the character's faces. The first panel depicts the mugger grinning and pointing his gun directly at the reader in what appears to be a display of aggression. The next panel depicts a close-up of Bruce Wayne's father's face, as he reacts to the appearance of the mugger in the previous panel with a look of paralyzed fear followed by the interjection of color that is the blast from the mugger's gun. This is then followed by a close up of the face of Bruce's dead mother. There is a clear subtext to these images, which can be elaborated upon through an application of Butler's theories as they have been discussed above. The gun held by the mugger in the images can be read as a clear symbolic manifestation of the "phallus" (Butler, 2008: 63), the sign which denotes "male" identity and the possession of cultural power and influence in a patriarchal society. The cultural power denoted by the gun as the symbolic manifestation of the phallus can be identified by the reaction of Bruce's father to it. The panel that shows the close-up of Mr. Wayne's face depicts a look of paralyzed fear and no trace of defiance. This suggests that Bruce Wayne's father is submissively accepting the dominance of the man with the gun. The wideness of Bruce's father's eyes and the fact that they are dilated denote that he is trying to "take in" the image and the situation visually. Such a display of "taking in" also suggests that Bruce Wayne's father is demonstrating to the mugger that he is "internalising" the situation through his "performative" "bodily" actions, thus incorporating his position as a submissive individual, subject to the "male," "masculine" identified will of the mugger. His willingness to submit and to passively accept "masculine" authority thus indicates a "feminine" tendency on the part of Bruce Wayne's father, a tendency that does not accord well with his socially gendered position as a "masculine" "male" patriarch in a patriarchal society. It must be stressed that it is Mr. Wayne's acceptance of the submissive role that results in his failure to protect his family, and perform adequately his role as the "masculine," "male" patriarch. This is indicated by the fact that the blast of the gun directly follows the image of the submissive expression of Bruce's father, thus denoting that it is a consequence of his inaction and reluctance to take a more affirmative, aggressive and normatively "masculine" response to the threat of the mugger. The subsequent image showing the dead Mrs. Wayne can be interpreted as the social sanction against Mr. Wayne's failure to "perform" his gendered social role correctly, with the destruction of his family, the physical deaths of both himself and his wife, as well as the metaphorical death of their son as the natural consequence of the mugger's usurpation of the dominant gendered social position in the situation. It is the father's "performative" display here that results in the crisis that causes young Bruce Wayne to lose his identity. The passive role that Bruce's father plays out in the nightmare flashback sequence can be said to adhere to "feminine" characteristics. Such characteristics acted out on a "male" "body" can be described as a performance of "drag," as it is defined by Butler: "The performance of drag plays upon the distinction between the anatomy of the performer and the gender that is being performed.... If the anatomy of the performer is already distinct from the gender of the performer, and both of those are distinct from the gender of the performance, then the performance suggests a dissonance not only between sex and performance, but sex and gender, and gender and performance" (187).

In *Gender Trouble,* Butler outlines various ways in which the "body" is perceived to be "feminine" in its role as a "passive" object upon which cultural identity is written. The quality of "passivity" can therefore itself be identified as a "feminine" character trait (176). The behavior that Bruce Wayne's father displays in his response to the threat from the mugger can be demonstrated as being denotative of a "passive" "feminine" interiority. Bruce Wayne's father's "performative" display of passivity qualifies as an example of a drag performance because, as noted above, "passivity" is a characteristic commonly associated with the "feminine" or "female" gender norm. However, Bruce Wayne's father's "performative" demonstration of his having a characteristically "feminine" passive "interior" personality conflicts with his obviously "male" "outer" body. The conflicting display of "female" "interiority" alongside "male" "exteriority" that Bruce's father performs thus creates the "dissonance" that Butler cites as a characteristic of "drag." This is achieved because both "male" and "female" gender norms are played out through their "performative" inscription onto Bruce's father's bodily actions. Consequently, the fact that these supposedly binary and, by definition, distinct norms are being played out on a common "bodily surface" means that the performance itself can be identified as neither male nor female thus creating dissonance and confusion in the identity of the performer and an existential crisis in his son, who is watching the "performative" display.

As outlined earlier in this essay, a sense of identity in a patriarchal society is, according to Butler, formed by the identification with and the "internalisation" (sic) of one or other of the binary gender norms: "male" or "female." As has also been stated earlier, as a heterosexual male, the forming ego of Bruce Wayne would have internalized and incorporated the perceived "masculine" normative identity of his father once his father had been "refused" as an object of desire. Bruce's subsequent relinquishment of his mother as an object of desire would similarly have been incurred for fear of his father's "masculine" authority and ability to "castrate" him. It is important to note that Bruce's emergence as a "heterosexual" "male" gendered identity is presupposed by the incorporation of those same characteristics that were apparent in his father's "heterosexual" "male" identity. The consistency of Bruce's "heterosexual" "male" identity is thus derived from the consistency of the "heterosexual" "male" identity of his father. Bruce's father's performance shows that this identity is anything but consistent, revealing that not only is the gender of his father's "inner" self not necessarily consistent with the gender of his father's "outward" bodily display but that different gender identities can be adopted in either the "inner" or "outer" spheres of an individual's character at any given time. Presumably, in the comfort of his own home, at the time when young Bruce's gender identity was developing, his father acted the role of the normative male patriarch in a way in which his inner gender identity consisted with that of his exterior, as would have been necessary in order for Bruce to "internalise" these characteristics and to develop into an individual subject with the gender identity of a "heterosexual" "male." In contrast, in the situation of the mugging, in which Bruce's father is standing opposite an individual whose display of "masculinity" is more potent than his own, he plays the "feminine" role in the "performative" display of his "internal" gender identity. As Bruce is alive to witness the event of the mugging, he also witnesses his father's "drag" performance. Due to the fact that Bruce's own sense of having a stable and immutable identity is based on a gender identification that is derived from the paternalistic and authoritarian role played by his father in his upbringing, bearing witness to his father demonstrating the discontinuity and contingency of such an identity inevitably throws the young boy into a state of existential crisis concerning his own sense of self. It can thus be suggested that it is the realization, on the part of Bruce Wayne, that his own identity within society is a discursively produced fiction that prompts a deconstruction of that identity and is perhaps what Batman refers to when he states that the boy he once was "died years ago" (DeMatteis, 1995: 7).

If the Bruce Wayne identity can be said to have been lost, the Batman identity can be read as a re-articulation of normative ideals in order to reinvest in the norms that the young Bruce Wayne had once believed to be substantial. The identity of Batman can be identified as having been formed through the second "loss" that Bruce Wayne experiences when his father dies at the hands of the mugger. Butler's musings on incorporation are therefore worth quoting again:

> The internalised losses of the ego are re-established as part of this agency of moral scrutiny, the internalisation of anger and blame originally felt by the object in its external mode. In the act of internalisation, that anger and blame, inevitably heightened by the loss itself, are turned inward and sustained; the ego changes place with the internalised object, thereby investing this internalised externality with moral power. Thus, the ego forfeits its anger and efficacy to the ego ideal which turns against the very ego by which it is sustained; in other words the ego constructs a way to turn against itself [84].

Batman is created when the child that was Bruce Wayne internalizes and incorporates his father into his ego a second time, thus repeating the process that formed his Bruce Wayne identity in the first place. However, the second incorporation of his father's identity also occasions the incorporation of unresolved feelings of resentment and anger at his father's inability to perform according to his prescribed gendered identity and subsequent belief that his father is the cause of his mother's actual death and his own metaphorical death. These feelings of "anger and blame" have been "turned inward and sustained." The former Bruce Wayne's ego has changed places with "the internalised object" that is his lost father, his ego has "turned against itself" and the "anger and blame" that the former Bruce Wayne had felt for his father is now manifested in the self regulating-function of his own superego. In other words, the Batman identity has been formed by the boy who was Bruce Wayne criticizing himself for his father's mistakes and failure to live up to the "masculine" normative ideal. As a result of this, Batman's only purpose in life is to engage in a constant battle to live up to the ideal set by his normative gender and sexuality, to become its living embodiment in order to silence the feelings of "anger and blame" which, previously directed towards his father, now criticize him for not living up to the "male" "heterosexual" norm and which challenge his very identity by suggesting that he does not accord with the normative role that he tries to embody. That this self-criticism is a constant source of doubt for Batman and a challenge to Batman's sense of self is evident in the fact that the passivity displayed by his father is also visible in Batman as he imagines himself in the nightmare flashback sequence in which his father is killed. He appears at the end of the sequence as a somber bystander having arrived "too late" to prevent the gun from being fired (DeMatteis, 1995: 7).

However, Batman's actual success at living up to the normative "heterosexual" "male" ideal is much greater than that of his father, despite his imagined doubts. Batman's self-appointed role is to provide a concrete example of the "masculine" "heterosexual" norm in its perfection. As such he challenges every threat to that order with a "performative" display that demonstratively consolidates his superiority. Batman's physical appearance is a perfect example of how he attempts to embody "masculine" characteristics. His costume is tight fitting, thus emphasizing his "masculine," muscled physique. In addition to this, the only part of Batman's face to be exposed by the cowl is his pronounced jaw, another supposedly "male" "bodily" attribute. Batman also seems to be attempting to offset any correspondence between his own "masculine" identity and the passivity of his father. In particular, whereas his father's eyes were wide open and inviting to the mugger, Batman's are concealed behind the sharp, scowling expression that has been designed into his cowl. Similarly, the costume has many "phallic," sharp edges, from the points at the end of his ears to the tips of his cape, denoting personal "sharpness" and aggressiveness. Batman's identity is, in fact, so tied to "male" "heterosexual" hegemony that any threat to it feels like a personal attack. This relationship is clarified at the end of Batman's nightmare flashback when the mugger responsible for the deaths of his parents and Bruce Wayne's own loss of identity is revealed to be Carnage, a homicidal maniac and an obvious threat to the social order. This also explains why Batman constantly reasserts his authority by physically beating the Joker, a character whose seemingly "feminine" mind and "male" body display a drag act that could be interpreted as a reminder to Batman of the one performed by his father. Batman's continual beating of the Joker is a show of strength, which illustrates the dominance and inevitability of the "male" "heterosexual" hegemony and society conceived according to patriarchal guidelines. The fact that physical strength is the attribute that Batman uses most frequently to literally beat the Joker into submission is itself no coincidence and is used by Batman as a "sanction" against anyone who implicitly challenges his own sense of identity by threatening the status quo (DeMatteis, 1995, 17). Batman, through these performances is attempting to act "male" "heterosexual" gender norms into concrete reality, thus justifying his existence, silencing his own doubts and making a second identity crisis and loss of self less likely. If Batman can be identified as a self defining representative of the hegemonic dominance of a discourse that attenuates power to normative "male" "heterosexuals," then Spider-Man's relationship with Batman can be, to an extent, explained by the former's own relationship to the patriarchal hegemony that the latter embodies so powerfully.

Spider-Man: The Normative Failure

Spider-Man's entrance into the narrative of *Spider-Man and Batman: Disordered Minds* is very similar to that of Batman and, indeed, seems to be included in order to suggest that the two heroes share a common origin. However, there are important differences which might help to explain the contrasting personalities of the two and why, in *Spider-Man and Batman:*

Disorder Minds, they manage to form a strained but ultimately productive collaborative friendship. Just as Batman's entrance into the narrative is prefigured by the murder of his parents at the hands of a mugger, Spider-Man's is prefigured by the murder of his uncle. The deaths of Uncle Ben and the Wayne parents are presented as parallel events. The layout of the page that presents the death of Peter Parker's uncle is the same as the layout on the page that showcases the death of Bruce Wayne's parents. There is a succession of panels across the top of the page depicting the grinning criminal with the gun and Uncle Ben's petrified wide-eyed face echoes the same fear and "feminine" passivity that characterizes Bruce Wayne's father's response to his own mugger (DeMatteis, 1995). Once again Uncle Ben, wide-eyed and open mouthed in his terror, appears to be demonstrating a "passive," "feminine" acceptance of the burglar's "phallic" power, as is again symbolized by the criminal's possession of a gun, as well as his dominance of the situation.

There are two key differences between the situation of the murder of Bruce Wayne's parents and the situation of the murder of Parker's uncle. The first of these is that it is Parker's uncle who is murdered, *not* his father. It is indicated in the script of the comic that Peter Parker indeed once knew his father and has not always lived with his aunt and uncle. This is made apparent when Spider-Man muses that "If Aunt May and Uncle Ben hadn't taken me in after my parents died, given me so much love and support—I might have grown to be bitter, angry. Hard" (DeMatteis, 1995: 7). It is important to note here that Parker originally grew up and developed under the influence of his mother and father. This would suggest that when young Parker's personality was forming, it was his father's normative gender traits that he incorporated in order to emerge as a "heterosexual" "male" (DeMatteis, 1995). These traits would have been reinforced through the second incorporation that took place upon the second loss that Parker experienced of his father, when the man died. The ego-superego relationship that exists in Parker is therefore derived from that of his father and not his Uncle Ben. This is important because any display of dissonance between "inner" and "outer" gender identities on the part of Uncle Ben would not necessarily prove to be a direct challenge to Parker's own identity because his sense of self as Peter Parker is derived from his father's gender identity.

Secondly, whereas the young Bruce Wayne is present to witness his father's "performative" "drag" act in front of the mugger, Parker is not present for the "performative" "drag" that his uncle displays when faced with his own assailant. In *Spider-Man and Batman: Disordered Minds,* Spider-Man arrives at the house after the event of the murder "too late" (DeMatteis, 1995: 1) to stop it. Even this appearance is probably symbolic of the fact that the Spider-Man identity performed by Parker as a coping mechanism for dealing with his Uncle Ben's death can never fully process the pain caused by the event, which no amount of atoning heroics can reverse. This theory is supported by the fact that in traditional *Spider-Man* cannon, Parker only arrives at the home of his uncle and aunt well after the immediate aftermath of his uncle's murder (Lee, 2009). That *Spider-Man and Batman: Disordered Minds* adheres to the Spider-Man cannon is made evident through a note printed on the page upon which Parker's relationship to Mary Jane Watson is being elaborated and which reads, "The events of this story occur before *the Spectacular Spider-Man #229.*" Butler suggested previously that any "performative drag" could challenge the assumptions that exist behind the prevailing "male" "heterosexual" cultural hegemony, and therefore Uncle Ben's "performative drag" could theoretically destabilize Parker's sense of self. However, as Parker is not actually present to witness it, he misses its effect. Parker's nightmare flashback could be read as an imaginative reproach to his Uncle Ben, which ascribes "feminine" characteristics to his uncle in response to his uncle's failure to perform the role of patriarch adequately. Ben fails to perform the role adequately because he fails to protect his own territory, which is his home and his family, when he "effeminately" submits to the dominance of the burglar when the latter presents a challenge to Ben's "masculine" authority.

Due to the fact that the "feminine" characteristics that his uncle displays in the nightmare-flashback sequence have actually been concocted in Parker's imagination, and due to the consequent fact that his own sense of "male" "heterosexual" identity is not decisively challenged when his uncle is murdered, Parker, unlike the young Bruce Wayne, does not lose his own sense of selfhood in the event of his uncle's death. However, one aspect of Parker's reaction to Uncle Ben's murder that *is* akin to Batman's reaction to his father's behavior at the scene of the mugging is that Uncle Ben's failure to protect his household and his family prompts Parker into forming feelings of "anger and blame" towards his uncle. These are then "incorporated" into Parker's ego and "reversed" as a result of the lost attachment that Parker feels after the death of Uncle Ben. It is these feelings of "anger and blame," incorporated, reversed and directed against Parker's own ego, accompanied by and sustaining the personal, "inwardly" directed feelings of guilt that he feels regarding his own failure to act and prevent the murder, which result in the creation of Parker's alternate identity, Spider-Man. However, because Parker's original identity is not dissolved by a display of dissonant gendered attributes on the part of Uncle Ben, it coexists with the more recently formed Spider-Man identity in a relationship that is characterized by conflict. Like Batman, Parker wishes to live up to the normative "masculine" ideal in order to prove that he is worthy of the privileged gendered sexual identity that has been bestowed upon him and to silence the constant self criticism that is the result of the incorporated feelings of "anger and blame" that were previously felt for his uncle and which suggest to him that, like his uncle, he is not fit to perform the role. However, Parker tries to accomplish this in both his Peter Parker and Spider-Man roles, the conflicting coexistence of which prevent him from ever truly embodying the normative "masculine" ideal in either, because one is constantly drawing his effort away from the other. When one life appears to be going well, it seems to be at the expense of the other, which inevitably starts to collapse as Peter Parker/Spider-Man has been directing his attention elsewhere. This phenomenon is not, however, much in evidence in *Spider-Man and Batman: Disordered Minds*, perhaps because the narrative of the comic is itself divided between two characters, thus not allowing for too much focus or development of one or the other. In this comic, Spider-Man's apparently happy marriage to Mary Jane Watson seems to suggest that he is coming close to being a relatively successful embodiment of a normative heterosexual male. However, as noted previously, the storyline of this comic occurs within the same continuity as the main line of *Spider-Man* comics. The *Spider-Man* comics released in that line in the year of 1995, when *Spider-Man and Batman: Disordered Minds* was also published, show that Parker's relationship with Mary Jane is becoming strained by his overzealous dedication to his Spider-Man identity. *Amazing Spider-Man: the Complete Clone Saga, Volume 1*, which features stories that were originally published in 1995, shows Mary Jane leaving New York to spend time with her family without the knowledge of her neglectful husband, who is spending almost all of his time in his Spider-Man identity. When musing on what Peter might be feeling about her decision to leave, Mary Jane asks, "I wonder if he found my note? Does he even know ... or care ... that I'm gone?" (DeFalco, 1995: 278). This suggests that Parker's family is breaking up because of his inability to cater for his loved ones and thus he is failing in his normative role as the male patriarch of his family. Similarly, the same volume also features an instance in which a new villain, the mysterious Judas Traveller, takes advantage of Parker's personal insecurities in order to beat Spider-Man in a fight (DeFalco, 1995:235), thus suggesting that the preoccupations in Parker's personal life are inhibiting his ability to perform the Spider-Man identity successfully and are preventing him from keeping challenges to the "male" "heterosexual" hegemony, represented by Judas Traveller and his fellow criminals, at bay.

Spider-Man: Success Through Failure

The aforementioned episodes suggest that Spider-Man's need to divide his attention between the competing responsibilities of his two identities result in his failure to live up to the normative role in either, thus rendering him a failure in both. This may appear to be a damning account of a superhero but Spider-Man's failures are, in fact, an intrinsic part of his appeal. Conflicting responsibilities and failure to live up to their ascribed gender norms is a characteristic of everyday being for real people. Butler herself relates to this difficulty when she describes gender norms as "impossible" (62). It is Spider-Man's status as a failure that makes it easier for his audience to relate to him. Stan Lee, Spider-Man's creator, even testifies to the fact that it was always his intention for Spider-Man to be a character with "human problems" and "human frailties" (200) in an early issue of *Amazing Spider-Man*. Furthermore, the fact that Spider-Man, for all his failures, is still a popular character suggests that "human frailties" are actually something that his readership looks for in a hero. Also, it is Spider-Man's everyman quality that helps to explain why he and Batman function as a successful team in *Spider-Man and Batman: Disordered Minds*. Initially, Batman is hostile to Spider-Man's offer of assistance. His sharp challenge, "What are you doing in my city?" (DeMatteis, 1995: 29), suggests that, at first, he views the presence of another superhero in his own territory as a threat to his hegemonic "masculine" authority, a threat which, since the death of his father, Batman has become attuned to meeting with corresponding aggression. Batman later relents for an unspecified reason and allows Spider-Man to work alongside him. However, it can be deduced that Batman has recognized in Spider-Man's "performative" display a "masculine" identity which, in contrast to his own, struggles to live up to the "male" "heterosexual" norm that has been set for him. Spider-Man's "heterosexual" "male" identity appears to be less potent than Batman's and thus does not threaten it.

Spider-Man thus demonstrates to his audience that failing to live up to an idealized vision of normative perfection can be productive; it can produce empathy between equally flawed individuals, to which Spider-Man's continuing popularity and the existence of this book testifies, as well as an understanding that sometimes cooperation is necessary for success. This is a realization that does not come easily to Batman, who is used to relying on himself in order to support his own belief in his normative perfection.

Works Cited

Brooker, Will. *Batman Unmasked: Analyzing a Cultural Icon*. London: Continuum, 2000.
Butler, Judith. *Gender Trouble*. New York: Routledge, 2008.
DeFalco, Tom, J.M. DeMatteis, Todd DeZago et al. *The Amazing Spider-Man: The Complete Clone Saga, Volume 1*. New York: Marvel Comics, 2010.
DeMatteis, J.M., Mark Bagley, Scott Hanna, et al. *Spider-Man and Batman: Disordered Minds*. New York: Marvel Comics, 1995.
Lee, Stan, Steve Ditko et al. *The Amazing Spider-Man Masterworks Volume 1*. New York: Marvel Comics, 2009.

V. Trauma Textual and Extra-Textual

The Loss of the Father: Trauma Theory and the Birth of Spider-Man

FORREST C. HELVIE

"The past is never dead. It's not even past."
— *William Faulkner*, Requiem for a Nun *(93)*

Introduction

When the reader sees the phrase "With great power comes great responsibility"[1] emblazoned across the final panel of *Amazing Fantasy 15*, the painful lesson Peter Parker learns over the course of this short but poignant story of one's coming of age becomes all-too clear. Although fate imbues Parker with the powers of the radioactive spider, it doesn't do so gently—biting instead of bestowing. He continues to feel the bite of the spider when he initially chooses self over his familial community, and this failure to act as a member of that community by policing it results in his fracturing that social group, which in turn allows Uncle Ben's soon-to-be murderer to run free. With the loss of his foster father, Uncle Ben—a traumatic experience he will not soon, if ever, overcome—Parker's misuse of his newly found powers forces him to recognize that one must be responsible to his community or else cause great suffering.

Trauma Theory and Comic Book Superheroes

It is important to understand first and foremost that the stories and characters of Stan Lee and Steve Ditko's *The Amazing Spider-Man* were meant to entertain young and old readers alike through a mix of comedy, action, and adventure. Unlike many other comics of yesteryear, however, there are certain Western metaphysical traces of humanity that show themselves from the very first story in *Amazing Fantasy #15*. And while one must be exceptionally careful not to trivialize the importance of the subject of trauma and those who are victims of such disruptions in their lives, it is worth considering how even "funny books" such as Lee and Ditko's *The Amazing Spider-Man* possess elements of the world in which we live. Such attempts at speaking to the human condition include elements of tragedy and trauma with which many readers past and present readily identify. Amidst the camp and conflict of costumed heroes, readers of *The Amazing Spider-Man* found the story of a young boy who struggled to come to grips with what he perceived as a tragedy of his own making; further, it carried the story of how a person can grow stronger from such difficulty in spite of the many opportunities to let it get the best of him.

It is also worth noting that this examination of comic superheroes and trauma theory is not an isolated one. In his 2009 essay, titled "Sixty-Five Years of Guilt Over the Death of Bucky," Rob Weiner explores Captain America's wartime experiences with his sidekick, Bucky Barnes, pointing to what may be viewed as post-traumatic stress disorder (PTSD) following the eventual death of the young boy. Weiner maps out the origins of the individuals in question as well as the fateful day Bucky is strapped to an experimental plane, which is subsequently blown apart, tossing Captain America into the freezing waters. As Weiner observes: "He could not bring himself to believe Bucky was dead.... Captain America was avoiding the reality of Bucky's death by wanting to go back and 'make sure' he was really gone" (93). Pointing to this form of "survivor's guilt" as one symptom of PTSD (among many others), Weiner argues that many of the creators who handled the Captain America stories were, in part, finding a vehicle for coping with this very real problem of trauma.

Furthermore, Shawn Gillen's work from the same collected anthology explores the relationship between comic heroes and post-traumatic stress syndrome (PTSD) in Steve Rogers' struggle to deal with his experiences from World War II during the explosive Vietnam era. While Gillen's work points to the ways in which Cap's association with the U.S. military and wartime experiences directly contribute to his PTSD, I would argue that we can expand the ways in which heroes are traumatized by examining experiences away from the battlefield (in much the same way non-active duty service members can experience PTSD and other sorts of trauma-induced difficulties, though the contributing factors differ). In this respect, there is precedent for this examination, and perhaps in bringing to light the presence in comics of experiences like these, we might better understand how sequential art can provide a voice for those who experience it in the real world.

The Call to Adventure and the Self-Inflicted Wound

Looking at Joseph Campbell's (1949) seminal work, *The Hero With a Thousand Faces*, one recalls the "call to adventure" that every hero answers, leading to a great adventure that forever alters his or her life trajectory. In the case of Spider-Man, Parker not only fails to initially respond to this call, he rejects it outright. At the end of shooting a scene for a television spot as another means of capitalizing on his sensational powers, Spider-Man sees a crook running away from the cop: "Stop! Thief! Stop him! If he makes the elevator, he'll get away" (Lee, 2009 [Vol. 1]: 8). Instead of making use of his superior physical abilities to stop the crook, Parker snarkily replies to the cop, "That's your job! I'm thru being pushed around — by anyone! From now on I look out for number one — that means — me!" (8). Most "journey" stories don't start in this fashion — otherwise, there would be no journey to follow and learn from. But as Campbell points out, there are usually dire consequences to the hero's failure to respond to the call: "The subject ... becomes a victim to be saved. His flowering world becomes a wasteland of dry stones and his life becomes meaningless" (59). Just as Sir Percival failed to bring restitution through his lack of response to the plight of the Fisher King and his kingdom in the Grail legends, so too does Parker's abject failure to respond to this call for a hero inadvertently bring about the traumatic destruction of his family community. Parker returns home to find that his home was broken into — the breaking of his kingdom — and this burglar shot his Uncle Ben — the death of the king. The call to heroism is no longer voluntary; it becomes internalized through this traumatic, life-changing experience as he walks down a dark city alley.

It is in these final two panels of this short, eleven-page story that the traumatic event sinks in. Parker sobs: "My fault — all my fault! If only I had stopped him when I could have! But I didn't — and now — Uncle Ben — is dead..." (Lee, 2009 [Vol.1]: 11). Spider-Man's failure to answer the call for a hero resulted in the continuation of chaos and violence in his community and that same destructive influence found its way into his home. Only after the fracturing of his home life does he recognize the trauma for which he is indirectly responsible; however, this recognition provides Parker with something few people who reject the role of hero are offered: a second chance. As the unnamed narrator states at the close of the final panel: "And a lean, silent figure slowly fades into the gathering darkness, aware at last that in this world, with great power there must also come — great responsibility" (11). With the realization that his powers are more than just sources of fame and fortune, Parker finds himself with a hard-earned opportunity to once again take up the mantle of Spider-Man and fulfill the hero's calling. Furthermore, it is this internalization of the trauma that provides the cure for the psychological wound that Peter Parker inflicted upon himself:

> Willed introversion, in fact, is one of the classic implements of creative genius.... The result, of course, can be a disintegration of consciousness more or less complete; but on the other hand, if the personality is able to absorb and integrate the new forces, there will be experienced an almost super-human degree of self-consciousness and masterful control [Campbell, 1973: 64].

Parker continually struggles with the isolation of his secret identity as Spider-Man, but it is through this continuous struggle that he eventually comes to not only accept his responsibility to protect those around him, but also to regain control over his life and recover from the trauma of his uncle's death in the form and garb of Spider-Man.

Trauma and the Fracturing of Community

To gain a better understanding of Spider-Man's origins, critics will find in trauma theory a useful approach in considering Parker and the ways in which he came to grips with the death of his uncle and the birth of his web slinging alter ego. Through viewing the Parker / Spider-Man dynamic through this critical lens, it becomes clear that the act of fighting crime serves as a vehicle by which Parker is able to reinvent a new identity for himself and, in turn, correct the mistakes of the past by preventing similar forms of trauma from being inflicted upon others in his community.

In medical terms, psychic trauma arises "when a sudden, unexpected, overwhelming intense emotional blow or a series of blows assaults the person from the outside. Traumatic events are external, but they quickly become incorporated into the mind" (Terr, 1990: 8). Other clinicians explain how "it is not the trauma itself that does the damage;" rather, it is the manner in which the mind of the individual finds itself without the necessary resources and abilities to navigate the traumatic experience that gives rise to long-term difficulties (Bloom, 1999: 2). From these two perspectives, one can surmise then that these sudden external events serve as a catalyst for an internal shift, which places the victim under a state of duress for a variable period of time. Furthermore, trauma acts as a "source that marks and defines ... individual identity" as much "as racial or cultural identity" (Belaev, 2010: 3), though certainly originating from a far more negative experience than one's race or culture. Therefore, one might begin to understand how trauma creates a lasting shift within the individual's psyche, whose effects will remain a part of that individual's conception and performance of self. Although this is a somewhat cursory view of a very complicated condition, it should provide a basic understanding of what is referred to as "trauma" and the effects it has on the traumatized victim.

In a medical study on trauma, psychiatrist Sarah Bloom (1999) notes that "we are physiologically designed to function best as an integrated whole ... [and] the fragmentation that accompanies traumatic experience degrades this integration and impedes maximum performance" (3). This seems to point towards the significance often placed on the individual's place and need for community — the need on the part of people in a community for unity and integration in their everyday experiences. It is then reasonable to assume that, in a sense, a traumatic experience is one that introduces some form of fracture in those affected and causes a displacement from the community.

Parker's Response to Trauma

Most comic book fans are all too familiar with the changes new artists and writers will enact upon a beloved series. For this reason, my analysis will limit itself strictly to the early years of *The Amazing Spider-Man*, and particularly those years where the creative team of Stan Lee and Steve Ditko were at the helm in steering the development of both Parker and Spider-Man. This narrowed focus will maintain a more accurate and consistent assessment of both creators' creative direction with this character. While Spider-Man regularly made appearances in other comic titles during his early years, the contributions would be marginal at best and would not contribute in a substantial way to this analysis. And while later creators would provide substantial contributions to the development of the Spider-Man mythos, it was Lee and Ditko who laid the foundation upon which all others would build.

While Bloom presents an extensive list of possible responses exhibited by trauma victims, there are a few that prove particularly relevant to Parker. These responses show how the traumatic events in Peter's life changed him, how the death of his Uncle Ben serves as the moment of his being fractured apart from his community, and his continual attempt to return that broken community to its original state of wholeness. Of the responses Bloom discusses, those that stand out most clearly are: Remembering Under Stress, Thinking Under Stress, The Loss of "Volume Control" (or emotional stability), Victim to Victimizer, and Traumatic Reenactment (3–11).

Shortly after Uncle Ben's death, Parker begins exhibiting behaviors that resemble the responses of Remembering Under Stress, Thinking Under Stress, and The Loss of "Volume Control." Remembering Under Stress refers to a condition where conscious memory is often impaired during a time of trauma, and "powerful images, feelings, and sensations don't just 'go away.' They are deeply imprinted ... [and can be] difficult or impossible to erase" (Bloom, 1999: 5). As a result, this can often lead the victim to the unconscious experience of flashbacks, temporarily disrupting the individual's relationship to linear time. *Amazing Spider-Man Annual #1* presents a clear example of these sorts of powerful memories surfacing and creating a break in the victim's temporal consciousness. Walking along the precipice of a New York skyscraper and wearing the protective garb of Spider-Man, Parker is lost in thoughts of his Uncle Ben. This is more than mere reminiscence, however. He becomes so lost in his thoughts that "the sure-footed adventurer loses his balance" (Lee, 2009 [Vol. 2]: 120) and falls from the building. Not only did this flashback cause him to lose track of his surroundings, it also brings about a temporary loss of his spider powers. It is no coincidence that Spider-Man loses his powers following his dwelling upon Uncle Ben's traumatic murder, and this becomes emblematic of the loss of control Peter is experiencing in his life. The traumatic loss of his father-like uncle leaves such a strong psychic imprint that it temporarily disempowers the superhero.

The next traumatic response Parker exhibits is Thinking Under Stress, which refers to those situations where the individual's ability to think clearly is significantly impaired and "decisions tend to be based on impulse and are based on ... a need to self-protect" (Bloom, 1999: 5). Furthermore, the individual is no longer prepared to think rationally and finds him or herself "geared towards action and often the action taken will be violent" (ibid.). Although one of Spider-Man's strengths is his ability to think under pressure, highlighted by his "spider sense," there are instances where his decision-making is seriously brought into question.

In *Amazing Spider-Man Issue #12*, Parker catches a debilitating flu that severely weakens him, and despite recognizing he is not physically well, the unnamed narrator informs readers: "But, shrugging off his own problem, Peter quickly rushes to an alley, where he changes to Spider-Man" (Lee, 2009 [Vol. 2]: 28). It is in this state that Spider-Man battles and loses to Doctor Octopus, who then unmasks him revealing the near-unconscious, weakened Peter Parker. While one expects Spider-Man to confront villains such as Doctor Octopus and prevent further crimes against New York (and by extension, his own family), he rashly jumps into violent action without considering his own ability to stop the criminal and avoid personal harm at the same time. With his secret identity shown to the world, he puts his beloved and sickly Aunt May at risk. Even his Spider-Man alter ego confronts him for his carelessness in his sleep that night as he dreams: "What are you? Some kinda nut or something?? You should have your head examined for appearing as Spider-Man when you were so weak" (30). Clearly, there is a part of Peter that recognizes his own failure to think clearly and resist such impulsive thoughts.

A third response Peter illustrates is The Loss of "Volume Control" (or emotional stability). Most people possess the faculty to regulate their inner emotions, but after being exposed to a violent, traumatic experience, many individuals will lose that ability. In particular, these individuals will be prone to substance abuse as a means of coping with their erratic feelings. In Parker's case, however, he does not turn to substance abuse but to his wrestling and television persona, Spider-Man, to find a means of compensating for the harm he allowed to happen. The robber (and eventual murderer of Uncle Ben) is allowed to continue on his way while Peter is donning his blue and red costume, and it is interesting to note that Peter then uses the same costume as a means of making up for his failure in the weeks, months, and years to follow.

One example (of many) of the strength of Parker's compulsion to maintain the Spider-Man persona as a means of containing his emotions can be seen in the final haunting panel drawn by Steve Ditko at the end of *Amazing Spider-Man #29*. In this picture, Parker is shown walking away dejectedly with the rejected Betty Brant crying in the background [2]. What is particularly poignant is the ghost-like image of Spider-Man interjected between the two with his arms spread out as though he were directly keeping the two star-crossed lovers apart. The message is clear: be Spider-Man and be without love. Parker's walking away from Betty further drives this point home — he cannot and will not abandon his role as Spider-Man even if it is to his own detriment. Throughout their relationship, Parker wants to open up and share his secret life with Betty but fears the consequences of doing so. As a result of being unable to negotiate this emotional territory, he opts to abandon it and Betty altogether in favor of the emotional isolation of the mask.

Parker's Attempts to Cope with Trauma

The next set of responses (Victim to Victimizer and Traumatic Reenactment) could best be viewed as Parker's conscious (and unconscious) attempts to cope with the trauma experience of Uncle Ben's death and find some methods of moving on with his life. During the Victim to Victimizer response, in an attempt to regain control over their lives, traumatized individuals assume the role of victimizer so they can assert some level of control over their lives and the world around them — unfortunately creating additional links in the chain of trauma. In the case of Parker, however, his creation of the Spider-Man alter ego demonstrates an interesting perspective on this particular response to trauma. Where it was a criminal who initially causes the trauma to the Parker family, Parker uses his Spider-Man persona to "victimize" the "victimizers." Parker realizes he could even use his superhuman abilities to impose order over the world around him through becoming like the criminal who forcibly imposed chaos into his life: "I can go anywhere! No one, nothing can stop me! Any amount of money could be mine — just for the taking!" (Lee, 2009 [Vol. 1]: 16). Instead of using his powers to further the violation of community forced upon him, however, he declares, "I'm not a thief! [...] it would break Aunt May's heart!" (16). Parker recognizes the dangers of fracturing the bonds of community and does not want the members of his community (represented by Aunt May) to experience such psychic trauma. Yet, he *will* become the "victimizer" of individuals who would make victims of members of his family and all of New York. He states that "fate gave me some terrific super-powers, and I realize now that it's my duty to use them ... without doubt ... without hesitation...!!" (Lee, 2009 [Vol. 2]: 255). Even months after Uncle Ben's death, Parker sits on a rooftop brooding over the effects of this traumatic experience and how "no matter what I do ... no matter how great my spider powers are, I can never undo that tragic mistake! I can never completely forgive myself!" (ibid.: 120). And this moment of vulnerability highlights the very reason for Spider-Man's continual battle against evil-doers: he is stuck in a cycle of continually reestablishing order in his world by battling those who would wrest that control for their own reprehensible interests. This leads to the final response Parker has through Traumatic Reenactment.

Traumatic Reenactment can be seen as connected to the notion of being locked in a cyclical battle with the forces of evil, with the Sinister Six at the forefront. This reenactment refers to the unconscious need for the individual to reintegrate him or herself into a functioning role in society; however, the traumatic event/s create a sort of disruption of the individual's routine. When we enact this day-to-day drama, we "secretly hop[e] that someone will give us a different script, a different outcome to the drama, depending on how damaging our experiences have been. The cure is in the disease" (10). In other words, reenactment serves as a means by which the traumatized subconscious attempts to right itself by reenacting the events that caused the disruption in hopes of eventually working through the trauma.

One might detect in Parker's adoption of the Spider-Man persona an attempt to develop a new identity script to perform — one whose identity is a clean slate, and therefore free of the traumatic death of his "father." Furthermore, looking at the previous incident of Spider-Man's loss of powers from *Amazing Spider-Man Annual #1*, he regains his superhuman abilities — those traits that differentiate Parker from Spider-Man — when he embraces his newly formed identity script: "I'm still alive!! I dodged his bolt! But ... nobody without super powers can do that!! That can mean only one thing ... my powers have returned to me!! I haven't lost them!! I'm still Spider-Man!" (ibid.:128). With the acceptance of his newly refashioned self, Parker (as Spider-Man) is able to come to power, and by extension, find some sense of personal renewal. The cure to Peter's trauma is found through this cathartic reenactment of the role he *should* have performed the fateful evening at the wrestling arena, and it is through this continued performance of his costumed-self that Parker can reach his full potential as he continues on the path towards adulthood. In his essay, "Captain America, Post-Traumatic Stress Syndrome, and the Vietnam Era," Shawn Gillen suggests that Steve Rogers' struggles with the trauma of his war-time experience and the death of Bucky result, in part, from his having to wrestle with the trauma alone, unlike many of his fellow World War II veterans who were welcomed home with open arms (ibid.: 106). In a similar way, Peter Parker cannot allow himself to fully grapple with the trauma of Uncle Ben's death else his identity as Spider-Man, who allowed the criminal to pass by unmolested, be exposed. Like Steve Rogers, Parker struggles with trauma alone but it is through his role as Spider-Man that he vindicates himself.

Conclusion

Spider-Man's abilities allow Parker the ability to find greater independence and self-reliance as a newly emerging adult. The point in time when Spider-Man came into existence runs concurrent with the same period in Parker's life when he would be experiencing the physical, mental, and emotional development of young adulthood. Young men grow taller, develop their physical prowess, strengthen their sense of self-discipline, and generally begin to move from a state of dependence on their parents to one of independence, relying more on their own abilities than that of their mother and father to meet their needs. Parker's newfound super strength, constitution, and speed allow far greater range of movement as well as endurance under hardship. He experiences jubilation in his newly acquired abilities and regularly seeks new ways in which to test his boundaries — again, not so dissimilar to most adolescents who "push boundaries" as they learn their capabilities. Just as young adults begin to break away from their parents and adopt personas of their own fashioning, so too does Parker break from his "bookish" image and recast himself as the Spider-Man. And while he initially rejects the responsibility of adulthood in the first call to exercise the use of power in a heroic way and must then undergo the trauma of being indirectly responsible for Uncle Ben's death, it is through this trauma that Parker receives his second opportunity to accept his place in society as the protector, Spider-Man.

Notes

1. While many fans of the first film directed by Sam Raimi will recall Uncle Ben as having uttered this iconic line, in fact, it was never actually spoken by any one character. Instead, an "unnamed narrator" coins the phrase in a text-box within the final panel in *Amazing Fantasy #15*.

2. Although many later Spider-Man comic book and movie fans may not recall Betty Brant, she was, in fact, Peter Parker's first love interest and someone who played a significant role in the development of his love life during the Ditko years (1963–1966). Their inability to continue on in their relationship would give way to later relationships between Gwen Stacy and then Mary Jane Watson which would further define and complicate both Peter Parker and Spider-Man's growth as a character.

Works Cited

Balaev, Michele. "Trends in Literary Trauma Theory." *Mosiac* 41:2 (2008): 148–167. *Academic OneFile*. Accessed 6/23/2010.
Bloom, Sandra L., M.D. *Trauma Theory Abbreviated*. Philadelphia: Community Works, 1999. Accessed 11/2/2011 PDF file. http://www.sanctuaryweb.com/PDFs_new/Bloom%20Trauma%20Theory%20Abbreviated.pdf.
Campbell, Joseph. *The Hero With A Thousand Faces*. Princeton, NJ: Princeton University Press, 1973.
Faulkner, William. *Requiem for a Nun*. New York: Random House, 1951.
Gillen, Shawn. "Captain America, Post-Traumatic Stress Syndrome, and the Vietnam Era" in Robert G. Weiner ed., *Captain America and the Struggles of the Superhero: Critical Essays*. Jefferson: McFarland, 2009.
Lee, Stan, Steve Ditko et al. *The Amazing Spider-Man Masterworks Vol. 1*. New York: Marvel, 2009.
_____, Steve Ditko et al. *The Amazing Spider-Man Masterworks Vol. 2*. New York: Marvel, 2009.
_____, Steve Ditko et al. *The Amazing Spider-Man Masterworks Vol. 3*. New York: Marvel, 2009.
Shay, Jonathan. *Achilles in Vietnam*. New York: Atheneum, 1994.
Terr, Lenore. *Too Scared to Cry: Psychic Trauma in Childhood*. New York: Harper, 1990.
Weiner, Robert G. "Sixty-Five Years of Guilt Over the Death of Bucky" in Robert G. Weiner ed., *Captain America and the Struggle of the Superhero: Critical Essays*. Jefferson: McFarland, 2009.

Artificial Mourning: The *Spider-Man* Trilogy and September 11th

TAMA LEAVER[1]

Spider-Man and his everyman alter ego Peter Parker have always lived in New York City, albeit an alternate New York situated within the Marvel comic book universe. The trilogy of *Spider-Man* feature films (Raimi, 2002; Raimi, 2004; Raimi, 2007) are also set in New York, although it is neither an historically accurate representation nor the comic book version, but a third cityscape which imaginatively borrows and builds on both of these precursors. This chapter argues that within that context, the *Spider-Man* films enact a form of artificial mourning, acting as a popular cultural arena in which some of the immediate tensions and traumas of the post–September 11th Western world are articulated and explored. From the outset, it is important to flag that the term artificial mourning is not necessarily positioning mourning facilitated through popular culture as "unreal" or necessarily "less" than trauma in the "real" world. Rather, the "artificial" in this term is consistent with deploying the artificial not as a marker of the unreal, but rather as a signifier of unstable boundaries, where easy binary divisions no longer make sense. Moreover, the artificial tends to highlight areas where technology, mediation and humanity intersect in unsettling ways, evident in the much-feared seeming oxymoron of artificial intelligence. In terms of Spider-Man as character, franchise and cultural icon, his artificiality is evident in the seeming incompatibilities of being both a human subject and a technological object, being both a hero and an everyday person with everyday problems, and being both a means of escapism for audiences, while engaging on some level with serious political and cultural concerns. Moreover, the movies situate Spider-Man and his various nemeses as artificial people — in that they are products of substantial technological transformation, whether purposefully or accidental — set in a New York largely facilitated by cutting edge special effects. This chapter begins by establishing some of the important connections between Spider-Man and New York from the more than 30 years of comic book history, then focuses on the influence of September 11th 2001 on both the comics and the feature films, before explicating some of the most important ways artificial mourning is played out in those films, concluding that the *Spider-Man* trilogy allegorically functions as a significant cultural arena in which aspects of the Western world's "Long September" have been explored.

Long before he came to the multiplex, Spider-Man's home and heart was firmly located in New York City. According to Bradford Wright, when Stan Lee and Steve Ditko originally envisioned Spider-Man in 1962, he was not a man of steel, nor a billionaire with a high-tech utility belt, but rather "an adolescent — one who had to contend with his own insecurities and confusion even as he had to fight the bad guys" (Wright, 2001: 210). After stumbling upon super-powers, Peter Parker first tried to exploit these gifts for financial gain, only becoming a hero after feeling responsible for his uncle's death, echoing the coda from the feature films that "with great power comes great responsibility" (Wright, 2001). However, unlike Superman or Batman, the best-selling superheroes at the time, Parker's Spider-Man did not inhabit a fictional Metropolis or dark Gotham, but rather lived and fought in the very city Stan Lee saw outside the window as he wrote: New York (Bukatman, 2003). Spider-Man quickly became Marvel Comics' most recognizable icon, a teenage everyman living in the same city as many of *Spider-Man*'s readers.

Comic book superheroes are often more deeply tied to their cities and surrounds than characters in non-visual narratives. As Scott Bukatman argues, Spider-Man's body is the "consequence of technology run wild. The superhero body is everything — a *corporeal*, rather than a *cognitive*, mapping of the subject into a cultural system" (Bukatman, 2003: 49), and that system is visualized through the cityscape. Just as New York is an icon of modernism and of technology, both in its positive aspects and its darker underside, so too is Spider-Man in his victories and his defeats. Bukatman argues further: "Superhero comics embody the grace of the city; superheroes are graced by the city. Through the superhero, we gain a freedom of movement not constrained by the ground-level order imposed by the urban grid" (Bukatman, 2003: 188). With a corporeality no longer anchored to the street, nor to the mundane horizontal, the numerous artists on the *Spider-Man* comic book could draw walls as floors and the space above the street, between buildings, as frantic pathways. Indeed, Bukatman explicitly links Spider-Man's abilities and relationship to the city with Michel de Certeau's tactics of spatiality (de Certeau, 1984); Spider-Man forges his own pathways transforming the metropolitan grid of place and modernity into tactical spaces of the resistant, struggling, embodied subject (Bukatman, 2003). The New York envisioned in the *Spider-Man* comics is thus a pre-digital artificial space, a tactical space which can be navigated and, to a considerable extent, reconfigured through the movement, motion and meaning of the subject. Indeed, the boundary between subjectivity and spatiality blurs just like the frenetic motion of a superhero in action.

Given Spider-Man's strong links to the city, it was no surprise when the promotional campaign for the first *Spider-Man* feature film was constructed around New York landmarks. The film was scheduled for release in May 2002 and advertising hit full momentum in August 2001 with a series of posters and one of the most expensive trailers ever made. In it, tech-savvy robbers plunder a New York bank and begin to escape in a helicopter, only for it to mysteriously stop mid-flight and then get yanked backwards. The helicopter finally stops and is snared in a gigantic spider web hung between the Twin Towers of the World Trade Center. The scene then cuts to the first ever visual of a computer-generated imagery (CGI) Spider-Man with the Twin Towers clearly reflected in his mirrored eyes, before he swings into the cityscape at full speed. The film's distributors removed the trailer the day following the September 11th attacks, less than a month after it debuted. In a CNN article published on September 13th, Columbia TriStar president of marketing Geoffrey Ammer stated, "the decision [to pull the trailer] was an easy one. [...] It's based on humanity. No cost can outweigh the sensitivity of the issue" (CNN Entertainment 2001). While sensitivity in the immediate aftermath of the fall of the Twin Towers is understandable, it is noteworthy that despite three *Spider-Man* films to date released on DVD, replete with extra material from across the history of the comics and films, the World Trade Center trailer is not amongst them. Nor have Columbia TriStar or their owners, Sony Entertainment, officially discussed the trailer since September 13th 2001. The first *Spider-Man* trailer is as much a ghost as the Twin Towers themselves.

However, while one aspect of the Spider-Man franchise chose to avoid any mention of the tragedy, the Marvel comic books went in a different direction.

Amazing Spider-Man 36, released with a cover date of December 2001, came with a completely black cover with nothing visible other than the outline of the comic book's title. The first page read: "We interrupt our regularly scheduled program to bring you the following Special Bulletin" (Straczynski, 2001: 1). This notice positioned readers within a tele-visual frame of expectation wherein images of the Twin Towers could still be found, but what the following pages contained was a tribute story to the firefighters, police women and men, the service personnel, and every other person who helped in the immediate wake of the September 11th tragedy. The following story sees the rest of the staple Marvel super-heroes arrive at Ground Zero, help out with the clean-up and rescue attempts, and show their deep respect for the "real" heroes. In an important scene, an exhausted and grim Spider-Man is drinking water with other emergency workers, his mask peeled halfway up, revealing the face of an ordinary New Yorker. In the last panel of that page, Parker laments, "I have seen other worlds, other spaces. I have walked with gods and wept with angels. But to my shame, I have no answers" (Straczynski, 2001, 15). While the Marvel universe had always existed alongside the "real" world in a *parallel* sense—with a similar cityscape but populated by different people, aliens, super-villains and superheroes—the sudden intersection of the comic book realm with "real" world events was a substantial change for Marvel. The comic emphasizes the role of superheroes alongside New York in its mourning, evident in Spider-Man's statements such as: "But we are here. Now. With you," emphasizing the grief that the Marvel superheroes are sharing with New Yorkers. More politically charged, however, was the dialogue. Spider-Man further states, "we live in each blow you strike for infinite justice, but always in the hope of infinite wisdom," explicitly critiquing the October 2001 invasion of Afghanistan by the U.S.-led coalition which was codenamed "Infinite Justice." Similarly, his line, "And All Wars have innocents" (Straczynski, 2001: 18) is far from a rallying cry for military action.

Given the deep ties between the Spider-Man and New York, it is hardly surprisingly that the impact of the 2001 terrorist attacks resonates powerfully throughout the *Spider-Man* trilogy. While the films are certainly less explicit than the comics in their engagement with the cultural impact of September 11th—it is never directly mentioned—the attacks resonate throughout the films, as will be demonstrated below. Moreover, this chapter situates these films as spaces of artificial mourning, that is, popular culture texts in which viewers can engage with the cultural aftermath of the terrorist attacks. The "artificial" here does not mean unreal, but rather is about mourning which takes place in the circuit of meaning negotiated between cinematic texts, the technologies of their creation, the socio-political landscape and, of course, each individual viewer. Artificial mourning, then, has to be subjective, but the markers inviting engagement with the emotional and cultural legacy of September 11th are largely unavoidable. The artificial marks where meanings are often unstable: the divisions between human subject and technological object, between entertainment and politics, between good and evil, are all in flux in an artificial space. Artificial mourning is an invitation to engage with the many legacies of September 11th rather than a single solution or perspective on those tragic events. It is with those ambiguities in mind that the first *Spider-Man* film comes into focus.

The graphics forming the title sequence for the first *Spider-Man* film, released in the American summer of 2002, immediately link Spider-Man and the sprawling metropolitan cityscape of New York. The images in the credits begin with spider webs as vectors, outlining the elements of Spider-Man's visualized corporeality, then showing the reds and blues of Spider-Man's upper body, bent with head bowed. The sequence then shifts to showing Spider-

Man crawling along a skyscraper rendered in the same colors, hues and with similar grid lines. Indeed, the similarity between Spider-Man's CGI costume and the visualized city almost suggests that the same grid lines at one point form the city, and at another are stretched around a human, forming a heroic costume. Significantly, as viewers see the last few images of the city, the buildings share the blues and blacks of Spider-Man's costume and reflect the reds in the windows, but a red glow is also visible on the horizon, a vista New York experienced the night the Twin Towers fell. These opening credits immediately link the superhero and the cityscape, intertwining their visual depictions and positing a shared ontology.

In an updated version of Spider-Man's origin story, Parker and his school class are visiting one of Columbia University's research facilities. Parker's geek credentials are displayed as he almost drools, "That's the largest electron microscope on the Eastern Seaboard." The class is introduced to a series of genetically engineered super-spiders that combine the skills of various species of spider. Rather than the 1960s technological bugbear of radiation, the early-21st century origins of Spider-Man are linked with one of the most contentious contemporary technologies, genetic engineering. When Parker awakens the next day after a feverish night, he discovers the he is stronger, faster and can shoot webbing from glands in his wrists. Spider-Man is thus a fusion of technologies and embodiment, a carnal superhero whose technological origins are as much cross-species as they are digital. Nevertheless, the synthesis of origins, technologies and species clearly mark Spider-Man as an artificial person.

It is worth noting, however, that the film does not unproblematically embrace new technologies, as it also emphasizes the difficulties entailed in adapting to the challenges of technological change. In the first scene with Parker's Uncle Ben, viewers discover that Ben has been fired after a lifetime's employment as an electrician. Looking through the employment section of the newspaper, he laments that the advertisements all seek experience with digital technologies: "Computer salesman, computer engineer, computer analyst — My lord, even the computers need analysts these days! I'm too old for computers." The technologies that facilitated the artificial origins of Spider-Man also hamper Parker's family. More significantly, once Parker has become Spider-Man, he no longer visibly engages with digital technologies. Despite being a science whiz and showing knowledge of the latest technologies, Parker never wields anything more advanced than a manual camera in any of the *Spider-Man* films. While this change is at odds with Parker's initial characterization — in the comic books he frequently uses technology, and even invented his web-shooters in the laboratory, rather than have them appear organically with his spider-powers — it does emphasize that for Spider-Man technologies are an inescapable part of life, but their utility and politics are determined through use, and are not intrinsic. Moreover, while Spider-Man does not appear to use digital technologies, viewers would be well aware that in many scenes Spider-Man *is the product* of the latest CGI techniques and thus *is* a digital technology. Although updating his hybrid origins, the films implicitly link Spider-Man and technology through the character's diegetic ontology and the CGI facilitating Spider-Man's amazing abilities, but rather than over-emphasizing the character's technological status, his lack of visible engagement with advanced technologies situates technology as a part of everyday life. Spider-Man is about a balance between the growing pains of adolescence, responsibility and an amazing but simultaneously banal engagement with technology. In effect, the films epistemologically situate artificial people such as Spider-Man not as differentiated "technological" entities, but rather, as simply one of New York's eight million citizens.

Just as Peter Parker became Spider-Man through engagement with the latest technologies, so too did his first nemesis, the Green Goblin. In *Spider-Man*, Norman Osborn (Willem Dafoe), a millionaire businessman half-way between Donald Trump and Victor Frankenstein, is about to lose a massive military commission to create both military hardware and nanotechnological "performance enhancers," designed to increase the abilities of humans in order to use their military devices. Despite their digital origins, performance enhancers sound like, and appear similar to, steroids and other performance-enhancing drugs, a symbolism reinforced by the need to ingest the enhancers. Thus, when Osborn pushes human trials of the enhancers forward, using himself as the guinea pig, he develops a megalomaniac split personality, steals the military tools including bombs and a human-sized glider, and becomes the Green Goblin. The Goblin's visceral desires and disdain for human life are dark mirrors of Parker's struggle to protect innocent life in the wake of his uncle's tragic death. In Slavoj Žižeks reflections on September 11th he argues that part of the horror of the attacks was that their incomprehensibility or otherness revealed a far deeper trauma, in that even in terms of terrorism, "every feature attributed to the Other is already present at the very heart of the USA" (Žižek, 2002: 43). If, as this chapter argues, *Spider-Man* offers an allegorical engagement with the trauma of September 11th, it is highly significant that the Other that Spider-Man must defeat shares very similar origins: he is a New York citizen whose engagement with advanced technologies had unintended consequences, giving him abilities beyond the norms of everyday corporeality. In many ways, the battle between Spider-Man and the Green Goblin, both artificial people, is as much a battle between similarities as between differences.

The *Spider-Man* films also present the relationship with media technologies as ambiguous and often problematic. Parker gets his first financial break in New York by using a timer function to capture pictures of himself in action as Spider-Man and selling them to the disreputable newspaper *The Daily Bugle* and its enigmatic editor J. Jonah Jameson. Although Jameson is, at times, a sympathetic character, he is certainly no champion of journalistic impartiality, evident when he purchases Peter's photos, ignores their context, and adds sensationalist captions. From a picture of Spider-Man simply scaling a wall, Jameson extracts a headline such as "Big Apple Dreads Spider Bite!" As Marcia Landy argues, the news media played a large role in both portraying and formulating the initial responses to September 11th (Landy, 2004). Just as the news media footage of the Twin Towers collapsing were the only sanctioned images, the media commentators who ran these segments had considerable influence in shaping the national response. Moreover, while the news media largely supported the U.S.–led 2003 invasion of Iraq, the following months and years included some hard questions about the journalism surrounding weapons of mass destruction which, most famously, led to the *New York Times* apologizing for their lack of investigative journalism before the invasion began (*New York Times*, 2004). In that context *The Daily Bugle* is an iconic representation of media sensationalism and irresponsibility. Indeed, in *Spider-Man 2*, after a series of articles from the *Bugle* attack Spider-Man's intentions, Parker briefly gives up on being a super-hero, and Jameson is seen celebrating after he purchases the discarded Spider-Man costume. Thus, the power and influence of media is both highlighted and, to an extent, critiqued in the *Spider-Man* films.

One of the core links facilitating the allegorical utility of the films is the entwining of the figure of Spider-Man and the New York cityscape. Earlier, Spider-Man's ties to the city were explored as enacted in the comic books, but through CGI and other techniques, the films further amplify these links. As Elizabeth Grosz argues, the links between corporeality and cities runs deep:

> The body, however, is not distinct from the city for they are mutually defining ... there may be an isomorphism between the body and city. But it is not a mirroring of nature in artifice; rather, there is a two-way linkage that could be defined as an *interface*. What I am suggesting is a model of the relations between bodies and cities that sees them, not as megalithic total entities, but as

assemblages or collections of parts, capable of crossing the thresholds between substances to form linkages, machines, provisional and often temporary sub- or micro-groupings. This model is practical, based on the productivity of bodies and cities in defining and establishing each other [Grosz, 1995: 108].

As the opening titles of the first *Spider-Man* attested, Spider-Man and New York share a similar grid-system, one delineating urban space, while the other is wrapped around a corporeal superhero. Building on Grosz's arguments, there are numerous other links between Spider-Man and the city. For example, when Parker first decides to accept the mantle of Spider-Man as a crime-fighter and moves to New York, the initial appearance of the iconic costume seemingly emerges from the heart of the city itself. With a camera pointing upward from street level, along a busy street ending with the Empire State Building, Spider-Man bursts forth, swinging down as if the streets have conjured their own embodied figure. Moreover, just as Spider-Man is frequently a CGI character, at times so, too, is the city. Many of the city streets were composited from existing footage and digital simulations and some of the live-action photography of New York took place on the streets of Los Angeles. The New York of the *Spider-Man* films is thus the New York of imagination, the city whose iconography most loudly speaks of the American Dream. For Spider-Man, the city is an artificial, tactical space being navigated and interfaced with by an artificial person. It is this synthesis between the idealized New York and Spider-Man that so powerfully and symbolically links the two.

After Spider-Man first bursts into New York, a montage of his fight against crime is seen and is followed by some candid on-the-street style interviews with the city's residents, who oscillate from recognizing a hero to being deeply suspicious of this seemingly non-human entity. At the end of these interviews, the film cuts to an image of Spider-Man with the New York skyline reflecting in his costumed eyes. This image is extremely significant because clearly visible in that reflected city are the Twin Towers, still standing tall. Indeed, a comparison with the withdrawn original trailer shows that this is exactly the same effects shot as was used in the trailer. For two full seconds, or roughly fifty individually rendered CGI frames, the Twin Towers are reflected in the eyes of New York's own superhero. Despite the World Trade Center being absent from the film's narrative *per se*, this CGI homage to the fallen Towers clearly establishes the ties between Spider-Man and New York both before and after September 11th 2001. Moreover, the use of CGI allowed the filmmakers to pay tribute to the Towers in a manner consistent with the comic books' meaningful engagement in the special tribute issue, but also in a fashion ostensibly recognizing the cultural taboo against the Towers being represented at this time. The Towers survive inscribed onto the body of Spider-Man. Moreover, the image being the same one from the withdrawn original trailer directly links both the narrative and the production of the *Spider-Man* film to the tragedy suffered by New York and its citizens.

While the *Spider-Man* films are clearly set in a science fictional world with superheroes and super-villains, they nevertheless engage with the historical realities of September 11th and its immediate cultural aftermath. In addressing films which engage directly with historical events, Sean Cubitt points out that: "History films invite us to inhabit our own societies, cultures and nations, but to do so they must construct all three.... Historical film presents as complete, at origin, what it seeks to create" (Cubitt, 2004: 301). History in cinema is thus always a reconstructing and visioning, never that impossibly historical dream of a reflection of unmediated events. Moreover, in analyzing films which attempt to change or challenge generally accepted versions of historical events, Cubitt argues that these "reversionary movies" often drawn on older models of representation and depiction, such as Japanese graphic arts (321). In the case of *Spider-Man*, the films do not seek to re-vision the historical event of September 11th, but rather address the West's Long September not just metaphorically but in an allegorical manner which, to some extent, attempts to remake the past of the Marvel comic book franchise. Following that line, the most significant re-characterization in adapting the comics for the cinema was the character of Mary Jane Watson.

In the comic books, Parker fell in love with Mary Jane only after the relationship with his first true love, Gwen Stacy, ended tragically with her shocking, uncomic-like death. However, as Marvel's editor-in-chief Joe Quesada notes in a featurette on the *Spider-Man 2* DVD, "when they created the Mary Jane character for the movie, it's pretty obvious that there's a mixture of Gwen and Mary Jane within that character. They sort of amalgamated the two girls into one sort of idealized character" (Raimi, 2004). Rather than the complication of two love interests in the space of a two-hour film, in adapting the comic for the silver screen the writers and director added elements of Gwen Stacy to the character of Mary Jane (Blumberg, 2003). However, when Mary Jane is kidnapped by the Green Goblin and held hostage atop a New York bridge, many viewers would immediately have feared Mary Jane would actually be murdered since this scene mirrors the moment when Gwen Stacy died in the comic books, a moment whose tragedy reshaped and led to a far darker comic-book universe (Blumberg, 2003). In the film, the Goblin gives Spider-Man a choice between rushing to save either Mary Jane or a tramcar full of children which is about to plummet to the ground. Luckily, Parker thinks outside binary choices and manages to catch the falling Mary Jane and save the cable-car. While a well-choreographed rescue scene in itself, the powerful significance of this sequence in terms of allegorically engaging with September 11th is that, in the revisioning of the *Spider-Man* films, the new Gwen Stacyesque character lives (Priest, 2002). Rather than revisioning the "real" politics outside of the fictional franchise, the films revision the Marvel universe and redeploy a fictional moment of tragedy deeply linked to New York. After heightening the fear of many viewers that *Spider-Man* would visualize the comic book's most shocking tragedy, the films actually present a far more optimistic city where the superhero can save the damsel in distress. At an allegorical level, this shift in the adaptation of the comics imbues New York with an optimism not so much about erasing history as renegotiating a cityscape shrouded in mourning. The artificial spaces of a revisioned New York and artificial personhood of a CGI Spider-Man facilitate a type of artificial mourning which both acknowledges New York's wounds but also points to a more hopeful future (even if located by, to some extent, re-visioning a fictional past).

The links between the *Spider-Man* film and New York's citizens are also explored in an overstated manner during the last fight sequences with the Green Goblin. As Spider-Man rescues Mary Jane and the children in the cable car, the Goblin's attack is interrupted by a group of ordinary New York citizens who throw bricks and stones at the Goblin; one screams out "You mess with Spidey, you messing with New York!" while another man yells, "You mess with one of us, you mess with all of us." These ordinary everyday New Yorkers coming to Spider-Man's aid emphasizes the ties and allegiance between the hero and the citizens of New York. More importantly, the crowd scene also situates an idealized viewer of the film as someone experiencing a deep connection with Spider-Man in his battle with the Goblin and, more broadly, against those who would hurt New York.

These feelings and images continue when the Goblin propels Spider-Man into a building, knocking it to the ground as Spider-Man struggles to regain his composure, his mask now shredded, revealing the ordinary man under the mask. As the conflict reaches resolution amongst the rubble of fallen buildings and with Parker's face apparent alongside the remains of his Spider-Man mask, this scene echoes the special post-September 11th issue of *Amazing Spider-Man* where Peter Parker's semi-revealed face highlights his link to the mourning New

Yorkers. Following these symbolic links, after the Goblin is defeated it is similarly telling that the last visual effects in the film show Spider-Man viewing New York from atop the Empire State Building. In the background, visible but ethereal and almost ghostly, the figures of the Twin Towers can be seen for a few moments on the distant horizon before Spider-Man swings back into his city with the American flag fluttering proudly in the background. These symbols serve to reinforce the links between Spider-Man, special effects and the New York cityscape, facilitating an artificial mourning which addresses September 11th by reinvigorating certain American icons, but in the midst of a storyline which continually reinforces the mantra "with great power, comes great responsibility."

In *Spider-Man 2*, both the plot and the central super-villain are substantially more complicated. Whereas Norman Osborn was an arrogant capitalist who developed weapons for the military even before his transformation into the Green Goblin, in the second film Doctor Otto Octavius (Alfred Molina) is actually one of Parker's personal heroes. Octavius thinks he has found a way to create a fusion reaction that would create a limitless energy source. Before his public test of the technology, Octavius meets with Parker who is writing a paper on the research. During their conversation, Octavius reflects on the role of the scientist, telling Parker, "Being brilliant's not enough young man. You have to work hard. Intelligence is not a privilege; it's a gift. And you use it for the good of mankind." Octavius thus appears to be a genius-scientist with, however patronizing, the best of intentions. In order to successfully stabilize his fusion reaction, Octavius has constructed artificial, metallic appendages that, owing to their difficult tasks, actually have their own artificial intelligence to assist in the processes. In the press conference preceding the first fusion test, Octavius explains their uses:

> OCTAVIUS: These smart arms are controlled by my brain through a neural link. Nanowires feed directly into my cerebellum, allowing me to use these arms to control fusion reaction in an environment no human hand could enter.
>
> REPORTER: Doctor, if the artificial intelligence in the arms is advanced as you suggest, couldn't that make you vulnerable to them?
>
> OCTAVIUS: How right you are. Which is why I developed this inhibitor chip to protect my higher brain function. It means I maintain control of these arms, instead of them controlling me.

Octavius' artificial limbs thus contain a physical version of Asimov's three laws of robotics, inasmuch as the inhibitor chip keeps the intelligence of the human user dominant, implicitly restraining the artificial intelligence whilst flagging the possibility that the limbs may prove influential in the right circumstances (Asimov, 1950). When the experiment goes awry, Octavius' wife and collaborator is killed, the arms are fused to his body and the inhibitor chip destroyed. At the hospital, Octavius' arms take defensive action when surgeons try to cut them away from the doctor's body; instead, the arms kill the entire medical team and, to some extent, influence the decisions and actions made by "Doctor Octopus." The corporeal line between "Otto Octavius" and the intelligent limbs shatters, and now multiple voices influence this one character. Octavius is clearly an artificial person through his hybridization of technologies, artificial intelligence, human intelligence and physical corporeality. Although, even as a villain, his motives are still driven by the idea of completing his work, that now becomes a threat to the city since Doctor Octopus has already proven unable to control the "power of the sun in the palm of my hand."

The major fight scene between Spider-Man and Doctor Octopus takes place in, on and around a New York train as it hurtles along on an unfinished track, ending in a sheer plummet, stories above ground level. In an effort to distract Spider-Man, Doctor Octopus sets the train to continually accelerate and then destroys the controls, leaving the train and its passengers hurtling towards their doom. During the fight, Spider-Man has fiery embers thrown onto his mask, casting it aside, revealing his face. Despite this, Parker immediately sets to work stopping the train's course, but fails in several attempts. Finally, using himself as the corporeal core, Peter shoots out many lines of webbing and holds tight to these at the front of the train, trying to use his strength and the webbing as a counter-force and bring it to a halt. During this scene, a maskless Peter has his arms spread wide with wounds and tears appearing as he struggles and screams under the enormous pressure. While he is successful, Parker collapses in a scene borrowing from the ubiquitous imagery of the Christian crucifixion. Having quite literally sacrificed himself for the people, Parker's limp form is cradled by the passengers and passed along the train-car above the heads of the people, before being gently placed on the ground. One passenger comments, "He's just a kid, no older than my son," and Parker's eyes flicker open, basked in the love of the people he has saved. After Parker realizes he has no mask, another passenger reassures him, "it's alright," and Parker and Spider-Man become even more deeply imbricated with the ordinary citizens of New York, having shared Parker's secret. In his symbolic crucifixion and rebirth, Parker rediscovers a new heroic identity tied to a sense of community and to links with a city still in the processes of reconfiguring its existence in its ongoing Long September. When two small boys hand Peter back the Spider-Man mask, he is renewed.

In the final confrontation between Spider-Man and Doctor Octopus, Peter's reconfigured sense of heroism is on display as he looks beyond the binary of good and evil and finds many shades of grey. In the finale, Doctor Octopus has rebuilt his fusion generator and has activated it, even as Spider-Man fights to try and turn it off before the enormous power destroys the city. After trading blows, Spider-Man knocks a power line onto Doctor Octopus who lies stunned, weakened, on the floor, only for Spider-Man to discover that the fusion reaction cannot be conventionally disconnected. Realizing the futility of violence, Spider-Man pulls off his mask and reveals his mundane identity as Peter Parker. He appeals to Octavius, who seems more balanced, as both he and his artificial limbs are weak after their ordeal:

> PARKER: You once spoke to me about intelligence. That it was a gift to be used for the good of mankind.
> OCTAVIUS: A privilege.
> PARKER: These things have turned you into something you're not. Don't listen to them.
> OCTAVIUS: It was my dream.

While Parker is ready to blame the artificial intelligence for Doctor Octopus' actions, Octavius points out that the artificiality was always working with his desires, not against them. However, after Parker's impassioned plea, Octavius and the artificial intelligence with which he has merged reach a decision and destroy the fusion generator, dragging it to the bottom of the river. In that moment, any clear cut distinction between good and evil falls away. So, too, does any remaining boundary between embodiment and artificiality, as Doctor Octopus is a hybrid artificially intelligent/artificial person whose sacrifice highlights the power of conversations and words over and above violence and conflict. Rather than Spider-Man saving the day through heroic conflict, Parker and Spider-Man are both present, with the former's face visible as he talks Octavius into seeing the errors he has made. Thus in conversations which entail corporeality and technology, good and evil, and conflict and resolution, Spider-Man and Parker save the day by convincing the artificial nexus that is Doctor Octopus to sacrifice himself for the sake of the citizens and city of New York.

In stark juxtaposition with the previous films, *Spider-Man 3* opens with Parker confident, self-satisfied and more than a little smug in his role as the city's superhero. Despite making a decent profit, the film was universally hated by critics and was highly derivative of the first two, evident in the plot and villains: Harry Osborn picks up his deceased father's legacy and becomes the new Green Goblin; just like Doctor Octopus, Flint Marko becomes The Sandman in a bizarre science accident which fuses him with sand on a molecular level; and finally, the Venom "symbiote" at least offers a new direction, being an alien parasite that feeds off and amplifies negative emotions. In an excruciatingly contrived plot point, Parker becomes infected by the alien "symbiote" that feeds off and encourages his darker tendencies, leading him to alienate Mary Jane, become even more arrogant and self-absorbed, and ultimately become far more violent and aggressive than before. It's not until Parker accidentally hits Mary Jane while influenced by Venom that he is finally contrite enough and figures out how to escape the symbiote. Unfortunately, it then bonds with Eddie Brock, a photographer who has been competing with Parker for a job. Ironically, within a film suffused with digital special effects, Brock is fired from *The Daily Bugle* after Parker reveals that one of Brock's photographs was faked in Photoshop. Given his clearly untrustworthy nature, Brock proves far more receptive to the evil symbiote, becoming a far more effective villain. However, it is Brock's many similarities with Parker that clearly resonate with Žižek's argument that our enemies are most unsettling because of how familiar they are (Žižek 2002).

As Spider-Man arrives for the final showdown with Venom and the Sandman, he lands in front of a fluttering U.S. flag to the cheers of a gathered crowd of New Yorkers, reminiscent of both previous films. Facing unbeatable odds, Spider-Man convinces his once-enemy Harry Osborn to again become an ally in saving Mary Jane, who has once again been taken hostage. While heavy-handed, the symbolism of overcoming old enmity for the common good is significant (even if that common good is a contrived damsel-in-distress). Reminding viewers of the ties between Spider-Man and New Yorkers, the finale sequence is intercut with news footage that literally states that Spider-Man's death would be a huge loss *for the city itself.* Venom is vanquished, symbolically defeating the darker side of Spider-Man, while Parker once again reasons with the other ostensible villain, Flint Marko/The Sandman. After hearing Marko's motivation — he's been trying to steal money to pay for his daughter's medical needs — Spider-Man actually forgives Marko for his involvement in killing Uncle Ben. This act of forgiveness and understanding lets Marko and Spider-Man reconcile to the point that the film ends with Marko dissolving into the sunset, ostensibly overcoming his criminal inclinations. Forgiving his uncle's killer concludes the trilogy's narrative arc, with a final act of compassion and empathy rather than a final act of violence or destruction. While contrived and awkward, the labored ending nevertheless champions understanding and diplomacy over conflict and is a fitting conclusion to a trilogy whose production and plots articulate moments of artificial mourning and, at their end, of hope for a future less replete with violence, fear and conflict.

The *Spider-Man* films reflect a markedly artificial culture in which old binary divisions blur and there are no longer easy divisions between subjects and objects, heroes and villains, and good and evil. The climax of *Spider-Man 2* shows New York's salvation coming when heroism means communicating convincingly rather than just overpowering an enemy, and this narrative resolution is largely repeated in *Spider-Man 3*. Along with the re-visioning of the comic book New York in the first *Spider-Man* film, these resolutions are indicative of the way the *Spider-Man* films can function allegorically as a space of artificial mourning. Artificial mourning is neither absolute, nor objective, but occurs where the *Spider-Man* films invite viewers to subjectively engage with the legacy of September 11th 2001, moving beyond trauma and perhaps embracing superheroes that can sway with words and ideas, not their fists.

Notes

1. Portions of this chapter are taken from: Copyright © 2011 From *Artificial Culture: Identity, Technology, and Bodies* by Tama Leaver. Reproduced by permission of Taylor and Francis Group, LLC, a division of Informa plc.

Works Cited

Asimov, Isaac. *I, Robot*. London: Panther, 1950.

Blumberg, Arnold T. "The Night Gwen Stacy Died: The End of Innocence and the Birth of the Bronze Age." *Reconstruction*. 3:4 (2003): accessed 11/2/2011 http://reconstruction.eserver.org/034/blumberg.htm.

Bukatman, Scott. *Matters of Gravity: Special Effects and Supermen in the 20th Century*. Durham & London: Duke University Press, 2003.

de Certeau, Michel. *The Practice of Everyday Life*. Trans. Steven Rendall. Los Angeles: University of California Press, 1984.

CNN Entertainment. "TV, film execs reassess scheduling, content." *CNN.com*, 9/13/2001. Accessed 11/2/2011. http://articles.cnn.com/2001-09-13/entertainment/terror.entertainment_1_film-execs-bombings-big-releases?_s=PM:SHOWBIZ.

Cubitt, Sean. *The Cinema Effect*. Cambridge, Mass. & London: MIT Press, 2004.

Grosz, Elizabeth. *Space, Time and Perversion: The Politics of Bodies*. London & New York: Allen & Unwin, 1995.

Landy, Marcia. "'America under Attack': Pearl Harbor, 9/11, and History in the Media" in Wheeler Winston Dixon ed., *Film and Television After 9/11*. Carbondale: Southern Illinois University Press, 2004.

New York Times. "From the Editors: The Times and Iraq." *The New York Times*, May 26 2004. Accessed 11/2/2011. https://www.nytimes.com/2004/05/26/international/middleeast/26FTE_NOTE.html.

Priest, Christopher J. "A Bug's Life." *View From the 27th Floor*, 2002. Accessed 11/2/2011. http://www.lamerciepark.com/legacy/viewpoint/spider.html

Straczynski, J. Michael, John Romita, Jr., Scott Hanna, et al. *Amazing Spider-Man 36*. New York: Marvel (December 2001).

Wright, Bradford W. *Comic Book Nation: The Transformation of Youth Culture in America*. Baltimore & London: Johns Hopkins University Press, 2001.

Žižek, Slavoj. *Welcome to the Desert of the Real*. London and New York: Verso, 2002.

VI. Issues of Gender in the Spider-verse

Three Stories, Three Movies and the Romances of Mary Jane and Spider-Man

Robert G. Weiner

> Spider-Man is a superhero who's always fretting because he needs money, money to take his girl out before she ditches him for a more generous escort.
> — *Glicksohn, 1974: 8*

> He wishes he were more popular with the guys.... He wishes the girls would pay a little more attention to him. He wishes he could make more money, because he worries about his aunt who has to pay the rent, and it's kind of tough for her. He doesn't want her to lose her house.... The thing about Spider-Man, one of the things that makes him so popular, is the fact that you can relate to him.
> — *Stan Lee, 2010*

> It's your basic kind of young love story.
> — *Tobey McGuire on* Spider-Man 2 *(De Laurzirika, 2004).*

Committed romantic relationships are somewhat of an anomaly in mainstream superhero comics, but there are plenty of "romantic entanglements" and passing relationships. Some of the most famous comic book relationships include Batman and Catwoman, Elektra and Daredevil, Green Arrow and Black Canary, Barry (The Flash) and Iris Allen, Ralph (Elongated Man) and Sue Dibny, and of course Sue and Reed Richards (from the Fantastic Four), who remain one of the longstanding marriages in comics. Perhaps the most well known relationship in the history of sequential art (next to Clark Kent/Superman and Lois Lane) is that of Mary Jane and Peter Parker/Spider-Man. Along with "With great power comes great responsibility" (from the first Spider-Man story), the line "Face it Tiger, you just hit the jackpot" (uttered when Peter Parker and Mary Jane first meet in *Amazing Spider-Man 42*) is one of the most famous lines in the history of comics. In nearly fifty years of various monthly comic titles, novels, three feature films (and a fourth on the way at the time of this writing), and numerous animated shows and graphic novels, Mary Jane and Peter Parker have remained a constant presence. This article examines the relationship between Spider-Man and Mary Jane through the three feature films, and contrasts it with three major events in the comic book series. These three events include: the first meeting of Peter Parker and Mary Jane and the circumstances that led up to that first meeting; Parker and Mary Jane's wedding ceremony and the subsequent press surrounding the marriage; and the recent "One More Day" storyline. There are plenty of romantically-oriented books related to Peter Parker and Mary Jane, including the prose novel *Mary Jane* (O'Brien, 2004), and graphic novels *Spider-Man Loves Mary Jane* (McKeever, 2007), *Amazing Spider-Man: Parallel Lives* (Conway, 1989) and *Spider-Man/Mary Jane: You Just Hit the Jackpot* (Lee, 2009). There also are comic titles like *Ultimate Spider-Man, Web of Spider-Man, Marvel Team-Up,* and *Spectacular Spider-Man*, but the three storylines examined in this article mainly come from the pages of *Amazing Spider-Man (ASM)*. Parker's other love interests (Gwen Stacy, Liz Allen, Felecia Hardy/the Black Cat, and Betty Brant) will not be discussed in any detail.

According to Susan Wood Glicksohn, romances "[become] increasingly important in the life of the superhero ... [and] their influence ... [is] destructive.... They mess up the hero's emotions, thus distracting him when he should be fighting" (1974: 3). Often, the romantic interests of the hero do not understand the duty behind the heroes' demand for justice. They rarely comprehend the inner turmoil between civilian and hero life.

While in the early *Amazing Spider-Man* comics, the stories were often built around the action, with romance creeping into Peter's life slowly and tangentially, the latter became increasingly more important as the series continued. In all three feature films, romance plays a pivotal role with much of the action predicated on the relationship between Spider-Man and Mary Jane. In both the films and the comic books, Mary Jane provided Spider-Man with both anxiety and joy.

The Comics

Peter Parker Meets Mary Jane

There are some key differences between the portrayal of Peter Parker and Mary Jane's relationship in the sequential art stories and the feature films. In the films, Parker has lived next to Mary Jane since childhood, and she rarely if ever has taken notice of him. In the comic, Aunt May always tries to "set him up" on a date with Mary Jane. Although Mary Jane's aunt (Mrs. Watson) is Aunt May's neighbor and friend, Peter has never seen or met Mary Jane before. In *ASM 15*, Aunt May plays matchmaker and tells Peter "she has arranged a date with a lovely girl." Peter is less than enthused at this prospect and thinks, "A Blind Date!! Oh brother that is All I need!!" (Lee, 1964: 11). At this point, Mary Jane is not named; Peter only knows that their neighbor (Mrs. Watson) has a niece who Aunt May thinks would make Peter a "... good housewife..." (Lee, 1964: 11), and later on in that issue, Peter refers to her as "that Watson girl." He promises Aunt May that he'll meet Mrs. Watson's niece for a date, but somehow something always comes up, and he avoids meeting her (Lee, 1964: 21). In *ASM 16*, he confesses to Aunt May that he just isn't interested in "blind dates" and feels as though his aunt is babying him by playing matchmaker (Lee, 1964: 2). Peter continually tells Aunt May that he has a girlfriend and makes up excuses, including going to a Spider-Man fan club meeting. His Aunt, however, is not dissuaded, and in *ASM 17* she argues that she "knows what's best" for her nephew (Lee, 1964: 10).

Mary Jane first appears in *ASM 25* (June, 1965), but readers do not actually see her because her face is covered. Betty Brant and Liz Allen are trying to track down the elusive Peter Parker, but find his Aunt and Mary Jane instead. They are surprised and a little jealous that Peter is possibly interested in this woman who looks like a "Screen Star" (Lee, 1965: 15). In the next issue, when Betty Brant confronts Peter about his other girlfriends, particularly "Mary Jane Watson," he replies, "I do not even know" her (Lee, 1965: 5). A subsequent rendering of MJ in *ASM 38*, a year later, also keeps her face from view. This was a highly effective storytelling technique to build suspense. Lee and Ditko kept readers in the dark about just who Mary Jane was. Was she ever going to meet Peter, much less have a relationship with him? Peter avoided Mary Jane through several years of *ASM*, and by the time they finally do meet, Steve Ditko had left the title and John Romita Sr. was doing the artwork. At the end of *ASM 41*, there is a hint that Mary Jane will finally be revealed. On the last page of *ASM 42*, Peter mulls to himself that he really had no interest in meeting Ms. Watson's niece, but the moment of truth is at hand. When the two finally meet, Mary Jane utters to Peter the famous line, "Face It Tiger.... You Just Hit the Jackpot!" (Lee, 1966: 20). After meeting her, Peter questions why he did not want to. She was not the ugly woman he was so fearful she would be.

For the next two decades, Mary Jane remains a constant presence in the pages of *ASM*. Peter goes through various other relationships and various trials and tribulations, including the death of his love Gwen Stacy. Mary Jane and Peter date on and off, but because of his commitments as Spider-Man, he often misses dates, much to Mary Jane's disappointment and annoyance. She is often portrayed as a party-loving woman without a care in the world. Underneath this façade, however, was a strong independent woman who becomes Spider-Man's rock. Eventually they end up as one the most exclusive couples in comics. Stan Lee is "proud" of the way he developed the original relationship between Peter and Mary Jane in the comics; building up to their first meeting made the climax of that meeting more potent (De Laurzirika, 2004).

Spider-Man/PP and Mary Jane Have a Wedding

The 1980s saw Peter and Mary Jane finally tie the knot. In *ASM 182–183*, Peter proposes and receives a definitively negative response. In his introduction to *The Wedding* graphic novel, Stan Lee points out that Marvel Comics had always been committed to giving their heroes real emotions and conflicts, which gives the stories a "fabric of reality." He goes on to ask, "what emotion could be stronger and more all pervasive than the emotion of love?" (Lee, 1991: n.p.). The relationship between Peter and Mary Jane continues to have its ups and downs, but at the end of *ASM 290*, Peter again pops the question. This is a difficult decision for him to come to grips with because of his life as Spider-Man and the danger into which she would be put should his enemies find his real identity. Mary Jane again answers him in the next issue with a resounding "No!" She does not know how she feels. She is taken aback by the question and tells Peter that she thought they "were just friends." Mary Jane has some personal issues to deal with (problems with her no-good father and with her sister), but she admits that she loves him. A Spider-Slayer follows Spidey to Pittsburgh to kill him, but Peter manages to help Mary Jane in a difficult situation, and finally in *ASM 292*, Mary Jane agrees to marry him. *Giant Sized Amazing Spider-Man Annual 21* finally sees the wedding of the couple come to fruition. Peter, who often second guesses himself throughout the issue, almost gets cold feet and wonders if he is making a mistake. While sleeping, he dreams that his major villains "crash" his wedding and make a mess of things. Mary Jane, meanwhile, still has other men sniffing around her. In the end, however, they do get married, and Mary Jane envisions them "living happily ever after" (Michelinie, 1991: n.p.). The wedding story was also featured in the *Spider-Man* syndicated newspaper strip written by Stan Lee, but the strip had none of the angst of the comic book stories. Lee's writing was much more celebratory and full of joy. Lee wanted to show the world that "Spidey's luck isn't always bad" (Lee, 1991: n.p.).

In addition to the comic book and newspaper strip story about the wedding, a "real-life" wedding was held in New York's Shea Stadium in June 1987. Spider-Man and Mary Jane took their vows thirty minutes before a Mets baseball game, in front of about 55,000 people. The wedding, which was attended by other heroes like Captain America, Hulk, and even Spidey villain the Green Goblin, was televised to the world, and Mr. Marvel himself, Stan Lee, performed the ceremony. Afterward, the heroes posed with Mets superstars like Darryl Strawberry for a poster. This type of mainstream media coverage was unprecedented in the history of sequential art characters. Major newspapers like *USA Today* and shows like *Entertainment Tonight* carried the story. Designer Willi Smith crafted the wedding attire for both the comic book and the "real" wedding ceremony shortly before he died (Dutter, 1991: n.p.). In part three of his massive four-part online essay, which outlines Mary Jane and Spidey's relationship history in the comics, J.R. Fettinger argues:

> MJ was truly the only character who satisfied both of the requirements for a permanent companion — she was an interesting character in her own right — and her motivations for marrying our hero were entirely consistent with that character.... The strength of her character literally forced its way into the foreground and the marriage was at the end of an entirely natural progression (Fettinger, 2008).

Sequential art/comic book romance had truly come of age.

Since the Wedding: One More Day—The End?

Since their wedding, Spidey and Mary Jane have had their obvious ups and downs. They have fought, been separated, and have gotten back together just like couples normally would. They have had to deal with villains like Venom and the Green Goblin, who used their knowledge of Spidey's real identity against him by putting Mary Jane's life in danger, thus confirming Peter's perpetual fears. They have had to deal with the infamous "Clone Saga," which resulted in Mary Jane having a complicated pregnancy that led to their child being stillborn. Mary Jane almost dies in a plane crash and Spider-Man briefly becomes a member of the Avengers. In the *Civil War* storyline, Peter Parker reveals to the world that he is Spider-Man, and the revelation leads several villains to come out of the woodwork seeking to harm him. When the Kingpin puts a hit out on Spider-Man, Aunt May is shot instead of the webslinger. But it is 2007's highly controversial *One More Day* storyline, in which scribes J. Michael Straczynski and Joe Quesada (2008) have Spidey lose his relationship with Mary Jane in order to save his Aunt, that causes Peter to regret most deeply his having revealed his true identity.

In order to save Aunt May's life, Spider-Man and Mary Jane make a deal with the demon Mephisto (a Satan-like character): In exchange for saving May, Mary Jane and Peter's marriage and life together "never happened" and Spidey gets his secret identity back. Twenty years after Spider-Man and Mary Jane are married, they are apart (at least for the near future). Mephisto adds more pain to their situation when he mentions the daughter they will never have. (In an alternate Marvel Universe storyline, Parker and Mary Jane do have a daughter, Mayday, who is Spider-Girl.)

Fans and critics alike were outraged at this change. One critic called the story "undoubtedly the worst comic Marvel published in 2007," and then went on to quip, "the funny thing is, though, it's not actually that badly crafted" (Schedeen, 2007). However, Stan Lee, in his afterword to the graphic novel, was optimistically philosophical about this decision, pointing out that Mary Jane and Spidey's marriage was equally controversial. Fans wrote in and complained that their marriage would kill the series. Lee points out that:

readers forget that a series can't continue going down the same road forever.... In real life, people may make friends, lose friends, stay single, get married, get divorced, get sick, die, whatever. All the (Marvel) Bullpen is brilliantly doing is giving you characters whose lives are as full of surprises as your own (Lee, 2008: n.p.).

The Movies

Spider-Man

The romance of Mary Jane and Peter Parker is the prominent plot device for the *Spider-Man* films. From the opening narration of the first film, Peter Parker (Tobey McGuire) tells us that "like any story worth telling, this is about a girl ... the girl next door, Mary Jane Watson (Kirsten Dunst)." She is *literally* the girl next door, having lived next to Peter since his childhood. There is no doubt in Peter's mind that she is the one for him; he has loved her since before he "even liked girls" (Raimi 2002), but in a direct inversion of the comics storyline, Mary Jane has for more than eleven years failed to notice him. Because just talking to her is difficult for Peter, he is often too bashful to take that first step at conversation. She dates jocks in high school (a science geek like Peter would have hardly made a blip on her radar), and because Peter never makes a move toward Mary Jane, his best friend, Harry Osborne (James Franco), dates her for a brief time (as he does in the comics).

In a pivotal scene, while Peter is taking out the trash, he hears Mary Jane's father yelling at her. In the movie, as in the comics, her father treats her poorly. In a conversation about life after graduating from high school, Mary Jane tells Peter that she wants to act (as she does in the comics). Peter tells her she was "awesome in all the school plays," and that he cried at her first-grade performance as Cinderella. Peter encourages her about her future telling her, "you're going to light up Broadway." While this is obviously the fantasy of an infatuated man, Peter really believes it. Mary Jane looks at him with an honest expression of wonder that he has such faith in her. When her jock boyfriend breaks up their conversation, calling Mary Jane to come for a ride in his car, Peter looks longingly after them, mistakenly thinking that if he had a car he might have a chance with her.

Throughout the film, Peter (as Spider-Man) rescues Mary Jane from various life-threatening encounters, including one in which she falls from a precipice as the Green Goblin (Willem Dafoe) is fighting with the hero. As he saves her, she looks longingly at the hero. She asks, "Who are you?" to which Spider-Man responds, "You know who I am" (tempting the revelation of his identity), and then he adds "your friendly neighborhood Spider-Man."

Harry is not amused by Mary Jane's comments about Spidey being "incredible," but this time Peter is quite amused about being called "incredible" by the girl who never gave him a second glance (even if he is in a Spider-Man suit). Throughout the film, as Spider-Man, Peter can be the romantic hero to Mary Jane that just plain old Peter Parker is not. When Mary Jane runs into Peter, she looks at him with eyes that do not speak romance, but when she is harassed by some thugs who intend to rape her, Spider-Man saves her, and Peter finally gets to kiss Mary Jane. This is perhaps the iconic scene from all three films: Peter/Spidey hanging upside-down, MJ pulling his mask down just enough to reveal his lips before going in for a rain-soaked kiss.

When Peter and Mary Jane visit Aunt May (Rosemary Harris) in the hospital to which she was admitted because of her encounter with the Green Goblin, Mary Jane tells Peter that she is in love with someone else, Spider-Man (she has no idea Spidey is Peter Parker). He tells her he knows Spider-Man (having been employed to take pictures of the hero for the *Daily Bugle*). When Mary Jane asks what Spidey has said about her, Parker tells her that Spidey asked him "what he thought about" her, and he responds that "the great thing about Mary Jane" is looking into her eyes and finding that everything "feels not quite normal. Because you feel stronger and weaker at the same time excited and terrified. As if you reached the unreachable and you weren't ready for it..." Softened by emotion, Mary Jane finally holds Peter's hand; his poetic words touch a chord within.

Even if Peter cannot admit his true feelings to Mary Jane, Aunt May makes mention of the fact that he is always smiling when she is around. She reminds Peter of the first time he saw Mary Jane at six years of age and thinking she was like an "angel." Aunt May advises him to finally let Mary Jane in on his decade-old crush because "everyone else around him is already aware of it" (Raimi 2002).

Harry ends up telling his father that there is no one "Peter cares for more" than MJ, which of course plants the seeds for the Goblin to kidnap her. Peter realizes that the Goblin knows too. He calls, but the Goblin already has her. In a tribute to the original "Death of Gwen Stacy" storyline, Mary Jane is held prisoner high up on a bridge-like structure, and the Goblin holds her over the ledge. The villain forces Spider-Man to make a choice between the women he loves or the kids on an air transport car. The Goblin lets go of both of them, and Spidey has to move fast to save both. Mary Jane gets thrown around like a rag doll, but Spidey does save her and the innocents he wants to protect. The Goblin nearly defeats Spidey in their hand-to-hand fight, but when he starts talking about killing Mary Jane, the hero gets his second wind.

At Norman Osborn's funeral, Mary Jane tries to speak with Peter about her feelings. However, because of his commitment as Spider-Man and after seeing what can happen to those who are close to Spider-Man, he gives up the idea of a romance with Mary Jane; he gives her the cold shoulder, thinking to himself, "[the] ones I love will always be the ones who pay." Mary Jane finally tells Peter that she loves him; it is not Spider-Man she loves, but Peter, the "only one man who's always been there for me." Peter is obviously happy to hear this, but he rejects her advances, after seeking them for so long, and tells her "I can't." He tells her he will always be there for her and will always be her friend, but that is all he has to give. Peter leaves Mary Jane in tears.

Spider-Man 2

As in the first film, Peter Parker's opening narration is about Mary Jane: "she looks at me every day. Mary Jane Watson. Oh, boy, if she only knew how I felt about her. But she can never know. I made a choice once to live a life of responsibility." It is "a life she can never be a part of."

Mary Jane by this time has found success as a model, appearing on billboards around the city. She seems to be living her dream of modeling and acting. Everything about Spider-Man is interfering with Peter's personal life: his schoolwork, his inability to keep a job. Mary Jane does find Peter mysterious. Harry tries to convince Peter that Mary Jane is "waiting for him," and all he has to do is reach out and take her by the hand.

Mary Jane wants Peter to come to her play, and tells him "she liked seeing him on his birthday." Peter cannot hide his affection for her, and when they are about kiss, Peter purposely ruins the moment by asking her where she lives. The passion they each have for the other is obvious, but Mary Jane tells Peter, who keeps a picture of Mary Jane in his apartment, that she is "seeing someone" who might be "more" than a friend. Peter promises Mary Jane he'll come to her play.

When Rosalie Octavius (Donna Murphy), asks Peter if he has a girlfriend, Peter responds with his usual aw-shucks "I don't know." Again the film plays up the romantic dimension, advancing the idea that ultimately the *Spider-Man* film series is about the girl. Otto Octavius (Alfred Molina) pokes fun at his noncommittal response, but Peter remains mum on the matter. Octavius goes on to say that if you keep something "as complicated as love stored up inside ... it's gonna make you sick," foreshadowing Peter's loss of powers later in the movie. Both Octavius and his wife explain how they met and fell in love, and they warn him that any romantic relationship requires work. When Octavius tells Peter to "feed" the woman he loves poetry, Peter reads and studies some poetry in the hopes of rekindling the love between him and Mary Jane.

Peter makes a good faith effort to come to Mary Jane's play; he even gets dressed up for the occasion. Just as it happens in the comics, however, his responsibility as Spider-Man interferes, and when Mary Jane looks at the empty seat where Peter should be she even forgets some of her lines. After the show, Peter looks longingly at Mary Jane, and when he sees her and her new beau kiss, he feels the pains of life as a hero destined to be alone.

Because his emotions got the best of him, he starts to lose his powers. His webs do not shoot, and his ability to stick to walls fails (see Peaslee, later in this volume, for a Freudian discussion of this highly-symbolic sequence). The emotional turmoil takes over. His regret at having to live the life of a hero causes him to doubt his whole being. He suffers immense personal duress fuelled by his longing for Mary Jane's love.

Peter calls Mary Jane and tries to explain "how complicated a simple thing like being someplace at 8:00 can become." He then tries to backpedal by blaming the usher, but Mary Jane does not buy any of it, and the movie audience sees the disappointment and disgust on her face. Peter wants to reach out, and tell her the truth of about his secret life, but he feels that would put her in too much danger. Because he is Spider-Man "he can't" be with her. It would put too much of a burden on her, and give his enemies something to use against him. He "could never forgive" himself if she ever got injured or worse. He wants so badly to explain to her that he confesses all into a vacant phone, but he has no resolution in this scene because he is only confessing to the empty air.

When Mary Jane and Peter meet at a party, it is apparent that she is annoyed with him and his excuses. She greets him with an obvious tone of disappointment, and she admits that thinking about Peter is "too painful" for her to deal with. He awkwardly tries to woo her with poetry, but it is to no avail. She tells Peter that everyone else in her life, including Aunt May and her father, has seen her perform, but her best friend, Peter Parker, cannot make it to the show on time. After she calls him an "empty seat," Peter cannot contain his emotions any longer. The weight of Spider-Man is too much to bear, and the loss of any personal life is too much; tears swell in his eyes. To make matters worse, John Jameson announces in public that he is going to marry Mary Jane. Peter is forced into the indignity of taking their picture, and ultimately this proves the last straw. He can no longer deal with his two identities, and his powers fail him. In homage to a scene in the storyline "Spider-Man No More" from *ASM 50*, Peter leaves his costume in the trash. According to director Raimi, "Peter can't watch her move off with someone else" which becomes "one of the main factors in Pete's decision to give up his powers" (de Laurzirika, 2004).

Mary Jane talks to a friend who convinces her that she does not really love John Jameson (Daniel Gillies), the man she has agreed to marry. When her friend asks her, "what's wrong in believing in love stories?" Mary Jane ponders the question and tries to determine who she really loves and whether she really wants to marry (Raimi 2004).

Another pivotal fantasy scene has Peter telling his Uncle Ben that he loves Mary Jane, but as the voice of his sub-conscious, Uncle Ben questions him about the "meaning of responsibility." Peter wants a "life of his own," but Ben tells him, "with great power comes great responsibility." Peter decides that he wants to be Peter Parker, not Spider-Man, and when he gives up the weight of being Spidey, his life seems better. For a brief moment, he knows what he thinks is happiness. Even Mary Jane sees the differences. He finally gets to see Mary Jane perform, and she is thrilled (again causing her to forget her lines). Peter tries to explain to Mary Jane that he has changed, and tries to talk her out of marriage. He wants to tell her that he loves her, suggesting instead that he is not "being a empty seat anymore."

While going through wedding invitations, Mary Jane is questioned by John Jameson about not inviting Peter, who she refers to as a "great big jerk." However, it is obvious that she loves him. The kisses that she gives Jameson are hollow; she is not in love with him. In another iconic scene, she meets Peter for coffee because she wants to confess her true feelings to him, but he pulls back again, telling her that he does not love her. The pain on her face is obvious, and, unbelieving, she asks for a kiss. Doc Ock ruins their coffee when he suddenly kidnaps her, right in front of Parker. Peter is used as a contact point because he is the wall-crawler's photographer. The kidnapping makes him mad enough that the Spider powers return. The very thing he wants to prevent has happened again, and Mary Jane's life is in danger. He is both Peter Parker and Spider-Man; as in the comics, his two identities are interwoven and he needs them both. Spidey has to save Mary Jane and New York from the villainous Doc Ock, and while he is fighting and being nearly beaten to death, Mary Jane's suspicions are confirmed; Peter and Spidey are one and the same. In this "moment of truth," he confesses his love for her, explains to her the risks involved in having a romantic relationship with him. He tells her that they can never be together because he "will always be Spider-Man" (Raimi 2004).

Actress Kristen Dunst pointed out that romance is "at the heart of the film" (De Laurzirika, 2004). Mary Jane cannot go through with her wedding, and she leaves her groom at the altar. She runs to Peter with a smile on her face, and in a very empowering moment at the end of the film, she states that whether she wants to take the risk is *her* choice to make. She chooses to be with Peter, and once again confesses her love for him; they kiss passionately. Mary Jane understands the sacrifices that must be made in order for them to be together. She has already had her life threatened by Green Goblin and Doctor Octopus, and she believes that together they can face whatever the future brings.

Spider-Man 3

As he does in the previous two films, Peter Parker provides the opening narration: "I'm in love with the girl of my dreams." Over this exposition, we see him looking at engagement rings. This film also introduces one of Spidey's major loves from the comics, Gwen Stacy (Bryce Dallas Howard), who becomes competition for Mary Jane.

Peter can finally go to the theatre and see Mary Jane on the stage without being late. He is proud that his girlfriend is in the spotlight. There is a great scene in which Peter and Mary Jane are on a web, suspended between trees, looking at the stars. In this scene, Peter promises that he will always be there watching her on the stage, and tells her that he has always loved her. Then they kiss under the stars, and later, Peter tells Aunt May that he plans to ask Mary

Jane to marry him. As Aunt May explains how Uncle Ben originally proposed to her, she gives Peter her original wedding ring. Peter nearly loses the ring in a fight with Green Goblin 2, Harry Osborn.

Mary Jane becomes annoyed at Peter's other life as Spider-Man because he cannot always be there for her emotionally. When Spidey saves Gwen Stacy (another damsel in distress) from falling to her death, Mary Jane, who is upset because she was fired from her musical, becomes a little jealous of Spidey's attention to Gwen. Then when Spider-Man is given the key to the city, and Gwen kisses him, Mary Jane is appalled and feels humiliated. The fact that it is front-page news just adds fuel to the fire.

Peter plans to ask Mary Jane to marry him on a special dinner date, but the date goes horribly wrong. Mary Jane is upset at being fired, and Peter only talks about himself and does not listen to her. Gwen happens to be at the same restaurant, and Mary Jane gets angrier and angrier while Peter just keeps fumbling over the words he is trying to express. Her jealousy becomes more and more apparent. She feels betrayed by Spider-Man's kiss with Gwen, and Peter never gets the chance to propose. Later Mary Jane does not answer the phone when he calls.

Complications start setting in. When Peter finds out who actually killed his Uncle Ben, he again pushes Mary Jane away from him and bottles his emotions up inside of him. Peter's landlord and daughter give him romantic advice. In a moment of confusion, Mary Jane visits Harry and kisses him, but immediately regrets it. Harry remembers that he hates Spider-Man. Harry does what he can to break them up, but this time the roles are reversed. Harry breaks into Mary Jane's apartment and threatens to kill Peter/Spider-Man. In order to protect Peter/Spider-Man from being killed by Harry, Mary Jane breaks up with Peter. He finally shows her the ring he wants her to have, but she tells him, "I've fallen in love with someone else." Harry looks with glee at his handiwork, and eventually tells Peter that he is the "other guy."

This causes Peter to become unglued, and the alien symbiote that had in the meantime bonded to him exacerbates the situation. In one of the silliest parts of the film, Peter takes on the look of a "goth" and his personality becomes obnoxious. The hate and pain are festering in him. When he goes out with Gwen and takes her to the same jazz club where Mary Jane sings, he is obviously trying to hurt Mary Jane and is using Gwen do so. He ends up involved in a fight, and inadvertently slaps Mary Jane. Both women find this behavior intolerable, and Peter realizes that the changes in him are due in large part to the alien bonded to him. Aunt May visits Peter at his apartment, and tries to give him romantic advice. When Peter tells her how he has hurt Mary Jane, May tells him to "forgive" himself. He can make things right again.

Once again, Mary Jane is kidnapped, this time by Venom (Topher Grace), working with the Sandman (Thomas Hayden Church). Spider-Man's enemies continue to use those he loves as bait, and Spider-Man must come to terms with himself and become the hero that he really is. Mary Jane is in a taxi suspended in the air by Venom's web, and nearly falls to her death. She is put through a traumatic experience for a third time. However, with the help of Goblin 2, Harry Osborn, they defeat the villains. The movie ends with Mary Jane singing a song about being "through with love." Peter stretches out his hand and she takes it. There is resolution and Spidey gets the girl after all.

Through all these dangers and tribulations, Mary Jane chooses to be with Peter/Spider-Man. In spite of the fact that she has nearly lost her life in three films, love triumphs. "Peter and Mary Jane know things between them will never be easy, but they believe the love they share is worth the heartache" (Couper-Smartt, 2006: n.p.).

Concluding Remarks: Mary Jane, Spidey and the Future

In all three movies, Mary Jane is caught in the "web" of the villains who use her as bait for Spider-Man, and Spider-Man always comes to the rescue. It is as if the villains have their own inner spider sense telling them that, somehow, kidnapping Mary Jane is leading them to Spider-Man. Mary Jane is initially portrayed as the typical damsel in distress that is a motif in many other films. The major difference, however, is that the audience sees Mary Jane grow and make her own decisions about the danger she is willing to be subjected to by being involved with Spider-Man/Peter Parker. Just like in the comics, Mary Jane becomes a strong character who knows and accepts the risks.

The movies are ultimately about Peter's relationship with Mary Jane from the first film onward. The comic stories in *ASM* did have a strong element of romance combined with lots of action and personal life struggles. Those early stories showed Peter's alter ego as the nerdy everyman who rarely got the girl anyway, fighting villains and trying to "live" life as a teenager/young adult with romance as a secondary objective. Eventually, in the pages of *ASM* the romance played a pivotal role through marriage, trials, near divorce, a stillborn baby, and the termination of the marriage by Mephisto. On the other hand, the movies brought out the romance from the first scene onward. The action in the *Spider-Man* movies is secondary to the romance with Mary Jane. In both the films and the comics, "Mary Jane is a woman strong enough to deal with Peter Parker's roller coaster existence" (Hopkins, 2006: 201).

Largely, one assumes, due to the differing imperatives vis-à-vis audience management (comics are not written for a four-quadrant audience), the films, unlike the comics, are ultimately about getting the girl. Who knows what the future holds for the two of them? With the reboot of the *Spider-Man* film franchise and the re-con of the comic series, it remains to be seen how the relationship between Spidey and Mary Jane will eventually play out. One thing is certain, however: Mary Jane will continue to be vital part of the adventures of Spider-Man.

Works Cited

Conway, Gerry, Alex Saviuk, Andy Mushynsky, et al. *Amazing Spider-Man: Parallel Lives*. New York: Marvel, 1989.

Couper-Smartt, Jonathan, Al Sjoerdsma, Mike Fichera, et al. *Official Handbook of the Marvel Universe: Spider-Man*. New York: Marvel, 2006.

De Laurzirika, Charles (director), Stan Lee, Sam Raimi et al., *Interwoven Women of Spider-Man*. Extras on Raimi, Sam (Director), Tobey McGuire, Kristen Dunst et al., *Spider-Man 2: Special Edition*. Sony Pictures, 2004.

Dutter, Barry. "Mets, Magic, and Marriage" in David Michelinie, John Romita, Jr., Vince Colletta, et al. *The Amazing Spider-Man: The Wedding*. New York: Marvel, 1991.

_____. "Wedding of the Century" in David Michelinie, John Romita, Jr., Vince Colletta, et al. *The Amazing Spider-Man: The Wedding*. New York: Marvel, 1991.

Fettinger, J.R. "'Why Did it Have to be You, Mary Jane?' Part 3: Happily Ever After?" *Spideykicksbutt.com*. 2008. Accessed 10/24/2010. http://www.spideykicksbutt.com/WhyYouMaryJane/WhyYouMaryJanePart3.html.

Glicksohn, Susan Wood. *The Poison Maiden & the Great Bitch*. Baltimore: T-K Graphics, 1974.

Hopkins, David. "Secrets and Secret-Keepers" in Gerry Conway, Leah Wilson eds., *Webslinger: Unauthorized Essays on your Friendly Neighborhood Spider-Man*. Dallas: Benbella, 2006: 189–203.

Lee, Stan, Steve Ditko, Art Simek, et al. *Amazing Spider-Man 15*. New York: Marvel (August 1964).

_____, Steve Ditko, S. Rosen, et al. *Amazing Spider-Man 16*. New York: Marvel (September 1964).

_____, Steve Ditko, S. Rosen, et al. *Amazing Spider-Man 17*. New York: Marvel (October 1964).

_____, Steve Ditko, S. Rosen, et al. *Amazing Spider-Man 25*. New York: Marvel (June 1965).

_____, Steve Ditko, S. Rosen, et al. *Amazing Spider-Man 26*. New York: Marvel (July 1965).

_____, John Romita, Sammy Rosen, et al. *Amazing Spider-Man 42*. New York: Marvel (November 1966).
_____, John Romita, Mickey Demeo, et al. *Amazing Spider-Man 50*. New York: Marvel (July 1967).
_____, "Introduction" in David Michelinie, John Romita, Jr., Vince Colletta, et al., *The Amazing Spider-Man: The Wedding*. New York: Marvel, 1991.
_____, "The Spider-Man Wedding Chronicle" in David Michelinie, John Romita, Jr., Vince Colletta, et al., *The Amazing Spider-Man: The Wedding*. New York: Marvel, 1991.
_____, Steve Ditko, Art Simek, et al. *Essential Spider-Man Vol. 1*. New York: Marvel, 1996.
_____, Steve Ditko, John Romita, et al. *Essential Spider-Man Vol. 2*. New York: Marvel, 2001.
_____, "Afterword" in Michael J. Straczynski, Joe Quesada, Danny Miki, et al. *The Amazing Spider-Man: One More Day*. New York: Marvel, 2008.
_____, Tom DeFalco, Kurt Busiek, et al. *Spider-Man/Mary Jane ... You Just Hit the Jackpot*. New York: Marvel, 2009.
_____, Rick Lee. "Stan Lee's Advice To 'Spider-Man' Star Andrew Garfield." *MTV.com* 10/ 14/2010. Accessed 10/22/2010. http://splashpage.mtv.com/2010/10/14/stan-lee-spider-man-andrew-garfield/.
McKeever, Sean, Takeshi Miyazawa, Valentine De Landro, et al. *Spider-Man Loves Mary Jane Volume 1*. Marvel: New York, 2007.
Michelinie, David, John Romita, Jr., Vince Colletta, et al. *The Amazing Spider-Man: The Wedding*. New York: Marvel, 1991.
O'Brien, Judith. *Mary Jane*. New York: Marvel, 2004.
Schedeen, Jesse. "*Amazing Spider-Man #545* Review: Can we make a deal with the devil to erase this? Please?" *IGN*. 12/28/2007. Accessed 10/22/2010 http://uk.comics.ign.com/articles/843/843196p1.html.
Straczynski, Michael J., Joe Quesada, Danny Miki, et al. *The Amazing Spider-Man: One More Day*. New York: Marvel, 2008.
Wolfman, Marv, Ross Andru, Mike Eposito, et al. *Amazing Spider-Man 182*. New York: Marvel (July 1978).
_____, Ross Andru, Bob McLeod, et al. *Amazing Spider-Man 183*. New York: Marvel (August 1978).

Women's Pleasures Watching Spider-Man's Journeys

Emily D. Edwards

Released in 2002, 2004, and 2007, the *Spider-Man* film trilogy would seem to be an example of Joseph Campbell's typical hero's journey (1949, 1988), in which a male protagonist ventures forth from the world of the common day into a region of supernatural adventure. Laura Mulvey's psychoanalytic film analysis has suggested that preexisting patterns of male spectatorship allow the male spectator to narcissistically identify with the male hero, while voyeuristically gazing upon the female object of the hero's desire. According to "gaze theory," female spectatorship struggles with an unhappy viewing position for most narrative action films, watching as a male protagonist actively drives the story forward, while the leading female character is little more than an object to ogle, displayed for the pleasure of the hero — as well as for the voyeuristic pleasures of the male spectator, identifying with his on-screen surrogate. This creates a traditional patriarchal structure for Hollywood's narrative films, limiting viewing positions so that male spectatorship enjoys a dominant ideology reiterated on screen, while female audiences experience the frustration of helplessly waiting for the female character's rescue. Moreover, attractive characteristics of the male movie star are not meant to be the erotic objects for the female spectator's gaze, but are intended to make up a more perfect, "more powerful ideal ego" for the male spectator to identify with as he looks into the screen "mirror" (Mulvey, 1990: 28–40).

While the *Spider-Man* trilogy might appear to be yet another example of a male dominated media story, Jungian analysis offers female spectatorship an alternate gaze through identification with archetypal characters. This view also recognizes the power of the spectator in interpretative play, "taking control of the fantasy material" rather than being imprisoned by it (Izod, 2001: 31). Through textual analysis and interviews with self-identified female fans of the trilogy, this essay will explore the promise of women's visual pleasures in the cinematic spectacle of Spider-Man's journeys. If movies are public dreams and the most popular movies resonate with audiences because characters are archetypes rather than stereotypes, then women may find pleasures in the narrative and visual contradictions within Spider-Man's cinematographic texts that open to the interpretive play of female audiences.

Spider-Man Movies As Public Dreams

Carl Jung's road map of the human psyche (1953, 1964, 1971) suggested three territories with permeable borders, where thoughts, symbols, and energies easily wander from region to region with or without conscious control. These territories include the conscious mind, the personal unconscious, and the collective unconscious. Jung's unique and still controversial contribution to this map is the territory of the collective unconscious, a universal region inhabited by archetypes. An individual's life and personal experiences create the conscious and personal unconscious regions of the mind, but Jung believed that the collective unconscious is inherited, like instinct, from the combined experiences of our ancestors, which an individual might access through dreams. All human beings inherit this collective unconscious. Like the evolution of the human body, the development of archetypes in the human psyche is slow, so that archetypes that resonated with Ancient Greek audiences are still recognizable today in modern media (Henderson, 1972).

While the Spider-Man comics, animations, live action television series, and musical stage performances might seem to be vaults rich with symbolic material for Jungian exploration, it is the sensuous pleasures of the *Spider-Man* films that come the closest to public dreams. Projected in a dark cinema house and saturated with color, fantastic imagery, vibrant sound, and intensely orchestrated musical scores, the films invite audiences into Spider-Man's gravity-defying world for a few short hours of emotional gratification. Watching film is a dreamlike experience (Rascarolli, 2002; Petric, 1981). The projections of film equipment augment psychological projections and identifications spectators have with characters on the screen. As public dreams, the Spider-Man films offer a rich and complex arena of both personal and collective meanings. A dream is not like a story told by the conscious mind, however, because the conscious minds that produced the *Spider-Man* trilogy can create, edit, and arrange thought in a logical and collaborative way that is not characteristic of dreams. But Jungian scholars believe that audiences respond to certain images and ideas in films because they resonate with these ancient archetypes that all people share.

William Indick (2004), Christopher Volger (1992) and others (Kaminisky and Mahan, 1986: 115–133) suggest that screenwriters might intentionally attempt to use Jungian archetypes in the construction of stories. The idea is that if a script and the resulting movie echo with the psychic traces of human memory, then the movie will resonate well with audiences. This psychic recognition creates stronger opportunities for the film's artistic and financial success (Izod, 2006:3).

It is hard to know if creators like Stan Lee and Steve Ditko (or screenwriters David Koepp, Alfred Gough, Miles Miller, Michael Chabon, Alvin Sargent, Ivan Raimi, and writer/director Sam Raimi) intentionally tried to include archetypes in their work or whether the characters spontaneously emerged from the collective unconscious into the region of the creators' personal consciousness and creative imaginations. The assumption is that contents of the unconscious mind exert a formative influence on the human psyche in all its creative work, from the writing and production, or encoding of a film, to the spectator's work of finding meaning or decoding it (Izod, 2001: 31). At any rate, all three *Spider-Man* films were financial and artistic successes, breaking box office records and winning multiple festival awards (Postrel, 2006; Smith, 2004; Sabbagh, 2007; Waxman, 2007; Xueling, 2007). This success suggests that the stories, characters, and imagery satisfied audiences in a fundamental way that does not exclude the female portion of the population. In fact, anecdotal evidence from female audiences indicates that Spider-Man may be among the most beloved of film superheroes among women.

Spider-Man's Journey

Joseph Campbell's concept of the mythic journey is closely correlated to Carl Jung's interpretation of dreams, drawing on his use of archetypes. Taken as a whole, the *Spider-Man* film trilogy closely resembles the complete hero's journey that Campbell described in *The Hero with a Thousand Faces* (1956), *The Power of Myth* (1988) and the PBS series dealing with his written work (1988). I argue that although the *Spider-Man* trilogy has special pleasures for female spectatorship, it is clearly a hero's journey and not the heroine's journey Maureen Murdock describes (1990).

Campbell's outline of the hero's journey starts with the hero's departure from the ordinary world (1949: 49). *Spider-Man's* journey also begins with this departure. In the first film, Peter Parker is a socially awkward teen, an orphan and science nerd. He lives with his Aunt May and Uncle Ben in a lower middle-class neighborhood, pining after the popular girl next-door, Mary Jane Watson (MJ). His best friend, Harry Osborn, is a privileged boy, booted out of several private academies and now attending public school. Parker's common world is one of ridicule and humiliation. Parker's departure from this world happens on a school field trip to the research lab at Columbia University's science department. As Campbell suggests, "A blunder — apparently the merest chance — reveals an unsuspected world, and the individual is drawn into a relationship with forces that are not rightly understood" (51). Someone blundered in the research lab, allowing a genetically altered spider to escape its terrarium. After the spider bites him, Parker transforms into a fledgling champion with superhuman powers, or with what Campbell calls "supernatural aid" (69–77). Parker initially refuses the true calling to heroic adventure, attempting to use the new powers for his own benefit instead. He enters a wrestling tournament hoping to win money to buy a car and impress MJ. It is only after losing his mentor, Uncle Ben, in a tragic carjacking and murder that Parker will come to understand the special burden of the hero: "With great power comes great responsibility."

Parker accepts his call to adventure and must pass the "guardian of the first threshold," who may hinder the hero's first steps into the unknown dangers of his journey. Campbell's "guardians of the threshold" are deceitful, dangerous presences who populate those abandoned or deserted "places outside the normal traffic of the village" (78). For Parker, this guardian will be the carjacker who murdered his Uncle Ben. At the wrestling match, Parker trounces his opponent only to have the tournament promoter cheat him out of his winnings. When a thief robs the promoter, Parker deliberately lets the man escape. But, there is chaos outside the sports arena: police sirens and a gathering crowd. Parker discovers that a carjacker has murdered Uncle Ben and stolen the family car. Parker immediately seeks vengeance. The carjacker leads him on a chase through the dark city to an abandoned warehouse. Parker confronts the man, who begs Spider-Man to give him another chance, but proves undeserving. After a struggle, the thief falls from the window to his death, but not until Parker recognizes the man as the robber he could have stopped back at the sports arena. Filled with guilt, Parker devotes himself to fighting crime. He is now fully immersed in Campbell's "Belly of the Whale" (90–94).

Part of the effort in all three films is for Parker to balance his persona as Peter Parker with his guise as Spider-Man. Parker finds part time work as a photographer for J Jonah Jameson, a tyrant who believes Spider-Man is a dangerous vigilante. Jameson will publicly question Spider-Man's humanity as well as his motives. Parker cannot defend Spider-Man's purpose without raising suspicion. The other central complication for Parker's ordinary life is his relationship with MJ, who is Harry's on-again, off-again girlfriend, creating an unstable romantic triangle. Parker's "road of trials" includes this inability to harmonize these complications of his ordinary life as Peter Parker with the difficulties of Spider-Man's assault on crime. When Harry's father, Norman Osborn, tests his company's dangerous new performance-enhancing drug on himself, Parker must also face the maniacal monster and super-villain that his friend's father becomes as Green Goblin. Parker additionally faces the reality that his best friend is dating MJ, forcing Parker to hide his love under the guise of mere friendship for both. In a scene where Harry introduces MJ to his father, Norman tells his son to dump MJ: "They're all beautiful until they're snarling after your trust fund like a pack of ravenous wolves." While Parker and MJ listen in an adjacent room, Norman rants, "A word to the not-so-wise about your little girlfriend. Do what you need to with her, then broom her fast." Even without his Green Goblin costume, Norman Osborn now has the heart of a villain.

Parker's life as superhero constantly intrudes on his life as a teenage boy. Parker will endure many ordeals, which also threaten his friends and family, but the first film ends without any real reward for Parker, only the reiterated heavy weight of responsibility. When Harry Osborn sees Spider-Man bringing his father's dead body back to the mansion, Harry believes Spider-Man is responsible and vows to avenge his father's death. The first film ends with Norman Osborn's funeral and Harry telling Parker about this sworn promise. It also ends with Parker unable to act on his love, fearing Spider-Man's enemies might hurt MJ. The journey is not over.

The second film begins with Peter Parker on his own and in dire financial circumstances, fully "initiated" into both the adult world of economic burdens and the mysterious world of superhero responsibilities. Having superpowers cannot solve the problems of Parker's ordinary world. They won't pay the rent and the responsibilities of Spider-Man have alienated him from both Mary Jane and Harry. Harry is now the head of his father's company, which sponsors the research of a smart, ego-driven nuclear scientist, Otto Octavius. Like Norman Osborn, Dr. Octavius experiments on himself and loses his own mind in the experiment, creating another monster for Spider-Man to battle. Parker will endure more trials and cruel choices, even going to a doctor when his powers become unreliable and the burden of Spider-Man seems impossible. He will throw away his costume, asking, "Am I not supposed to have what I want?" His Aunt May's answer reveals her to be the nurturing and caring mother—or feminine part of the psyche—with whom the hero must unite; what Campbell calls "The Meeting with the Goddess" (109–120). Aunt May tells him, "I believe there is a hero in all of us that keeps us honest, gives us strength, makes us noble, and finally allows us to die with pride." Because Aunt May is an older woman as well as Parker's aunt, the audience understands that this union of purpose is a sacred marriage and asexual. Parker's encounters with Aunt May provide him with the emotional strength he needs at his weakest moments.

In opposition to Aunt May, MJ as anima represents the romantic interest for Parker. It is an on-going romance in all three films that meets with recurring barriers. Because Parker believes his superhero responsibilities forbid the pleasures of home and family, MJ becomes engaged to John Jameson, a handsome astronaut and the son of Parker's boss at the newspaper. She betrays her love for Parker in exchange for a normal marriage that will offer security and social standing. However, she will ultimately abandon her groom. At the end of the second movie she leaves the church and runs to Parker's apartment in her wedding dress. She professes her love and vows to Parker, "I'll always be standing in your doorway." Still the journey is not complete.

The "rescue from without," where others rescue the hero and carry him to safety, occurs earlier in Parker's journey than in Campbell's model. Not every element of Campbell's model is included in the trilogy, but as Indick (2004) notes, the stages are "structural elements and not a formula" (159). One example of this rescue comes in the second film when passengers of a runaway subway train lift an exhausted Spider-Man to safety and promise to protect his identity. There are additional rescues for Parker, when a little girl he attempts to save from a burning building actually returns the favor and saves him. Another example occurs when Aunt May clomps Doc Ock with an umbrella, giving Spider-Man a momentary advantage in battle.

In the third film, Peter Parker will face his shadow. These ordeals finally fully transform him into a superhero with wisdom and powers that can benefit his world, but these special abilities will continue to be a difficult burden to bear. Unlike the second film, the third film will open with the city safe and sound and Parker in balance. He appears to have succeeded, living up to the legacy of his Uncle Ben. But the balance is temporary, an illusion. As Robert Johnson notes, "All paradises fail; each one has a serpent of some kind in it. That's the nature of paradise" (1977: 18). This is also the fundamental nature of movies; each must have a serpent or multiple serpents to provide the conflict viewers expect. The serpents in the third film come from multiple sources: the world of super-villains, the ordinary world of common frustrations and misunderstandings, and even from Parker's own psyche.

MJ's dreams of stardom fall short with a bad review, leaving her depressed and self-absorbed. MJ's disappointment derails Parker's determination to marry her. Harry, bent on vengeance, attacks Spider-Man with the Green Goblin technology that was his father's legacy. A battle with Spider-Man injures Harry and he suffers amnesia. Meanwhile, Flint Marko, an escaped convict, wants to make up for his failures to his family by resuming his criminal activities. Parker learns that Marko was the real culprit in his Uncle Ben's murder; the carjacker dispatched in the first film was only an accomplice. Marko falls into a particle accelerator, which transforms him into the super-villain, Sandman.

While Parker's troubles become increasingly complicated, his supreme ordeal or "apotheosis" will come when a symbiote literally overtakes him in a dream. Because this invasion happens while Parker is asleep, the psychic nature of the assault is clear. This black alien sludge fuses to Parker like tar, giving him enhanced powers, even turning his costume black. In Jungian analysis, a person's shadow includes those "Mr. Hyde" qualities and impulses a person may be aware of, ashamed of, and attempt to hide. Repressed tendencies create an "ever-present and potentially destructive 'shadow'" (Jung, 1964: 93). The symbiote retrieves Parker's repressed "shadow," which surfaces from the basement of his sleeping psyche. Parker becomes jealous, belligerent and vengeful. His new aggressive personality helps Parker to humiliate a rival freelance photographer, Eddie Brock, and win a staff position at the *Daily Bugle*. Parker behaves like an ogre; but then, following Campbell's model, Parker recognizes the need to free himself of these destructive impulses. He defeats the ogre within, and is miraculously reborn, becoming "more than he was" (162). In a scene that signifies the symbolic death and spiritual rebirth in the hero's journey, Parker goes to a church where the loud bells help dislodge the symbiote. The religious imagery appears at that point in the journey where the hero sacrifices human drives for spiritual purposes. Eddie Brock is conveniently at the same church praying for Parker's death, when Parker expels the symbiote. The symbiote then attaches to Brock, remaking Brock into the super-villain, Venom. Now as Venom, Brock gleefully gives himself over to his own shadow, claiming that being bad "...makes me happy."

Venom joins forces with Sandman in an attempt to vanquish Spider-Man. The two super-villains kidnap MJ, hanging her in a taxicab above a construction site. Parker will convince a disfigured and bitter Harry to join him in battle in order to save MJ. Once Harry has learned the truth about his father, he agrees to help. The united friends are successful in defeating the villains and rescuing MJ, but Harry will die in the fight, sacrificing himself for Parker. With this sacrifice, Harry shares in Parker's heroic journey, taking the role of martyr.

After Venom dies, Parker forgives Sandman (Marko), showing that he is now freed from his need for personal vengeance. With confessions and forgiveness, Parker can return to the common world of ordinary events. Spider-Man is now in control of his human emotions: master of both the common world and of the superhuman world. In ordinary street clothes Parker enters a jazz club where MJ is singing, "I'm through with love." The closing scene and last embrace contradict the lyrics of the song, suggesting that Parker will receive the final reward of MJ's love.

Female Spectatorship, Animus and the Romance of Spider-Man

At first glance, the journey the *Spider-Man* trilogy offers might appear to limit the female spectator to narcissistic identification with the cinematic female object (the frustration of identification with poor MJ) or force her into a masculine gaze by causing her to identify with the male hero, Peter Parker. However, female spectatorship may include more complex methods of viewing than masochistic identification or transsexual voyeurism (van Zoonen, 1994: 91). The playful aspect of viewership is that projection and identification need not be continuous or faithful, particularly for post-modern audiences. Spectatorship in the movies is not necessarily a committed marriage but a flirtation with possibilities. I suggest that for some viewers Peter Parker can be interpreted as a manifestation of the animus, allowing the viewer to identify with the masculine side of her self but not suffer "masculinization" of the male gaze. Contradictions within the narrative, Spider-Man's departures from the typical male attributes for the protagonist, and "playful" readings of the film's text make it comfortable for female spectators to identify with the hero without "masculinization." This is not to suggest that all women will choose to view a film the same way. Some may even view the *Spider-Man* films with an inconsistent perspective, seeing themselves momentarily reflected in MJ, then withdrawing the projection to identify with another character.

Jung believed that, in developing a sense of sexual identity as a woman, a girl comes to distinguish certain characteristics as typically male and others as typically female. Culture, biology, or myth may cause her to suppress certain aspects of experience as masculine. Through the process of gender identification, she will consider some responses to experience as proper and others as alien. Jung believed that women project those alien responses or the sexual "other" onto her animus figure. However, to be a whole person, a woman must accept her animus, embracing responses that culture or biology may reject as inappropriate. In Western culture, accessing the masculine side encourages women to embrace reason, assert physical strength, and intellectual control. The positive side of the animus can personify "enterprising spirit, courage, truthfulness and, in its highest form spiritual profundity" (von Franz, 1993: 194–195).

Interestingly, the root of Spider-Man's power, the spider, has strong mythological associations with female characteristics: spinning, weaving and the patience to wait for prey. Yet, Spider-Man's tactics are not subtle; he doesn't set inert snares and wait for his villains to get caught. His webs are more often employed in a way that allows him to swing Tarzan-like through an urban jungle. However, Spider-Man's violence does tend to be reactive, defensive rather than offensive. Spider-Man uses his webs to prevent carnage, to catch falling objects or people, and to stop speeding vehicles. More importantly, Peter Parker is tender, sweet, and vulnerable in ways we don't expect of a superhero, especially the hero of an action film. While a hero like Superman puts on the meek persona of Clark Kent, this is a mask intended to hide Superman's *true* identity. Peter Parker's meek persona was in place long before the spider bit him. And, unlike Bruce Wayne, Parker doesn't have the mask of great personal wealth. Parker candidly displays his vulnerabilities. He cries openly when his Uncle Ben dies. As Tobey

Maguire portrays him, Peter Parker acts with his heart and wears it on his sleeve. He is not beefy, aloof, aggressive, or sardonic. This departure from the stereotypical heroic qualities invites female audiences to confront the text with alternate readings. As critic Virginia Postrel (2006) suggests, on an emotional level, superheroes create glamour for all audiences: "The elements that create glamour are not specific styles — bias-cut gowns or lacquered furniture — but more general qualities: grace, mystery, transcendence" (140).

During the course of my textual analysis of the *Spider-Man* films, I had the opportunity to interview nine women who identified themselves as admirers of the trilogy and two who claimed to be fans of the comics as well. Each of these women had interpretations of the film texts that suggested playful negotiations of meaning. These fans suggested that the prominent Spider-Man storyline in the movies is basically a romance that wears the mask of an action film so that male audiences won't be threatened by it. Like Spider-Man, they felt the movies hid their true identity. Some female viewers expressed disappointment that MJ wasn't a very strong character but appreciated that the movies didn't go the way of the comics in their frequent depiction of female characters as overly endowed characters in tight, skimpy clothes. Because these women didn't consider the female characters to be openly displayed as erotic spectacles, it was easier to deny that the *Spider-Man* films occupy a male gaze. Some might argue that the films do provide MJ with plenty of wet T-shirt moments, but these aren't exaggerated, and Spider-Man doesn't leer in the manner of a film character like James Bond, which makes it more comfortable for women to identify with Spider-Man.

Another fan of both the movies and the comics further suggests that the departures these films made from the comics were welcome in at least one other regard: the absence of the "refrigerator syndrome," or the tendency for female characters to die horrible deaths in order to motivate superheroes to valor (Simone, 1999). Even Gwen Stacy, whose neck is broken when Spider-Man tries to save her in the comic, is spared a grisly death in the third film, though some fans questioned whether she needed to be in the third film at all. In the comics Gwen Stacy was Parker's first girlfriend, and seemed misplaced in the third film but — happily — the movie didn't kill her off just to make Spider-Man feel bad.

The female fans I interviewed all recognized the *Spider-Man* trilogy as a romance. The domineering thread of romantic involvement within the *Spider-Man* films creates ambiguity about the actual meaning of the journey, opening it for viewer interpretation. The recognized goal of the "chick flick" is for the female protagonist to find and secure romantic love, whereas the goal of the action film, the hero's journey, is for the male protagonist to protect the world. Peter Parker has both ambitions: he wants to secure personal love and happiness as well as protect his community from crime. He seems desperate for MJ's love and uncomfortable with the hero's duties. This is especially clear in the second film, when Parker attempts to surrender his role as a superhero in order to have the life he really wants. A stranger in an elevator comments on his "cool Spidey outfit" and that the costume "looks uncomfortable"; Parker agrees that it's "kinda itchy" and "rides up in the crotch a little bit, too." Later, Parker will throw away the costume but can't discard the heroic impulse the costume represents.

One fan explained that women truly relate to the wearing of an uncomfortable costume, hiding ordinariness under the glamour of a tight outfit, makeup, or a "couture dress." All are masquerades. Both men and women seem to require masquerades for the illusion of *being in love*, because these masks hide the ordinary person, creating the fantasy of someone exceptional. To love is to draw close to another person, to merge with that person, but to "*be in love*" is to substitute the individual for an ideal (Johnson, 1977: 35).

The act of loving is not an illusion but rather the work of valuing another person for his or her personal uniqueness within the context of an ordinary world. However, *"being in love"* is an intrusion of an archetypal, super-personal or divine world. A god or goddess is suddenly mirrored in the beloved. Being in love is divine insanity. People in love look *through* each other rather than *at* each other, "each in love with an idea, an ideal, or an emotion. The worst thing about being in love is that it doesn't last. The transpersonal, god-like quality dims, revealing the personal, down-to-earth, ordinary man. This is one of the saddest and most painful experiences in life" (Johnson, 1977: 31). The faithful love Peter Parker continues to express for MJ can be interpreted as his love for her personal uniqueness, however flawed. This is the kind of love that can live to celebrate 50th wedding anniversaries (unless a comic book villain like Mephisto wipes the memory clean). This is the love we say we want but it's not the kind of love that makes someone giddy. Being in love with a mystery makes a person giddy.

Another fan of the films believes that because of its restraint as well as its mystery, the first film in the trilogy has perhaps the "sexiest kiss in all of screen history." The famous scene occurs after Spider-Man saves Mary Jane from rapists in a dark alley. He hangs upside down from a web facing her. MJ asks if she gets to thank him and reaches for his mask. Spider-Man's hands are preoccupied with hanging from the web, so Mary Jane tenderly pulls down his mask, just uncovering his lips — nothing else — and they kiss. No groping, no frantic tearing of clothes, no clichéd trail of discarded garments in a littered path to a rumpled bed — just this long, sweet, soft, wet kiss in the rain. MJ is not kissing a man she knows and loves for himself; she is kissing an ideal — a god. MJ is an ordinary woman who survives this divine touching. The scene has the excitement of *"being in love,"* of caressing a mystery. The romantic intensity may have as much to so with the unknown and unfulfilled promise as the actual kiss. MJ's response might not be the same if she knew that Spider-Man is not really a god but "dorky Peter Parker." When she has suspicions about Spider-Man's identity, MJ asks Parker to kiss her, but kissing Peter Parker in a café couldn't possibly be the same as kissing the mysterious Spider-Man in a dark, wet alley. Violence must interrupt the experiment.

Even though identifying with MJ permits the possible excitement of kissing a god, the female spectator is in on the secret of Spider-Man's identity, which deadens the giddiness a bit. Furthermore, MJ will eventually learn the truth about Spider-Man. It seems to be part of the heroine's journey to cast a light on the face of a god, to unmask the superhero and reveal what is of value as well as uncover the illusions. As Murdock (1990) suggests, a heroine's journey involves slaying the delusions of several myths, even if in the process it also destroys the delights of giddiness. However, this is clearly Spider-Man's journey, not MJ's.

Although MJ, as played by Kirsten Dunst, might seem to offer an idealized media mirror image with which women can narcissistically identify, the character lacks the heroic determination that invites projection and admiration. As one fan suggested, Mary Jane is "whiney and self-absorbed, especially when her career ambitions go down the toilet." MJ is not a hateful character; she just isn't Spider-Man's equal. Female fans seemed to connect more strongly with Peter Parker than with MJ. Another fan thought the last scene in the second film showed MJ's potential to be Spider-Man's partner. She now knows Spider-Man's identity and is willing to take whatever risks come along. But, by the third film, MJ is disappointed in her own failures and the bright vision of Spider-Man has dimmed. She has seen behind the mask to the ordinary man. He cannot magically understand her disappointments. He is not magically able to fulfill her desires and he will additionally give away their "special kiss" to Gwen Stacy as part of a publicity stunt. Mary Jane doesn't trust Parker. She gets jealous and turns to Harry. She allows herself to be used, proving that Parker should not trust Mary Jane either. She doesn't know her own heart.

Both male and female critics of the films seem to have the least admiration for the third film in the trilogy. For critic Roger Ebert of the *Chicago Sun Times*, Peter Parker is a "sap" in the third film and the romance is "dopey," but for both male critics and female fans it is Parker's shadow in the third film that becomes really problematic. Under the influence of the symbiote, Parker becomes mean, leering, and egotistical — as one female viewer put it, "just like any other man." Critic Todd McCarthy complains that although the shadow allows Peter Parker to suspend "his goody two-shoes personality" and gives him a cool new black costume, all it "really amounts to is an interlude in which Peter struts around with a trendy new haircut ogling women and humiliating Mary Jane with some aggressive nightclub antics" (2007). Ebert agrees that while Peter Parker is under the influence of the symbiote, "he combs his hair forward, struts the streets, attracts admiring glances from every pretty girl on the street, and feels like hot stuff" (2007). But, female fans argue that the glances from women characters can hardly be interpreted as "admiring." The women watching Peter Parker "strut his stuff" seem more revolted than impressed. The dark, symbiote-infected Peter Parker just isn't cool. He isn't socially powerful in his shadow self, he's just a more formidable jerk.

Without the illusion of Spider-Man, MJ must learn to love the unique qualities of Peter Parker, which have always included his "dorky" vulnerability and now include observations of his blemished shadow. At the end of the third film there is the hint that she might be able to do this. The song suggests she's giving up on *being in love*, but the kiss suggests she's not giving up on the work of loving. Loving takes effort and forgiveness for the boorish behavior of Parker's shadow, and the sometimes-careless behavior of his ordinary self. This work may explain why so many other action heroes must have a succession of love interests: eventually the female character will unmask the hero, damaging the god and exposing the man. The hero will see his own clay feet mirrored in her knowledge. Equally possible is for the hero to see the humanity in his love interest, destroying the illusion of the goddess that even a couture masquerade cannot secure. This is part of why Spider-Man is a special hero to female spectators: he continues to love the unique and flawed qualities of MJ (though it probably doesn't hurt that she was popular and considered a social prize from the beginning).

Finally, some female spectators point out that all three films carry a repeated message: it is male hubris and male intellectual ambition that threaten humanity. The egotistical scientists (Norman Osborn and Otto Octavius), the pretentious and dishonest journalists (J Jonah Jameson and Eddie Brock) and the multitude of male criminals bent on self-gratification (which include Flint Marko and the carjacker who stole Uncle Ben's car) are threats to be defeated. As one fan noted, it's not women who cause problems in these movies: the problems are all male.

The mythological hero is principally a symbol of the self, constantly changing on a journey toward balance and wholeness. This journey reflected in Hollywood films has traditionally been the journey of a white man. This is also true of the *Spider-Man* film trilogy. However, social changes in the last few decades have made it possible for American women to share the masculine hero myth. At least in the ideal, American women can enjoy social equality and friendship with men and the opportunity to compete with men in the public sphere. For a modern American woman with education and some means of economic independence, life is something to be controlled as an act of her own heroic resolve. Feminist interpretations of the animus suggests that relating to the heroic male opens a woman to unrealized capacities in herself to be assertive, logical, and show leadership. The animus in its stages of transformation can encourage the development of a strong feminine personality (Ulanov, 1971: 242). In its most developed form, the animus can make a woman more receptive to new possibilities. When a woman "knows she has an animus and can relate to him, she is no longer subservient" (Johnson, 1977: 24).

For decades, women, minorities, and homosexuals have learned to apply the mental gymnastics necessary to be able to project themselves into the active role of Hollywood's white male protagonists and subject those narratives to alternate readings. The other choice would be to internalize oppressive readings for the symbols of white patriarchal society (Wehr, 1987). In actual practice, problematic viewership may not belong to women and minorities but to white men, whose gaze Hollywood has traditionally privileged. Unused to mental gymnastics, the heterosexual male spectator might find identification with a female protagonist threatening. Yet, as social roles for men begin to change and Hollywood offers more diverse possibilities for protagonists and stories, the white male spectator may learn to develop the same mental flexibility to find and enjoy heroic adventure, even in romances or more domestic, character-driven adventures that do not hide behind a mask.

Works Cited

Campbell, Joseph. *The Hero with a Thousand Faces*. Princeton, NJ: Princeton University Press, 1949.
_____. *The Power of Myth*. Doubleday, 1988.
Ebert, Roger. "*Spider-Man 3*." *Chicago Sun-Times*. 11/16/2007. Accessed 11/4/2010. rogerebert.suntimes.com.
Henderson, Joseph L. "Ancient Myths and Modern Man" in Carl G. Jung and M. L. Franz, eds. *Man and His Symbols*. Garden City, NY: Double Day, 1972: 104–157.
Indick, William. *Psychology for Screenwriters*. Studio City, CA: Michael Weise, 2004.
Izod, John. *Myth, Mind and the Screen: Understanding the Heroes of Our Time*. Cambridge: Cambridge UP, 2001.
_____. *Screen, Culture, Psyche: A Post-Jungian Approach to Working with the Audience*. New York: Routledge, 2006.
Johnson, Robert. *She: Understanding Feminine Psychology*. New York: Harper and Row, 1977.
Jung, Carl. G. "Archetypes of the Collective Unconscious" in H. Read, M Fordham and G. Adler, eds. *Collected Works*. Princeton: Princeton University Press, 1953.
_____. "Approaching the Unconscious" in Carl G. Jung and M. L. Franz, eds. *Man and His Symbols*. New York: Doubleday, 1964: 18–103.
_____. *The Portable Jung*. Joseph M. Campbell, Ed. New York: Viking Press, 1971.
Kaminsky, Stuart M. and Jeffrey H. Mahan. *American Television Genres*. Chicago: Nelson-Hall, 1986.
McCarthy, Todd. "*Spider-Man 3*." *Variety*. 4/26/2007. Accessed 11/3/2011. http://www.variety.com/review/VE1117933393.html?categoryid=31&cs=1
Moyers, Bill (producer). *Joseph Campbell and The Power of Myth*. (Six Part Documentary Series) with and PBS, 1988.
Mulvey, Laura. "Visual Pleasure and Narrative Cinema." *Screen*. 16 (3), (1975): 6–18.
Murdock, Maureen. *The Heroine's Journey: Woman's Quest for Wholeness*. Boston: Shambhala, 1990.
Petric, Vlada, ed. *Film and Dreams: An Approach to Bergman*. South Salem, NY: Redgrave, 1981.
Postrel, Virginia. "Superhero Worship." *Atlantic Monthly*. 298:3 (Oct 2006): 140–144.
Rascaroli, Laura. "Like a Dream: A Critical History of the Oneiric Metaphor in Film Theory." *Kinema: A Journal for Film and Audiovisual Media*. 18:3 (Fall 2002): 4–22.
Sabbagh, Dan. "Spider-Man Lures Audiences to the Cinema." *The Times London*. 5/7/2007: 43.
Simone, Gail. "Women in Refrigerators." Accessed 11/1/10 http://www.unheardtaunts.com/wir/.
Smith, Sean. "Along Came Spidey." *Newsweek*. (June 28, 2004): 7.
Ulanov, Ann Belford and Barry Ulanov. *Transforming Sexuality: The Archetypal World of Anima and Animus*. London: Shambhala, 1994.
van Zoonen, Liesbet. *Feminist Media Studies*. London: Sage, 1994.
Vogler, Christopher. *The Writer's Journey: Mythic Structures for Writers*. 2nd ed. Studio City, CA: Michael Wiese, 1998.
Von Franz, Marie-Louise. *The Feminine in Fairy Tales*. 2nd ed. London: Shambhala, 1993.
Waxman, Sharon. "*Spider-Man 3* Conquers Box Office and Bodes Well for Summer." *New York Times*. (May 7, 2007). Section E: 1.
Xueling, Huang. "Pow! *Spider-Man 3* Smashes Local Box Office Records." *The Straits Times, Singapore*. (May 5, 2007).

The Incorrigible Aunt May[1]

ORA C. MCWILLIAMS

Imagine for a moment that your brother-in-law and his wife die tragically in an airplane crash and leave you and your husband with the responsibility of caring for a little boy. A few years later your own husband gets murdered tragically during a robbery. All that is left of your burgeoning family is yourself and the little boy. Tragedy defines your life.

May Riley-Parker, or "Aunt May," was created by Stan Lee and Steve Ditko as a mother figure for Peter Parker/Spider-Man. Her first appearance was in *Amazing Fantasy* #15 (August 1962). Since that time Aunt May has been many things: Parker's aunt, Spider-Man's foil, Doctor Octopus' bride — she's even been a Herald of Galactus. The character wasn't truly fleshed out in the first issues in which she appeared, but even by then many of the tropes through which we came to know Aunt May were established. In *Amazing Fantasy* #15 and *Amazing Spider-Man* #1, the stage was set for some 30 years of Aunt May's characterization. These issues set the precedent for Aunt May as domestic goddess, single mother, and moral compass. In the wake of Uncle Ben's tragic death, Aunt May clearly becomes the rock in Parker's life, paramount to the moral development of his character. Throughout most of her history Spider-Man, who is her own nephew in disguise, is an abhorrent horror and in her mind she fears the wall crawler, often to the point of fainting at the sight of him. As this was the case, Peter feared revealing his secret identity for many years. Eventually when Aunt May finds out that Peter is Spider-Man she unconditionally accepts him, as any parent would.

Within the Spider-Man comics, Aunt May's presence shows several contradictions. There are several tellings and retellings of Spider-Man's origin story, and Aunt May is portrayed differently within each of them. This paper will examine several issues of *Amazing Spider-Man* from the 1960s to present day, the *Trouble* mini-series, and issues of *New Avengers*, of which Spider-Man was a member. It will then conclude with the current status quo of Spider-Man in "Brand New Day." The inquiry will ask what Aunt May's place is within the Spider-Man comic universe and use theories from Eco, Jung, and Campbell. The paper will also ask about her status as a feminist or non-feminist figure.

Aunt May: A Stumbling Block or Stepping-Stone for Spider-Man?

Aunt May has been one of the few constants in Parker's life. She is Parker's heart. However, her presence represents Ben's absence. She serves as a constant reminder of Parker's failure to save Ben and that "with great power comes great responsibility." Aunt May's first appearance on-panel is on the second story page of *Amazing Fantasy #15*. The exposition states, "As for Pete's Aunt May, she thought the sun rose and set upon her nephew." She then says to Peter, "I cooked your favorite breakfast, Petey—Wheatcakes!" (2). The first story establishes her continuing love for Parker.

The love and respect that Aunt May has for Peter is not a one-way street. He feels the same way about her, and many Spider-Man writers consider this relationship to be a part of the core of the comic book. When speaking of his motivations to write the story of Aunt May's death in *Amazing Spider-Man #196—200*, DeFalco writes to Wolfman, "I believe that you are the first Spider-Writer to kill Aunt May." Wolfman responds, "That was just a game. [...] I knew upfront that Aunt May hadn't really died because I would never do that. I believe she's the root that keeps him balanced. But I wanted to set up a mystery that wasn't solved in one issue. I really wanted to tear Peter down a bit. That's why I set up the whole 'death' of Aunt May" (DeFalco, 2004: 82). Fettinger (2006) states that "without [May and Mary Jane], Peter, and Spider-Man, would likely have fallen apart. May's inner strength and will to live are an incalculable benefit. For all her maladies, she is almost too stubborn to die as long as she believes that someone needs her. Spider-Man's equally stubborn refusal to give up even in the face of overwhelming odds is due directly to May's influence" (152). A common trope for Aunt May is that she is often on the brink of certain death. Fettinger aptly states that Aunt May is "too stubborn to die" as long as someone needs her, and that someone is Parker. Further, Fettinger also argues that May and Mary Jane represent a connection to "non-superhuman race," that his "great power does not separate him from the rest of humanity and set him above it" (152). In this formulation, May represents grounding for Peter. Not only is she the keeper of his morality, but also she insures that he is beholden to human frailty.

In the early issues of *Amazing Spider-Man*, Aunt May is primarily concerned with paying the rent and worrying about her nephew. Paul Lytle (2006), in his essay "Power, Responsibility and Pain: the Price of Being Spider-Man," attempts to save May as a character despite her neurosis. He states, "Ben's death did something to Aunt May. She became weak where she was not before, and the bills began to pile up. Grief had struck her in the most horrible ways [...] Her judgment began to slip as well. It began with a real hatred for Spider-Man, but progressed to a sympathy and even love for Doctor Octopus" (178–179). Lytle posits that Aunt May's unexplained and erratic behavior is linked to her melancholic feelings of loss for her beloved husband.

May is not the only one that feels these melancholic feelings. In *Amazing Spider-Man #32* (1/1966), Aunt May falls ill and need a blood transfusion. Peter donates his own blood but her condition worsens because of the radioactivity of his blood. In other words, May could die because of his powers. Spider-Man tracks down a cure with the help of Dr. Curt Connors. However, on the way back with the cure as Spider-Man, he gets into a tussle with Doc Octopus and gets pinned under building rubble. B.J. Oropeza (2008), in the essay "'Behold! The Hero Has Become Like One of Us': The Perfectly Imperfect Spider-Man," suggests that "as the hero contemplates his fate, he interprets Aunt May's cure as a way to stop being 'haunted' by the memory of his dead uncle. He determines that if he does not deliver the serum he will be responsible for his aunt's death too" (136). This gives him the strength to overcome the unbearable weight; whereas not using his powers made him responsible for Uncle Ben's death, in this case it is his powers that would be directly responsible for his Aunt's death. In other words, he views delivering the cure as redemption for letting Uncle Ben die.

It hadn't happened yet, but this fate does come to pass later when Spider-Man attempts and fails to save Gwen Stacy in *Amazing Spider-Man #121–122* (1973). As Leaver outlines earlier in this volume, fans have argued for years whether or not she was dead before the webbing broke her fall and her neck. Ultimately, it didn't matter, because Peter blamed himself. After Gwen's death, Peter lives with a new tension. According to writer Gerry Conway, "Uncle Ben died because Peter didn't use his power. Gwen dies as a consequence of his power" (DeFalco, 2004: 47). Spider-Man lives in a no-win world. If he stands by and does nothing, then people he cares about die; if he uses his powers he may be directly responsible for their deaths. He declares revenge on the Green Goblin and catches him, but is finally unable to murder him.

As Emily Edwards outlines above, Carl Jung, and later Joseph Campbell, described the archetypes of our collective conscious. Jung's psychology, like Freud's, is problematic and not without its flaws, but it remains useful for the interpretation of literature, and in the case of Aunt May (and in particular Uncle Ben) Jung is useful for examining their archetypical characterizations. One of the types Campbell describes is the "wise old man" or the "helper figure." The most logical formulations would fit this character with Uncle Ben. Indeed, Uncle Ben fits the criteria of being supernatural (Campbell, 2008: 51–63); however, Aunt May fits some of the characteristics of the wise old man (person) as well. Sometimes Ben has been known to appear as a ghost and give advice in Peter's life, but more often it is May that offers advice in practical matters. A critical contradiction within the character of Aunt May is that while May is the "helper" to Peter, to Spider-Man she is the evil "crone." She is wicked and hateful toward Spider-Man: she even shoots at Spider-Man to defend Doctor Octopus in *Amazing Spider-Man #115* (1972).

Does May Represent a Feminine Ideal or a Feminist Critique?

Depending on who is writing her, Aunt May could either be a tragic suffering widow or a wacky wisecracking spinster. One particular oddity, occurring as part of a gimmick called "assistant editors month," was published in *Marvel Team-Up #137*. In the issue, Aunt May is transformed by a being with limitless power into a superhero—a herald of Galactus named Golden Oldie (a riff on the Silver Surfer). At the end of the story, none of it matters because it turns out to be a dream. In some ways, the story is simply preposterous, but of course the draw of the issue is the comedy that the most unlikely candidate, Aunt May, could be imbued with the power cosmic.

This issue plays on the comedy that it would be silly for frail old Aunt May to be a mighty herald of Galactus. Aunt May represents an "intersectionality" between expectations of feminine gender roles and expectations of the elderly. Intersectionality is defined as the intersection of two forms of oppression (Hill-Collins, 2006). However, May's role is further problematized by the fact that she is a single-mother and has a child to raise. I believe that since there was already a female herald (Nova), the comedy in the above issue derived from the fact that she was elderly. The *Marvel Team-Up* issue brings into focus the double standard that society has for the elderly. It is fully believable that an alien we know nothing about could wander the galaxy as a herald of Galactus. But "old" Aunt May? That's just silly. It should be noted that depending on the writer and time period, Aunt May's age can be used as both a weakness and a form of cleverness. In later issues, Aunt May shows her own cleverness against even the toughest of Spider-Man foes.

Aunt May was created in 1961 as a kindly old woman. However, the 1960s were a tempestuous time for gender relationships. Comic books have often struggled with the feminine and the 1960s were no exception. Feminist theorist and comics scholar Laura D'Amore in her forthcoming article observes of female superhero characters that "the superheroine was intimately linked, as a symbol and an idea, to American cultural history, making it a particularly suitable icon for the identity struggles of American feminists" (D'Amore, forthcoming: n.p.). In many cases these women shared the same struggles as other women — were beholden to the same social constructions — but were able to exert power in certain circumstances.

The women's liberation movement was going on concurrently with the introduction of Aunt May. Nevertheless, for many years she represents an older generational idea of femininity, one that is still subject to and dependent upon the man of the house, her nephew. Even in situations where May is not dependent on Peter financially, she is still dependent upon Spider-Man to elude capture or injury. The relationship between Peter and May only reinforces gender normative roles. This is not an isolated situation, as D'Amore explains: "Sue Storm did for the Fantastic Four 'family' what Friedan's 1950s mother did for hers; she kept them 'together,' admonished them for fighting, apologized for her own (insignificant) role, and reminded them of their moral duty" (D'Amore, 2008: n.p.). Sue's presence in the team is that of a typical or ideal woman of the time. Further, D'Amore states of Sue Richards: "Sue as captive," "Sue as beauty," and "Sue as housewife" are recurrent themes throughout the 1960s (ibid.). Like Sue Storm (cum-Richards), Aunt May's role in the *Spider-Man* comics of the 1960s, and well into the 1980s, was as a captive or housewife.

D'Amore does leave room for the subverting of gender roles on the part of superheroines. She suggests that the superheroine of the 1960s may represent a feminine ideal which allows one to "work outside the home, in a profession that was traditionally male," and that "battle with villains was a regular condition of employment" (D'Amore, forthcoming: n.p.). These superheroines, moreover, represent a new manifestation of characters already present in popular culture. Sherrie Innes (2004) states that "tough" women existed throughout 20th century popular culture: in the 1950s and 1960s, comic books featured the "jungle girl" woman and Modesty Blaise, while television introduced *The Avengers'* Emma Peel and, later, *Charlie's Angels* and *The Bionic Woman*. Jeffery Brown describes the contradictory nature of the action heroine as "tough and sexual, violent but desirable ... [which] constructs the emerging roles for women as both heroic subject and as a sexual object" (Brown, 2010: 7). Brown describes the body as the place at which women are objectified.

Although Aunt May fits many of the molds of the other female characters of the 1960s, one way in which she does not is in her sexuality or in her body — particularly in her frailty. Although Aunt May's beauty is not at issue, her role as a potential beauty or potential mate is played in the books for her foolish love interests, particularly Doctor Octopus. Not only does Aunt May exhibit the obvious frailty of her body, but also less obviously of her ego. She is not like the tough "Supermoms" that D'Amore describes as being in the mold of Sue Richards: "never let em' see you sweat," juggle work and home effectively, and do it all with a smile. Aunt May *cannot* juggle it all and laments loudly about not being able to make rent or buy Peter nice things. Despite this constant state of alarm, however, Aunt May seems ultimately to be able to weather any storm and make ends meet.

Parker has also had other women in his life but none as stable as May. In a recent storyline, May becomes a wedge in the relationship between Parker and Mary Jane, the next closest constant in Parker's life. However, one might contend that May has always been a wedge in Peter's love life. When he was interviewed about the death of Gwen Stacy, artist John Romita Sr. said of Aunt May that "they were going to kill somebody in the strip for shock value and I think they settled on Aunt May. I didn't like that idea. If you kill Aunt May, Peter Parker's secret identity isn't a problem anymore because there's no one for him to protect, and you'd lose the whole teenage nerd factor" (DeFalco, 2004: 32). Peter's down-on-his-luck nerd routine was a clear story reason to leave Aunt May alone.

Lawrence Watts-Evens posits in his 2006 essay "Peter Parker's Penance" that all aspects of his life, including his choice to be Spider-Man, his career choice, and even his love interests are intricately linked to a self-imposed penance: "Peter Parker feels he doesn't deserve happiness. After all, he let Uncle Ben get murdered, when he could have prevented it. [...] Ben isn't there to see it. Ben Parker was encouraging him in his plans to study science, so with Ben gone, science is no longer where he's meant to be" (21). Parker cannot bring himself to be a brilliant scientist because that is what Ben wanted for him. Working in science would be a constant reminder of his Uncle Ben. In that way, Aunt May serves as a constant reminder of his failure as well. May's presence represents Ben's absence. "Ben would tease [Peter] about girls, and offer him advice, and Ben and May provided his role models of a loving couple, so with Ben gone he can't have that [...] so he screwed up his love life" (ibid.). As a result, Peter limits himself in his relationships.

The character of Aunt May also represents containment for Parker's own burgeoning sexuality. Aside from theoretical-psychological considerations, there are other practical considerations. Living with one's elderly aunt would have rendered it difficult to bring a girl home. As a result, the archetypal Spider-Man story rules suggesting that Peter Parker is a down-on-his-luck young man make it difficult to "grow Peter up" with his Aunt May wandering so prominently around his life. Said Romita, Sr. of Parker/Spider-Man, "It didn't matter how good-looking he was or how well he was doing if his Aunt was still telling him to bring his umbrella whenever he went out in the rain" (DeFalco, 2004: 32). A recent storyline further drives home the point about Aunt May being the wedge in Peter's sexual development. In "One More Day" (2008), it becomes clear that May is a full containment on Peter's sexuality. In that story, Aunt May gets shot and fatally wounded. Spider-Man attempts all of the avenues available to him through his superhero friends. Science, magic and medicine all fail him. He ends up making a pact with Mephisto, Marvel's equivalent of the devil, through the surrogate of Mary Jane, to save his aunt. He chooses to wipe his marriage, which Mephisto refers to as a rare love, from existence in order to save the life of his dying Aunt. If one takes May to be Peter's "mother," it doesn't take much to read the Oedipus complex at work in his choice. The idea that he'd save his Aunt-cum-surrogate-mother over his happy marriage to his wife is one that gave Spider-Man's writers more freedom in storytelling. Joe Quesada said in an interview shortly after the story, "When Peter Parker got married, it caused the character to be cut off from many of the social situations and settings that put him at conflict with his family, friends, and especially the girl he was dating" (Weiland, 2008: n.p.).

Peter's love life isn't the only complicated one featured in *Spider-Man* comics. Aunt May's first romantic snafu mentioned on panel was in *Amazing Spider-Man #131* (4/1974), when Doc Octopus attempts to marry Aunt May. He wants to marry her because he has inherited some land that contains uranium. The romance had been building up through several issues of the series, and this issue establishes that Aunt May is not simply beholden to Uncle Ben as her sole/soul mate. However, it does establish the uniqueness of Ben as good man in Aunt May's choice of men.

Another example of Aunt May's trouble with men comes with an explanation in the B-story in *Amazing Spider-Man #370* (1992), which tells a story of Aunt May's past wherein she was abandoned at a young age by her father and blamed by her mother for the break-up. May expresses that she was worried Peter's presence in her and Ben's life would do the same to her marriage. It remains unclear why May unloads that emotional baggage on Peter. But the 1990s were a different time for comic books. It seems every character had to have an extreme look or origin—including Aunt May.

Another example of May's bad choices in the romantic department emerges in the limited series *Trouble*, published in 2003. *Trouble* was written by Mark Millar, and its art was created by Terry Dodson. The hype around the book was that it would be the "secret origin" of Spider-Man. The book coyly played with the names Ben, Richard, May and Mary. Essentially, *Trouble* was a modern romance comic that attempted to revive a 30-years-fallow genre. The book involved an accidental and covered-up teenage pregnancy, a topic that the older romance comics couldn't address due to considerations of Comics Code approval. Marvel divested themselves from the Comics Code a year earlier and were eager to stretch their storytelling wings a bit. Ultimately the book did not reach its intended audience and is by and large regarded as a misfire. The book's modern romance and pregnancy story might have done well on its own merits. However, the prerelease buzz around the book implied that that May and Ben were actually Parker's birth parents and that good friends Richard and Mary took care of the child. As one can imagine, the fans were livid and the book was never assimilated into the canon. Although the book itself isn't important to Spider-Man continuity, as an interesting derivation it nevertheless does do two things. Firstly, it shows the amount that Marvel might have been willing to adjust the Spider-Man origin. Secondly, it explores a genre shift that loosely involves the same characters.

In multiple interviews prior to the release of *Trouble*, everyone involved stated that the book could supply the true origin of Peter Parker. Then-Marvel President Bill Jemas stated, "There've been a lot of half-rumors and some misreported stories if this is really Peter Parker, Ben, Aunt May, etc.... That's not confirmed right now because frankly we don't know if that is what it should be." Further, "we think the final answer ought to come from the comics community based on the acceptance of the story" (Weiland, 2003: n.p.). In other words, if the book was popular enough, Marvel stated they would let it stand as Parker's origin story. Whether or not that was simply Marvel attempting to attract attention to the new book may never be known.

The problematic presence of *Trouble*, however, creates an interesting thought experiment; what if the Spider-Man comic were told from the point of view of Aunt May? The genre would probably be a romance comic of sorts about a single "mother" interspersed with horror as she is "menaced" regularly by the villain known only as Spider-Man. Theorist Umberto Eco writes about comic book temporality in his essay "The Myth of Superman" (2004/1972). Drawing on the work of Heidegger, Eco points to the idea of causality in comics, wherein a character is not responsible for their past or their future and only partially responsible for their present (157). Applying this concept to Aunt May, wherein all the reader knows about her in most or all of her daily life is Peter Parker/Spider-Man-centric, Aunt May could cease to exist when Peter or Spider-Man are not present. This is much the same as in theater, for example, in the sense that when a character walks off stage, it is fair to assume nothing has happened to them since the audience last saw them. There are relatively few events that occur in the *Spider-Man* comic universe where Aunt May is not acting somehow as an agent intrinsically linked to the events of Peter Parker/Spider-Man. As a result, we know that Aunt May is only a supporting character and not the main character of the book.

Aunt May as an incorrigible character never learns and repeats the same mistakes over and over. Simply as an example, she continuously becomes embroiled in bad love life choices—not just bad, but probably the worst choices. Throughout her history, Aunt May also fails to learn lessons, as she is often an unwitting hostage. Indeed, one would assume that she would learn to protect herself after each encounter. Aunt May's character remains relatively static for 30-plus years of publication, never learning, never changing. The story-run of J. Michael Straczynski-written issues of *Amazing Spider-Man*, however, changed this. Lasting from June 2001–November 2007, the Straczynski era had its ups and downs. There was the 9/11 issue which, tragedy aside, is one of the best single issues ever published. On the other end of the spectrum, there was also the incoherent Gwen Stacy and Norman Osborn tryst that resulted in two cloned children (huh?). Most important for this inquiry, however, is that Aunt May really comes into her own as a strong character.

Aunt May finds out that Peter is Spider-Man in Vol., 2, *#37* (2002). After 478 issues of *Amazing*, and a few hundred more issues of *Marvel Team-Up*, *Web of Spider-Man*, and *Spectacular Spider-Man*, Marvel finally provides the big reveal, and a great thing happens: the next issue Parker explains his motives for keeping the secret. He says that he has blamed himself for Ben's death all these years and that is why he did it. Aunt May retorts that she and Ben got into a fight just before he died and that she'd been blaming herself too. She also says that she knew that he was hiding something all this time, but she figured him to be homosexual. She also states that a part of her will always hate that he is Spider-Man. This simultaneously shows Aunt May's care for her nephew and respects story precedent, ensuring that his worries about the reveal were not unfounded, and that Aunt May was not simply acting hysterical toward Spider-Man. The move also respects the growth of the characters occurring in Spider-Man's and Aunt May's appearances in *New Avengers*, which ran concurrently. In that book Aunt May could continue to grow as a character, even to the point of having an implied relationship with Jarvis, the Avenger's butler. Although this is only one example, during the Straczynski era Aunt May grew as a character and truly showed promise to become more complex.

However, it was not to last. After Peter and Mary Jane's marriage is undone in "One More Day," the next story is titled "Brand New Day." The storyline holds onto some of the strong character elements but regresses May somewhat to a frail old woman and, more importantly, takes back Parker's Spider-Man secret identity reveal. This retrograde backslide of the characters was done in theory so that creators could have more latitude in storytelling. However, it is unfortunate that so many babies were thrown out with some of the last 25 years of bathwater. The deal effectively undid several years of character growth and progressive thought on the part of several characters, but Aunt May was the character most affected.

In conclusion, Aunt May has been many things in her 40-plus years of publication. Throughout her appearances in comics, Aunt May has been portrayed differently in different time periods. She has been a doting Aunt and solid rock in Peter Parker's life. Sometimes she is a helpless old woman and an unwilling dupe to Spider-Man villains. Sometimes she is a powerful woman that knows what she wants. She may also be a cosmic being, or even [temporarily] dead. As a result, Aunt May becomes a reflection of how we feel about mother figures and women in general from the 1960s through the 2000s. She has grown as a character, died, come back, and loved and lost. She's made good choices and bad.

Aunt May could very well be a hero for us all.

Notes

1. I must give a special thank you to Dr. Claude E. Taylor (Monmouth University) who pointed out the "sexual containment" observation to me at a conference and really spring-boarded sections of the discussion. Thanks to Rachael Rost and Laura D'Amore, to the esteemed editors of the text for keeping me sharp, and to all those who discussed this project with me over the years: you know who you are.

Works Cited

Brown, Jeffery A. *Dangerous Curves: Action Heroines, Gender, Fetishism, and Popular Culture* Jackson: University of Mississippi Press, 2011.
Campbell, Joseph. *The Hero with a Thousand Faces.* Novato, CA: New World Library, 2008.
Carlin, Michael, Greg LaRocque, et al. *Marvel Team-Up 137.* New York: Marvel Comics (Jan 1984).
Conway, Gerry, John Romita, et al. *Amazing Spider-Man 115.* New York: Marvel Comics (Dec 1972).
_____, Gil Kane, et al. *Amazing Spider-Man #121–122.* New York: Marvel Comics (Jun/Jul 1973).
_____, Ross Andreu, et al. *Amazing Spider-Man #131.* New York: Marvel Comics (Apr 1974).
D'Amore, Laura. "The Accidental Supermom: Superheroines and Maternal Performativity 1963–1980." *Journal of Popular Culture* (forthcoming).
_____, "Invisible Girl's Quest for Visibility: Early Second Wave Feminism and the Comic Book Superheroine." *Americana: The Journal of American Popular Culture (1900-present).* Fall 2008, 7:2. Online: accessed 11/7/2011. http://www.americanpopularculture.com/journal/articles/fall_2008/d'amore.htm.
DeFalco, Tom. *Comics Creators on Spider-Man.* London: Titan Books. 2004.
Dematteis, J. M., Mark Bagley, et al. *Amazing Spider-Man 400.* New York: Marvel Comics (Apr 1995).
Eco, Umberto. "The Myth of Superman" in Jeet Heer and Kent Worcester, eds. *Arguing Comics: Literary Masters On A Popular Medium.* New York: University Press of Mississippi, 2004: 146–64.
Fettinger. J.R. "The Absent Father and Spider-Man's Unfilled Potential" in Gerry Conway, ed. *Webslinger: Unauthorized Essays on Your Friendly Neighborhood Spider-Man.* Dallas, TX: Benbella, 2006: 149–163.
Hill-Collins, Patricia. "The Politics of Black Feminist Thought" in Carole Ruth and Seung-Kyung Kim, eds. *Feminist Theory Reader: Local and Global Perspectives.* New York: Routledge, 2003: 318–33.
Inness, Sherrie A. *Action Chicks: New Images of Tough Women in Popular Culture.* New York: Palgrave-MacMillian, 2004.
Lee, Stan, Steve Ditko, et al. *Amazing Fantasy 15.* New York: Marvel Comics (August 1962).
_____, Steve Ditko, et al. *Amazing Spider-Man 1.* New York: Marvel Comics (March 1963).
_____, Steve Ditko, et al. *Amazing Spider-Man 32.* New York: Marvel Comics (Jan 1966).
Lytle, Paul. "Power, Responsibility, and Pain: The Price of Being Spider-Man" in Gerry Conway, ed. *Webslinger: Unauthorized Essays on Your Friendly Neighborhood Spider-Man.* Dallas, TX: Benbella (2006): 175–187.
Michelinie, David, Aaron Lopresti, Mark Bagley, et al. *Amazing Spider-Man 370.* New York: Marvel Comics (Dec 1992).
Millar, Mark, Terry Dodson. *Trouble, 1–4.* New York: Marvel (2003).
Oropeza, B.J. "'Behold! The Hero Has Become Like One of Us': The Perfectly Imperfect Spider-Man" in B.J. Oropeza, ed. *The Gospel According to Superheroes: Religion and Popular Culture.* New York: Peter Lang (2008): 127–144.
Straczynski, J. Michael, John Romita, Jr., et al. *Amazing Spider-Man Vol.2: 37–38.* New York: Marvel (Jan/Feb 2002).
_____, Joe Quesada, et al. *Spider-Man One More Day.* New York: Marvel (2007).
Stern, Roger, Marie Severin & John Romita. *Peter Parker, Spectacular Spider-Man Annual 3.* New York: Marvel (1981).
Watta-Evans, Lawrence. "Peter Parker's Penance" in Gerry Conway, ed. *Webslinger: Unauthorized Essays on Your Friendly Neighborhood Spider-Man.* Dallas, TX: Benbella, 2006: 17–24.
Weiland, Jonah. "Marvel Comics Press Conference 6/6/03, 'Trouble' Preview." 2003. Accessed 3/1/11. http://www.comicbookresources.com/?page=article&id=2216.
_____, "The 'One More Day' Interviews with Joe Quesada, Pt. 3 of 5." *Comicbookresources.com.* 1/2/2008. Accessed 3/1/11. http://www.comicbookresources.com/?page=article&old=1&id=12681.
Wolfman, Marv, Stan Lee, Keith Pollard, & Sal Buscema. *Amazing Spider-Man 196–200.* New York: Marvel (Oct 1979 — Jan 1980).

Spidey Meets Freud: Central Psychoanalytic Motifs in *Spider-Man* and *Spider-Man 2*

ROBERT MOSES PEASLEE

Introduction

At the very beginning of *Spider-Man* (2002), a teenage Peter Parker (Tobey Maguire) relates in narrative voice-over that this story is "all about a girl," a girl that he has "loved since before (he) even liked girls." The girl is Mary Jane Watson (Kirsten Dunst), Peter's ultra-popular longtime neighbor, who despite this proximity has remained out of the reach of the nerdy Parker. From the outset, the audience is given, in very clear terms, the parameters for understanding what will become an enormously fantastic narrative: this is a love story. While there are many features of this film and its sequel, *Spider-Man 2* (2004), which lend themselves to a psychoanalytic interpretation, it is the fixation of Parker on Watson, the first love, which drives the films and, in turn, the following analysis.

Mary Jane (MJ) is the axis around which most plots and subplots spin. While such an operationalization of the female lead may be said to be characteristic of the superhero film genre, her presence in these films is of a more crucial nature given the lack of mothers anywhere in the span of two films. The role of mother in the lives of major characters is one either ignored or fulfilled by a surrogate. The first part of this discussion, then, will analyze the several Oedipal triangles which are set up in the films, with special attention paid to the patriarchal role played by Parker's omnipotent half, Spider-Man himself.

But MJ's role is a complex one. As a "mother" figure, MJ also acts as a catalyst for the many revolutions in the character of Peter/Spider-Man. Specifically, an analysis of the triangle set up between Peter, MJ, their mutual friend Harry Osborn (James Franco) and, later, John Jameson (Daniel Gillies), will illustrate a number of dynamics theorized in Freud's essay "The Most Prevalent Form of Degradation in Erotic Life" (1912). I will posit that MJ, while a clearly maternal character in Oedipal terms, also fulfills other Freudian roles such as the madonna/whore, and finally, exhibiting her own agency in the narrative, an Oedipal role of her own in seeking to possess the omnipotent father figure.

Finally, this chapter will also look at the overarching construct of the conscious/unconscious split as it is so plainly illustrated in many characters, both heroic and villainous. Specifically, I will consider the ego/repression dichotomy as portrayed in two villains—Norman Osborn/Green Goblin (Willem Dafoe) and Otto Octavius/Doc Ock (Alfred Molina)—one ambivalent character (James Franco's Harry Osborn), and, of course, the hero himself. Each of these characters offers different levels of psychoanalytic complexity, and none more than the titular character. For there are many important questions to ask of Parker/Spider-Man from a Freudian perspective, questions that address, I think, the changing nature of the superhero in popular culture.

Writers of superhero texts, it should be said, are no doubt familiar in various ways with Freudian concepts; that this awareness should be harnessed in the creation of these characters, therefore, is not surprising. What is most interesting to me is the degree to which super characters are created in this way by necessity — that is, is it necessary to address these themes because audiences respond to them in specific and largely circumscribed ways? Are the lines that form for these films on opening days in the U.S. and abroad the clearest indications that superheroes work out Oedipal issues, unconscious desires, and other motifs paramount to psychoanalysis in ways that other texts cannot? This is a larger question than I might address here, but the analysis of films with regard to psychoanalytic themes is a crucial one in the ongoing literature concerning heroes and villains in American cinema. That writers are aware of how they construct characters, or that characters are not consciously and freely acting agents, is therefore less important to this study than an understanding of these characters and films as coded texts which, taken as a whole, shed light on our national cinematic discourse, what it values, and what it rejects.

Couching Superheroes and Psychoanalysis

The superhero in American culture, as one of that culture's most immediately recognizable tropes, has been theorized largely as a product of historical and ideological circumstances. Various periods of upheaval (e.g. the Great Depression, World War II, Watergate) are often said to be behind the initial appearance and continual evolution of these characters who, in their extremity, outline the borders of human activity, aspiration, and understanding. According to these analyses, the movement from a sure-footed, morally upright, and distinctly American Superman to a more ambivalent, sometimes openly hostile Spider-Man, reflects an ongoing sea change in the mass audience's understanding of and interaction with the American capitalist ideology. Despite the American origins of this character type, however, a discussion of the superhero as a device that expresses a broadly psychological in addition to a nationalistic dissonance has maintained itself across diverse paradigmatic and disciplinary boundaries. Perhaps what can be said about the variety one finds in reviewing this literature is that the role of the superhero in cultural texts is one which functions in a particularly multi-nodal fashion, illustrating conflicts within the social sphere while expressing at the same time eminently individual and unconscious desires and needs.

Areas of emphasis within the literature addressing superheroes in more psychological terms may be divided into four sub-categories. These areas can be termed as, first, the superhero as a place of wish fulfillment (the return to primary narcissism); second, the "mythic" function of the superhero, both in an American and supra-national context; third, what E. Ann Kaplan (1990) terms the "material pressures of social institutions" (3) or what we might more succinctly call "morality"; and, fourth, the ongoing discussion of the superhero's Oedipal function and, related to this, the role of the superhero in the field of feminist Lacanian psychoanalysis. The literature outlined thus concerns the superhero as presented in both the comic book and the film. Much of the richest scholarship on the topic has been conducted in studying the former,

Freud, Superheroes and Wish Fulfillment

Freud (1908) famously relates the activities of the poet — and, by extension, the literary practitioner in general — to the process of daydreaming. The writer, according to Freud, "does the same as the child at play; he [sic] creates a world of phantasy which he takes very seriously; that is, he invests it with a great deal of affect, while separating it sharply from reality" (45). He goes on to relate that play in childhood "is determined by (one's) wishes," and that "happy people," in adulthood, "never make phantasies, only unsatisfied ones. Unsatisfied wishes are the driving power behind phantasies" (47). Daydreaming, like the unconsciously created products of its nighttime counterpart, offers the opportunity for the adult, "ashamed of his phantasies as being childish" (ibid.), to explore his or her ideal world and place within it. These "phantasies," according to Freud, exist in the "three periods of our ideation" — the past experience, the current situation, and the future desire (49). "Nocturnal dreams," minus their inherent distortion, "are fulfillments of desires in exactly the same way as daydreams are" (50).

The poet, then, is seen by Freud to express desires and wishes in much the same way. His or her work is the reification of a daydream, the creation of a scenario in which a phantasy may derive from and take the form of past events, "current" narrative developments, and repressed wishes. One of the principle wishes Freud identifies in literature is the central presence of the hero. Although Freud wrote in a historical and cultural context in which the concept of the superhero as we understand it was unavailable, he nonetheless points out the characteristics of "invulnerability," "good," and attraction of the opposite sex as consistent themes within the hero character (51). These are not unfamiliar to us, and may be said to be the groundwork of the classical superhero model.

Behind the construction of the pervasive, central hero character is, for Freud, "His Majesty the Ego, the hero of all daydreams and novels" (ibid.). Our identification with the omnipotent hero, in all its manifestations (be it super- or anti-hero, or somewhere in between), rests in two places. First, there is the wish for characteristics of invulnerability in ourselves that we understood well as children. Freud reminds us that these wishes (such as, for example, the ability to fly or remain invisible) are not only endemic to childhood fantasy, but remain with us in our unconscious. Also embedded in the netherworld of our unconscious is our constant propensity to return to a state of primary narcissism. The hero, again, provides a link for readers of literature to attain, either through the sheer omnipotence or the extreme asceticism (often masochistic in nature) of the central character, this oneness with and in the world. This process is achieved primarily through poetic license since, as Freud points out, "only one person — once again the hero — is described from within; the author dwells in his soul and looks upon the other people from outside" (51). Thus, in identifying with a character of prodigious strength and moral rectitude, we play this role ourselves.

The satisfaction we find in possessing the persona of the superhero can be described in any number of forms. Our narcissism may be satisfied through feelings of power, independence, or physical beauty. In this final sense, the corporeal presence of the superhero becomes crucial. Scott Bukatman (2003) points out that

> superhero comics present body narratives, bodily fantasies, that incorporate (incarnate) aggrandizement and anxiety, mastery, and trauma. Comics narrate the body in stories and envision the body in drawings. The body is obsessively centered upon. It is contained and delineated; it

becomes irresistible force and immovable object.... The body takes on animal attributes, merges with plantlife, is melded with metal. The body is asexual and homosexual, heterosexual and hermaphroditic...the superhero body is everything — a corporeal, rather than a cognitive, mapping of the subject into the cultural system [49].

And while Bukatman is writing here about the print medium, the same is no less true for representation of cinematic superheroes. Director Kevin Smith recalls the importance of the male hero's costume, especially the codpiece, in establishing his masculinity: "they're all powerful, they can do no wrong and, apparently, they are hung like (late pornography star John) Holmes" (92). Lawrence and Jewett (1977) offer that

> Clint Eastwood, one of the superstars who enacts the role of the cool, violent redeemer, says, "...It's not the bloodletting or whatever that people come to see in the movies. It's vengeance. Getting even is very important with the public. They go to work every day for some guy who's rude and they ... have to take it. They go see me on the screen and I just kick the shit out of him." Assuming Eastwood is correct, his screen action amounts to a vicarious gratification for audience members who confront abuses of power in real life [211].

Thus the sexualization and omnipotence of the superhero, coupled with the reader/viewer's tendency to read the narrative from the point of view of him or her, marks a clear point of narcissistic pleasure for that reader/viewer.[1]

The Supermyth: Archetypal Understandings of Superheroes

Though generally connected with the work of Carl Jung[2], an archetypal approach to the analysis of myth is not unfamiliar to psychoanalysis. In his *Introductory Lectures*, Freud understands symbols, which often work in dreams to create distortion and interference for the dreamer, as "not something peculiar to dreamers or to the dream-work through which they come to expression." Rather, "this same symbolism is employed by myths and fairy tales, by the people in their sayings and songs, by colloquial linguistic usage and by the poetic imagination. The field of symbolism is immensely wide, and dream symbolism is only a small part of it" (165). This is not to suggest the superhero is solely a symbol (though, in most cases, we might conceive him or her to be at least that), but that, for Freud as well as for Jung, the hero or superhero has a history.

The most complete work on this subject is, of course, Joseph Campbell's *Hero with a Thousand Faces* (1949), but more recent studies have cast greater light on the modern and post-modern role such characters have come to play. Richard Reynolds (1994) offers a "first-stage working definition of the superhero genre" (16), which requires, for example, that the hero be portrayed as outside society, more concerned about innate justice that explicit laws, and extraordinary in comparison both with his surroundings and his alter ego (e.g. Clark Kent). The two former attributes, offers Christian Pyle (1994), are "accepted facets" of a particularly American brand of hero, "as true of Natty Bumppo and Huck Finn as they are of Superman and Batman" (2). Eco (1972) and Lawrence & Jewett (1977, 2002) suggest the nationalist tendencies of superhero mythology. Eco points out that Superman is obliged to perform acts of local and civil significance, since taking up the mantle of "justice" worldwide would mean questioning cornerstone American values such as capitalism. Superman is therefore "obliged to continue his activities in the sphere of small and infinitesimal modifications of the immediately visible ... each general modifications would draw the world, and Superman with it, toward final consumption" (124). Lawrence and Jewett, meanwhile, offer that the myth of the American superhero is one primarily of deliverance and redemption. Crucial to their analysis is the passive nature of the populace in such narratives, which they see as transferable to the reader/viewer. They contend in *The American Monomyth* (1977) that

> the American monomyth is an escapist fantasy. It encourages passivity on the part of the general public and unwise concentrations of power in ostensible redeemers. It betrays the ideals of democratic responsibility and denies the reliance on human intelligence that is basic to democratic hope [211].

And so we come back to fantasy. Revenge, redemption, and deliverance resurface in the mythological understandings of superhero character types; yet the undercurrent here is that the fantasy is more societal than individual, a collective fantasy of a super-advocate in an increasingly atomized and serialized society. This understanding of the superhero, then, is different in important ways from the fantasy that feeds individual narcissistic tendencies. It is a social fantasy.

"Spider-Man no more": Morality, Alter Egos and the Conscious/Unconscious Split

In *Spider-Man 2*, Parker makes the decision to cease his activity as a superhero due to its inconvenient schedule and the resultant chaos it causes in his "ordinary" life. Most directly, this decision concerns his feelings for the significant other, Watson, and his desire to be with her without secrecy and restraint, but he also sees himself increasingly reviled and feared by the people he has pledged to serve. This plot device is not uncommon in superhero literature and film history; it might, in fact, be termed essential in the sense that truly omnipotent characters have little to fear but their own inequity or selfishness.

Such confrontations with self are frequent in superhero texts also because of the bifurcated nature of their characters. They most often, as we have seen, live two separate and widely dissimilar lives, the unremarkable and usually socially inept alter ego balancing the prodigious capital of the "super" side. The initial enjoyment of super powers in a character like Spider-Man/Parker gives way to a kind of despondence born of isolation and misunderstanding. This ambivalence of mission is, historically, something that has evolved into the superhero ethos. Jeffrey Lang and Patrick Trimble (1988) point out that

> the superhero's awareness of his place (or lack of it) in society ... is one of the few things that has changed about superhero comics in the history of the genre. The new heroes feel ambivalence toward society and their place in it. Not coincidentally, these heroes began to emerge in the early 1960s, an era when many Americans began to entertain serious doubts about the viability of using old methods to solve new, more complex problems. It was an era that promoted self-doubt [167].

Implicit in this encroachment of doubts is a graying of the concept of morality. Bradford Wright (2001) offers that "it is difficult to overstate the impact of ... early Spider-Man comic books on the subsequent development of the industry" since the "young, flawed, and brooding antihero" became the new archetype, especially in the work produced by Marvel Comics. Jean-Paul Gabilliet's (1994) study of The Silver Surfer and Jesse Moore's (2003) work on the Green Lantern offer excellent historical studies of the shifting moral compass of the comic superheroes. Their cinematic counterparts, coming to screen largely after the cynical impression left by the 1960s, have either followed suit or skipped the moral high ground altogether.

Where this concerns psychoanalysis is in the very concept of morality itself, since the latter is merely one expression of an ego-driven set of constraints on the unconscious. In the halcyon days of Superman and moral rectitude, the villain in the story represented the unconscious. The hero was repression, "an operation whereby the subject attempts to repel, or to confine to the unconscious, representations (thoughts, images, memories) which are bound to an instinct" (Laplanche & Pontalis, 2003: 390). Such instincts might concern lust for power, greed, monomaniacal tendencies, and, of course, sexual gratification, either in the form of seduction or orgiastic violence. And yet, as reader/viewers, we still identify with the hero who has deprived us of these instinctual pleasures because, simply, he wins. The villain is destroyed (either actually or figuratively, as in Superman's tendency to expose Lex Luther for his pride, vanity, folly, etc.). The reader/viewer is left with little choice but to identify with the power of repression.

And yet this character must always remain alien lest we imagine ourselves to be omnipotent. Whether from outer space (Superman), a mishap of science (Spider-Man), or the ashes of childhood trauma and the inheritance of great wealth (Batman), superheroes share an originary exceptionalism that allows the spectator to see them as other. The fact that this is generally agreed to be less and less true over time is significant in psychoanalytic terms, since it presents us with a cultural closing of the gap between the conscious and the unconscious. If heroes as "heroic" in the classical sense are less and less believable, and villains are becoming, in their frailty and proneness to instinct, more so, where does the identification rest? Is it enough for the villain to lose, as he or she ultimately does, or has a shift occurred in our cultural relationship with the unconscious?

Oedipal Themes and the Place of the Woman in Superhero Texts

It is difficult to talk about the genre of superhero comics and films without sensing the presence of Oedipus. To name only a few, Superman, Spider-Man, and Batman share the following characteristics:

- They are all orphans. Superman is brought up by "adoptive" Earth parents after his departure from Krypton, where his own parents perished. Batman sees his own parents murdered and chooses his crime-fighting lifestyle in dialectical conversation with that moment. Spider-Man lives with an aunt and uncle, the latter of whom dies as a result of Spider-Man's (Peter's) refusal to apprehend a suspect at an earlier crime scene.
- All three pine, to varying degrees, for female companionship. Clark Kent and Peter Parker have feelings for women who are not superheroes, and, therefore, are off limits, while Bruce Wayne's many dalliances pale in comparison to Batman's sexual tension with Catwoman.[3]
- All three superheroes hold an influence over the emotions and passions of these female characters that their alter egos do not.

What is crucial in these admittedly reductive plot summaries is the triad that is set up between the superhero, the female, and the alter ego. It is a clear reflection of the parents/child trilogy that is at the heart of the Oedipal theory. The superhero almost always acts as an impediment to the alter ego's possession of the female; the superhero is the figure of power and authority, the female is the object of desire[4]. The tension which has crept into the superhero genre, which we have discussed above, concerning the moral ambivalence of the lead character, is often a direct result of the hero's wavering commitment to heroism in the face of loneliness or jealously. All three characters, at one or more times in their respective mythologies, let down their guard or unmask themselves to the female objects of desire. It is a metaphorical slaying of the father figure in the triad for the sake of possessing the mother; and yet, this is a perpetually temporary victory. The unconscious, in the form of the perceived moral responsibility of the hero to the society he has come to protect, represses the Oedipal desire and causes the resurfacing of the superhero identity. Spider-Man pulls his jumpsuit out of the trash and returns to fighting crime, subjecting himself to the asceticism that has come to define the modern superhero.

The female lead of the superhero genre, then, becomes the mother figure par excellence. But while they are often the focal point of desire, they often perform other dramatic roles. Susan Wood Glicksohn (1974) offers that

> women ... grow increasingly important to the life of the superhero. Usually, their influence is as destructive as the (Black) Widow's bite. They mess up the hero's emotions, thus distracting him when he should be fighting, or resting up between fights; they leave him in his hour of triumph, thus emphasizing his loneliness, the price of alienation he must pay for his powers; they hysterically reject his violent alter-ego, or demand attention for themselves, thus depriving him of the sympathy he needs after a hard day of saving the world; and worst of all, they expose him to danger on their fragile behalf, thus threatening him through their own vulnerability. Women are increasingly, negatively, important in the masculine comic world [3].

Laura Mulvey (1975) offers, from a Lacanian perspective on audience reception, the notion of the male gaze, whereby the female characters in film are viewed in a scopophilic manner by both the spectator qua spectator and by the spectator through the patriarchal point of view of lead male characters. Tania Modleski (1988) counters that the "male spectator is as much 'deconstructed' as constructed" in such ways, since this form of filmic technique reveals "a fascination with femininity that throws masculine identity into question and crisis" (87). Superhero films, I think, support both sides of this argument. There can be little question that the female form is idealized in such films, and that stories are told largely through the point of view of the superhero/alter ego. Yet the hamstrung nature in which these central characters pursue their mission or their mistress suggests as much uncertainty as it does mastery. Catwoman (both as a foil to Batman and as her own central character) plays a much different role than, say, Lois Lane, and may be seen as empowering. As Orr points out, Catwoman "'see(s)' phallocentrism and patriarchy, and is seen by it, more specifically than Batman" (179). While she may fulfill female redemptive wishes, however, she is also highly sexualized in her black leather catsuit and no doubt performs a different function for the male gaze. Wonder Woman, similarly, is an area of feminist and queer theory subversion clothed (barely) in the red, white, and blue terms of American patriarchy.[5]

Mary Jane Watson, then, deserves analysis as a contemporary representation of superhero femininity. As the girlfriend, to what degree does she represent Glicksohn's (now potentially outdated) solely problematic woman? As a character in her own right, where does her agency lie? Psychoanalysis, I think, can help readers/viewers to better understand the embedded discourse of MJ, especially as she relates to her male (super- and non-super-) counterparts.

Understanding the Spider-Man Films Psychoanalytically

Oedipal themes

In the first film, Parker is lectured by his uncle on the proper use of his power, couched in terms of adolescence rather than super-heroism. Parker, in true teenager mode, reacts negatively to the lecture. "I know I'm not your father...," Ben says, to which Parker replies thoughtlessly, "...then why are you trying to be?!" The comment clearly stings, and Parker leaves his uncle immediately aware of the gravity of his words. It is at this point that Parker eschews the library for the financial promise of the wrestling match, making these his final words to the man who was, for all intents and purposes, his father.

The following sequence, as is well known, involves the escape of the thief—an escape made possible by Parker's refusal to act—and the resultant murder of Uncle Ben. This crucial moment in the development of Spider-Man displays two moments of parricide, one metaphorical and one actual. Parker, in affirming Ben's role as only a surrogate father, semantically destroys the father/son bond. In pointing out, rather harshly, that Ben, as surrogate, has no grounds on which to lecture him, Parker reaffirms Ben's proper role and removes him from that of father. More obviously, a few moments later, Ben is actually killed through a series of events leading back to a key moment of decision on Parker's part. In this way it could easily be posited that Parker, like Oedipus, accidentally killed his father.

After this moment, Parker is the lone caretaker of his Aunt May. In Freudian terms, he has achieved the unconscious desire to remove the patriarchal figure and possess the mother. Indeed, for most of the duration of the two films, Aunt May is continually, though reluctantly, looking to either Parker or Spider-Man for assistance, a responsibility Parker takes with the utmost seriousness. It is the attack on Aunt May by the Green Goblin, in fact, that sets Parker's mind against a union with MJ, since it becomes clear to him that his identity had been learned and his loved ones put in danger as a result.

Another interesting Oedipal triangle is established in the first film by the relationship between Harry Osborn, his father Norman, and MJ. Harry's mother is never mentioned. One can only assume that Norman, immersed as he appears to be in his business affairs, alienated her in much the same way he has Harry. But the underachieving Harry remains fiercely loyal to his father, anxious to please him however he can, especially after Norman, a scientist as well, takes a liking to the intelligent Parker.

Shortly after Harry and MJ begin a romantic relationship, the group—Parker, MJ, Aunt May, Harry, and Norman—gather in Parker and Harry's midtown apartment for Thanksgiving. Parker and Norman, fresh off a battle between their alter egos, both arrive late, and Parker unknowingly reveals himself to Norman by displaying a laceration that Norman recognizes as having been sustained during the recent scuffle. Norman—shocked by the discovery and pained by the loss of his preferred "son"—leaves abruptly, but not before telling Harry to separate himself from MJ. He bitterly describes her as, essentially, a gold-digger (a view, one is led to believe, he had toward Harry's mother), well within earshot of the group. MJ protests Harry's unwillingness to defend her and Harry, confused, takes the side of his father.

The preceding sequence illustrates the problem as it is presented to Harry. He is horribly inept as a male partner, offering nothing to MJ but his money. His conflicted feelings toward his father—a true love/hate relationship—leave him unable to deal with women. It will be necessary for him to remove his father in order to achieve the personal happiness he desires, and one gets the impression that at least part of the anger Harry feels toward Spider-Man for his father's murder is that of having the opportunity taken from him to do it himself. Now, without a father to slay, Harry is trapped in the shadow of the omnipotent patriarch, a position illustrated in the later in the film as Harry is visited by the spectre of his dead father. Here, as we have seen, Harry again tries to slay the father by throwing a dagger through his image in the mirror, only to reveal the trove of his father's alter ego. In his inability to kill his father, we are led to believe, Harry is destined to become him.

The Harry-Norman relationship, however, is problematic in Oedipal terms for its lack of a mother. We could, as we have seen, substitute MJ here, but her presence between them is more catalytic than as an object of desire. An interesting position one might take here is to posit a homoerotic competition between Harry and Norman to possess Parker. Both have strong feelings of affection toward Parker, and Harry's rage at Parker's choice to protect Spider-Man rather than reveal his identity has all the drama of a jilted lover's despondency. Thus his abject horror at finding that Parker and Spider-Man are one. This triangle is further complicated by Norman's appeal to Parker in the scene of his death. "I've been like a father to you," Norman pleads, "be a son to me now." Parker replies by reaffirming Uncle Ben's status as his true father, thereby slaying another patriarchal pretender. Norman's final words, "Don't tell Harry," serve then as much to keep his illicit love for Parker a secret as they do to keep quiet his identity as the Green Goblin.

The most elegant and fruitful triangle to explore in Oedipal terms is, however, that between Parker, MJ, and Spider-Man himself. In the first film, as we have seen, Parker submits to the will of Spider-Man in the sense that he rejects the advances of MJ and commits himself to a life of superheroic service. Clearly, the admonishment against selfish sexual satisfaction and the adulation of repression act here to reify the conscious dictum against parricide and incest, for there can be little doubt that MJ, whose first name after all *is* Mary, acts as a mother figure in this triad. She is enthralled with Spider-Man, who saves her life on two occasions. The hero is in full libidinal possession of her, as a highly erotic kissing scene — whereby Spider-Man hangs upside down, half-unmasked in the pouring rain — reveals. And yet her feelings for Parker, more tender than erotic in nature, also intensify. At the conclusion of the first film, Parker has withstood the passionate desire for the mother and submitted to the will of the repressive patriarch, Spider-Man.

In the second film, however, Parker's situation becomes increasingly untenable. He comes to resent his omnipotent alter ego for its imposition on the consummation of his feelings for MJ. As MJ drifts away from him, Parker sees a doctor in hopes of explaining a mystifying inability spin webs (more on this later). The doctor tells him that his problem, pointing to his head, is "all up here," and reminds him that he has a choice. The doctor, of course, has no idea of Parker's alter ego, but nonetheless his advice makes Parker's path clear to him. He must reject, abandon — in effect, kill — Spider-Man in order to possess MJ and be finally happy. This he does, rejecting the dream-sequence pep-talk of his deceased uncle, and pledging to be "Spider-Man no more."

Parker then sets about making things right with MJ, who by this time, as we have seen, has agreed to marry another man. Despite a considerable decrease in his powers (eyesight, strength, etc.), he is visibly unburdened by this decision. He is ultimately successful in his pursuit of MJ, but, interestingly, a talk with his primary mother figure, Aunt May, reestablishes the primacy of the authoritarian, patriarchal Spider-Man as necessary to society. In Freudian terms, we can also posit the sudden realization of the proximity of sex with the mother, the immediacy of the possibility of the act itself, as a catalyst for the return to repression. Peter in any case rethinks his position, rejects once again the utterly confused MJ, and returns to crime-fighting with renewed vigor once MJ is taken hostage by Doc Ock. In the end, the mother figure, MJ, consents to a *ménage-à-trois* of sorts, accepting both Spider-Man and Parker — both father and son — as her lovers, a decision the wisdom of which remains clearly in doubt.

Degradation and Impotence

Another interesting Freudian angle to take in consideration of these films is in the continually evolving nature of Parker's feelings for MJ and, in turn, MJ's evolving role in the construction of those feelings. The central metaphor in such a discussion is Spider-Man's web-spinning ability, the raw material for which (the webs themselves) serve as a clear metaphor for semen throughout the two films. Parker's initial discovery of the substance in the school cafeteria, where his inadvertent adhesion to various objects gets him into conflict with Flash, illustrates the embarrassing first discovery on the part of the human male of his ability to ejaculate. The silky, white, sticky nature of the substance is a clear corollary to its reproductive counterpart, a comparison which makes Spider-Man's later inability to spin webs an equally clear representation of psychical impotence.

Freud asserts that such impotence stems from the incestuous desire of the male to have sex with the mother, a condition that leads to a bifurcation of filial and sensual love. The former is reserved for the mother or sister, the latter for presumably unattached females encountered during and after puberty. "The sensual feeling that has remained active," Freud relates,

> seeks only objects evoking no reminder of the incestuous persons forbidden to it; the impression made by someone who seems deserving of high estimation leads, not to a sensual excitation, but to feelings of tenderness which remain erotically ineffectual. The erotic life of such people remains dissociated, divided between two channels.... Where such men love they have no desire and where they desire they cannot love [1912: 177].

Freud goes on to posit that, in those individuals for whom this bifurcation remains — must remain — solid, the need surfaces to view those with whom successful sexual relations might be had as somehow "lower" or "inferior." One manifestation of this lowering is to see the woman as attached in some way, thereby generating an "injured third party." In this way, the male, according to Freud, is able to see himself as erotically involved with a lower woman, involved as she is in the cuckolding of another male. Moreover, the male in this subversive position often sees himself in the role of a perpetual savior, constantly shepherding the lower women from danger. It is in the context of the latter two points that I would like to consider the impotence of Spider-Man and its relationship to the Parker/MJ dynamic.

Spider-Man experiences no problems with vitality in the first film. In the initial episode, he rescues MJ from mortal danger on two occasions, and partakes in the aforementioned rain-soaked kiss despite her ongoing relationship with Harry. Parker, for his part, attracts the love of MJ, but is forced to renounce that love for the sake of his alter-ego. Spider-Man has thus, essentially, cuckolded not one but two competitors for MJ's attention.

In the second film, however, the combination of Parker's resolute refusal to consummate any erotic feelings he might have for MJ, along with the eventual disappearance of Spider-Man, moves MJ into the arms of Jameson. It is at this moment, immediately after it becomes clear to Parker that MJ has accepted a proposal from this new man in her life, that he first falls as a consequence of his inability to spin webs. This inability continues sporadically throughout the film until the very moment when, first, Peter is about to kiss the betrothed MJ and, second, she is abducted by Doc Ock (thus putting her once again in mortal danger). At this crucial time, Spider-Man regains his focus and is once again at full strength.

This short timeline serves, I think, to illustrate a clear need on the part of Spider-Man/Parker to hold MJ in a very particular position. Parker's tender feelings, running back many years into pre-pubescent childhood, no doubt necessitate the kind of lowering Freud posits. The "injured third party," whether in the role of Harry or Parker himself, serves this purpose for Spider-Man. Once he himself becomes the injured third party, however (at the moment of MJ's engagement), his impotence sets in. Later, when he is able to see himself once again as both subversive lover and as savior, his vitality returns.

The savior motif, however, is somewhat complicated for Spider-Man/Parker. Spider-Man, as we have seen, is able to restore his prowess largely through the physical act of salvation—doing battle with Doc Ock, performing acts of great strength and skill, and lifting the heroine to safety. On the other hand, Parker sees himself as saving MJ through his denial of their romantic relationship, since in his view such a relationship would bring her into the cognizance of his enemies. Perhaps it could be said that the eventual reunion of Spider-Man and Parker into one person, effected through MJ's realization of their/his true identities, achieves the kind of fusion of "tenderness and sensuality" Freud finds so uncommon in human love relations (180).

Finally, it should be pointed out that MJ's role as the madonna/whore in Spider-Man/Parker's sexual life is supplemented by her action as an Oedipal agent in her own right. As the daughter of an abusive patriarch, MJ sees in Spider-Man an apt representation of her father. Though he acts in diametrically opposite ways toward her (saving her rather than condemning her), she is nonetheless attracted to the vitality of Spider-Man as a symptom of her larger desire to possess the powerful patriarch. Since there is no mother in the way, MJ moves her way past a number of lesser male suitors (Harry, Parker, and Jameson) in her quest to conquer the hero. That she succeeds in doing so is met, as her ambivalent gaze out the window to close the second film illustrates, with some level of apprehension and disappointment.

The Conscious/Unconscious Split

Norman Osborn, though distracted, ambitious, and largely absent as a parent, nonetheless reifies traditional Protestant values such as a rigid work ethic, advancement and accumulation through wisdom and frugality, and responsibility. His alter ego, the Green Goblin, is by contrast without restraint and appeals to Osborn's sense of pride, entitlement, and revenge. The Goblin, created as he was with faulty, aggression-heightening performance-enhancement drugs, is a powerful, vicious, remorseless creature, an uber-mensch with the power to destroy those who would stand in his way. He is a clear representation of the unbridled ego, cackling at one point that "no one says no to me!" Were it not for the presence of Spider-Man, New York, at least, would be lost.

Similarly, Otto Octavius, though brilliant and equally ambitious, is at pains to lecture Parker, who has been missing class, about the responsibilities associated with the "gift" of intelligence. Again, he preaches hard work and obligation. When Octavius' experiment goes awry, and he becomes Doc Ock, he loses any kind of restraint in the pursuit of his goal. Needing money to buy equipment for a new fusion device, he resorts to robbing banks. Needing tridium (the magic ingredient in the reaction), he figures simply to take it from Harry. When Harry posits the deal whereby Ock brings Spider-Man to him, Ock is merciless in his pursuit of the hero. Only by Parker's coaxing out of Octavius' conscious self, removing him from the influence of his cybernetic arms, is disaster averted.

In both cases, we can clearly see the repressive role of the conscious self at play, especially in contrast to the explosive, narcissistic ego that emerges through scientific mishap. Osborn and Octavius are clearly framed as the wiser, more sustainable alternatives to their alter egos. The Goblin and Doc Ock are passion, ambition, hate, and pride unburdened by the restrictions of the conscious, social self. They are thus cataclysmically dangerous to humankind, the very embodiment of social impropriety and the rejection of human community. It is immediately understandable, then, that these characters are villains, villains whose exploits must be thwarted.

Harry Osborn, similarly, vacillates between two poles. As the best friend of Peter Parker, he often works on his behalf, giving him advice about his relationship with MJ, arranging a meeting with Octavius (on whom Parker is writing a paper), and even, in the end, when he has already named Parker to Doc Ock as the conduit through which to find Spider-Man, advocating to Ock's unhearing ears that he not "hurt Peter." As the arch-enemy of Spider-Man, however, he rejects all feelings of fraternity with Parker and sees him only as an impediment to the fulfillment of his desire for revenge. He drinks constantly, obsessing over the location of his father's "murderer," until finally relinquishing any concern for human society by knowingly giving the tridium — which he has every reason to believe will produce catastrophic results — in exchange for his moment of narcissistic redemption.

But Spider-Man/Parker himself (themselves?) complicates this clean split between the morally upright, restrained symbol of consciousness and repression on the one hand, and the omnipotent, childlike superhuman ego on the other. In the aforementioned characters, the ego represents the omnipotent ability, potential or realized, to do what one wants. By contrast, omnipotence for the *hero*, since it is ostensibly used for "good," represents *repression*. Being Spider-Man, rather than rejecting him for a normal life with MJ, is presented to Parker as being the "steady" alternative; the rejection of personal desires, one's "dreams," is posed as the ideal. In this case, then, omnipotence is to be embraced rather than feared, and what is to be rejected is the selfish desire to ignore such powers and be what can only be described as "normal." Might it be posited, then, that the ego is represented in these films not by sheer omnipotence, but by the somewhat simpler construct of selfishness? Even if this is the case, defining what is selfish for Spider-Man/Parker is difficult. In his desire to keep MJ safe from harm, and thus maintaining a position of savior, it might be said that Parker is catering to narcissistic tendencies. Conversely, his abandonment of his super powers in hopes of possessing MJ is clearly a symptom of narcissistic object-love. Finally, the resolution that both sides, in fact, of the Spider-Man/Parker dichotomy get the girl and continue to fight crime leaves us wondering just how we should feel about this character. To whom is his allegiance most securely attached? Us or her?

Conclusion

In *Spider-Man 2*, Aunt May tells Parker that society needs someone who is "courageous, self-sacrificing" to teach them "how to hold on a second longer." She believes, in one of the tag lines of the film, that "there is a hero in all of us." What might also be intimated here is that there is also a villain in all of us, a conclusion easily drawn not only from these films, but from the genre in general. How this apparently ubiquitous hero/villain dichotomy plays out in extraordinary individuals is, I think, meant as a blueprint for how it might or might not play out in each of us. In Freudian terms, then, Spider-Man allows us to see the potential inherent in unconscious desires, and the emancipation that can come from knowing them.

The bitter irony presented to Parker in this story is that he is able to achieve his desires (the attainment of MJ) only through the confidence he attains from his newfound power. In the end, however, it is this very power that necessitates his refusal, through much of the two films, to consummate the relationship for which he has pined for so long. Staring out a window as he ponders his decision to return to crime-fighting, Parker asks himself, "am I not supposed to have what I want?" If we view the relationship between Parker and MJ in Freudian terms, the clear answer is, of course, no. None of us are, since what we really want is the return to primary narcissism, the disposal of the father, and the possession of the mother for all time. That Parker achieves a middle way in this narrative is thus enormously interesting, both terms of psychoanalytic theory and in terms of the genre.[6]

Notes

1. In addition to fulfilling the wishes of the reader/viewer, superheroic characters may also be psychoanalyzed in their own right. Michael Brody (1995), for example, points out that "Bruce Wayne's vow to fight crime is a compensatory wish" made in response to the loss of his parents to a homicidal mugger (174).
2. See, for example, Jung (1990), Hopcke (1992), and Iacchino (1997).
3. See Orr (1994).
4. I will describe below in greater detail the ways in which this structure is facilitated in the Spider-Man films.
5. See Peters, 2003.
6. This article is reprinted from its original publication in 2005 with only minimal edits. I have not chosen at this time to modify the text with an additional analysis of *Spider-Man 3*, released after this piece's initial publication. Peaslee, Robert Moses. "With great power comes great responsibility: Central Psychoanalytic Motifs in *Spider-Man* and *Spider-Man 2*" *PSYART: A Hyperlink Journal for the Psychological Study of the Arts.* (July 2005) Accessed 6/10/2011. http://www.psyartjournal.com/article/show/m_peaslee-with_great_power_comes_great_responsibil.

Works Cited

Brody, Michael. "Batman: Psychic Trauma and Its Solution." *Journal of Popular Culture* 28:4 (Spring 1995): 171–8.
Bukatman, Scott. *Matters of Gravity.* Durham: Duke University Press, 2003.
Campbell, Joseph. *Hero with a Thousand Faces.* New York: Pantheon, 1949.
Eco, Umberto. "The Myth of Superman." Rpt. in Robert Con Davis, ed. *Contemporary Literary Criticism: Modernism Through Poststructuralism.* New York: Longman, 1986: 330–344. (Originally published in 1972).
Freud, Sigmund. *Introductory Lectures on Psychoanalysis.* New York: Norton, 1965.
_____. "The Most Prevalent Form of Degradation in Everyday Life." *Four Collected Papers.* Joan Riviere, trans. New York: Basic Books, 1959. (Originally published in 1912).
_____. "The Relation of the Poet to Daydreaming" in *On Creativity And The Unconscious.* New York: Harper, 1958: 44–54.
Gabilliet, Jean-Paul. "Cultural and Mythical Aspects of a Superhero: The Silver Surfer, 1968–1970." *Journal of Popular Culture* 28:2 (Fall 1994), 203–13.
Glicksohn, Susan. *The Poison Maiden and the Great Bitch: Female Stereotypes in Marvel Superhero Comics.* T-K Graphics, 1974.
Hopcke, Robert. *A Guided Tour of the Collected Works of C.G. Jung.* Boston: Shambhala, 1992.
Iacchino, James F. "Jungian Archetypes in American Superhero Comic Strips: the Hero's Shadow Side" in Ken Nordin and Gail Pieper, eds. *Understanding the Funnies: Critical Interpretations of Comic Strips.* Lisle, IL: Procopian Press, 1997.
Jewett, Robert, and John Shelton Lawrence. *The American Monomyth.* Garden City, NY: Anchor, 1977.
_____, and John Shelton Lawrence. *The Myth of the American Superhero.* Grand Rapids, MI: W.B. Eerdman, 2002.
Jung, Carl. *The Archetypes of the Collective Unconscious: The Collected Works.* R.F.C. Hull, trans. Princeton, NJ: Princeton University Press, 1990.
Kaplan, E. Ann, ed. *Psychoanalysis & Cinema.* New York: Routledge, 1990.
Lang, Jeffery. S. and Patrick Trimble. "Whatever Happened to the Man of Tomorrow? Examination of the American Monomyth and the Comic Book Superhero." *Journal of Popular Culture* 22:3 (Winter 1988): 157–173.
Laplanche, Jean. and J.B. Pontalis. *The Language of Psycho-analysis.* London: Hogarth, 1973.
Modleski, Tania. *The Women Who Knew Too Much: Hitchcock and Feminist Theory.* New York: Methuen, 1988.

Moore, Jesse. "The Education of Green Lantern." *Journal of Popular Culture* 26:2 (2003): 263–72.
Moran, Patrick. "The Retired Superhero." *Southern Review* 38:3 (Summer 2002): 506–7.
Mulvey, Laura. "Visual Pleasure and Narrative Cinema" in *Visual and Other Pleasures*. Bloomington: Indiana UP, 1989: 14–26. (Originally published in *Screen*, 1975.)
Orr, Philip. "The Anoedipal Mythos of Batman and Catwoman." *Journal of Popular Culture* 27:4 (Spring 1994): 169–82.
Peters, Brian Mitchell. (2003). "Qu(e)erying Comic Book Culture and Representations of Sexuality in Wonder Woman." *CLCWeb: Comparative Literature and Culture: A WWWeb Journal* 5:3 2003. Accessed 11/3/2011. http://docs.lib.purdue.edu/cgi/viewcontent.cgi?article=1195&context=clcweb
Pyle, Christian. "The Superhero Meets the Culture Critic." *Postmodern Culture* 5:1 (September 1994). Accessed 11/18/2004. http://infomotions.com/serials/pmc/pmc-v5n1-pyle-superhero.txt.
Reynolds, Richard. *Superheroes: A Modern Mythology*. Jackson, MI: University of Mississippi Press 1994.
Smith, Kevin. "The Superhero." *Rolling Stone* (May 15), 2003: 92.
Wright, Branford. *Comic Book Nation*. Baltimore: Johns Hopkins University Press, 2001.

VII. Under-Examined Spider-Texts

Reinterpreting Myths in *Spider-Man: The Animated Series*

David Ray Carter

Lewis Spence makes an audacious statement in the opening section of *An Introduction to Mythology*. "Once the terms of a story become fixed," he writes, "he will be bold who will attempt to alter them when recounting them to children or savages" (2005: 38). Spence bases his observation not on historical or scientific but personal and anecdotal evidence, and one wonders if the author is being overzealous in his warning against revising or recontextualizing myths. In addition to being ironically placed in the preface of a work that does both of those things, Spence's statement seems to ascribe to mythology a type of narrative death; a chiseling into stone or placement on the apocryphal "permanent record."

The ancients certainly did not believe as Spence did; revisions of myths and legends are both innumerable and easily found through a cursory review of important works. His warning also went unheeded by twentieth century storytellers in their efforts to create the modern mythology of the superhero. The connection between comic book superheroes and classical mythology has been exhaustively examined in several works, and any attempt to repurpose those ideas here would do disservice to their complexity. In the interest of brevity, let us simply point out that both comic books and mythology rely heavily — but not exclusively — on recounting the lives and adventures of beings with abilities beyond the scope of normal humans, be they aliens, exceptional mortals, or gods themselves.

It is within this similarity between superheroes and myths that Spence's statement, though still perhaps too far-reaching, has some merit. Retroactive continuity, or *retcon*, is a popular and frequently used device in comic books. There are, however, certain aspects of the narrative which must remain "fixed," to borrow Spence's phrasing, otherwise readers would no longer be able to relate to a character in the same manner. The details of how millionaire Bruce Wayne received the training to become Batman can and have changed over the years, but the fact that he was orphaned by violent crime at a young age has not. Superman's powers may wax and wane depending on the authorship of a particular story but his infant journey from the dying planet of Krypton is an immutable part of the character. Iron Man's origin can be updated as necessary to any recent war or international conflict, but Captain America is inexorably tied to World War II, regardless of when his story is retold. To amend Spence's statement, a myth, be it a classic or modern one in the form of a superhero tale, can be revised as long as certain key identifying facets remain.

So superheroes can change. Powers can come and go, ages can be modified, and pieces of their history can disappear without explanation. Wont as comics are to do this, stories are most often altered when they are transferred into a different medium. Rare is it that a superhero makes the transition from the pages of a comic book to the movie or television screen without some occasionally significant changes occurring. Various media have different strengths and weaknesses, and stories and characters are modified to take advantage of these. The adaptations from one medium to another are never without controversy, and many works are judged solely on how authentically they conform to the originals.

There are some works that transcend the quibbles about exact duplication because they are faithful to the key facets of a work to such a degree that minor changes become irrelevant. One such work that goes beyond the realm of merely being an adaptation is *Spider-Man: the Animated Series* (*SMAS*). The show was one of the longest running Marvel Comics adaptations and the most successful of their single character cartoon efforts, but had significant differences from the Spider-Man of the comics. Despite these differences, the version of the character in *SMAS* was certainly recognizable to fans as it synthesized thirty years of the character's history into a new, more cohesive storyline. By recontextualizing the character as a cartoon, the writers were given a chance to weave a more perfect web; to take the best parts of hundreds of Spider-Man comics and rewrite the history of one of the twentieth century's most beloved myths.

SMAS was not the first attempt to bring Marvel's flagship character into a new medium. His first appearance outside the comic panel was in the ABC animated series *Spider-Man*, which ran from 1967 to 1970. The series utilized many of the scenarios from the five years of Spider-Man comics produced at the time, but also contained episodes featuring newly created characters such as Parafino and Dr. Vespian. While it remained true to the origins of the character, *Spider-Man* ultimately did not distinguish itself from action-oriented cartoons of the period. It lacked the qualities that make Spider-Man unique among his peers in the superhero world — his vulnerability, his self-doubt, and his willingness to sacrifice himself for the greater good.

Spider-Man's further adventures on the small screen would be hampered by similar problems. The live-action *The Amazing Spider-Man* developed the Peter Parker aspects of the character well, but completely eliminated the colorful villains synonymous with Spider-Man. A highly entertaining version for Japanese television dispensed with every aspect of the Spider-Man character, save the costume. Two more animated versions were created in 1981, the syndicated *Spider-Man* and the more popular NBC property, *Spider-Man and His Amazing Friends* (*SMHAF*). The latter is perhaps the most fondly remembered of the Spider-Man adaptations made up to that time, as it featured a wise-cracking Spider-Man familiar to fans of the comic and frequent guest appearances from other Marvel characters such as the X-Men and Captain America.

SMHAF, though well made and largely true to the character, was still a flawed adaptation in many regards. It rewrote Spider-Man's adventures to include the mutants Iceman and Firestar, eliminating the loneliness and solitude that are large parts of the Spider-Man mythos. Part of Spider-Man's appeal has been based in the fact that — for most of his career — he has had no one to turn to, no one to rescue him from danger, no teammates waiting in the wings should things prove to be too difficult. Spider-Man is not a loner but he is alone, and his greatest stories frequently involve celebrating this self-reliance. Teaming him with two partners, especially two with greater offensive superpowers, fundamentally undercuts this aspect of the character.

Furthermore, like the previous animated versions of Spider-Man, *SMHAF* was aimed at a young audience. Programmed on Saturday mornings among other, more obvious children's fare, it was clear that *SMHAF*'s intended audience was pre-teen or younger. At this point in his history, Spider-Man had been around for almost twenty years. Someone who began reading the comics as a pre-teen would have been approaching thirty years of age, meaning that the show, by design, excluded these long-term fans. The comics adjusted over the years to be inclusive of a wide range of demographics and for an animated adaptation to be successful, it would need to do the same. That adaptation would be *SMAS*.

One only need look to the series' first episode, "Night of the Lizard," to understand how greatly *SMAS* deviated from the adaptations that preceded it. The classic villain the Lizard is not introduced as a swamp-dwelling would-be conqueror (as he had been in the 1967 series) or as reptilian Pied Piper (as in the 1981 solo series) but as a monster — a snarling, red-eyed creature more animal than man. The piercing red eyes of the Lizard terrify two sewer workers, hypnotizing one with fear to the point that he recklessly careens through downtown New York with Spider-Man in tow; a scene that displays the series' dedication to exciting plots and showcases the vast improvements in animation technology since Spider-Man's last appearance on the small screen.

More to the point, this version of the Lizard is informed by all of the previous incarnations of the character that appeared in the comics, as every aspect of *SMAS* would be. Facets of the character are derived from his initial appearance in 1963's *The Amazing Spider-Man* #6 as well as from the more recent incarnation in 1990's *Spider-Man* #1. The plot of the episode is an amalgamation of old and new; classic and contemporary. *SMAS*'s strength is in its ability to take the best parts of the Spider-Man mythos and present them in a manner that still feels original. Here in the first episode, we have a Spider-Man that is informed by thirty years of history squaring off against a Lizard that is a mixture of Lee and Ditko's tragic victim of science and Todd McFarlane's feral monster. *SMAS* privileged neither version over the other and operated with the realization that die-hard fans of Spider-Man would be familiar with both. Rather than a compromise or a revision, this plot — and those that would follow — is a synthesis of Spider-Man's thirty year history, condensed, but elegantly retold.

Modernized versions of Spider-Man's classic tales would be the series' most defining characteristic, with many of the first season's plots taken directly from the first fifty issues of *The Amazing Spider-Man*. Episode 2, "The Sting of the Scorpion," is a near-verbatim retelling of *The Amazing Spider-Man* #20, complete with a rooftop showdown and an uneasy alliance between Spidey and J Jonah Jameson. The episode's story was classic, but the Scorpion's abilities and appearance were based on the then-modern incarnation of the character. Other episodes in the first season would feature classic/modern amalgamations of Doctor Octopus, Mysterio, the Chameleon, and Dr. Smythe and his robotic Spider-Slayers.

These early episodes would see a handful of characters undergo drastic changes. However, these changes would be done logically and with the narratives from the comic series taken into consideration. Kraven the Hunter is transformed into a far more sympathetic character than in his 1964 debut, depicted as a victim of science gone wrong much like Spider-Man himself. The saga of the alien symbiote costume and Eddie Brock's transformation into Venom is shortened primarily for narrative length reasons, although this Venom is depicted as villainous in keeping with his original appearances, rather than as the anti-hero into which he evolved. The Hobgoblin is the only other modern villain to make an appearance during the first season and, like Venom, his origin is shortened considerably, eliminating his associate the Rose but retaining the mystery around his true identity.

The first few episodes of *SMAS* showcased two other traits that were integral to the comics but had yet to be seen in previous animated version. Spider-Man had frequently been depicted as having an acerbic wit in other cartoons, but this incarnation of Spider-Man brought humor to the forefront. Even joking when under attack, this self-deprecating, sarcastic Spider-Man was more in line with his comic incarnations than his bad-pun spewing television predecessors. Several early episodes featured meta-humor, such as references to the non–Marvel cartoon series *The Tick* and an in-joke for comic fans in the form of Spider-Man's gargoyle of choice being named Bruce after Batman's alter ego.

The other trait of the series introduced in these initial episodes was foreshadowing. One truly gets the impression that the scriptwriters were conscious of future plot developments and wrote scripts with their implications in mind. Long-term storytelling was a rarity in American animation and even less common in children's programming of any type. Characters beyond Spider-Man himself are given a character arc in Season One, with Eddie Brock being introduced seven episodes prior to his Venom transformation and Norman Osborn featured heavily as well. Those viewers familiar with the comic would be aware of how their stories would conclude, but the gradual introduction of them into the Spider-Man universe was a departure from previous versions. It favored plot development over the typical format of superhero cartoons, where villains are introduced and summarily defeated over the course of a single episode.

SMAS was written with long-term narrative goals in mind. Filler episodes or short-term payoffs are rare in the series and anything that feels superfluous in seasons one and two took on a greater meaning as the series progressed. This "slow-burn" approach is one that is unique among comic book adaptations into other media, which typically rush their heroes into battle with their arch-nemesis at the first opportunity. Here, we see patience. To immediately have Spider-Man face off against the Green Goblin—as has been done in not only previous animated series, but the filmic *Spider-Man* as well—lessens the emotional impact of their confrontation. To accomplish its long-term narrative goals, *SMAS* began employing multi-episode story-arcs during the Venom and Hobgoblin portions of its first season. The second season saw the multi-episode story arc expanded to encompass the entire season, the format in which the show would remain for the rest of its run.

"Neogenic Nightmare" is the subtitle of *SMAS*'s second season, one that introduces a larger number of characters into the Spider-Man universe and takes the show into more uncharted territory for an animated series. Episode one ("Chapter One," to use the series' nomenclature) is not only typical of the season, but of the entire series as a whole. We begin with another first for superhero animation: our hero in a state of emotional doubt and in danger of losing his powers. *SMAS* visits this and similar concepts frequently, examining the notion of what being a "superhero" means. Our Peter Parker spends as much time worrying about paying bills and his relationship troubles as he does locked in battle with fantastic villains—a defining characteristic of the Spider-Man character. The appeal of Spider-Man is that he is both a regular person and a superhero, and it is in this second season that this becomes explicit within the confines of an animated series for the first time.

Chapter One is also an excellent example of *SMAS*'s attention to detail. Early in this episode, we see the Kingpin addressing the assembled leaders of various crime organizations. Present are not only the Spider-Man villains Silvermane and Hammerhead, but also minor crime figures from other comic series, like the Daredevil villain the Owl. The Owl doesn't factor much into the plot of the episode, or of any subsequent episodes; his presence is there simply to subtly remind the viewer that the events are taking place in the larger Marvel universe. Rather than introducing a new character or having an anonymous placeholder, the show included a character that might not have been recognizable to casual fans but would have excited long-term comic readers.

The main plot of the episode involves the assembled New York crime bosses putting pressure on the Kingpin to rid them of the problem of Spider-Man. To this end, he assembles the "Insidious Six," the animated version of the comic's Sinister Six, consisting of the first season villains Doctor Octopus, the Chameleon, the Rhino, Mysterio, and the Scorpion. The group's makeup differed considerably from the comic incarnations, but again the decision to change the line-up was logically made rather than change for change's sake. A new name and new members does not stop the six villains from having a clash of egos, their typical downfall in their comic appearances.

The Insidious Six are merely a diversion from a subplot that would become the overall theme of the season, Neogenic recombination and its effects on Spider-Man and those around him. Neogenics is the catch-all, faux-science term used by the series to explain the various superpowers of Spider-Man, the Scorpion, and others. It is also in this subplot that we are first introduced to Michael Morbius, who appears as a rival to Peter Parker both for his place in the university's science department and for Felicia Hardy's love. Morbius figures heavily into the events of "Neogenic Nightmare" but, more importantly, represents the first wholesale revision of a character in *SMAS*.

The revisions to the Morbius character occur for two primary reasons. The first is essentially practical: the concept of an unsympathetic vampire draining blood out of his victims was a bit too mature a topic for a Saturday morning cartoon. To work around this, Morbius is introduced as a human first and his non-lethal "feedings" are for plasma, rather than blood. The second reason the Morbius character was changed was to better serve as a foil for Spider-Man. Much of the "Neogenic Nightmare" storyline involves showing Spider-Man the necessity of turning to his friends in his times of need and to open himself up emotionally to those around him. His declining powers have him seek out the help of Kraven's wife, Dr. Moira Crawford, and after losing Felicia Hardy to Morbius, he becomes closer to Mary Jane Watson. This is juxtaposed against Morbius' predicament in order to demonstrate the two potential methods one can take when faced with difficulties. Morbius withdraws from his colleagues and from Felicia, essentially worsening his problem because of his refusal to accept help. Though he and Spider-Man are essentially suffering from the same Neogenic-caused affliction, Morbius dooms himself by choosing the solitary path.

The second season, like the first, takes the basis of its stories from the comics, although it jumps ahead several years. While most of the plots from the first season are from Spider-Man's earliest adventures, season two begins in the early 1970s, specifically with *The Amazing Spider-Man* #100's story "The Spider or the Man?" The plot of "The Spider or the Man?" is one that echoes throughout *SMAS* as it relates to Spider-Man having to choose between being a hero or a normal person. Spider-Man chooses the heroic path, but the consequence of his moment of doubt was the growth of four additional arms. *SMAS* also features this strange mutation, but makes it something beyond Spider-Man's control rather than a consequence of his poor judgment. Furthermore, instead of the quick solution to his problems he found in the comics, *SMAS* would turn his extra limbs into an ongoing ordeal, from which he would emerge a greater hero than ever before.

The climax of the two-episode Insidious Six saga was followed up by an anomaly for the series, a self-contained episode that, on the surface, had little relevance to the "Neogenic Nightmare" storyline. The episode "Hydro-Man" features the titular villain as Mary Jane Watson's obsessive ex-boyfriend turned small-time crook. The inclusion of such a minor character in the Spider-Man universe is a bit odd, and the show's creators have gone on record as saying that Hydro-Man was simply a stand-in for the more famous Sandman, who the show was unable to use due to his appearance in a potential James Cameron film adaptation. The same reason would prevent the show from using Electro, but Hydro-Man's episode is strange for reasons greater than simply its choice of villain. The episode's plot deals more with Peter Parker than Spider-Man and focuses a great deal on his relationship with Mary Jane. The inclusion of an episode dedicated to character rather than plot development is further proof of the creators' commitment to delivering a more robust depiction of Spider-Man than had previously been seen. Though it is easy to dismiss the Hydro-Man episode as "filler," it is ultimately one of the more important episodes in the series because it reiterates the fact that Spider-Man is still human, despite the dramatic changes he would undergo in the following episodes.

After a two-part crossover with *X-Men: The Animated Series*, Spider-Man squares off against Morbius in a five episode arc that is among the best in the series. Here, the creators' ability to take existing storylines from the comic and modernize and incorporate them into the show is at its creative peak, using the arc to introduce the Punisher and Blade the Vampire Hunter into Spider-Man's animated universe. The episodes are action-packed, but curiously, the true focus of these storylines lies elsewhere. Relationships are at the heart of these episodes: Peter and Mary Jane, Felicia Hardy and Morbius, Kraven and Dr. Crawford, the Punisher and Microchip, and Blade and Whistler. Each has not only an emotional attachment to the other but an actual reliance on that person to effectively perform their role as a hero. Just as Morbius' love for Felicia prevents him from giving in to his vampiric urges, Mary Jane's love for Peter stops him from giving up in the face of his greatest challenges. The conclusion of the season sees the series take a turn towards the supernatural, introducing the "Tablet of Time" and both the young and old versions of the Vulture.

Season Two ends with a cliff-hanger that is immediately continued in Season Three along with the final episodes' focus on the supernatural over the scientific. Subtitled "Sins of the Fathers," Season Three once again forms a cohesive storyline throughout its fourteen episodes but more overtly places an emphasis on interpersonal relationships. This is clearly seen in the mystical first episode "Doctor Strange," wherein Marvel's resident Sorcerer Supreme challenges his arch-nemeses Baron Mordo and Dormammu, with Spider-Man and Mary Jane caught in the middle. Mordo's scheme involves preying upon emotionally vulnerable people like Mary Jane by falsely reuniting them with their estranged loved ones and then turning them into psychic slaves in his war against Strange. His gambit works temporarily but he is ultimately defeated by Strange and Spider-Man when, in one of the series' more bizarre twists, the pair travel to another dimension to confront Dormammu face-to-face.

This first episode of Season Three features a brief introduction of Madame Web, a minor character in the comics but someone who would figure prominently into the remainder of *SMAS*. She is introduced fully in the season's second and third episodes, "Make a Wish" and "Attack of the Octobot," a two-part storyline that combines comic plots both old and new — 1967 and 1984, respectively. Madame Web appears to guide Spider-Man through the use of cryptic advice and, at least in his opinion, she is more hindrance than help. Madame Web is perhaps the most important secondary character in *SMAS*, however, because it is through her that Spider-Man sheds the weaknesses that prevent him from fully realizing his potential. These two episodes explore Spider-Man/Peter Parker's two main problems, self-doubt and self-pity—the two faults that Madame Web focuses on during their initial meetings. This is done explicitly in "Make a Wish," which sees Parker ready to abandon the Spider-Man mantle, and metaphorically in "Attack of the Octobot," wherein Spider-Man suffers from amnesia, literally forgetting that he is a hero. Madame Web's reasons for guiding Spider-Man to be a better hero are kept mysterious at this point but will be revealed in the final season, in the series' most bizarre and poignant twist.

Elevating Madame Web from a handful of cameo appearances to the architect of Spider-Man's destiny was a major revision of the comic narrative. However, it would be the following episode, "Enter the Green Goblin," that was the biggest departure from the Spider-Man mythos. The Green Goblin is Spider-Man's arch-nemesis, his foil, and his antithesis. Delaying his appearance until the third season subverts the audiences' expectations for Spider-Man media. All other adaptations, be they animated or filmic, introduce the Green Goblin first, as it is expected that audiences will want to immediately see Spider-Man face his greatest foe.

I would argue that delaying the introduction of the Green Goblin is the among the best attributes of *SMAS*, because doing so allows his conflict with Spider-Man to have a level of pathos impossible were he the first villain the young hero faced. To make the conflict with the Goblin meaningful, there has to be an established relationship not only between Spider-Man and Norman Osborn, but between the audience and Osborn as well. Delaying his transformation into the Goblin until this point imbues Osborn's appearances in the first two seasons with suspense, another dimension that would be diminished by an earlier introduction. The added tension of these early episodes gives way to a more sympathetic depiction of the Goblin later, as the audience is well aware that his villainy is not by choice. Furthermore, by exploring the Osborn aspects of the Green Goblin first, the series is able to avoid the petty torments the Goblin first visited upon Spider-Man in the comics in favor of an all-out personal assault on Peter Parker. It also taps into the surrogate father relationship Osborn has with Peter, stretching the meaning of "Sins of the Fathers" to new definitions that would be expanded further during the season.

"Enter the Green Goblin" is one of the series' highpoints and one of the better single episodes of an ongoing superhero animated series. In addition to a compelling plot which sees Spider-Man and all of the series' recurring characters in mortal peril at the hands of the Green Goblin, the ending of the episode marked a shift in several of the series' subplots, making the culmination of the Goblin storyline the *denouement* of the series. It would not be the final appearance of Osborn's Goblin, but this was the beginning of several changes in *SMAS*. Elements of the comic mythos were still integral to the storylines, but more risks would be taken from this point forward. This animated version of Spider-Man was now narratively whole; he could stand separate from his comic predecessor. The already rich storytelling on display in the series would be used to tell stories even more atypical for the action/superhero cartoon genre.

The following episode, "The Rocket Racer," introduces two obscure characters from the Spider-Man universe and breaks an unwritten taboo of children's entertainment—discussing race and class. The Rocket Racer is a young African-American who turns to crime because he sees it as the only way to escape his poverty. The series does incorporate his motivation from the comics—a desire to get money to help his ailing mother—but the animated series illuminates the fact that his social status makes earning the money through legal means nearly impossible. In the Rocket Racer, we have a representation of African-American issues that were typically neglected in children's programming. *The Super Friends* had incorporated a multi-racial cast, but their differences from their Caucasian counterparts were often in skin tone only. *SMAS* had a robust depiction of both super-powered and human African-Americans, with characters like Blade, the Rocket Racer, and Robbie Robertson, and deftly avoided the clichés and stereotypes that often appear in mainstream media. This inclusiveness of race does not feel forced, however, but rather a natural extension of the very real world in which Spider-Man is set.

The remainder of the season continued to focus on the father/son dynamic through arcs featuring Venom and the introduction of his "son" Carnage, albeit in a form more suitable for Saturday morning consumption. We are shown how the transgressions of the father are passed to the son in the episodes "The Ultimate Slayer" and "Tombstone," with the back-to-back placement of these episodes subtly hinting that a father's presence in a son's life can steer his choices away from evil. The season closes with the return of the Green Goblin in a trio of episodes that see him squaring off against Osborn's technological progeny, the Hobgoblin. The concluding episode of this saga lives up to its title, "Turning Point," as it takes the series in a direction unexpected by viewers or followers of the comics. The Goblin's use of the Time-Dilation Device invented by the Spot results in he and Mary Jane Watson being sent to another dimension with no hope of return. This de facto simultaneous "killing off" of Spider-Man's greatest foe and his love interest is a huge departure from the source material and marks the beginning of *SMAS*' trek in to more original storylines and uncharted narrative territory for Spider-Man.

The shortened Season Four was subtitled "Partners in Danger," and focuses largely on Spider-Man's relationship with the newly super-powered Felicia Hardy in her guise as the Black Cat. The Black Cat depicted in the animated series was significantly different from her comic counterpart. The fact that these revisions to the character feel organic rather than unnecessary is a testament to the strength of the narrative in *SMAS*. By this season, the animated series represented a continuity all its own. It would have been illogical to turn the established character of Felicia Hardy into a petty crook overnight simply to make the Cat's origin follow the comics' storyline. A wholly original device would have to be created to turn the spoiled little rich girl into the formidable hero, and the series did so by harkening back to a comic icon that predates Spider-Man: Captain America. Hardy is given the super-soldier serum as part of one of Kingpin's schemes, eliminating the need to retcon her story to include years of acrobatics and combat training. Furthermore, the animated series adds another twist to both the Cat and the well-established properties of the Captain America serum by making its effect something that Hardy could turn on and off. This would allow Felicia to maintain her secret identity so that Peter/Spider-Man would be unable to tell that she and the Cat were one and the same.

After the Spider-Man/Black Cat duo take on Kraven, the Vulture, the Scorpion, the Shocker, and an army of vampires, the season shifted focus away from the Black Cat and back to the storyline of the third season. The episode "The Return of the Green Goblin" marked not only the transformation of Harry Osborn into the second Green Goblin but saw Mary Jane mysteriously return from her exile in another dimension. She immediately finds herself as a target for super-villains once again, as Mysterio's girlfriend kidnaps her for taking a role she originally played. The episode "The Haunting of Mary Jane" is especially notable because it features a female villain and the actual death of Mysterio, an event that had yet to occur in the comics. Mysterio's heroic sacrifice at the climax of the episode inspires Spider-Man to reveal his true identity to Mary Jane and, unlike the previous seasons, Season Four ends on a positive note with Spider-Man and Mary Jane reunited and without danger looming overhead.

Season Four is an anomaly in Spider-Man's animated universe because of its short format but also because of the lack of narrative movement. It is paced considerably more slowly than previous chapters and introduces no new characters to Spider-Man's world, save for the obvious Black Cat and a one-shot episode featuring the Prowler. The overall narrative progresses very little; the open question of the Green Goblin's whereabouts creates an unspoken dread that hangs over the plot of the season. His brief appearance via Harry Osborn's visions further cements him as Spider-Man's greatest foe — able to strike at him from beyond even the confines of reality. Though Season Four is less exciting by the standard set by previous installments, the creators of *SMAS* made a wise decision not to replace the Green Goblin with a new threat to Spider-Man. Harry's Goblin is but a shadow of his father's and the lack of any credible threat to Spidey temporarily shifts the focus of the series away from action.

By eschewing action and super-villainy in the fourth season, *SMAS* is able to focus primarily on character development. Such development was always a significant part of the series, but here it becomes the sole narrative driver. Spider-Man spends most of the episodes grieving for the loss of Mary Jane and, to a lesser extent, the loss of Norman Osborn. His eventual acceptance of the Black Cat as his partner is not just an acceptance of assistance and of a woman as his equal, but his acceptance of a replacement for Mary Jane. After the Black Cat's departure with Morbius, Spider-Man resigns himself to being perpetually alone. Mary Jane's unexpected return therefore gives him a renewed sense of purpose, one that he would need for the events of the fifth and final season.

The fourth season began to establish *SMAS* as having a continuity all its own, but it would be in Season Five where we first see vast portions of the Spider-Man's history — and even the history of Marvel Comics — rewritten. It is during this final season that we see Spider-Man faced with his greatest challenges to date, yet the first episode "The Wedding" is a recreation of the happiest day of Peter Parker/Spider-Man's life, his marriage to Mary Jane. The events of the episode are a recreation of the comic version from a decade prior, with necessary changes made to better fit the continuity of the animated universe. The largest revision of the comic's story is the inclusion of villains in contrast to the peaceful wedding depicted in *The Amazing Spider-Man Annual #21*, giving a hint to the heightened action on display in the remainder of the season.

The second episode begins the five-part story arc "Six Forgotten Warriors," one of the most ambitious plots ever featured in a superhero animated series — a feat that would only be superseded by *SMAS*'s concluding episodes. The spy-centric action of the first installment is unique among the stories the series had told up to that point and, despite featuring a reformed Insidious Six, is closer to James Bond than Spider-Man. Spider-Man (as Peter Parker) journeys to Russia with Robbie Robertson in an effort to find out the fate of his parents and to investigate the rumor that they were traitors. Both Parker and Robertson have their own agendas that they keep hidden from the other, with Robertson's secret eventually taking center stage in the third installment (which sees the reintroduction of Golden Age heroes from Marvel's Timely Comics years into the modern day).

Spider-Man teams up with five of the "Six Forgotten Warriors," Black Marvel, the Whizzer, the Thunderer, Miss America, and the Destroyer, to face off against the Kingpin's Insidious Six for control of the keys to a "Doomsday Device" created by the Red Skull. The fourth chapter sees the return of the Red Skull and the sixth "forgotten warrior," Captain America, from limbo to renew their conflict in the present day. This, of course, is a significant revision to the history of the Marvel Comics universe, where Captain America had been found frozen in ice by the Avengers in 1964. Furthermore, it was a revision of the Marvel animated universe continuity as well, as Captain America had appeared in *X-Men: The Animated Series* a few years prior. This wholesale continuity change is a strong indicator of *SMAS*'s universe being separate from other Marvel worlds, a world wholly crafted by the series' creators and able to exist on its own apart from established timelines and stories. In larger sense, this story arc is indicative of the creator's desire to tell good, compelling stories regardless of Marvel continuity or the standard tropes of the superhero cartoon genre. The introduction of five characters that would be completely unfamiliar to all but a select few comic fans shows a desire to take risks that other superhero media have been historically reluctant to take. The "Six Forgotten Warriors" arc is proof that the creation of a strong narrative was the creators' primary goal for the series; a goal that I would argue they certainly achieved.

"Six Forgotten Warriors" also sees some rather dramatic changes made to one of Spider-Man's classic foes, Electro. When James Cameron's proposed filmic Spider-Man failed to materialize, *SMAS* was free to use Electro, but rather than introducing him as yet another super-powered crook, they choose to reinvent him as a significantly more powerful being, the Red Skull's "Doomsday Device." No longer a small-time crook that suffered an accident of science, the animated Electro is the son of the Red Skull, imbued with a complete control of electrical energy in much the same way that Magneto controls magnetic fields. This Electro is one not before seen in the comics or in any of Spider-Man's forays into other media — a new creation of the animated series designed to showcase Spider-Man's ability to defeat a more powerful foe. Despite the presence of Captain America, S.H.I.E.L.D., and the Golden Age heroes, it is ultimately Spider-Man who is able to defeat Electro. He does so through cunning, agility, and intelligence — the very things that define Spider-Man as a hero and make him more attractive to readers than his brawnier counterparts. Even though distracted when Mary Jane is injured, Spider-Man succeeds where the others have failed because he perseveres even to the point of personal sacrifice. This is a Spider-Man that is confident in his abilities and in his role as hero; a vast departure from the insecurities on display in earlier seasons.

After Spider-Man's greatest triumph comes his greatest setback in the two-part episode "The Return of Hydro-Man." The B-league villain seemingly returns from the dead to ruin Peter and Mary Jane's delayed honeymoon in Niagara Falls, kidnapping Mary Jane in the process. With the Black Cat's help, Spider-Man is able to track him down where he receives the shocking news that he is simply a clone that retained the memories of the original Hydro-Man. Furthermore, it is revealed that Mary Jane is also a clone of herself, meaning that the real Mary Jane is still lost in an alternate dimension along with the Green Goblin. Compounding Spidey's tragedy of discovering his wife to be a clone, the Mary Jane clone disintegrates at the episode's climax and Spider-Man is faced with having lost the love of his life twice.

In addition to being a storyline created exclusively for the show, "The Return of Hydro-Man" was a thinly veiled criticism of the Spider-Man comic series by *SMAS*. All of the Spider-Man comic titles had just recently wrapped up the controversial "Clone Saga," which saw Peter Parker replaced by a (possible) clone, Ben Reilly, who took up the mantle of Spider-Man. The confusing storyline eventually wore on readers and, by wrapping up their "Clone Saga" in two episodes, this arc can be seen as *SMAS*'s attempt to correct an error the comics had made. For five seasons, *SMAS* had been refining the Spider-Man character into one who was confident, strong, and capable; to incorporate the actual "Clone Saga" and replace Peter Parker as Spider-Man would have been counterproductive, an erasure of the continuity of the animated series. Instead we are given a brief homage to the "Clone Saga," complete with Miles Warren (the Jackal in the comics) making an appearance and an ending that hints at the potential for more Spider-Clones.

Spider-Man is not given time to grieve or to pursue Warren before Madame Web reappears to reveal to him the culmination of the plans she began in Season Three and to start perhaps the most ambitious revision of Marvel Comics continuity ever undertaken by one of its forays into other media. Madame Web and the Beyonder have tapped Spider-Man to be the lynchpin of their "Secret Wars," based on the comic mini-series of the same name. Rather than being inclusive of all of the Marvel Universe as it had been in the comics, *SMAS*'s version of the story drastically pared down the roster of heroes and villains to a mere handful with Spider-Man as their leader. In a shortened retelling, Spider-Man leads the Fantastic Four, Iron Man, Storm of the X-Men, Captain America, and the Black Cat against Dr. Octopus, the Red Skull, and Dr. Doom on an alien world to prove to the Beyonder that good is stronger than evil. We see Spider-Man take on a leadership role yet unseen in the comics, and he proves himself to be as capable in a large-scale battle as he is fighting crooks in downtown New York.

This is a depiction of Spider-Man that could only take place in *SMAS* due to its gradual building of Spider-Man's confidence and its focus on long-term narrative planning to set the stage for such an event. The comic incarnation of the character has never progressed to the level of "Earth's savoir" in the way that a character like Superman has, and, indeed, his limitations are part of his appeal. Spider-Man could fend off the Hobgoblin and the Vulture, but Marvel had always left the battles with Galactus, Kang the Conqueror, or Magneto up to the Fantastic Four, the Avengers, or the X-Men. Spider-Man's role in the "Secret Wars" arc is proof that this version of the character is a unique creation; a different and perhaps better Spider-Man.

Madame Web again appears after Spider-Man's victory in the Secret Wars to transport him to yet another reality for the two-part series finale. Another jab at comic series, part one, "I Really, Really Hate Clones," takes on the sticky issue of comic continuity again and provides a visual and narrative depiction of the many incarnations of Spider-Man throughout the years. Here we see the Spider-Man of *SMAS* confronted by multiple versions of himself, further proving the animated series' Spider-Man to be a character now fully separate from his print counterparts. This episode recaps several of the comic Spider-Man's less stellar moments, including Ben Reilly's Scarlet Spider and the Spider-Armor donned in *Web of Spider-Man #100*. The episode uses humor to address the issue of the many Spider-Men, as Spider-Man says when he sees Ben Reilly, "Whoa, I don't think I even want to hear your story;" a swipe at these other, less-authentic interpretations of the character.

The main villain for the two-parter is Spider-Carnage, who appeared briefly during the "Clone Saga," but in their tradition of refining and expanding on the comic's narrative, *SMAS*' creators do much more with the character than previously seen. The animated Spider-Carnage is a villain on a cosmic scale; so full of loathing for his lot in life that he plans to destroy not only his own universe, but all universes as revenge. This Spider-Carnage is the dark inversion of Spider-Man; a character who dwells on his problems rather than overcoming them. He represents all of the weakness in the Spider-Man character that *SMAS* had been slowly eliminating over the course of the five seasons. Much like the symbiote itself, *SMAS* depicted self-doubt, anger, and jealousy as parasites which, left unchecked, would have consumed Spider-Man. Spider-Man and company's final battle with Spider-Carnage serves as a literal interpretation of the metaphorical battle that ran throughout the series.

The final ten minutes of the second episode, "Farewell, Spider-Man," serves as a fitting coda to the story arc and to the entirety of *SMAS*. Spider-Man journeys to our reality, the world where he is just a fictional character whose adventures are depicted in comic books and cartoons. He takes Stan Lee on a web-slinging tour before the two have a discussion about the differences between their worlds, and Spider-Man expresses that, in spite of his trials, he is grateful for his life. Lee responds, somewhat puzzled, "Gee, you're definitely not the same guy I've been writing about all these years!"

Stan Lee was correct. The Spider-Man of *SMAS* was not the same one he'd written about, nor was he the same one that could have been found in contemporary Spider-Man comics. He was a more mature, more refined version of Spider-Man; the same character, but one that had different experiences and, most importantly, different reactions to those experiences than his comic counterpart. *SMAS* is such a successful "reinvention" of a comic book property because it is not truly a reinvention but rather a reinterpretation. Having the benefit of knowing what worked and what had not worked, the creative team behind *SMAS* was able to perfect a comic book superhero in a way that no adaptation had before or, it could be argued, has since.

Works Cited

"Jim Krieg Talks Spider-Man: The Animated Series." *Marvel Animation Age*. Accessed 10/18/10. http://marvel.toonzone.net/spideytas/interviews/krieg.

Lee, Stan, Steve Ditko, Art Simek, et al. *The Essential Spider-Man Vol. 1*. New York: Marvel, 2002.

_____, Steve Ditko, Art Simek, et al. *The Essential Spider-Man Vol. 2*. New York: Marvel, 2007.

LoCicero, Don. *Superheroes and Gods: A Comparative Study from Babylonia to Batman*. Jefferson, NC: McFarland, 2007.

Spence, Lewis. *An Introduction to Mythology*. New York: Cosimo, 2005.

Finding the Milieu of the *Spider-Man* Music LPs

Mark McDermott

With the Broadway musical *Spider-Man: Turn off the Dark* spinning through the news cycle at the time of this writing, it is surely appropriate to explore some of the previous cultural artifacts that set Peter Parker's story to music. It is not hard to find musical interpretations of the web-spinner. The theme song from the 1960s cartoon series remains one of the best-remembered of American Saturday morning TV themes in America, having been covered by fellow Queens natives the Ramones, referenced by Aerosmith guitarist Joe Perry in his theme for the 1994 animated series, and heard throughout the three theatrical films. The fourth season of PBS' *Electric Company* (1974–75) debuted a series of "Spidey Super Stories" skits with a funky theme song of its own. The skits were spun off into a juvenile-reading-level comic book, and to an album on the children's label Peter Pan Records, which later included Spider-Man in its "Book and Record" comic series on the Power imprint.

It is in the world of commercial pop music, though, that Spider-Man and the rest of the merry Marvel menagerie have gone mostly unrepresented. Despite Marvel's popularity among comic fans during the 1960s, its impact on the wider world at the time was muted. Since 1957, Marvel's newsstand distributor — which was owned by DC Comics — would only handle eight titles each month (Daniels, 1991: 80–81). In the 1960s, Batman got the prime-time TV series, Broadway got *It's a Bird... It's a Plane... It's Superman*, and Donovan's number-one hit boasted, "Superman or Green Lantern ain't got nothin' on me!" (1966). Lucky is the collector who today finds a 45 copy of the Traits obscure 1969 garage/psych record, "Nobody Loves the Hulk" (QNS 101). Spidey finally made his first dent in the *Billboard* charts in 1976 with a jazz-dance single by Ramsey Lewis that asked the musical question, "What's the Name of this Funk (Spider Man)?"

By the 1970s, though, Marvel had graduated from its cult status to the mainstream. After getting a new distributor, they finally saw *The Amazing Spider-Man* outsell the Superman titles. In 1971, Marvel won out in a standoff with the Comics Code Authority over their depiction of the consequences of drug abuse in *The Amazing Spider-Man* ("Green Goblin Reborn!" 1: 96–98). On January 5, 1972, Marvel celebrated its cultural ascendancy with a "Marvel-ous Evening with Stan Lee" at Carnegie Hall, in which Tom Wolfe, French director Alain Resnais (*Hiroshima Mon Amour*) and other "elites" proclaimed Lee's eminence as a creator of modern culture. Among the show's participants was actor René Auberjonois, then known for playing Father Mulcahey in the movie adaptation *M*A*S*H* (1970). The event was recounted in a *Bullpen Bulletin* appearing in Marvel comics cover dated July 1972:

ITEM: January 5, 1972! Mark that date in your memory-book, faithful one—'cause that's the night the batty Bullpen got it all together at Carnegie Hall, in the hectic heart of New York City!

As we told you last month, the whole magilla was called "A MARVEL-OUS EVENING WITH STAN LEE"—and it was a way-out compendium of music, magic, and madcap Marvel mayhem! Smilin' STAN himself was Master of Ceremonies—presiding over the frantic goings-on while images of mighty Marvel superheroes flitted across a giant movie screen. A trio of our titanic artists got into the act, too, as Jazzy JOHNNY ROMITA, Happy HERB TRIMPE, and Big JOHN BUSCEMA did sensational sketches of Captain America, ol' Greenskin, and Thor —which in turn were projected onto that selfsame screen. (There was a passel of our cavortin' characters in actual attendance, too, including Spidey, Daredevil, Doc Doom, and even J. Jonah Jameson himself!)

The standing-room-only crowd exploded with applause, also, at the roster of famous names who had gathered to pay homage to the madness that is Marvel: World-famous film director ALAIN RESNAIS translated a few of the Silver Surfer's soliloquies into his native French; and there were also a few pungent paragraphs about our heroes which were intoned by radio personalities ALEX BENNETT and EARL DOUD, by actors RENE AUBERJONOIS and CHUCK MCCANN (you've seen the latter a zillion times as the "Hi Guy" neighbor on the other side of the medicine cabinet in those Right Guard commercials), and neo-journalist Tom Wolfe, resplendent in red, white, and blue as he read about—you guessed it—Captain America.

As for the music mentioned above, most of it was provided by the far-famed CHICO HAMILTON PLAYERS—but some more Marvel Madmen got into the act, too, as Hectic HERBIE and Bashful BARRY SMITH plunked a couple of wild electric guitars while Rascally ROY THOMAS belted out a rousin' rocker or two! Then, for the grand finale, just about everybody in the blamed Bullpen crowded onto stage to sing the Merry Marvel Marching Society theme-song—while, not to be outdone, dozens of cheering fans rushed onstage as well, and the show closed amid a revel of handshaking and autograph signing all 'round. And that was that! All in all, it was a wildly successful evening—and not necessarily the last of its kind, either! And, if there were a few bleary eyes and sore throats among the Bullpenners come the morning of the 6th well, that's show biz, people!" ["Bullpen," 1972].

Indeed, in this era, Stan Lee or one of the Bullpen Bulletin writers would boast that Marvel was "gonna take over the world" by expanding into other media. With live-action television projects still some years away, Marvel's first cross media foray came from third parties wanting to exploit the comics in the medium of rock concept albums.

In 1972 and 1975, two LPs were released that attempted to re-imagine Spider-Man's story as a combination of audio drama and pop music; a rock opera comic book, even. Nearly 40 years later, and despite interest from both comics and music fans in these audio artifacts, it remains uncertain whether someone at Marvel came up with the idea, or the record companies involved brought the concept to the publisher. Yet the albums remain, both of them reissued on CD with the requisite bonus cuts and available from the inheritors of their defunct record labels, or downloadable online.

The Amazing Spider-Man: From Beyond the Grave (1972)

I remember when I first heard about this album. As a pre-teen music fan, I was a member of the Record Club of America, a club whose appeal lay in its low prices and shipping charges, and no minimum purchase requirements. During 1972, its fliers had a listing for *Beyond the Grave* on the Buddah label (the misspelling may have been deliberate, to avoid the appearance of exploiting Buddhism—when the trademark was reactivated in 1998 as a reissue label by the BMG/Arista group, its name was properly spelled "Buddha"), promising the unique experience of a "Rockomic," with contemporary-sounding song titles like "It's a Groove to be Free." While at the age of 13 I was still solidly in the DC Comics camp, I soon began to pick up on Marvel. I later found a remaindered copy of the LP in 1979, when a regional discount store chain went out of business and was clearing three aisles of remaindered vinyl at $1 apiece.

The "Rockomic" aspect of the album was in the gatefold of its sleeve, which featured a wordless comic story, one row of panels for each song, accompanying the music on the disc. The comic was by Spider-Man artist John Romita, who also drew the cover showing Spidey in his familiar pose: crouching in a huge web, hand poised to "thwip!" his webbing at the reader. The cover was reproduced on a foldout poster also included in the record. While the album announced itself as first in a series of "Rockomics," no follow-up issue appeared.

Underneath the production credits on the back cover, next to a small Buddah logo, was the credit: "A VASHTI PRODUCTION: A licensee of the Marvel Comics Group. All material under the supervision and control of the Marvel Comics Group." This may have indicated that someone at Marvel had the idea for this production, or it was their method of proclaiming copyright protection: all the figures drawn on the back cover—Spider-Man, Aunt May, the Green Goblin, and Kingpin—had their own ™ symbols hovering nearby.

The cover credits include "Music and Lyrics by:" Stephen Lemberg, whose only other notable credit seems to have been Merle Haggard's Bicentennial hit "Here Comes the Freedom Train." Musical arranger Tony Camillo later won a Grammy for his production of Gladys Knight & the Pips' "Midnight Train to Georgia," though he is best known publicly for the 1975 hit "Dynomite," released under the name "Tony Camillo's Bazuka," which capitalized on Jimmy Walker's catch-phrase from the TV comedy *Good Times*.

The only credit for the musicians involved was: "All tunes performed by: The Webspinners." Another credits list on the back of the poster included the line "Spinner of the Web—Ron Dante." Dante was a singer and songwriter, later Broadway producer, who had been the anonymous vocalist of the Archies cartoon band. After singing the original McDonald's "You Deserve a Break Today" jingle written by Barry Manilow, he became Manilow's producer in the mid- to late–1970s.

Other voice credits included Earle Doud in several small roles. Besides the Carnegie Hall appearance, Doud was a voice artist who had co-written and produced a string of political humor albums, starting with *The First Family* (1962). Chuck McCann was a veteran actor, puppeteer and kiddie show host. The performer that fans might most likely encounter at the next ComiCon, though, was the voice of Peter Parker: René Auberjonois, best known today as the shape-shifting Odo in *Star Trek: Deep Space 9*, and who shared the scenery being chewed by William Shatner in *Boston Legal*. About this early credit in a lengthy and busy show business career, Auberjonois could only tell me, "Steve Lemberg was a classmate from my University days. He asked me, and I said yes. That's really all I remember about that project" (personal communication, 2010).

Reviewing the Album

The tracks alternate between "set piece" songs and dialogue: each episode plays out as bits of audio drama leading into the songs. In "Episode I: Peter's Nightmare," Parker narrates a dream sequence in which he is pursued by police and tormented by visions of his major foes. The Green Goblin, the Vulture and the Lizard taunt Spider-Man with the knowledge of his secrets, and the fact that he'll "always be a loser." It's hard to tell the villains apart here, as they all deliver their lines cackling like Macbeth's three witches. In this nightmare, Parker also hears another voice calling out for help, just as he's awakened by the phone ringing. On the line is New York's crime boss, the Kingpin, with the kidnapped Aunt May. Knowing that Parker is the one who gets photographs of Spider-Man for the *Daily Bugle*, Kingpin demands that he take one more picture using a camera somehow rigged to kill the wall-crawler.

This segues into the first song, "Theme from Spider-Man," with some competent pop-funk in its instrumental backing. The first verse seems somewhat tuned in to the Spider-Man ethos: "Crawl like a spider, love like a man / Ev'rybody's talkin' 'bout that normal Spider-Man / Amazing! Amazing! / How does he ever win?" But the very next lines call Spidey "No one lady's sex machine / he makes all the little girls sigh!" a sign that maybe the writer didn't quite understand Spider-Man's appeal after all. The song has showed some staying power, though, by appearing in the soundtrack of *Austin Powers: The Spy who Shagged Me* (1999).

"Episode II: Spider-Man Remembers" opens with a scene in the Kingpin's office, with the strains of "Santa Lucia" in the background. The Kingpin's henchman Carlo tells him the time by calculating "The big hand is on the six..." and wonders if Aunt May could make a good pan of lasagna, all as if to ask the listener, "Am I Guido enough for you?" After the Kingpin obliges the listener with exposition on his place as head of the Maggia crime family, Marvel's equivalent of the Mafia, the soundtrack cross fades to Parker reminiscing the story of his own origin.

The next song, "Such a Groove to Be Free," has a Ron Dante vocal over an electric keyboard tuned to harpsichord, in the style of many easy-listening acts of the time, but especially, perhaps, the Partridge Family single, "I Think I Love You." "Episode III: Spider-Man's Dilemma" finishes the recap of Spidey's origin with the death of Uncle Ben. The album's Side One ends with a choir singing "Rock of Ages" at Uncle Ben's funeral.

"Episode IV: A Strange Ally" has Parker pondering whether he should let Spider-Man "die" after all, since his heroic identity has caused nothing but pain to those around him. The voice from his dream returns, calling for Spider-Man, and Parker realizes it's the voice of his late Uncle Ben. He remembers that Uncle Ben would always remind him: "The stronger the man, the heavier the load. With great power comes great responsibility." Parker decides, "A man might quit. But Spider-Man is more than a man! I'm a super-hero! I must fight on, no matter the personal sacrifice! Because that's what being a super-hero is all about!" This succinct summation of Spider-Man's personal obligation suggests that maybe the album's writers knew the character after all, and makes up for the "sex machine" line. This sentiment is amplified in following track, "The Stronger the Man," a digestible piece of early 70s power pop.

"Episode IV: A Strange Ally (cont'd)" brings Doctor Strange into the story. Here his purpose seems to be to use the Eye of Agomotto as more exposition, to show Aunt May feistily resisting Kingpin's enforcers. Strange decides to help Spider-Man on this seemingly mundane crime-fighting task, to which Spidey declares "Let's head cross town!" Indeed, the next cut, "Goin' Cross Town," is what Jackie Gleason would call their "travelling music," a slow boogie in which we are assured that our heroes are going to "kick a tail or two."

"Episode V: From Beyond the Grave" has Strange and Spider-Man arriving at the Kingpin's secret lair, where the Sorcerer Supreme dispenses with the gunsels and allows Spidey to take on Kingpin. Spider-Man calls out, "Maestro, if you will?" as cue for an instrumental version of "Goin' Cross Town," laid under a battle fought with sound effects. Kingpin attempts to flee, only to meet Doctor Strange who, apparently, casts him into Hell. But no, explains Strange, he has only trapped Kingpin within an illusion. Strange further reveals that he was moved to act on Spider-Man's behalf because he heard Uncle Ben's voice calling for help as well.

Spider-Man: Rock Reflections of a Super-Hero (1975)

Most fans learned about this second Spider-Man album from a full-page ad in Marvel comics headlined "The Biggest Rock Event of the Decade!" Beneath that banner is a caricature of Stan, ballyhooing:

> Hi, rock fans! This is Stan (Music Lover) Lee soundin' off! I'm here to tell you about a great, new album—"Reflections of a Super-Hero!" It's not just for the younger set, either! No, it's an honest-to-Aunt May Rock-and-Roll album that's the answer to every disc jockey's prayer! And every one of the sensational songs deals with another aspect of Spidey's tumultuous life! Don't miss this one, True Believer—be in on the beginning of a musical revolution! And if you're wondering why I'm making like a Dee Jay here myself—guess who'll be narrating the whole amazing album? Aww—someone musta told you! [Superhero, 1976].

The ad was run by Superhero Merchandise, a New Jersey store featuring comic book merchandise whose mail-order catalog was a design project of the students at The Joe Kubert School of Cartoon & Graphic Art. Superhero Merchandise later formed Heroes World Distribution, which Marvel purchased in 1994 and made its sole retail distributor.

The album was another studio project, this one on Lifesong Records. The label was formed in 1975 by the production team of Terry Cashman and Tommy West, with Philip S. Kurnit, attorney to the late singer Jim Croce. *Spider-Man: Rock Reflections of a Superhero* was only their second album release.

The album's cover was a more finished version of the sketch shown in the ad: Peter Parker staring into his reflection as Spider-Man in a full-length mirror. The cover was laid out by Romita and finished by Nick Cardy, an artist known for his work on DC's *Aquaman* and *The Teen Titans*, doing one of his few jobs on a Marvel property (Cronin, 2011). The back cover had the usual album production credits, but surrounded by inset drawing of various Marvel characters also "performing": The Incredible Hulk on drums; The Fantastic Four on background vocals; Conan the Barbarian on strings; Captain America on tambourine; and Hand Claps by The Falcon.

Reviewing the Album

This album sounds like an unproduced Spider-Man musical of the 70's, and "High Wire," the first cut, would have been Spidey's introduction number. It is a decent rocking song with the chorus, "I'm a free flyer on the high wire / I'm a man, I'm the Spider-Man." Following the number, Stan Lee begins to narrate the events of the story, setting up each song to follow.

"Peter Stays and Spider-Man Goes," the introspective character examination, was written and sung by Mike Ragogna, a Lifesong signee (and current *Huffington Post* music feature writer), with some psychedelic flourishes.

Stan then provides the flashback to Spidey's origin. And the musical narrative shifts to 1950s style music, with a doo-wop style reading in "Square Boy." The track's composer/singer, Marty Nelson, was a member of the first incarnation of Manhattan Transfer (1969–71). His song recapped the familiar narrative of Peter and the radioactive spider.

"New Point of View" is another "this is what I'm feeling" number, describing Spider-Man's ill-fated television debut from his origin story. Nelson then sings "Spider-Man," a song opening with some barrelhouse boogie in the style of Elton John's "Hercules," or more appropriately, Wings' "Magneto & Titanium Man": "Once I was helpless / Now I rescue those who need me when I can / Spider-Man!" This song was released as a single to radio stations, with "Hero" listed as the artist on the label.

"No One's Got a Crush on Peter" seems to return to a point already made about the pitfalls of Spider-Man's dual life. Stan's narration then has us turn the clock back again, this time to the Gwen Stacy romantic plot, described by "Gwendolyn," another Marty Nelson doo-wop number, and "Count on Me," a modern power pop number.

Rather than establish a plot, Stan continues into another "reflection," relating that Peter has a dream of Dr. Octopus, sung by John Palumbo (lead singer of Lifesong's progressive rock group Crack the Sky). Doc Ock "counts the dozens" on Spidey and all his superhero colleagues in song, backed by a full rock orchestra and vocal section representing all of Spider-Man's foes: "Power Man ... and you, Silver Surfer! You messed me long enough ... now I'm gonna hurt ya-a-a-a!"

After the dream sequence, Stan describes the sudden appearance of the Green Goblin: "Tingling with anticipation, Spider-Man would be more reluctant to fight the emerald fiend if he could foresee Gwen Stacey's body falling, as it will, out of his spider-reach." So much for any thread of suspense here. Rather than dramatize Spider-Man's battle with the Green Goblin and Gwen's death musically, Stan continues to narrate the story as if he was reading a movie review. Spider-Man's reaction to Gwen's death is sung, though, to a string and choir backing somewhat recalling the Rolling Stones' "Lady Jane," titled "A Soldier Starts to Cry." Stan wraps up by proclaiming, "He's a hero, if you will. A hero whose dreams have turned to nightmares; who walks in step with tragedy and death. But still he perseveres! For such is the haunting fate ... of Spider-Man!" Finally, we get a curtain-closer in Nelson's "Time Will Show Me the Way."

Critical Analysis

Having heard "Boy Falls from the Sky," the first song publicly performed from the 21st-century musical *Spider-Man: Turn Off the Dark*, I can't say it's that much better than anything done on LPs 35 years before. Each of these albums has marked similarities and differences. The similarities mark them more as products of their times. Both were produced as special projects by small labels, with the involvement of label studio personnel or other talents that were well-known within the industry, but unknown to the public.

In 1972, Buddah was one of the major suppliers of hit records. It was established in 1967 as a spinoff of Kama Sutra Records, then successful as the label home of the Lovin' Spoonful. Buddah branched out from its early bubble-gum hits to a diverse range of artists from Bill Withers and Gladys Knight & the Pips to Captain Beefheart and Charlie Daniels (Hyde, 2000). *From Beyond the Grave* is the product of a company at a stylistic crossroads: Ron Dante brought a well-honed sensibility for bubble-gum to his production work, abetted by popular comedy and voice talent, while some of the songs involved R&B and funk leanings that would serve the label in the disco era. The funk elements in *From Beyond the Grave* were not entirely new to the Spider-Man oeuvre, either. The 1970s PBS show *The Electric Company* featured a heavy urban groove in its soundtrack, which carried over to the "Spidey Super Stories" segments. An *Electric Company* soundtrack album featured yet another retelling of Spidey's origin story, with a contemporary R&B musical bed–the effect of which was somewhat marred by the nasal delivery of the voice actor attempting to play a teenaged Peter Parker. Auberjonois, on the other hand, went for a natural delivery that did not attempt to conceal his 32 years, and helped to expand the appeal of the album beyond the confines of the Children's Records section. The Buddah project as a whole played like a modern radio drama.

Lifesong was a much smaller label than Buddah at the time of their Spider-Man project. Much more of the new label's personnel were involved, and the music overall had a more professional sheen. Every fan blogger who writes about the album takes aim mostly at the Dr. Octopus song, though it could be seen as no more over the top than the songs in *Rocky Horror Picture Show,* also released in 1975. The impression I got from listening to *Rock Reflections* in 2011 was of the pitch for a Spider-Man musical being presented to a group of potential backers: the songwriters are present to sing the show's songs, while Stan Lee lends his celebrity presence and narrates the show's book. This happened to be Stan's function when he moved to Los Angeles in the 1970s to pitch Hollywood on Marvel TV or movie projects.

It seems, though, that these projects were made with minimal involvement from Marvel Comics, aside from approval for the use of characters and artwork. Except for the outside ad for *Rock Reflections,* there was no mention of either album in Marvel's "Bullpen Bulletins" text pages of the time. Roy Thomas, Marvel's Editor in Chief from 1972 to 1974, wrote: "I've racked such brains as I have, but since I wasn't involved in either rock album, I'm afraid I don't know much of anything that might help you. I never got the idea that Stan was intimately involved in the albums, either ... in particular, I seem to recall that *Reflections* was readied by someone else and then brought to Stan for such participation as he may have had" (personal communication, 2010). In a later correspondence, Thomas noted that he had also tried his hand at a song: "Wish Gary Friedrich and I had been able to place our 'Spider-Man' recording, made with the vague blessings of Marvel, in 1966 ... but only our little private copies of the session remain. Maybe if Gary's lawsuit is ever settled, we can get permission to run it as a quasi-giveaway sometime" (2011). Friedrich filed a lawsuit in 2007 against Marvel and Sony Pictures, et al., claiming damages for Marvel's use of the Johnny Blaze Ghost Rider character he'd created (DeMott).

No matter whether Marvel's involvement in *From Beyond the Grave!* was peripheral or hands-on, the album seemed to be an attempt to create a new reader experience, albeit one based on juvenile "read-along records," a media form starting with Bozo the Clown's 1946 debut in *Bozo at the Circus* (Raymond, 2005). In the 1970s, the children's label Peter Pan Records started the Power Records imprint for a "Book and Record" line of complete comic book stories, sometimes repurposed from already published stories, accompanied by a dramatization on 7-inch disks. Power Records adapted not only DC and Marvel characters, but TV and movie properties like *Star Trek, The Six Million Dollar Man, Planet of the Apes,* and *Kojak.*

The popularity of these children's records is hard to compare, since their sales were not reported on music industry charts. *Billboard* did a tongue-in-cheek review *From Beyond the Grave!,* alongside reviews of albums by Pete Townsend, Elvis Presley and David Bowie, declaring:

> There are many (mostly parents) who say that there are many similarities between comic books and rock music (both are abhorable non-functional destroyers of youthful brain tissue, or so they say). Spider-man faithfully vanquishes the forces of evil and underground rock right before your very ears. The songs are all buoyantly sung by (who else) the Wedspinners [sic] ... [*Billboard,* 1972].

The same issue of *Billboard* carried a one-column ad for the album on its front page. The caption beneath the album cover assured readers it would be "The Christmas smash of the year!" *From Beyond the Grave!* did appear in *Billboard's* "Bubbling Under the Top 200 LP's" chart, tracking for six weeks and peaking at #201 the week of January 27, 1973. This was the same level as an album of songs by the cast of *The Brady Bunch*. The Number One album of that time was *Seventh Sojourn* by the Moody Blues.

The 1975 *Rock Reflections* album seems to have been produced with a greater expectation of radio play, and many of my references suggest it did receive some play at college stations. The album's music tracks were separate from Lee's narrative segues, making airplay easier, whereas Auberjonois' narrations on *From Beyond the Grave!* often ran right up the "ramp" (the instrumental introduction) of the songs that followed them.

The Lifesong label released *Rock Reflections* before its brief string of mid-1970's hits: "Shannon" by Henry Groce, "Ariel" by Dean Friedman, and a few mid-charting posthumous releases from Jim Croce. Its main contribution to the pop culture arcana was co-founder Terry Cashman's 1981 release, "Talkin' Baseball (Willie, Mickey and 'The Duke')," which became a folk anthem during the 1981 Major League Baseball strike. Cashman would re-record the song with new lyrics to fit nearly every major league team. The best-known version of his song, though, was "Talkin' Softball," heard under the end credits of the 1992 *The Simpsons* episode, "Homer at the Bat."

From Beyond the Grave showed off its bubble-gum pop heritage, while *Rock Reflections* strived some for credibility among both music and comics fans. Musically, the failure of the latter may have stemmed from its attempting to cover too many musical styles so it could play up the strengths of each contributing artist. "Gwendolyn" and "Square Boy" were too kitschy in revisiting 50s pop styles when compared to the more earnest "Spider-Man" or the camp of "Dr. Octopus." Narratively, the production's error was in taking the "Reflections" part of the title too literally. Too many grooves are spent revisiting Spider-Man's origin in song. Then the death of Gwen Stacy, which could easily have dramatized in a tragic way, was instead simply narrated by Stan between tracks, one of which was yet another dream sequence. Here, *From Beyond the Grave!* better succeeded in creating a dramatic narrative in the style of an old radio drama; even with the gatefold comic strip narrative and the Kingpin's stereotypical Maggia goons. Its narrative still succeeds as a drama played out in the mind's eye.

The Marvel World of Icarus

The author's fanboy penchant for over-completeness and too much detail compels a mention of an album which is even harder to find in its original pressing than the two discussed above. In 1972, a British progressive band named Icarus recorded an album titled *The Marvel World of Icarus*. Rather than attempting a rock-opera style narrative, the band instead wrote and recorded twelve songs about Marvel characters. The album's front cover was a collage of comic strips, and the back showed photos of the band members' heads pasted over drawings of Spider-Man, Thor, Conan, etc. After a spoken "Prologue" that built in speed and intensity like the opening "Departure" from the Moody Blues' *In Search of the Lost Chord*, the album starts with "Spider-Man." Like the rest of the album, it brings in all the standard tropes of British prog and psychedelia: an instrumental backing including flute and clarinet, with organ driving most of the melody, punctuated by brief flourishes of guitar, flute or organ solo. Lead vocalist Steve Hart had a gravelly tone not unlike John Kay of Steppenwolf. The whole effect, though, was of a generic acid rock soundtrack to any exploitation "Mondo" documentary about hippies running wild. The lyrics to "Spider-Man" include couplets like "Gonna catch a fly / Right between the eye…. He's always reeling in and out of town/Jonah's always trying to bring him down," and the chorus: "Spider-Man is on the prowl! / Look out! The threat's behind you now!" (Plotel, 1972). Hardly a show-stopper. The album has a few surprises, like an ode to the Iron Man femme fatale "Madame Masque" which was a close simulation of any Rod Stewart ballad of that time. *The Marvel World of Icarus* was pulled shortly after its release, and legend claims that after initially approving the release, Marvel demanded more royalties than Icarus' label, Pye Records, wanted to pay. Whether the story is true or not, the Icarus album never saw release in the U.S., and became another rare piece of Marvel ephemera, until it was re-issued in the 1990s. The writers of TV's *Law and Order* franchise tipped their hats to this album as well. The June 19, 2011, episode of *Law and Order: Criminal Intent* featured Dets. Robert Goren and Alex Eames (Vincent D'Onofrio and Kathyrn Erbe) investigating the apparent stunt-releated death of the leading man in a long-delayed, injury plagued rock musical. The play's name and the title of the episode: *Icarus* (Ng, 2011: n.p.).

The Rock Opera Context

Although the dramatic and musical enactment of a comic book story would seem like a quirky project for a record label, there were plenty of similar recordings whose success could suggest that the Spider-Man LPs might have a chance to turn a profit. Foremost were the concept albums that defined the "rock opera" genre by combining music with a clear narrative beyond a collection of thematically related songs. Rock historians cite *SF Sorrow* by Pretty Things (1968) as the first true rock opera, but the genre was best defined by The Who's *Tommy* (1969). *Jesus Christ Superstar* was first produced on album in 1970 before any idea of a stage production. *Superstar* was realized as a motion picture in 1973, and *Tommy* in 1975, perhaps fuelling the hope that dramatic albums could profitably cross over into other media. Pink Floyd's 1970s string of themed albums culminated in *The Wall* (1979), which itself became a motion picture. Other acts such as Rush, Frank Zappa and Jethro Tull also recorded whole albums around individual themes or stories.

Rick Wakeman's *Journey to the Centre of the Earth* (A&M, 1974), which followed the Yes keyboardist's first solo outing, *The Six Wives of Henry VIII* (1973), was produced as an avatar for the entire progressive rock genre. This musical interpretation of Jules Verne had only four songs, banded as one continuous track on each side. It is the most successful LP on this list, having hit #3 in the *Billboard* Albums chart. Though the album showed signs of the self-indulgent pretentiousness that sank the prog movement before the decade was out, it may also have been one of the reasons Homer Simpson proclaimed "Everyone knows rock attained perfection in 1974. It's a scientific fact!" (Forrester, 1996). The following year, Wakeman debuted his next album, *The Myths and Legends of King Arthur and the Knights of the Round Table*, with a live performance of *King Arthur on Ice* at London's Wembley Arena.

Flash Fearless vs. the Zorg Women, Pts. 5 and *6.* (Chrysalis, 1975), which includes work from various artists, is a campy rock rendition of a sci-fi serial, which anticipates George Lucas' trick with the *Star Wars* narrative by starting in the middle of its own story. The LP came with a comic book adaptation. Flash was played by one of that year's hottest artists, Alice Cooper, with character or musical parts by John Entwistle and Keith Moon, "Jim Dandy" Mangrum of Black Oak Arkansas, Justin Hayward (The Moody Blues), Carmine Appice (Vanilla Fudge) and more. Unfortunately, the songwriting ability was not equal to the big-name cast. The project had been intended as a stage musical, but the album's commercial failure sent the concept into hibernation until it ran briefly onstage in Los Angeles in 1981, retitled *Captain Crash Versus the Zorgwomen, Chapters 5* and *6* (Joseph, 1995).

Considering the swath Wakeman laid across the musical landscape, it's odd that so few other musicians mined literature as subjects for concept albums. Alan Parsons was a studio engineer at London's Abbey Road, where his first credit was on *Abbey Road*. He significantly contributed to the sound of Pink Floyd's *Dark Side of the Moon*, and formed his own studio group — the Alan Parsons Project — with songwriter Eric Woolfson. *Tales of Mystery and Imagination* (20th Century, 1976) offered musical reinterpretations of Edgar Allan Poe works. Parsons eschewed the "all star" approach in the studio, working instead with members of 70s groups he had produced, Pilot and Ambrosia. First pressings of this album featured a lyric insert booklet by the Hipgnosis design studio, "wrapped" with a sheet of tissue guard, as was used to protect engraved plates in old books. Parsons continued to release themed prog rock albums into the 1980s.

Another various-artists studio project that failed to dent the charts was *Intergalactic Touring Band* (Passport, 1977). The concept was a performance set list by the imaginary IGTB on its tour of far-flung planets in a far-flung future. It featured an illustrated lyric booklet and yet another all-star collection of vocalists: Meatloaf, Ben E. King, Rod Argent, Arthur Brown, members of Status Quo, and Clarence Clemons on saxophone.

Jeff Wayne's Musical Version of The War of the Worlds (Columbia, 1978) has the most gravitas of any of these albums, due mostly to Richard Burton's narration. Previously known largely for producing a David Essex album, Wayne was nonetheless able to fund production of this ambitious project and attract contributions from more of the 1970s' heavy musical hitters. In the U.S., it peaked at #98 in *Billboard's* album chart and spun off a Top 40 hit in Justin Hayward's "Forever Autumn." In Britain, it remained on the charts for over five years and was reissued in several anniversary editions — including a 7-CD box set. Its rock-classical-disco fusion kept it much sought-after by club DJs.

Various Artists: White Mansions (A&M, 1978) achieved some promotional buzz in its time as a Country counterpart to *War of the Worlds*. Its narrative of the Civil War from a Confederate point of view involved a cast including Waylon Jennings and his wife Jessi Colter, Steve Cash of the Ozark Mountain Daredevils, and guitar parts by Eric Clapton.

Conclusion

From a the perspective of the comics fan, the Spider-Man music projects do not add much to the "Spider-verse." Both of the narrative albums spend much of their time rehashing Spidey's origin story, while *Rock Reflections* also delves into the Gwen Stacey tragedy. Both albums also feature Peter Parker taunted by hallucinations of his many villainous foes. *From Beyond the Grave!*'s plot of the Kingpin having Aunt May kidnapped to coerce Peter Parker into killing Spidey does sound like an original story, but as with most non-comics stories, it has probably never been referenced in any Marvel comic — though if Grant Morrison ever writes *The Amazing Spider-Man*, bet on him making that story part of canon somehow.

A Spider-Man narrative on a long-playing album presents a different listening experience than the same narrative on CD or in an MP3 library. Just as in a live performance, the audience is obliged to listen to an LP from the start to finish — of each side, at least — with little chance to skip the bad parts or just delete unwanted cuts altogether, as today's music consumer can do.

Since its inception, the LP format has been explored as a medium for performances beyond the standard two-hits-plus-filler-songs format of most pop albums. Genres like classical and jazz could easily stretch out to an LP's up to 60 minute capacity, and well before the "rock opera," artists from Frank Sinatra on down recorded "theme" albums meant to stand on their own with the extraction of singles a secondary consideration. Millions of people experienced Broadway musicals from albums recorded by the cast one Sunday after matinees. Among the cast albums and soundtracks atop the sales charts in the early 1960s were comedians like Bob Newhart and Bill Cosby, and *The First Family,* hinting at the LP's narrative potential. At the time, there was also a steady trade in albums of old radio shows, voice tracks from old movies, and spoken word albums, now called "audiobooks." Among many acts creating original narrative projects for LP was Stan Freberg, with his 1961 "Album Musical" *Stan Freberg presents the United States of America, Volume One: The Early Years,* and freeform radio performers the Firesign Theatre.

Placed against the history of "concept albums"—some deservedly successful, others deservedly obscure—we can see that perhaps the Spider-Man albums fit well within the parameters of the pop concept album, at least before it became the exclusive province of progressive rock bands. The packaging of *From Beyond the Grave!* went a further step in trying to re-integrate the album with its roots in comics' sequential narrative. The effect of trying to follow the album's action along in the gatefold seems to this Baby Boomer more like sitting through a filmstrip of the Easter story in Catechism, missing only the "beep" from the accompanying album to remind the presenter to advance the strip. Since the dialogue-less gatefold adds little to the story that isn't already told in the grooves, the album works out better as a musical performance than a new hybrid of music and comics.

The Spider-Man LPs can be seen as sharing a common thread: using the long-playing format to tell a narrative beyond the usual collection of pop songs. Whether rooted in progressive rock, kid's records, jazz or radio drama, the Spider-Man records can be seen as part of an effort to create a narrative form exclusive to the 40-plus minutes of a long-playing record.

Works Cited

Auberjonois, René. (9/11/10). E-mail correspondence with the author.
Awarehouse, The. Merchandise Catalog for Record Club of America, 1972.
"Billboard Album Reviews." (11/11/72). *Billboard* 84:46. New York: Billboard, 73
"Bullpen Bulletins." *The Amazing Spider-Man 110.* New York: Marvel (July 1972).
Cronin, Brian. "I Saw It Advertised One Day #21." *Comic Book Resources: Comics Should Be Good!* 1/17/11. Accessed 3/9/11. http://goodcomics.comicbookresources.com/2011/01/17/i-saw-it-advertised-one-day-21/comment-page-1/.
Daniels, Les. *Marvel: Five Fabulous Decades of the World's Greatest Comics.* New York: Harry N. Abrams, 1991.
DeMott, Rick. "Ghost Rider Creator Sues Marvel, Sony & More." *Animation World Network.* 4/11/07. Accessed 6/20/11. http://www.awn.com/news/business/ghost-rider-creator-sues-marvel-sony-more.
Forrester, Brent "Homerpalooza." Episode of *The Simpsons.* Television program (5/19/96).
"From Beyond the Grave." *Billboard* 84:46. New York: Billboard. Cover.
Hyde, Bob. "The Kama Sutra/Buddah Records Story." *Both Sides Now Publications.* 4/11/2000. Accessed 3/14/11. http://bsnpubs.com/buddah/buddahstory.html.
Joseph, Tim. "Flash Fearless." *Sickthings UK* (Alice Cooper fan site). 1995. Accessed 2/15/11. http://www.sickthingsuk.co.uk/albums/a-flash.php.
Leitch, Donovan. *Sunshine Superman.* Donovan. Epic, 1966. Vinyl recording.
Lemberg, Stephen. *The Amazing Spider-Man: From Beyond the Grave.* Perf. The Webspinners and René Auberjonois. Buddah,1972. Vinyl recording.
Ng, David. "'Law & Order' episode feels the pain of Broadway's 'Spider-Man' musical." *L.A. Times Blogs: Culture Monster.* 6/20/11.Accessed 6/20/11 http://latimesblogs.latimes.com/culturemonster/2011/06/law-order-spider-man.html.
Plotel, David, & Icarus. "Spider-Man." *The Marvel World of Icarus.* Pye International (UK), 1972. Vinyl recording.

Ragogna, M. & Nelson, M., et al., *Amazing Spider-Man: Rock Reflections of a Super-Hero*. Perf: Ragogna, Nelson, J. Palumbo et al. Lifesong, 1976. Vinyl recording.

Raymond, Tom. "The Unusual History of Bozo the Clown." *Clown Ministry*. 2005. Accessed 2/10/10. http://www.clownministry.com/index_1.php?/site/articles/the_unusual_history_of_bozo_the_clown_attempting_to_unravel_who_did_what_wh/.

Superhero Merchandise. Advertisement. *The Amazing Spider-Man 153*. New York: Marvel (Feb. 1976): 32.

Thomas, Roy. (11/5/2010, 6/13/2011). E-mail correspondence with the author.

Games Are Not Convergence: *Spider-Man 3*, Game Design and the Lost Promise of Digital Production and Convergence

CASEY O'DONNELL[1]

Introduction

It is common to hear that games, and people are frequently referring to videogames, are exemplary of what is meant by convergence. Some game developers wax whimsical, saying that games are "the convergence of everything" (Irwin, 2008). These remarks, when combined with widespread confusion between convergence and cross-media synergy, and then coupled with brand leveraging in a multi-platform world, results in mystification over what convergence is or isn't. This article draws on more than five years of ethnographic participant observation amongst "AAA" game studios as well as independent and hobbyist game developers. The bulk of the material presented in this article is drawn from ethnographic fieldwork amongst videogame developers at a large game studio in New York State. This studio has produced numerous titles for console game systems and PCs over the course of its 20-year history. Participant observation, structured and unstructured interviews, and analysis of industry news sources provide the bulk of the material presented.

I argue that there are facets of convergence that have fallen out of the current frame of analysis and this is demonstrated by examining two particular aspects of the production of videogames. The first is the way technological systems and their interoperability (or lack thereof) shape and constrain production. Secondly, the article examines how "game mechanics" must always be created for games, regardless of the kinds of technological hurdles that over time may be made simpler. Combined, these demonstrate that the perception of media "flow" between platforms is often based on the creative collaborative work of numerous media workers. Production, as a whole, is largely neglected in the analysis of convergence. Perhaps most importantly, the complexity of "flow" increases dramatically when examining cross-media/cross-platform/synergistic media production endeavors.

The material presented in this article demonstrates that "production" as a core-category has largely escaped our analysis, and this omission has significant implications for the producers of media. Simultaneously, these repercussions also have significant impacts on the "users" of media. While the article focuses explicitly on those developers at the "center" of the game development world, the issues they face are magnified and exacerbated when you extend your analysis to the "periphery" (independent or hobbyists content creators) or the user.

This article first examines the disconnects between convergence as a conceptual category and issues related to media production. The article then turns to an ethnographic account of cross-media videogame production to demonstrate this disconnect. The analysis then delves deeper into two aspects of this disconnect, related to production tools and videogame "mechanics." Finally, the article examines the implications of this lack of attention to media production and the broad sweeping implications this has for the concept of convergence, with particular attention to users.

Production and Convergence

Production, which is the sets of activities and practices associated with creating media/technologies, is an often-neglected area of academic scholarship. This is doubly true in the context of videogame development. In part this follows from difficulties researchers have in their ability to access field-sites and the temporal restrictions that game developers often face in the production timelines associated with their work. Scholarship is further limited by the inclusion of Non-Disclosure Agreements (NDAs) and other mechanisms by which game companies attempt to control and structure communications out of their companies. However, these difficulties do not excuse the dearth of attention paid to the implications on media production practice in the Web2.0/Convergence/Cross-Media/Cross-Platform moment.[2]

As Henry Jenkins notes, "[c]onvergence is a word that manages to describe technological, industrial, cultural, and social changes depending on who's speaking and what they think they are talking about" (Jenkins, 2006: 2–3). Indeed this makes it difficult to pin-down what precisely is being discussed with regard to convergence. The particular component of convergence that this article examines has been described as follows:

> Perhaps most broadly, media convergence refers to a situation in which multiple media systems coexist and where media content flows fluidly across them. Convergence is understood here as an ongoing process or series of intersections between different media systems, not a fixed relationship [ibid.: 322].

This article attempts to grapple with the "flow" of media content, especially when conceptualized as "fluidity." It argues that the appearance of media flow and fluidity, when it does occur, which it often doesn't, is the product of massive human labor. The "convergence" on digital media technologies promised fluidity and labor reducing opportunities. Digital media technologies promised the ability to record, create, produce, and deploy on numerous devices, with scaling and customization, for each platform "just happening," since it was all digital anyway. Even with the acknowledgement that, "[f]or the foreseeable future, convergence will be a kind of kludge — a jerry-rigged relationship among different media technologies — rather than a fully integrated system" (Jenkins, 2006: 17), it continues to be talked about as something more magical. The impact of these kludges resounds throughout the worlds of media producers. While users may be content to jerry-rig, it is important to understand that the same is true for content producers at the center, just as much as those at the constructed periphery, and jerry-rigging for one's livelihood can be a particularly uncomfortable position.[3]

Users, consumers, players, or, more generally, the people that put convergence at play, culturally speaking, tend to be the focus of our understandings of convergence. While this article turns the tables, focusing on the loci of "big media" production, it remains relevant to those interested in remix or convergence culture. It is certain that "[p]articipation ... is shaped by the cultural and social protocols" (ibid.: 137) in which they are situated, it is also structured by numerous technological elements. These same technological components are highly influential in the shaping of media production in this state of convergence. Thus, the examination of a large — often referred to as an "AAA"— videogame production studio has significant relevance for understanding "user" convergence as well. The labor required to enable the flow of media between devices when unavailable to users or restricted to only large media production companies becomes significantly enmeshed with disconnects or kludges that emerge amongst users.

Convergence began as an important concept linked to the rapid adoption of digital technologies associated with digital media production and distribution.[4] One of the original promises of digital convergence and its associated technologies was the ability for multiple devices to make use of a single-source piece of data and display it in multiple contexts. It was this ability to use and deploy the same data in numerous locations that was a huge promise for the producers of digital media/technologies.

Two major structuring issues inhibit this in the case of videogame production. The first category, broadly considered, is the role of the numerous technologies in the different spaces of media production and how they shape creative collaborative practice, which applies to numerous areas of media production practice. The second category has to do with the particular characteristics of videogames. Games are played by a user and thus require internal feedback systems, often called "mechanics" to provide compelling user experiences. Though I use the lens of videogame development practice here as a means to unpack the "something that happened on the way to convergence," it is by no means limited strictly to the worlds of videogame developers.

(Non-)Convergence in Videogame Production

In May 2007, *Spider-Man 3* was released to theaters across the USA. Though not critically acclaimed, the movie was exceptionally successful at the box office as the 18th highest-grossing domestic film at more than $330 million over 16 weeks. Amongst fans of the comic it marked the first appearance of "Venom," one of the more popular villains of the series (Staff, 2010). At the same time two different games, bearing the same name, were released for the Sony Playstation 3 (PS3), Sony Playstation 2 (PS2), Microsoft Xbox 360 (360), and Nintendo Wii (Wii). Much later, in October 2007, a version of the game was also released for the Sony Playstation Portable (PSP). Though the game was also later brought to other gaming platforms, this article examines specifically the production of the PS2, Wii, and PSP versions by the game studio Vicarious Visions (VV). This same studio also produced a substantially different version for the Nintendo Gameboy Advance (GBA), which is not included in this article's analysis.

Spider-Man 3, or SM3, as it came to be known amongst the development team, is actually two different games released on five different game platforms. Two different game studios, both owned by Activision, were responsible for the production of these two different games. Treyarch was the game studio responsible for the creation of the PS3 and 360 versions, while VV was responsible for the Wii, PS2, and PSP versions. Activision acquired Treyarch in 2001 after successfully porting several videogame titles for other Activision subsidiary companies. Activision purchased VV in 2005 under similar circumstances. This corporate activity demonstrates the value placed and, to a degree, the significant labor necessary for games to "flow" between different videogame platforms. This becomes drastically more apparent when examining the production of these games day to day over the course of months and years.

During the nearly year and a half production time for SM3 there was moderate cooperation and contact between the Treyarch and VV teams. VV would be responsible for the "current gen," or generation, of consoles, while Treyarch would approach the "next gen" systems. This alone is interesting, that a division was made at the time of production to have two different teams responsible for creating, ostensibly, the same game. This division of labor focused on individual media platforms is important. When talking about concepts like convergence, analysts must understand that significant differences exist between devices and the resulting implications for users and producers of media.

While filming was largely complete nine months prior to the release of the videogame, little data flowed between the companies. Much of the movie script remained out of the hands of the games producers until late in the production of the game. Basic story lines were known, but little information flowed from the team producing the movie to those producing the game. Digital effects were produced independent of the game development teams. This was of course in part because the models and animations associated with Spider-Man on the console game systems had started months prior to their development by the film's visual effects teams.

The storyline presents problems of its own. A videogame is typically expected to provide a great deal more playtime than the two to three hours movies are expected to capture their audiences. In addition, a videogame must stretch the story and supplement it in different ways by introducing either storylines from the worlds of the characters or providing hurdles for players that increase the amount of time it takes to progress through the game. These story changes must then be filtered through numerous other media organizations involved in the process, such as Marvel comics, who ultimately owns the rights to the *Spider-Man* franchise. Thus game developers quickly encounter a difficult situation in how to stretch a story designed to be resolved in two hours and may only include a small set of obstacles that challenge the main character.

Time and again during the production of SM3, it was apparent that making a game based on the Spider-Man character was a very different undertaking than the production of a movie. SM3 required the invention of gangs of thugs that would roam the city providing battle fodder for the web-slinging protagonist. The addition of new enemies, drawn from *Spider-Man* comics, provided additional gameplay duration. New audio voiceovers were done by the original actor, Tobey McGuire, who had to be flown in to provide adequate vocal isolation for Spider-Man's lines. Bruce Campbell, who has appeared in all of the Spider-Man movies as a cameo actor, returned as the narrator on only the PS2, Wii, and PSP games.

The models and animations for on-screen game characters differed significantly on each platform from those used in the movie and even across development studios. One team used 3D Studio Max to create these models and animations, while another team used Maya; both 3D graphics packages are owned by Autodesk. Textures were significantly different as well, based largely on the available graphics processing memory of the target consoles. The number of buildings that could be displayed diverged markedly from system to system based on its processing and graphical capabilities. One point of convergence was the use of Google Earth's 3D Model data of New York City as a resource for the development teams. It would be interesting to know if this was a resource used by the special effects teams producing graphics for the movies. Development rework was constantly required when attempts were made to share artistic "assets" between the two teams and two entirely different mission systems had been developed between the current and next generation console platforms.

Perhaps most important, at least for Spider-Man, is the extensive effort that went into making "web slinging" and "web swinging" look like it "should." Significant amounts of engineering were invested in making the fundamental aspect of Spider-Man work within the games. This was combined with the complex development of animation sequences for the Spider-Man character model, which appeared in the game. All movements had to be disassembled and recombined in ways where even the slightest glitch would cause the games player to see noticeable "hiccups" in the player's movements on screen.

As is apparent, there was a significant disconnect between each one of these projects all focused on the same franchise, and seemingly the same "product." The notion that *Spider-Man 3* simply flowed or web-slung from device to device oversimplifies the situation. It might be expected that convergence would be a kludge for users; it also remains largely a kludge for media producers at the center of these worlds. More differences can be found across these three creative collaborative efforts than overlaps. Yet, this project is exemplary of what most cross-platform/cross-media production looks like. There is more divergence than convergence when examined from the perspective of media producer. Synergy across the project was more about leveraging marketing muscle than about synergy between those creating the resulting projects.

Ultimately, cross-media and cross-platform production, as currently configured, is more about "synergy" than convergence[5] and any sense of "flow" is the product of human labor rather than any real fundamental shift occurring in the worlds of media producers. The later portion of this article attempts to understand this disconnect between convergence as it is understood more broadly and convergence as it is understood by cross-media content creators.

Convergence/Synergy and the Role of the Socio-Technical

Many game developers imagine a world where digital "assets," or content created for one platform, can "flow" to others. One of the goals of VV's *Alchemy* Game Engine, purchased and continually developed by VV, is the ability for multiple game platforms to be supported while minimizing the work required of the game development team. During the same period of time when SM3 was being created, another team within VV was working on a game for the Nintendo DS. This game was to mirror the release of the new *Transformers* Movie, another cross-media project. The VV team was abuzz that a team at another studio, working on *Transformers* for the Xbox 360, had successfully used the same models for the game as those used in the movie. Of course the hardware limitations of the DS made that impossible for the VV team, but it was newsworthy for many of the developers. Despite the ability for those teams to use the same models, they still required massive rework, given that they had been "rigged" for animation with full motion video, rather than for a game. However, for some developers it has become only a matter of technological advancement. "Convergence" as a sense of flow from platform to platform will get better as technology advances.

However, I argue that convergence will always be a kludge, for users and media producers alike. I make this argument from the perspective of a scholar of Science and Technology

Studies (STS) and an analytic framework drawing upon Actor-Network Theory and Heterogenous Engineering. This illuminates why socio-technical assemblages stabilize in the ways they do. Thus the argument is that digital "flow" is not in the interest of the socio-technical assemblages as they have now constructed themselves. As a consequence, it will continue to be a promise that remains to be realized and convergence will remain a category that inherently carries with it a host of people and labor when media does flow across media/platforms. As noted by one of my informants, this lack of understanding of digital production extends well beyond a lack of familiarity of what media producers do:

QUESTION: How would you go about explaining what you do every day?

ANSWER: Really, I've given up on explaining. Most people think that I do work like what comes out of Pixar. The majority of people only think they comprehend Pixar's animation and that is what they think I do. They see a 3D animation and they are like, "Oh, look!" Most people know I work in games, but they have no real concept of what it is. Some people think I do graphic design. There is also this misconception that when you're working on a licensed title that all we do is take someone else's game and convert it into something that can be played on another platform. They have no idea that most games are totally recreated. A DS game may be completely different from its corresponding PC game. I'm sure some gamers know that, because they play them both and see that they are different. But so many people think, "Oh, you just take their art assets and convert them." They assume that there is no difference across platforms. There is so much design and creativity that goes into those new games. They are literally largely created from scratch. We just use the same characters as a launching point.

(NOTE: When I first arrived at the studio, my informant had asked: "Can't we just take their models and sort of optimize them?" Her supervisor had replied: "It is just faster to make them ourselves really. At least that way we know ours aren't going to give us any goofy problems in the tool chain.") [Informant and O'Donnell 2006].

One of the promises of digital media production was the notion that all things digital carry with them some sort of innate interoperability. The rise of digital media production carried the promise that a single digital data source could provide numerous platforms with custom tailored art assets that could be readily incorporated and deployed. The word convergence, in and of itself, indicates this predilection. However, as the example of videogame production indicates, the reality of convergence is something quite different. Even in a simple form one imagines convergence to be "cooperation between multiple media industries" (Jenkins, 2006: 2–3).

As the more senior artist noted in the quote above, regardless of developers using the same tools, they may be used in different ways or in a broader context that differs from other game developers. Typical practices or "tool chains" may differ in ways that render it "faster" to do it oneself rather than even attempting to work with the materials provided from other teams. Even the overlap with a specific software package may be insufficient. Particular plugin packages may have been used by one development team or another and objects may be tagged with data in different ways that make them inaccessible to game designers or game engine programmers. Thus, the broader "actor-network" that the tools are situated in renders the "same" tool quite different.

One approach to understanding the continual kludginess of convergence might be to posit that "platforms matter" and all the various baggage that goes along with those platforms (i.e. hardware specificities, operating systems, programming languages, software development kits, supported data formats, and the various ways these systems layer together [Montfort and Bogost, 2009: 2–3]) makes a significant difference. Indeed, this is part of the equation. Put simply, technology does matter, and technologies that layer on top of one another, as they do in these digital realms, often do so in ways that make them less rather than more interoperable.

The argument is that platforms carry with them assumptions about uses and means by which they can be interacted with. While transitioning the *Spider-Man* movie from the large screen to a smaller screen may be a simpler task than its transition to the videogame realm, questions must be asked about that hardware's capabilities. When platforms differ significantly, as is often the case in the creation of a "movie videogame," questions quickly multiply. How would one go about playing *Spider-Man* the movie? What would that look like and what would a typical videogame player expect from such an experience?

The enormity of the work of convergence begins to emerge. Something quite different must be created when platforms diverge significantly. This shifts the task from one of translation or re-encoding to one of re-creation in a new technological environment with different affordances. To better understand this process, Heterogenous Engineering and Actor-Network Theory offers us insight into how the process of technological development is a socio-technical assemblage. Thus the process of creating a new technological system, in this case SM3, is a massive undertaking of human labor that is constantly connected with and shaped by the broader social and technological systems within which they take place. Or, as John Law puts it, "the stability and form of artifacts should be seen as a function of the interaction of heterogenous elements as these are shaped and assimilated into a network." The work of incorporating these diverse elements is due to there "almost always" being a "degree of divergence between what the elements of a network would do if left to their own devices and what they are obliged, encouraged, or forced to do when they are enrolled within the network" (Law, 1989: 112–114).

Thus, the remainder of the article re-examines the story of SM3's development by further illuminating why given shifts occurred or did not occur by following some of the numerous other actor-networks to which they are attached. It is attention to the shaping and assimilation of the elements as they are drawn into "the network" or "game." Two primary core issues emerge as fundamental blockades to convergence as it has often been conceptualized. These core categories, data flow and game mechanics, represent where the majority of cross-media labor is expended. In the case of data flow, the socio-technical assemblage is very much at play, as corporations attempt to gain leadership positions through the very structure of their data formats. In other cases it is less deliberate, with data formats being largely dictated by their underlying technologies, though nonetheless effective at limiting "flow." Game mechanics, the second classification, deals with one of the fundamental differences between games and other forms of media. Games, though they can still be message or story delivery platforms, are composed of systems with numerous feedback loops that inevitably engage the user.[6] This multiplicity of complexity and interactivity thus leads to a much different storytelling platform, that in many cases tears open the thin veil of formulaity surrounding the stories being offered.

The Devil Is in the Details: Proprietary Data Formats

Videogames are assembled from a massive number of different files that reference one another. Source code is compiled into machine-readable code, which differs from platform to platform. The compiled source code references design data, which is constructed by game designers to describe the functioning of a game. Design data references art assets generated by artists in a variety of file formats. These art assets are read into the game through the compiled source code of the game's engine. Art assets my be directly read, or exported from one program into an intermediate format that is then read by the game's engine. This entire piece of "software" is incredibly complex and highly interconnected and iterated on over the lifecycle of a game's development. It is possible, in some cases, that pieces of the game's engine, art, or design data do "flow" from one project to the next. However, the majority of the files were new or significantly modified for this project. The 3D models, created with 3D Studio Max (or just "Max"), were exported using the proprietary set of software tools, often called a "toolchain" by game developers. These tools, known as Alchemy, performed customizations and assorted automations to each model being exported. Custom information that had been added to the models by artists is read by the file export system. This information is then used to link art assets to design data, which is then interpreted by the underlying game engine. An intermediate file is generated that can then be interpreted by other components within the toolchain.

For VV to use the same 3D models as Treyarch, multiple parts of Alchemy would have had to be significantly modified. Maya, used by Treyarch, and Max, used by VV, have different internal representations for models. The ways data are stored throughout the system and the ways in which this information is then stored in the file formats is largely proprietary and different from application to application. This isn't to say that Max and Maya don't have various intermediate "compatible" file formats. Indeed they do, but each also has a different representation or understanding of how data should be stored and must then be interpreted by each application. In some cases, certain aspects of models or animations are discarded, as there may be no logical corollary between the two applications.

In many ways, the fact that Max is the more prevalent software package amongst game developers has lead to it becoming a critical aspect of the game development process. Its "naturalization" has also lead it to being a forgotten aspect of what game development looks like. The same could be said of Visual Studio, the most widely used programming environment used by engineers in the videogame industry. Thus these products, which are part of their own corporate and socio-technical actor-networks, "sink into the community's routinely forgotten memory" (Bowker and Star, 1999: 299). Despite the amount of work necessary for each game development studio to support these tools and their accompanying proprietary formats, these systems have disappeared from the analysis of accounts of the game development community. So despite their idiosyncrasies, unusable character, and potential for collapse, they still recede from analysis.

To make matters even more complex, each application has a significant history prior to their acquisition by AutoDesk, who now owns both software applications. Max and Maya were originally the two leading competitors in the 3D modeling and animation space. Each product was independently developed in competition with one another. Interoperability was never a priority, as each company had an investment in their own implementation. Locking users into a data platform was just as important to these companies. The black boxes of Max and Maya then demonstrate the point that "[t]he more automatic and the blacker the black box is, the more it has to be accompanied by people. In many situations, as we all know all too well, the black box stops pitifully because there is no salesperson, no repairer, [and] no spare part" (Latour 1987: 137). As a company acquired or created a large catalog of models, their investment is not only in the software, but in the underlying data formats creating a level of inertia, especially in the case of videogame development, because other systems and software technologies depend on the idiosyncrasies of those technologies and formats.[7]

Even when a complex system like Alchemy is used to process data into intermediate formats, in the hopes of protecting your production practice from the variability of other software formats, problems can still occur. Each target console game system expects data in different formats. These formats are dictated yet again by typically proprietary systems. The hardware compromising these systems is by no means remotely standardized and what may work perfectly in one case will often not work in another. Each console game system also uses a different kind of Digital Rights Management (DRM) that further affects how data is encoded and written to a disk and then read back off, or more frequently "streamed" from the disk. At each step, it is possible that systems will stop functioning as a result of undocumented bugs, also called "features," with tongue in cheek, by developers. Furthermore, the DRM that accompanies these systems locks content creators into the licensing agreements dictated by the devices' manufacturers (Gillespie, 2007).

Combined with the sheer weight of the number of files being created for a project of this scope, format specifications creep into numerous aspects of a project. However, it is not simply technological. Naming conventions, or standards, for files may differ from studio to studio. Naming conventions and the means by which extra information is linked to an object may differ project to project. Software written by videogame engineers then interprets the tools that videogame designers use to reference the work of artists and the additional information they provide. Particular conventions and proprietary data types are used to define the underlying behavior of the game. These expectations allow the connections between numerous systems to function. They enable the feedback loops that occur between artist, engineer, designer, and videogame (O'Donnell, 2009: 3.1–3.4). In many ways the videogame production process itself mimics the behavior of a videogame system. That isn't to say that making games is anything like the play of a videogame, only perpetuating the myth of what game developers do. Game development, in terms of information flow, is very similar to the systems that make up a videogame.

As can be seen throughout the development process, "flow" is not a particularly good term for understanding how assets of any kind move through the production process any more. Data does not flow through this system. Humans or computers process it, or it is parsed and presented on the screen mediated by software applications. Cross-media production converges less than it diverges. Data multiplies and is re-created in different applications bringing new capabilities. Human labor and computer processing power are leveraged through these systems to bring the semblance of convergence.

Mechanics vs. Narrative: Games Are Played, Not Read or Watched

The second major issue standing in the way of games and convergence is that games are quite different from film, music, television, or the myriad of other media industries interested in "flowing" content to videogame players. What gamers and game developers have long been aware of, and many executives and decision makers in other creative industries have not yet come to understand, is that games are complex information systems. Their rules and logics are governed by game mechanics. Narratives can of course be placed in games, but if the player is too constrained in a linear fashion, it ceases to be a meaningful play experience. It must be coupled with game mechanics that provide the player with meaningful means to interact with that narrative (Salen and Zimmerman, 2004). Many "platformer" games, *Super Mario Bros* for example, have fairly static narratives. At the same time, those games provide mechanics that produce meaningful interaction with the game. "Saving the princess" must be coupled with jumping, running, block breaking, and the myriad of other elements of the game. The story cannot exist divorced from the game's mechanics. Gamers will often refer to this as the "rail" within games, along which one travels. If made too linear, the player is left with little feeling of input. Narratives must be in line with the underlying mechanics of a game. Put another way, the feedback loops between the systems that comprise a game are just as important as the narrative placed on top of that system. This is what gamers and game developers alike refer to, perhaps vaguely, as "gameplay."

> The message that gamers have been broadcasting should be loud and clear by now. At the end of the day, it's about gameplay. All of the "entertainment device" functionality in the world wasn't enough to sell PS3s without games. We don't want to play movies, we do not want the game industry to resemble the fickle music industry, we don't want games to emulate our real lives or our real relationships [Carless, 2008].

The story of SM3, at least in part, deals with rather complex issues ranging from the ambiguous position that the hero, avenger, and vigilante Spider-Man occupies. "Black-Suit" Spidey, though powerful and nearly unstoppable, is rooted in something very different from who Peter Parker is, or who he believes himself to be. It is about pride, forgiveness, and redemption. Yet, these rather abstract story messages are harder to conceptualize in terms of "gameplay." Much of the gameplay focuses on the "fun" of web-slinging and traversing New York City. The action focuses on missions of one kind or another, Spider-Man combat, and attempting to deliver the climatic battle sequences featured in the film. To provide the player with enough to do to encompass a playtime gamers expect, rival gangs are created and deployed throughout the city. These provide the fodder for Spider-Man's heroic exploits. Though the game features the villains also found in the movie — Venom, New Goblin, and Sandman — it also includes other villains from the *Spider-Man* comic world. The game attempts to recreate the events of the movie without any of the sub-text storytelling that occurs within the script of the film.

Thus, the message of the game is not the same as that being communicated in the movie. The game mechanics remain quite similar to the original *Spider-Man* games. To capture the essence of those more complex stories is more difficult, though they are the elements which viewers like best. There is a disconnect between the mechanics of SM3 the game and the story being told in the movie. So how would SM3 capture those story elements in actual gameplay? One answer can be found in a feature cut from the PS2 and Wii versions of the game. In these versions of the game, if the player spends too much time as "Black Suit Spidey," which carries with it negative consequences over time and simultaneously makes the player more powerful, the city itself begins to become corrupt. More and more garbage appears on the streets, the sky takes on a smog-ish look, and the overall appearance of the city becomes dingier. Thus the game creates a connection back to the movie's more ambitious storytelling (this feature was removed from the final game, though it can be seen as part of several missions in the game).

One need only look as far as game design textbooks or industry trade publications to see that narrative and gameplay are constantly in conversation. Perhaps more important, though, is the fact that games contain systems and mechanics. So, despite the fact that "[g]ames usually limit players to a very narrow range of potential actions ... in stories [and film] the number of possible actions that characters can engage in seems nearly limitless." This is because games are systems: "the actions and all their effects must be simulated on the fly, while in stories it is all worked out ahead of time" (Schell 2008: 143). Meaning, story, and narrative are products of those narratives that can be inserted in the game, but also through the gameplay itself.

Meaningful play is found in the conversation between the actions of a player and the outcomes, within the simulation, being "discernible and integrated into the larger context of the game." Perhaps most importantly though, it is not so much about the text of the game, but about the "emotional and psychological experience of inhabiting a well-designed system of play" (Salen and Zimmerman, 2004: 34).

This isn't to say that the developers' hopes for SM3 were not ambitious enough or that they did not have the requisite understanding of the story of *Spider-Man*. Quite the contrary, many of the developers involved in the project were avid readers of the comic books and fans of the film series. The development team toiled for nearly two years on a project that was ultimately panned by videogame reviewers. This seems to indicate a disconnect between what was necessary from the outset: a collaborative vision that spanned platforms and told the story in a way appropriate to the means available to it. Or as stated by a developer of the soon to be released game *NightSky*:

> Don't just utilize narrative and gameplay in your products according to typical convention. Equally senseless is the idea to use both simultaneously with the blind hope that the outcome will somehow be better than just having one or the other. Be deliberate in how you select and architect the medium that's best at conveying what you want the player to experience [Shirinian, 2010].

But this "convergence storytelling" is about deliberate thought and consideration of the platforms upon which stories will be told. Convergence is about how these deliberate instances of stories must be individually architected and constructed in ways that each deliver the message. Convergence, from the view of media producers, is not so much flow as it is the massive set of activities, technologies, and systems that must be carefully considered and labored around to ensure that stories are told in ways that match each platforms' experience. In all cases, it is a labor that is largely ignored as the natural "flow" of media in our current social and technological moment.

Conclusion

Thus, the successful assemblage, SM3, was the product not of "flow" or some natural process, but of "heterogeneous engineers" (meaning in this case, 3D artists and animators, technical artists, software engineers, tools engineers, game designers, and game producers) being capable of "associat[ing] entities that range from people, through skills, to artifacts and natural phenomena." The game developers ability to "maintain some degree of stability in the face of the attempts of other entities or systems to dissociate themselves into their component parts" (Law 1989: 129) is what makes the work of game development a creative collaborative practice. This labor is a critical aspect of what appears on the outside to be convergence. However, from the inside, there is no flow, or even feeling of convergence. There is only the daily grind of working to produce a product, which is largely viewed as derivative or un-unique.

Convergence, then, is not a space where "media systems coexist and where media content flows fluidly across them" (Jenkins, 2006: 322), but rather a labor space where media producers work extensively to keep media technologies, digital encoded data in proprietary formats, and media organizations with little interest in cooperating with one another beyond economic gain from flying apart into their "component parts." Thus the convergence kludge for user/producers is far more complex for those that make it their livelihood to work in this productive space. It has more to do with a passion for those underlying system than the challenge associated with their "absurd labor conditions" (Deuze et al., 2007: 350). It is a passion for game systems, game mechanics, and creating an engaging gameplay-driven user experience that makes them willing to continue working in this space.

The repercussions for users can be seen in how user/players continually (mis)understand the game production process. Often fueled by confusing imagery from popular culture, game development is not understood to be at the intersection of diverse disciplinary boundaries, between art, computing, and game design. This crossroads is further convoluted by the numerous technologies and software systems that are used to produce games. Thus, for the user, it becomes an impenetrable mass only made accessible through user-targeted tools, which often have a very different set of functionalities than those available to large videogame production companies.[8] Even when an "engine" is released to users, its context is removed. The company that sells an engine often does not provide information regarding how it is used and connected broadly throughout their organization. It is divorced from its actor-network context.

It may prove true that some media and devices flow more readily than others and that videogames are just more prone to disaggregation, though I suspect that is not actually the case.[9] While some suggest that the flow of cross-media is "accelerating" (Jenkins and Deuze, 2008: 6), I would not argue that some innate aspect of media production has changed or that convergence brings flow, but rather that greater labor is being spent for this to occur. Companies have expanded their efforts to increase earnings by leveraging existing brands and intellectual property. As one examines the actor-networks of production, in the cross-media and multi-platform space, for producers the notion of convergence will continue to have a very different meaning. This meaning is one much more akin to synergy and less linked to any special notions of media flow. While "game mechanics" may remain specific to videogame production, in all likelihood, parallels can be found in all areas of media production. Where specificity lies, media producers and their labor can be found.

Notes

1. A modified version of this essay was originally published in the journal, *Convergence*, published by Sage Publications (O'Donnell, August 2011). *Convergence* has published several issues examining other aspects of cross-media practices with a focus on emergent issues of ownership, authorship, and the policing of (prosumer) users in our current media moment. In particular, Bonner and Jacob's examination of the chronology of Lewis Carroll's character Alice is particularly relevant to this essay. The amount of labor involved in each of the productions mentioned in this essay speaks directly to what is necessary for convergence "flow" in the context of transmedia (2011). While Zhao's account of cross-platform user-generated books in the same issue does not indicate significant labor in the shift of a book from one platform to another, that may be in part due to the form ("a text") and smaller numbers of authors. The production of "additional channels" in the form of applications, or "client software," enabling the use of these book sites on mobile platforms indicates a labor necessary for the flow from one platform to another (2011: 92).

2. While one notable article examines the "professional identity" of videogame developers, it does not engage with what game developers actually do, day-to-day. The authors index, "the answer to what drives developers to deal with this list of problematic circumstances may be similar to what drives their audience to break through the progressively more difficult levels of the games developers create" (Deuze et al., 2007: 350), yet offer little insight to what that process looks like. They also fail to critically examine the lack of "standards" with regard to technology or even job titles. Other analysts have examined the lack of standards more closely and how it blurs lines between work and play in the game industry. In particular, the marking of game development work as "different" is what makes it special or interesting, it also denotes its participants as exceptional or as having gained access to a particularly exclusive play group (O'Donnell, 2008: 37). While I suspect the authors are correct in their assessment of why developers work so hard, they miss that this is a broader phenomenon when one looks at the work of scientists or other technology workers (O'Donnell, 2009). The drive to find answers, is a deep seated one that is not particular amongst game developers. The

drive to "test" or pursue science or technology is a deep one. "When Nietzsche installs love as a motor force behind the scientific urge, he does so to open the scene for an unprecedented generosity of being capable of melting the moral ice age and a history of intellectual arrest.... To this end, love supplants the deep freeze of moral valuations, rendering the scientific pursuit on a par with what is felt to be irresistible" (Ronell, 2005: 178).

3. For a sense of the kind of precariousness this results in for media workers, an introduction can be found in an article about the rising importance of "Quality of Life" for videogame developers (Dyer-Witheford and de Peuter, 2006). For a more visceral sense of the situation, the actual blog entry cited in that article is still available (ea_spouse 2004).

4. When adopting CDs as a new format of choice in the early 1980s, record companies, and the record industry more broadly, saw them not as a digital media technology, but as a kind of updated LP, which was read with a laser rather than a needle, preventing degradation over time and play. What I suspect is that many involved didn't understand that CDs contained, in a raw, uncompressed, and unencrypted format, the digital data associated with audio recordings. It was the introduction of the CD that ultimately led to encoding technologies like MP3 and the desire for users to shift their digital media from one media and device to another. It also altered significantly the production processes in audio recording studios. This is an inverse case to what is actually seen in the game development work place. Because data formats in these spaces are proprietary and closed, they do not lend themselves to being manipulable and capable of flow in the same way the CD was. Proprietary formats and encryption become tools to control information, but they also exhibit significant control over production practices (O'Donnell 2009).

5. Recently, there has been extensive discussion in industry and in the academy as well about "transmedia" and "cross-media." It is clear that more and more content creators and cultural analysts are thinking more robustly about what "transmedia" and "cross-media" might be. Forums such as Power to the Pixel and Transmedia Hollywood, are two such examples. These gatherings' goals have been to think through some of the issues presented in this essay. Given that storytelling, social elements, play, and "gamification" are the galvanizing points for these discussions, it should also be important to address how these efforts might be produced. At a conceptual level, transmedia is something that is already happening, yet does little to engage with the complex issues for content creators. This essay's focus on creation and the kinds of issues that face game creators will only come to impact greater numbers of creative workers.

6. In fact, games need not be story-telling systems at all. Games can engage the user/player without attempting to tell a story; for example, *Tetris* and other puzzle games. However, in the context of cross-media game development, there is almost always a corresponding story or message that is attempting to be delivered. The cross-media possibilities for *Tetris* are quite limited.

7. Proprietary data formats, especially when combined with encryption technologies, are the "thing that happened along the way to convergence." The idea that digital data would be broadly useful and capable of being used by multiple platforms and software packages was one of the hopes that made convergence a compelling argument for media producers. However, most software and technology platforms have tended to lock users in, rather than enable more efficient production practices. A notable exception to the analysis of file formats in the context of convergence is the ways in which digital file formats have significant importance for archivists. In particular, the "appropriateness" of a file format is difficult to determine, as these are rooted both in the applications that create them, and in the domain of application for a file (Ruppel, 2009).

8. I have argued that "user-facing tools" shape the possible interventions that user/players can make in videogames. This is an important aspect of co-creative work that is under-studied. It is important to examine the roles, sites, and means by which users are allowed to engage with co-creative technologies.

9. I would imagine that the labor of creating a theme park based on Disney intellectual property would be an undertaking not dissimilar in scale to the production of a game based on Disney IP. The very notion that convergence can include theme parks, which often includes working actors, demands that we further unpack the labor involved with the flow of cross-media (Brown, 2007). Even in the case of a digital theme park, massive human effort is involved in the creation of entities, art assets, technologies, design of queues where attendees must wait etc, which must be included in assessing flow.

Works Cited

Bonner, Frances, and Jason Jacobs. "The First Encounter: Observation on the Chronology of Encounter With Some Adaptations of Lewis Carroll's Alice Books." *Convergence.* 17:1 (2011): 37–48.

Bowker, Geoffrey C. and Susan Leigh Star. "Sorting Things Out: Classification and Its Consequences" in Wiebe Bijker, Bernard W. Carlson, and Trevor Pinc, eds. *Inside Technology.* Cambridge, MA: MIT Press, 1999.

Brown, Tom. "'The DVD of Attractions'?: The Lion King and the Digital Theme Park." *Convergence.* 13: 4 (2007): 169–83.

Carless, Simon. "Opinion: The Case Against Entertainment Media Convergence." *Game Set Watch*. 2/7/2008. Accessed 1/17/2010. http://www.gamesetwatch.com/2008/02/opinion_the_case_against_enter.php

Deuze, Mark, Chase Bowen Martin, and Christian Allen. "The Professional Identity of Gameworkers." *Convergence*. 13:4 (2007): 335–53.

Dyer-Witheford, Nick, and Greig de Peuter. "'EA Spouse' and the Crisis of Video Game Labour: Enjoyment, Exclusion, Exploitation, and Exodus." *Canadian Journal of Communication*. 31:3 (2006): 599–617.

ea_spouse. "EA: The Human Story." *Live Journal*.11/10/2004/ accessed 6/24/2010. http://ea-spouse.livejournal.com/274.html.

Gillespie, Tarleton. *Wired Shut: Copyright and the Shape of Digital Culture*. Cambridge, MA: MIT Press, 2007.

Informant, and O'Donnell, Casey. "Interview With Art_Ds_Ogre_1." (2006):

Irwin, Mary Jane. 2008. "Games Are the Convergence of Everything." *Forbes.com*. 13/3/2008. Accessed 1/17/2010. http://www.forbes.com/2008/12/03/ken-levine-bioshock-tech-personal-cx_mji_1203levine_print.html

Jenkins, Henry. *Convergence Culture: Where Old and New Media Collide*. New York: NYU Press, 2006.

_____, and Mark Deuze. "Editorial: Convergence Culture." *Convergence*. 14: 1 (2008): 5–12.

Latour, Bruno. *Science in Action: How to Follow Scientists and Engineers Through Society*. Cambridge, MA: Harvard University Press, 1987.

Law, John. "Technology and Heterogeneous Engineering: The Case of Portuguese Expansion" in Wiebe Bijker, Thomas P. Hughes, and Trevor Pinch eds. *The Social Construction of Technological Systems: New Directions in the Sociology and History of Technology*. Cambridge, MA: MIT Press, 1989: 111–34.

Montfort, Nick, and Ian Bogost. "Racing the Beam: The Atari Video Computer System" in Ian Bogost and Nick Montfort, eds. *Platform Studies. Vol.1*. Cambridge, MA: MIT Press, 2009.

O'Donnell, Casey. "The Everyday Lives of Videogame Developers: Experimentally Understanding Underlying Systems/Structures." *Transformative Works and Cultures*. 2 (2009). Available online: http://dx.doi.org/10.3983/twc.2009.0073.

_____. "Games Are Not Convergence: The Lost Promise of Digital Production and Convergence." *Convergence*. 17: 3 (2011): TBD.

_____. "Production Protection to Copy(right) Protection: From the 10NES to DVDs." *IEEE Annals of the History of Computing*. 31:3 (2009): 54–63.

_____. "The Work/Play of the Interactive New Economy: Video Game Development in the United States and India." Dissertation, Rensselaer Polytechnic University, 2008.

Ronell, Avital. *The Test Drive*. Chicago, Illinois: University of Illinois Press, 2005.

Ruppel, Marc. "Narrative Convergence, Cross-Sited Productions and the Archival Dilemma." *Convergence*. 15: 3 (2009): 281–98.

Salen, Katie, and Eric Zimmerman. *Rules of Play: Game Design Fundamentals*. Cambridge, MA: MIT Press, 2004.

Schell, Jesse. *The Art of Game Design: A Book of Lenses*. New York, NY: Elsevier, 2008.

Shirinian, Ara. "The Uneasy Merging of Narrative and Gameplay." *Gamasutra.com*. 2010. Accessed 1/26/2010. http://www.gamasutra.com/view/feature/4253/the_uneasy_merging_of_narrative_.php?print=1.

Staff. "Spider-Man 3." *Boxofficemojo*. 2007. Accessed 1/17/2010. http://www.boxofficemojo.com/movies/?id=spiderman3.htm

Zhao, Elaine Jing. "Social Network Market: Storytelling on a Web 2.0 Original Literature Site." *Convergence*. 17:1 (2011): 85–99.

Afterword

Gary Jackson

The essays in this anthology offer contemporary interpretations of Spider-Man that I've never considered; how television and films offer re-contextualized meaning on Spider-Man's original 1960s mythic origin; how, despite a myriad of creative interpretations, there are certain modifications of the character that the general populace doesn't readily accept (a black Spider-Man?); how the absence of Uncle Ben and his parents influence Peter's reality. These essays explore many different facets of the famous webslinger, yet they share a common thread. Peter Parker, himself.

Spider-Man is merely a mask; unlike the Man of Steel or The Dark Knight, the superhero persona is a façade for Peter Parker. Time and time again, Peter throws those old red-and-blues in a trashcan, only to realize that "with great power, comes great responsibility" and thus to resume his Sisyphean task of fighting evil in New York. He uses humor to cope with his hopelessly impossible goal: to rid the city of evil, but also to make up for the guilt over his perceived role in Uncle Ben's death. Spider-Man — that obsessive part of Peter — is unrelenting in his pursuit of righteousness; and Peter welcomes it. After all, when Peter is Spidey, his everyday problems temporarily disappear. But his normality is what draws us to him; it's why we see him as more complex than other superheroes. He reminds us too much of ourselves. It's why we love him. It's why I love him.

I'm nine again, lying on my bed, reading The Amazing Spider-Man #336. *It's the second comic book I've read, and I'm thinking I should be outside playing with my friends instead of having my nose jammed between the flimsy stapled pages of a "funny book"— my grandparents' words. I'm not entirely sold on comics myself—granted, I've only read one other* (The Incredible Hulk #372), *but there was no denying that they were fun.*

So this Spider-Man guy seems to have all the usual superhero tropes: an alter-ego, a colorful costume, cool powers. And he fights ridiculous villains like The Vulture in this issue. Typical superhero stuff—until the Vulture decides to snatch Aunt May's fiancé as a hostage. In the end, The Vulture gets away and her fiancé dies of a heart attack in Aunt May's arms. The story closes as Spider-Man learns "the helpless knowledge that there are some battles even a hero can't win."

Man, this superhero has problems.

Over the years, I've grown in and out of — and back in — love with comic books, superheroes, and Spider-Man, but looking back on that issue, I feel it points to the core characteristic that makes Peter Parker so goddamn personable — he fails. A lot. He's got the big failures we've all come to recognize: failing to stop the criminal that would eventually kill his Uncle Ben; his failure to save his true love, Gwen Stacy, from the Green Goblin. But Spider-Man is also riddled with the daily stresses that we all experience — making rent, holding down a job, keeping a high GPA, maintaining his relationships—and he overcomes these problems with the same modicum of success we do. He's moved back in with his Aunt May from time to time, he's gotten low grades, his marriage with his wife dissolved (and the less we get into the "details" behind that editorial decision, the better). We could argue that, where it counts, he saves the day—the world, even—but just like in *The Amazing Spider-Man #336*, he reminds us that we can't always win. People die, the world moves on. But after fifty years, Peter is still cracking wise while jaw-socking criminals, trying his best to keep his head above water, reminding us of our own vulnerabilities and faults while simultaneously exemplifying the human ideal.

Not bad for a guy who sews his own tights.

Gary Jackson • May 2012

Gary Jackson (MFA) is the winner of the 2009 Cave Canem Poetry Prize for his first book *Missing You, Metropolis*. He was nominated for a Pushcart Prize, and his poems have appeared or are forthcoming in *The Laurel Review*, *Callaloo*, *Tin House*, *Blue Mesa Review*, *Pilgrimage*, and *BorderSenses*.

About the Contributors

Christina C. **Angel** is an English professor at Metropolitan State College and Arapahoe Community College in Denver, teaching a range of courses in literature, humanities, writing, and rhetoric. She holds a B.A. in creative writing and English, an M.A. in literary and film studies, and a Ph.D. in literary studies from the University of Denver. Her teaching experience includes courses in developmental English, rhetoric, creative writing, pedagogy, film, and literature (classics, Old and Middle English texts, medieval, renaissance, and children's literature).

Phillip **Bevin** is a Ph.D. student based at Kingston University, UK. He has studied undergraduate level English at the University of Leicester and cultural studies at the master's level at the University of Edinburgh, when he developed his lifelong interest in the study of superheroes.

David Ray **Carter** is a film critic for Film Fanaddict Magazine and NotComing.com. His book *Conspiracy Cinema* was published in 2012. His areas of study are cinema, conspiracy theories, and pop culture. Carter has previously published book chapters in *From the Arthouse to the Grindhouse* and *In the Peanut Gallery with Mystery Science Theater*.

James Bucky **Carter**, Ph.D., is an assistant professor of English education at the University of Texas at El Paso. He has written many articles and book chapters on the intersections of comics-and-literacy. His larger works include the edited collections *Building Literacy Connections with Graphic Novels: Page by Page, Panel by Panel* (NCTE, 2007), *Rationales for Teaching Graphic Novels* (Maupin House, 2011), and *Super-Powered Word Study: Teaching Words and Word Parts Through Comics* (Maupin House, 2010), co-authored with Xeric grant winner Erik A. Evensen.

Phillip Lamarr **Cunningham** (Ph.D.) is a visiting assistant professor of media studies at Quinnipiac University. His scholarly work has appeared in the *Journal of Graphic Novels and Comics, Journal of Popular Music Studies, Journal of Sport and Social Issues, Captain America and the Struggle of the Superhero* and in several forthcoming anthologies.

Aaron **Drucker** is a Ph.D. student at Claremont Graduate University. His contribution to this collection was honored as a runner-up for the Lent Award, presented by the Popular Culture Association to outstanding scholarship in the area of comic book and graphic novel studies. He is preparing for publication his own collection on Neil Gaiman and feminism.

Emily D. **Edwards** (Ph.D.) has been the writer, director, editor or animator on many films, ranging from short animations to narrative feature films, and has published books and articles on popular media. She is a professor of media studies at the University of North Carolina Greensboro and the director of the Center for Creative Writing and the Arts.

Martin **Flanagan** is a senior lecturer in the faculty of Arts and Media Technologies at the University of Bolton, UK. His doctoral thesis (Sheffield) was concerned with the cinematic relevance of Bakhtinian theories, concentrating on issues around genre, narrative, spectatorship and technology. His book *Bakhtin and the Movies: New Ways of Understanding Hollywood Film* was published in 2009. An article exploring textual and thematic issues in comic book adaptations, including *Spider-Man* (2002), was published in 2007.

Forrest C. **Helvie** is an instructor of developmental English at Norwalk Community College in Norwalk, CT. He is a Ph.D. student in English literature and criticism at Indiana State University of Pennsylvania and his research interests include the development of American comics of the 20th and 21st centuries.

Lisa **Holderman** is an associate professor in the Department of Media and Communication at Arcadia University. Her research focuses on narratives of social class and intellectuality in popular media. She has published in journals including *Mass Communication and Society* and *Popular Communication*, contributed to books such as *Stardom and Celebrity: A Reader*, and published an anthology entitled *Common Sense: Intelligence as Presented on Popular Television*.

Rick **Hudson** is a professional writer and has produced short stories and comic strips for numerous markets. He was a senior lecturer in writing at Southampton Solent University from 1999 to 2008 and now conducts research under the aegis of Bath Spa University. Rick specializes in the study of science fiction, fantasy and horror and was one of the first British academics to subject the comic book–graphic novel to academic analysis.

Tama **Leaver** teaches in the department of Internet Studies at Curtin University in Perth, Western Australia. His work has appeared in journals such as *Comparative Literature Studies* and *Media International Australia*. His forthcoming book is entitled *Artificial Culture: Identity, Technology and Bodies*.

Peter **Lee** is a graduate student at Drew University, with a focus on American cultural history. He has contributed to *Americana: The Journal of American Popular Culture*, and the upcoming collections *Coded: Comic Books and the Cold War* and *Understanding Superman*, also from McFarland.

Mark **McDermott** earned his MA degree in popular culture at Bowling Green State University. He has published encyclopedia articles on TV, comics, and DJs, and academic essays on James Bond movie themes, Captain America, *Marvel Zombies*, and *Star Wars* fans.

Matthew **McGowan** is a journalism graduate of Texas Tech University. Now a professional editor/journalist, he has been the higher education reporter for the *Lubbock Avalanche-Journal* in West Texas and a reporter for the *Odessa American*, as well as features editor for the *Daily Toreador*.

Ora C. **McWilliams** is a Ph.D. student in American studies at the University of Kansas. A former managing editor of the *American Studies Journal*, he has taught classes on American studies, sociology and popular culture.

Casey **O'Donnell** is an assistant professor at the University of Georgia. His research examines the socio-technical interactions that occur during the design/development of videogames and power dynamics that occur in professional "AAA" organizations and "independent" game development communities.

About the Contributors

Robert Moses **Peaslee** (Ph.D.) is an assistant professor in the College of Mass Communications at Texas Tech University. His academic writing includes work published in *Visual Communication Quarterly, Tourist Studies, NMEDIAC: Journal of New Media & Culture, Mass Communicator*, and *Reconstruction*.

Derek Parker **Royal** has taught as an associate professor of English at Texas A&M University-Commerce, and is the founder and executive editor of *Philip Roth Studies*. His essays on American literature and graphic narrative have appeared in a variety of scholarly journals and edited collections. He is the editor of the comics-related special issues of *MELUS* (Fall 2007), focusing on ethnicity and American comics, and *Shofar* (Winter 2011), devoted to Jewish comics and graphic novels.

Cord A. **Scott** (Ph.D.) has written for several encyclopedias and academic journals, and has collaborated previously with Robert G. Weiner on the book *Captain America and the Struggles of the Superhero*. Cord has also been published in the *International Journal of Comic Art*. He teaches at several institutions in the Chicago area.

Jeremy **Short** (Ph.D.) holds the Rath Chair in Strategic Management at the University of Oklahoma. He published a graphic novel management textbook titled *Atlas Black: Managing to Succeed*, as well as the sequel, *Atlas Black: Management Guru?* He also co-wrote the first Harvard Business Case in graphic novel format, as well as short graphic novel works for journals such as *Journal of Management Inquiry* and *Business Horizons*.

Andrew A. **Smith** (MA) is a designer/copy editor at *The Commercial Appeal* in Memphis, Tennessee, and an adjunct professor at the University of Memphis. Since 1992, he has written a weekly newspaper column on comics syndicated by Scripps Howard News Service. He has served as a contributing editor for *Comics Buyer's Guide* since 2000.

David **Walton** studied graduate level literature and languages at Texas A&M University, Commerce. He contributed an essay to *Captain America and the Struggle of the Superhero: Critical Essays* and a book review to *Shofar*.

Robert G. **Weiner** is an associate humanities librarian for Texas Tech University Libraries. He is the author of *Marvel Graphic Novels: An Annotated Guide*, and the editor of books on libraries and graphic novels, Captain America, and the Grateful Dead and co-editor of books on James Bond, Mystery Science Theater, and transgressive film.

Index

Abbey Road 231
ABC 24, 211
Across the Universe 50
Activision 46, 236, 237
Actor-Network Theory 239, 240
Aerosmith 222
Affleck, Ben 24
Afghanistan 125, 156
Alan Parsons Project 211
Alchemy Game Engine 238
Alger, Horatio 24
Allen, Barry 25
Allen, Iris 166
Allen, Liz 167
Allen, Woody 44
Alonso, Axel 25
Amazing Fantasy 1, 5, 6, 7, 66, 90, 92, 93, 102, 121, 122, 128, 146, 187, 188
Amazing Spider-Man 1, 4, 5, 6, 8, 12, 16, 22, 23, 24, 25, 26, 29, 33, 34, 43, 49, 50, 82, 83, 84, 86, 90, 91, 92, 93 95–99, 101–110, 116–117, 118, 121, 123–125, 129–131, 142, 143, 146, 149–151, 156, 160, 166–168, 187–191, 193, 211, 212, 214, 218, 222, 223, 231, 249, 250
Amazing Spider-Man Annual 99, 104, 106, 129, 149, 151, 168, 218
Amazing Spider-Man: Official Index to the Marvel Universe 4
Amazing Spider-Man: Parallel Lives 167
Amazing Spider-Man: The Complete Clone Saga 142
Ambrosia 231
American Dream 159
American Monomyth 199
"American Son" 49
Ammer, Geoffrey 155
"Andrea del Sarto" 64
Angel, Christina C. 13, 74, 251
anti-villain 15, 128, 129
Appice, Carmine 230
Aquaman 226
Aquirre-Sacasa, Roberto 10
Arkham Asylum: A Serious House on Serious Earth 132
Armageddon 48, 60
Art of John Romita 5

The Atlantic 63
Atlas Comics 92
"Attack of the Octobot" 215
Auberjonois, Rene 222, 224, 227
Aunt May 1, 6, 9, 11, 16, 31, 65, 85, 93, 99, 106, 108, 121, 141, 150, 151, 167, 169–174, 179–181, 187–193, 202, 203, 206, 224–226, 231, 250
Austin Powers: The Spy Who Shagged Me 225
Avenging Spider-Man 8

Bacon, Lloyd 44
Baker, William 130
Bakhtin, Mikhail 41
Banner, Bruce 27, 82
Barker, Kyle 25
Barris, Jeremy 63
Bather, Neil 45
Batman 4, 5, 9, 15, 47, 50, 51, 79, 82, 87, 113, 128, 131, 132, 133, 134, 135, 137, 139–143, 155, 166, 198, 200, 201, 210, 213, 222
Batman and Spider-Man: Disordered Minds 15, 135, 137, 139–143
Batman: Dark Victory 82
Batman: Haunted Knight 82
Batman: The Long Halloween 82
Bay, Michael 48
Beck, Quentin 131, 133
Bells, Jamie 22
"Belly of the Whale" 179
Bender, Thomas 42, 46
Bendis, Brian Michael 8, 11
Benjamin, Paul 8
Berger, Glen 10
Bernardin, Marc 22
Best of Spidey Super Stories 10
Betty and Veronica 1
Bevin, Philip 15
Bible 77, 78
The Big Man 108
Billboard 222, 228, 230, 231, 232
Bin Laden, Osama 115
The Bionic Woman 190
"Birth of a Super Hero!" 106
"Birth of Spider-Man" 19, 146
Birth of Venom 8
Black Canary 166

the Black Cat 167, 217, 218, 219, 220
Black Marvel 218
Black Oak Arkansas 230
Black Panther 26
"Black Suit Spidey" 243
Black Widow 76, 201
Blackcrow, Charles 35
Blade 215, 216
Blair, Jayson 117
Blake Bell 102
Blank Theatre Company Young Playwrights Festival 11
Blaxploitation cinema 47
Bloom, Harold 63
Bloom, Sarah 149
Bond, James 42, 130, 183, 218, 252, 253
Bono 11
Bordwell, David 44
Bowell, Stephen 32
Bowie, David 228
The Boy Wonder 37
Bozo at the Circus 228
Brad Bird 49
"Brand New Day" 187, 193
Brant, Betty 104, 106, 110, 150, 167
Brant, John 31
Brantley, Ben 10
Brazil 124
Broadway 4, 8, 10, 11, 46, 170, 222, 224, 232
Brock, Eddie 43, 163, 181, 185, 212, 213
Brodheim, Adam 11
Bronze Age 47, 83
Brook, Vincent 26
Brooklyn Bridge 3
Brooklyn Dreams 13, 70, 71
Brown, Hobie 36
Brown, James 49
Brown, Jeffery 190
Browning, Robert 64
Bruckheimer, Jerry 45
Bucky 5, 10, 12, 13, 63, 128, 147, 152, 251
Buddha 223
Buffy the Vampire Slayer 8
Bukatman, Scott 44, 155, 197
Bullit, Sam 36, 108
Bullpen Bulletins 32, 222, 223, 228

Bumppo, Natty 198
Buscema, Sal 8
Butler, Judith 15, 134

Cage, Luke 26, 47
Caine Mutiny 107
Callahan, Harry 122
Cameron, James 215
Campbell, Bruce 237
Campbell, Joseph 147, 148, 177–181, 187, 189, 198, 237
Captain America 9, 12, 25, 47, 79, 81, 82, 90, 92, 120, 123, 124, 125, 126, 128, 147, 152, 169, 210, 211, 217–220, 223, 226, 251, 251, 253
Captain America: White 81
Captain Beefheart 227
Captain Marvel 6
Captain Queeg 107
Captain Stacy 97
Cardy, Nick 226
Carnage 9, 140, 182, 217, 220
Carpenter, John 48
Carradine, Robert 23
Carroll, Lewis 246
Carter, David Ray 16, 210, 251
Carter, James Bucky 10, 13, 63
Cash, Steve 231
Cashman, Terry 226, 229
Castle, Frank 121, 122, 127
The Cat 109, 217
Catwoman 82, 166, 200, 201
Catwoman: When in Rome 82
Cave Canem Prize 17
Celluloid Skyline 47
Central Park 121
Chabon, Michael 178
Challengers of the Unknown 82
Chameleon 1, 130, 212, 214
Charlie's Angels 190
Checker, Chubby 49
Chicago Sun Times 185
Chile 132
Choi, Ryan 25
Christian crucifixion 162
Christianity 14, 77, 162, 198
Church, Thomas Hayden 174
CIA 123
Cinderella 170
Cirque du Soleil 11
Citizen Kane 82
Civil War 15, 120, 125, 169, 231'
Clapton, Eric 231
Clone Saga 8, 9, 82, 142, 169, 219, 220
Clooney, George 24
Cloverfield 41, 48
CNN 155
Cockburn, Rooster 8
Cold War 121, 252
Colter, Jessie 231
Columbia Studios 12
Columbia Tristar 155
Columbia University 55, 157, 179
Comedy Central Presents 25

Comic Book Curriculum 10
"Comic Books, the Menace to American Childhood" 92, 95
Comic Creators on Spider-Man 4
Comics Alliance 25
Comics Chronicles 6
Comics Code 13, 14, 37, 90–92, 192, 222
Comics Magazine Association of America 90, 92
Comics Magazine Publishers code 95
Communication Quarterly 5
Community 24
computer generated imagery 41, 45, 155, 157–160
Conan the Barbarian 226
concept albums 223, 231, 232
Connors, Curt 31, 129, 132, 188
"Contemporary Trends and Issues in the Graphic Novel" 63, 68
Continuum: Journal of Media and Cultural Studies 5
convergence 17, 234–246
Conway, Gerry 4, 8, 87, 81, 121, 124, 189
Coogan, Peter 7
Cooper, Merian C. 48
CORE 32
Cosby, Bill 232
Cosmopolis 44
Crack the Sky 227
Crawford, Dr. Moria 214
Crime-Master 105, 108, 109
"Crisis on Campus" 33, 34, 35, 36
Cronenberg, David 50
Cross-media 17, 234, 235, 238, 240, 242, 245, 246
Cruise, Tom 44
Csikszentmihalyi, Mihaly 63
Cubitt, Sean 159
Cunningham, Phillip Lama 12, 22, 251

Dafoe, Willem 43, 157, 171, 195
Daily Bugle 14, 23, 29, 34, 91, 92, 99, 101, 103, 104, 108, 109, 113–116, 129, 158, 161, 171, 181, 225
Daily Planet 129
Daily Show 24
D'Amore, Laura 190, 193
Dandy, Jim 230
Daniels, Charlie 227
Dante, Ron 224, 225, 227
Daredevil 42, 44, 45, 81, 82, 87, 109, 112, 124, 131, 166, 213, 223, 231
Daredevil: Yellow 81, 82, 87
Dark City 45, 148, 179
Dark Knight 41, 45, 49, 51, 87, 249
The Dark Knight 41, 45, 241
"Dark Reign" 29
Dark Side of the Moon 231
Dassin, Jules 46

Day After Tomorrow 41, 48
DC Comics 9, 25, 41, 71, 134, 222, 224
DC Universe 25, 82
Death of Gwen Stacy 8, 83, 87, 128, 129, 171, 190, 229
Death of Spider-Man 8
De Certeau, Michel 155
Deconstruction 63, 65, 139
Deep Impact 60
DeFalco, Tom 1, 2, 4, 6, 7, 8, 9, 12, 18, 34, 37, 38, 112, 142, 143, 176, 188, 189, 191, 194
Dekker, Thomas 75
DeLillo, Don 44
DeMatteis, J.M. 8, 13, 15, 18, 23, 27, 42, 70–73, 139–140
Department of Health, Education, and Welfare 97
Derrida, Jacques 63
Derridean theory 13
Destroyer 218, 228
Diamondback 125
digital media production 236, 239
digital rights management 242
Dillane, Frank 22
Dillon, Max 130
Dirty Harry 47, 122, 123
Disney 46, 51, 74, 246
Ditko, Steve 5–8, 12, 17, 42, 49, 78, 90, 101, 102, 104, 118, 121, 128, 130, 146, 149, 150, 154, 168, 178, 187, 212
Dr. Doom 130
Dr. Octopus (Doc Ock) 9, 31, 42, 43, 56–59, 87, 105, 115, 130, 133, 150, 161–163, 172–173, 180–181, 187–191, 195, 203, 204, 205, 206, 212, 214, 227
Dr. Strange 76, 214, 215, 225
Dr. Vespian 211
Dodson, Terry 192
"Donald Glover for Spider-Man" 12, 22–27
Donen, Stanley 44
Donner, Richard 51
Donovan 222
"Doomsday Device" 218, 219
Dormammu 215
Drucker, Aaron 14, 90, 251
Dunst, Kirsten 45, 170, 184, 195

Easter story 232
Eastwood, Clint 198
Ebert, Roger 185
EC 92
Eco, Umberto 26, 54, 187, 192, 198
The Edge 11, 47, 49
Edwards, Anthony 23
Edwards, Emily D. 16, 177
Eglash, Ron 24
Eisner, Will 6
Eisner Award 82, 87
Electric Company 9, 222, 227

Electro 130, 131
Elektra 166
Elizabeth I 75
Elliot, Billy 22
El Salvador 132
Emmerich, Roland 41
Empire State Building 159, 161
"Enter of the Green Goblin" 216
Entertainment Tonight 169
Entwistle, John 230
Erbe, Kathryn 230
Escape from New York 48
Eva, Little 109
Everett, Bill 42
Excelsior 101, 107, 108, 110
Eyes Wide Shut 44

"Face It Tiger, You Just Hit the Jackpot" 166, 168
Facebook 10, 22, 24, 115
The Falcon 226
Family Matters 24
Fantastic Four 1, 9, 45, 76, 90, 92, 96, 125, 166, 190, 220, 226
"Farewell Spider-Man" 220
Fast and Furious 26
Faverau, Jon 45, 49
Fein, Eric 83
Fettinger, J.R. 169, 188
Fingeroth, Danny 81, 83
Finn, Huckleberry 198
Firestar 211
First Family 224, 232
Flanagan, Martin 13, 40, 252
The Flash 25, 45, 166
Flash Fearless vs. the Zorg Women 230
Fletcher, Bill 33
The Fly 6, 243
Ford, Gerald 124
Fort Apache: The Bronx 48
42nd Street 44, 46
Foswell, Frederick 104, 105, 108
"four-quadrant" audience 16
Fox News 115
Franco, James 170, 195
Freberg, Stan 232
Freeman, Morgan 9
French Connection 47
Freud, Sigmund 16, 134, 135, 172, 189, 195-207
Friedkin, William 47
Friedman, Dean 229
From Beyond the Grave 223, 225, 227, 228, 229, 231, 232
Front Line 110, 111, 116, 117
Fury, Nick 76
Future Foundation 9

Gabilliet, Jean Paul 199
Gaiman, Neil 8, 13, 35, 251
Garfield, Andrew 8, 26, 27
Gargan, Mac 103
Garrick, Jay 25
"gaze theory" 177
Gender Trouble 134, 136, 138

General Electric 118
George Washington Bridge 59, 82
Ghede, Baron 132
The Ghost of Milton 64
Ghost World 67
Giant Size Spider-Man 124, 127, 168
Gibson, Mel 41
Gillen, Shawn 147, 152
Gillies, Daniel 172, 195
Giuliani, Rudolph 48-49
Gladys Knight & the Pips 224, 227
Gleason, Jackie 225
Glicksohn, Susan Wood 167, 201, 210
Glover, Donald 8, 12, 22-28
Glover, Elaine 36
The Goblin 43, 46, 97, 98 108, 158, 160, 161, 171, 205, 216, 217
"The Goblin and the Gangsters" 108
God 71, 73, 75, 81, 83, 86, 99, 132, 184, 185
Goldbug 125
Golden Age 90, 115, 218, 219
Golden Gloves 34
Golden Oldie 189
Goodman, Martin 5, 102
Google 11, 237
Gorbachev, Mikhail 70
"The Gospel According to Spider-Man" 19, 62, 77, 80
Gotham 41, 50, 61, 113, 155
Gough, Alfred 178
Grace, Nancy 115
Grace, Topher 43, 174
Grail legends 147
Grand Theft Auto: San Andreas 47
graphic novel 10, 13, 63, 64, 65, 67, 68, 82, 168, 169, 251, 252, 253
Great Depression 196
Greek mythology 74
Green Arrow 12, 40, 166
Green Goblin 9, 11, 12, 42, 43, 49, 56, 57, 59, 82, 86, 97, 108, 109, 110, 128, 129, 130-133, 157, 158, 160, 161, 163, 169, 170, 171, 173, 174, 179-181, 185, 189, 193, 195, 202, 203, 205, 213, 216-219, 222, 224, 227, 249
Green Goblin's Last Stand 8
Green Hornet 8
Green Lantern 40, 99, 222
Greenberg, Oscar 71
Greenberg the Vampire 71
Grey, Jean 12
Groce, Henry 229
Gross, Edward 5
Grosz, Elizabeth 158, 164
Groth, Gary 6
Ground Zero 50, 156
Gruenwald, Mark 8

Hajda, David 90
Hammerhead 213

Hancock 24
Hardy, Felicia 167
Harlem 34, 47
Harris, Rosemary 170
Hart, Steve 229
"Haunting of Mary Jane" 217
Hayward, Justin 230
Healy, Patrick 11
Heidegger, Martin 192
Hell's Kitchen 44
Helvie, Forrest C. 15, 146, 252
herald of Galactus 187, 189
Hermeneutics 74, 77, 78
Hermes 74
"Hero for Hire" 47
Hero with a Thousand Faces 147, 179, 198
Herzberg, Frederick 116
Heterogenous Engineering 239
Hill, Walter 48
Hindu 72, 73
Hipgnosis 231
Hobgoblin 9, 126, 212, 213, 217, 220
Holderman, Lisa 13, 53, 252
Hollywood 11, 13, 40, 48, 51, 53, 55, 58, 59, 185, 186, 228, 246, 252
Holmes, John 198
Holy Grail 16
"Homer at the Bat" 229
House Un-American Activities Committee (HUAC) 95
How to Read Superhero Comics 67
How to Train Your Dragon 74
Howard, Bryce Dallas 173
Hudson, Rick 9, 15, 128, 252
Hulk 8, 11, 42, 81, 82, 90, 92, 106, 110, 169, 222, 226, 249
Hulk: Grey 81, 82
Human Fly 104
Human Torch 12, 22, 29, 90
Hydro-Man 214, 215, 290

I Am Legend 48
"I Really, Really, Hate Clones" 220
Iceman 37, 212
In Search of the Lost Chord 229
Inception 45, 231
Incredible Hulk 226, 249
Incredibles 49
Indick, William 178
"Infinite Justice" 156
Information Age 114
Innes, Sherrie 190
The Inquisition 76
Insidious Six 214, 218
Intergalactic Touring Band 231
International Journal of Comic Art 5, 253
Introductory Lectures 198
Iraq 125, 158
Iron Man 6, 45, 49, 87, 92, 125, 220, 230
It's a Bird...It's a Plane...It's Superman 10, 222

Jack-O-Lantern 125
Jackal 9, 107, 123, 219
Jackson, Gary 3, 17, 249
Jackson, Peter 41
James I 75, 76
Jameson, J. Jonah 1, 6, 11, 14, 16, 29, 30, 31, 34, 36, 42, 89, 91, 93, 95, 98, 99, 101, 102, 104, 105, 110, 114, 115, 122, 128, 129, 158, 223
Jameson, John 30, 94, 102, 172, 173, 180, 195
Jeff Wayne's Musical Version of The War of the Worlds 231
Jekyll/Hyde 31
Jemas, Bill 192
Jenkins, Henry 12, 17, 235
Jenkins, Paul 8
Jennings, Waylon 231
Jensen, Bill 24
The Jester 125
Jesus Christ 78, 230
Jesus Christ Superstar 230
Jethro Tull 230
Jiminy Cricket 108
Jimmy Corrigan 67
JJJ 102, 107, 133
Joe Kubert School of Cartoon & Graphic Art 226
John, Elton 226
John Birch Society 35
Johnson, Mark Steven 45
The Joker 131, 132, 133, 140
Jonah, Jolly 107
Journal of Child Abuse & Neglect 5
Journal of Criminal Justice and Popular Culture 5
Journal of Popular Culture 5
Journey to the Centre of the Earth 230
Jung, Carl 177–178, 181, 182, 187, 189, 198

Kama Sutra Records 227
Kane, Gil 99
Kang the Conqueror 220
Kaplan, E. Ann 196
Ka-Zar 107, 110
Kelly, Gene 44
Kendall, Lori 23
Kennedy, John F. 121
Kent, Clark 25, 166, 182, 198, 200
Keopp, David 178
Kernaban, Stevie 24
Kersey, Paul 122
Key, John 229
Killing Joke 132
King, Fisher 147
King, Dr. Martin Luther, Jr. 33
King Kong 48
King of Death 126
Kingpin 96, 105, 109, 110, 126, 169, 213, 214, 224, 225, 231
Kirby, Jack 6, 7, 42, 82
Klock, Geoff 67
Kool-haa, Rem 44

Kraven 9, 13, 70–73, 86, 103, 110, 130, 131, 133, 212, 215, 217
Kraven's Last Hunt 8, 10, 13, 70, 131
Kravinoff, Sergie 130, 131, 133
Kress, Gunther 63
Kristeva, Julia 63
Krypton 200, 210
Kubrick, Stanley 44

Landy, Marcia 158
Lane, Lois 128, 129, 166, 201
Lang, Jeffery 199
Law, John 240
Law and Order 230
Lawrence, Francis 48
Leaver, Tama 15, 252
Lee, Ang 11
Lee, Peter 12, 29, 47, 252
Lee, Stan 1, 4–9, 12, 14, 17, 23, 29–37, 42, 45, 47, 57, 77, 78, 81–110, 118, 121, 128, 130, 141, 143, 146–151, 154, 155, 166, 167–170, 178, 187, 212, 220, 222, 223, 226, 228
Lenin, Vladimir 70
Letrell, Lamar 24
Lewis, Ramsey 222
Lieber, Larry 8
Lifesong Records 226–229
Lilith 72
Lion King 11
Lizard 31, 86, 106, 128, 129, 212, 224
Loeb, Jeph 14, 81, 86
London 27, 75, 76, 230, 231
"Long September" 16, 154, 160, 162
Lord of Misrule 132
Lord of the Rings 41
Lovin' Spoonful 227
Lowe, Gilbert 23
Lucas, George 230
Luthor, Lex 130, 131
Lytle, Paul 188

Macchio, Ralph 81
Mackie, Howard 8
MAD Magazine 11
Madame Web 215, 216, 219, 220
Madoff, Bernie 115
Madureira, Joe 8
Magneto 219, 220, 226
"Magneto & Titanium Man" 226
Maguire, Tobey 27, 195
Major League Baseball 229
Malcolm in the Middle 24
Malik, Joe 32
Man of Steel 38, 154, 249
The Mandarin 26
Manhattan Transfer 226
Marine Corps 122
Marko, Flint 56, 130, 161, 181, 185
Marty, Nelson, 226, 227
Marvel Comics 1, 4–6, 9, 10, 12–14, 22, 25, 30, 32–34, 37–38, 40–43, 46, 47, 49, 50, 70, 75, 76, 81–87, 90, 92, 95–99, 117, 120, 121, 126, 134, 154–156, 160, 168, 169, 192, 193, 199, 211, 213, 218–220, 222–224, 226, 228–230, 237, 252–253
Marvel Masterworks 102, 110
Marvel 1602 13, 14, 75, 77, 78, 79
Marvel Team-Up 101, 167, 189, 193
Marvel Universe 4, 8, 11, 76, 77, 82, 83, 120, 126, 156, 160, 169, 213, 220
Marvel Universe Vs. the Punisher 120, 126
Marvel Universe Wiki 82
Marvel World of Icarus 239, 230
"Marvelous Evening with Stan Lee" 222, 223
Marvels 3, 35, 91
*M*A*S*H* 222
"Material History of Spider-Man: A 50th Anniversary Observance" 4
Matrix 40, 41, 45
Matrix Reloaded 45
Maus 63
Maya 72, 73, 237, 241
Mayday *see* Spider-Girl
McCarthy, Todd 115, 185
McCloud, Scott 63
McDermott, Mark 17, 222, 252
McGowan, Matthew 14, 113, 252
McWilliams, Ora C. 16, 31, 187, 252
"Meeting of the Goddess" 180
Menace 92, 96, 99
Mengele, Joseph 124
Mephisto 169, 175, 184, 191
Metropolis 17, 41, 43, 133, 155, 250
"Michael Cera 4 Shaft" 26
Microchip 215
Microsoft Xbox 360 236, 238
Millar, Mark 192
Miller, Frank 8, 99
Miller, Miles 178
Milton, John 64
Miss America 218
Missing You Metropolis 17
Mr. Hyde 181
Mr. Marvel 169
Moby Dick 70
Modern Age 84
Modern Language Association 4
Modesty Blaise 190
Modleski, Tania 201
Molina, Alfred 43, 161, 172, 195
"Mondo" documentary 229
The Moody Blues 229, 230
Moon, Keith 230
Moonshadow 72
Moore, Alan 132, 133, 199
Moore, Jesse 199
Morales, Robert 25
Morbius, Michael 214
Mordo, Baron 215

Index

"Most Prevalent Form of Degradation in Erotic Life" 195
The Motivation to Work 116
MSNBC 115
MTV.com 10
Mulcahey, Father 222
Mulvey, Laura 201
Murdock, Maureen 179
Murphy, Donna 172
Mysterio 103, 105, 130, 131–133, 212, 214, 217
"Myth of Superman" 192, 194, 207
Myths and Legends of King Arthur and the Knights of Round Table 230

Naked City 43, 46
Namor 90
National Association for the Advancement of Colored People (NAACP) 32
National Observer 32
National Public Radio 10
National Treasure 49
NBC 24, 211
Neo 26, 45, 223
"Neogenic Nightmare" 213, 214
New Avengers 187, 193
New Criticism 65
New Goblin 243
New World 76
New York 10, 11, 13, 31, 34, 40–51, 65, 98, 102, 103, 108, 110, 116, 117, 128, 126, 133, 142, 149–151, 154–163, 169, 173, 205, 212, 214, 220, 223, 234, 237, 243, 249
New York Public Library 51
New York Review of Books 10
New York Times 10, 11, 34, 48, 98, 117, 158
Newhart, Bob 232
Newsrama 25
Night Fighter 6
NightSky 244
9/11 11, 13, 15, 40, 47, 48, 49, 50, 120, 125, 193
Nintendo DS 238
Nintendo Gameboy Advance (GBA) 236
Nintendo Wii 236
Nixon, Richard 47, 123, 124
"Nobody Loves the Hulk" 222
Nolan, Christopher 41, 45
non-disclosure agreements 235
Nova 189
Now magazine 29
NPR 10

Obama, Barack 8
Octavis, Rosalie 172
Octavius, Otto *see* Dr. Octopus
O'Donnell, Casey 17, 252
Oedipus 16, 42, 43, 134–135, 191, 195, 196, 200–203, 205

Olbermann, Keith 115
Old Testament 122, 123
On the Town 44
One More Day 8, 166, 169, 176, 191, 193, 194
Online Computer Library Center 4
O'Onofrio, Vincent 230
Operation Iraqi Freedom 125
O'Reilly, Bill 115
Oropeza, B.J. 77, 188
Orwell, George 126
Osborn, Harry 38, 56, 86, 97, 98, 163, 170, 174, 179, 180, 195, 196, 202, 206, 217
Osborn, Norman *see* Green Goblin
Oscorp Industries 56
The Owl 213
Ozark Mountain Daredevils 231

Page, Karen 82
Page, Max 50
Palmer, Ray 25
Palumbo, John 227
Paradox Press 71
Parafino 211
Parker, Ben 128, 131, 133, 191
Parker, Peter 1, 4–6, 8–9, 11–12, 15–16, 22–23, 25–26, 29, 31–32, 36, 44, 47, 49–51, 55–59, 63, 65–68, 73–79, 81–86, 90–93, 95–98, 101, 110, 113, 115–116, 118, 121, 123, 141–142, 146, 148, 150, 152, 154–155, 157, 160, 162, 166–167, 169–173, 175, 179, 180–185, 187, 190–195, 200, 211, 213–216, 218–219, 222, 224, 226–227, 231, 243, 249
Parquagh 14, 75, 76, 77
Parsons, Alan 231
Passion of the Christ 49
Patient Zero 126
PATRIOT Act 126
PBS 179, 222, 227
Peace Corps 121
Peaslee, Robert Moses 4, 16, 123, 195, 253
Peel, Emma 190
Perry, Joe 222
Peter Pan Records 222, 228
Peter Parker: Fur Klavier sol 4
Petersen, Wolfgang 41
Petrie, Daniel 48
Philip, Kurnit S. 226
Photoshop 117, 163
Pink Floyd 230, 231
Pittsburgh 168
Pixar 49, 239
Planet of the Apes 228
Planetary 67
Plato 13, 63, 64, 67
"Plato, Spider-Man and the Meaning of Life" 63, 68
Platonic philosophy 13
Poe, Edgar Allan 231

Poole, Dan 8
"Pop Art" 63, 67
Postrel, Virginia 183
post-traumatic stress disorder (PTSD) 147
Potter, Harry 79
Power and Responsibility 13, 14, 63, 65, 67
Power of Myth 179
Power Records 222, 228
Prabhakar, Pavitr 22
Presley, Elvis 228
Pretty Things 230
Protestant values 205
The Prowler 217
Proyas, Alex 45
PsyArt: An Online Journal for the Psychological Study of the Arts 5
The Pulse 109
Punisher 14, 47, 120–127, 215
Pye, Christian 198
Pye Records 230

Queen Elizabeth 75
Queens 11, 22, 42, 44, 65, 222
Quesada, Joe 8, 160, 169, 191

Ragogna, Mike 226
Raimi, Ivan 178
Raimi, Sam 5, 13, 15, 40–51, 53, 129, 152, 154, 160, 170, 171, 172, 173, 175, 178
Ramones 222
Rausch, Jason 25
Raymond, Ronnie 25
Reagan, Ronald 70, 124
Reconstruction: Studies in Contemporary Culture 5
Red Hulk 8
The Red Scare 95
Red Skull 218, 219, 220
Reeves, Keanu 45
Reilly, Ben 219, 220
Resnais, Alain 222, 223
"Return of the Green Goblin" 217
Revenge of the Nerds 23, 24
Reynolds, Richard 198
Rhino 85, 214
Richards, Reed 125, 166
Richardson, Niall 77
Riley-Parker, Mary 187
Riverdale 1, 37
Roanoke 76
Robertson, Cliff 42
Robertson, Joe "Robbie" 34–38, 42, 98, 104, 108–109, 216, 218
Robertson, Randy 36–38
Robin 1, 5, 12, 37, 128
"Rock of Ages" 225
Rock Reflections of a Superhero 226, 228, 229, 231
Rocket Racer 216
Rocky Horror Picture Show 228
Rogers, Steve 25, 47, 147, 152
Rolling Stones 227

Romita, John 5, 34, 37, 86, 121, 224
Romita, John, Sr. 5, 8, 168, 190
Romita Legacy 5
Rourke, James 10
Rowling, J.K. 79
Royal, Derek Parker 81, 253
Rudow, Martin 34
Rush 213, 230
Russia 218

Saffel, Steve 4
Sale, Tim 14, 18, 86
Sanders, James 46, 48
Sanderson, Peter 75
Sandhu, Sukhdev 22
Sandman 9, 30, 56, 60, 105, 130, 163, 174, 181, 214, 243
"Santa Lucia" 225
Santini, Carl Vincent 71, 72
Santo 9
Sargent, Alvin 178
Satan 169
Savage Land 106, 110
Schatz, Thomas 45
The Schocker 217
Scorpion 9, 31, 103, 104, 105, 109, 212, 214, 217
Scott, Cord A. 14, 120, 253
Scott, Larry B. 24
"The Second Coming" 76
"Secret Wars" 220
Seduction of the Innocent 92, 93, 94
Senate Subcommittee on Juvenile Delinquency Hearings of 1954 95
September 11, 2011 11, 13, 15, 40, 41, 47–50, 120, 125, 193
Serpico 47
Sex and the City 44, 48
SF Sorrow 230
Shadow 8, 71, 72, 73, 181, 185, 202, 218
Shadowland 44
Shakespeare, William 10
Sheldon, Phil 3
S.H.I.E.L.D. 219
Shiva, Lady 26
Shoedsack, Ernest B. 43
Short, Jeremy 14, 253
Siege 43, 49
Silver Age 40, 49, 83, 90
Silver Spider 6
Silver Surfer 90, 189, 199, 223, 227
Silvermane 213
Simmonds, J.K. 129
The Simpsons 229
Sims, Chris 25
Singer, Bryan 45, 49
Singh, Greg 46
Sinister Six 9, 15, 128, 129, 130, 131, 133, 151, 214
"Sins of the Fathers" 215
"Sins Past" 82, 87
"Sins Remembered" 82, 87
Sir Nicholas 76

Sir Percival 147
"Six Forgotten Warriors" 218, 219
Six Million Dollar Man 228
Six Wives of Henry VIII 230
Skolnick, Lewis 23
Skywalker, Luke 8
Slott, Dan 8
Smith, Andrew 14, 36, 101–112
Smith, Kevin 91, 92, 97, 198
Smith, Will 24, 26
Smith, Willi 169
Smythe, Spencer 31, 110
Society of Professional Journalists Code of Ethics 112, 118
Socrates 63
Sony Entertainment 155
Sony Pictures 41, 228
Sony Playstation Portable 236, 237
Sony Playstation 2 236, 237, 243
Sony Playstation 3 236
South America 124
Spectacular Spider-Man 36, 105, 124, 141
Speedball 8
Spider, Scarlet 83, 220
Spider-Armor 220
Spider-Carnage 220
Spider-Girl 2, 9, 169
Spider-Man 1–17, 22–27, 29–37, 40–50, 53–60, 63, 65–68, 70–79, 80–86, 90–110, 113–152, 154–163, 166–175, 177–185, 187–193, 195, 196, 199–206, 210–232, 234, 236–238, 240, 243, 244, 249, 250
Spider-Man and Batman: Disordered Minds 134, 135, 137, 139–143
Spider-Man and His Amazing Friends 211
Spider-Man: Blue 14, 81–87
Spider-Man Confidential 18
Spider-Man: Edge of Time 8
Spider-Man Handbook 19
Spider-Man: India 9, 22
Spider-Man Loves Mary Jane 167
Spider-Man: Manga 9
Spider-Man/Mary Jane You Just Hit the Jackpot 167
Spider-Man: Noir 8
Spider-Man/Parker 86, 128, 129, 199, 204, 205, 206
"Spider-Man Plays to Packed House!" 90
Spider-Man: Shattered Dimensions 22, 46
"Spider-Man Slated for New TV Series!" 90
Spider-Man: The Animated Series 16, 210, 211, 213, 215, 217, 219, 221
Spider-Man The Icon 4
Spider-Man: The Ultimate Guide 2, 4
Spider-Man 3 44, 46, 57, 58, 60,

106, 162, 163, 173, 234, 236, 237, 238, 240, 243, 244
Spider-Man trilogy 25, 54, 55, 154, 156, 177–179, 182, 183
Spider-Man: Turn Off the Dark 10, 11, 222, 227
Spider-Man: Turn Off the Lights 11
Spider-Man 2 44, 45, 49, 56, 58, 59, 105, 158, 160, 161, 163, 166, 171, 195, 199, 206
Spider-Man 2099 9, 22
"Spider-Man Wins Showbiz Award!" 90
"The Spider or the Man?" 99, 214
Spider-Slayer 104, 168
Spider Spry 6
Spider-verse 12, 165, 231
Spider-Woman 8, 9
"Spidey Super Stories" 9, 10, 222, 227
Spidey Super Stories 9, 10, 222, 227
Spirit magazine 6
Spivak, Gayatri 63
Spurgeon, Tom 5
Squaresville 33
Stacy, George 31, 87, 105, 107
Stacy, Gwen 3, 8, 11, 12, 59, 81–87, 124, 128, 129, 133, 160, 167, 168, 171, 173, 174, 183, 184, 190, 193, 227, 229, 249
Stadium, Shea 169
Stan Freberg Presents the United States of America 232
Stan Lee Conversations 101, 107
Stan Lee's Mutants, Monsters & Marvels 91
Star City 43
Star Trek 224, 228
Star Wars 230, 252
Steppenwolf 229
Stern, Roger 8
Stewart, Rod 230
Stillwell, Farley 31, 103
Storm, Johnny 26, 29, 190, 220
Story, Tim 45
Stott, Jon C. 74
Straczynski, J. Michael 99, 169, 193
Strange and Stranger: The World of Steve Ditko 102
Strawberry, Darryl 169
Super Friends 216
Super Mario Bros 242
Superboy 1
Superhero films 27, 108, 201
Superman 4, 6, 9, 10, 12, 37, 43, 45, 51, 78, 82, 92, 94, 113, 121, 128, 129, 131, 133, 155, 166, 182, 192, 196, 198, 199, 200, 210, 220, 222, 252
Superman: A Man for All Seasons 82
Superman Returns 45
"Supermoms" 190
Suspense 83, 93, 100, 168, 216, 227
Swing Time 46

Index

Tales of Mystery and Imagination 231
Tarantula 124
Tarzan 107, 182
Tasker, Yvonne 45
Taymor, Julie 10, 50
The Teen Titans 226
The Ten-Cent Plague: The Great Comic-Book Scare and How It Changed America 90
Tetris 246
Theakston, Greg 6, 7, 8
"Theme from Spider-Man" 225
The Thing 8, 64, 66
Third Reich 36
30 Rock 24
Thomas, Roy 8, 91, 98, 99, 101, 223, 228
Thompson, Flash 95
Thor 223, 229
3D animation 239
3D Studio Max 237, 241
Thunderer 218
The Tick 213
Timely Comics 92, 218
Times Square 46, 50
Titus 50
"To Kill a Spider-Man" 110
Todd, Jason 12
Tombstone 217
Tommy 230
Tony Awards 11
Toomes, Adrian 130
Tourette's syndrome 132
Tower of London 76
Townsend, Pete 228
Traits 222
Transformers 238
"transmedia" 18, 245, 246
Traylor, Craig Lamar 24
Treyarch 236, 237, 241
Trimble, Patrick 199
Tristar 155
Trotsky, Leon 70
Trouble 187, 192
Troy 41, 49
Trump, Donald 157
Truth, Red, White & Black 25
The Tudors 75
Turtletaub, Jon 49
Twin Towers 155–159, 161
Twitter 10, 22, 24, 115
Two Face 132

"The Ultimate Slayer" 217
Ultimate Spider-Man 10, 11, 13, 41, 63, 65, 67, 68, 82, 167
Ultimate Spider-Man Volume 1: Power and Responsibility 63, 65

Uncle Ben 5, 6, 15, 42, 43, 51, 65, 66, 68, 82, 91, 121, 141, 142, 146, 148, 149, 150, 151, 157, 163, 173, 174, 179, 181, 182, 185, 187, 188, 189, 191, 202, 203, 225, 249
Uncle Tom 35
Understanding Comics 63
Universal Studios 16
Unstable Molecules 67
Urich, Ben 109
Urkel, Steve 24
USA Today 12, 169
U2 11, 17

van Gelder, Lawrence 98
Vanilla Fudge 230
Venom 8, 9, 33, 43, 127, 163, 164, 179, 181, 212, 213, 217, 236, 243
Vermin 70, 73
Vietnam 14, 32, 33, 47, 120–123, 126, 132, 147, 152
Village Voice 24
Visual Studio 241
Vivacious Visions (VV) 17, 236, 237, 238, 241
Voldemort 22
Volger, Christopher 178
Vulture 1, 83, 85, 105, 106, 116, 117, 118, 130, 131, 215, 217, 220, 224, 249

Wachowski, Andy 40
Wachowski, Larry 40
Waid, Mark 99
Wakeman, Rick 230
Wald, Malvin 46
The Wall 230
Wall-Crawler 29, 30, 94, 101, 104, 110, 173, 225
Walton, David 13, 70, 253
"War on Terror" 15
Warren, Miles 219
The Warriors 48
Watchmen 67
Watergate 196
Watson, Anna 108
Watson, Mary Jane 16, 45, 141, 142, 160, 167, 170, 171, 179, 195, 201, 214, 217
Watson, Mrs. 167
Watts-Evans, Lawrence 191
Wayne, Bruce 27, 135, 138, 139, 141, 142, 182, 210
Web of Spider-Man 83, 167, 193, 220
Web 2.0 247
Webb, Marc 41
Weber, Max 123

Webslinger 4, 12, 15, 81, 83, 113, 169, 249
Webslinger: Unauthorized Essays on Your Friendly Neighborhood Spider-Man 4
Web-Spinner 102, 104, 109, 222
The Wedding 8, 168, 169, 175, 176, 218
Weiner, Robert G. 4, 16, 79, 147, 166, 253
Well, Daniel 37
Welles, Orson 83
Wells, Zeb 8
Wertham, Dr. Frederic 14
West, James 26
West, Tommy 226
"What's the Name of This Funk (Spider-Man)?" 222
Whistler 215
White, Jaleel 24
White, Perry 129
White Mansions 231
Whizzer 218
The Who 230
"Who Is Spider-Man?" 90
Wicked 11
Wii 236, 237, 243
Wild Wild West 26
"Will the Real Dragon Please Stand Up?" 80
Wings 226
Wolfe, Tom 222, 223
Wolfman, Marv 8, 188
Wolverine 8, 82
Wolverine/Gambit: Victims 82
Woman magazine 101
Wood, Dave 82
World Trade Center 40, 49, 50, 155, 159
World Unity Festival 50
World War Hulk 110
World War II 25, 121, 147, 152, 196, 210
World Wrestling Federation 49
WorldCat 4
Wright, Bradford 154, 190

X-Men 40, 49, 76, 211, 215, 218, 220
X-Men: The Animated Series 215, 218

Yeats, W.B. 76

Zappa, Frank 230
Zeck, Mike 13
Žižek, Slavoj 49, 158

www.ingramcontent.com/pod-product-compliance
Ingram Content Group UK Ltd.
Pitfield, Milton Keynes, MK11 3LW, UK
UKHW050538150426
5217IPUK00026B/1981